# Writing Strategies for the Education Dissertation

*Writing Strategies for the Education Dissertation* offers a unique take on doctoral writing. It uses composition and rhetoric strategies to identify key activities for generating thought to keep students writing. It demythologizes the view of writing as a mere skill and promotes the view of writing as thinking.

It uses writing to help students invent, think through, write, rethink, and rewrite as they develop and present their innovations. The book opens with this mindset and with the purposes of the task (adding to knowledge); it helps define a "researchable topic," and provides advice on invention ("brainstorming"). It then addresses each of the key sections of the dissertation, from Problem Statement, through Literature Review and Methods, to Findings and Conclusions, while underscoring the iterative nature of this writing. For each chapter, the book provides advice on invention, argument, and arrangement ("organization") – rhetorical elements that are seldom fully addressed in textbooks. Each chapter also looks at possible missteps, offers examples of student writing and revisions, and suggests alternatives, not rules. The text concludes with an inventive approach of its own, addressing style (clarity, economy, and coherence) as persuasion.

This book is suitable for all doctoral students of education and others looking for tips and advice on the best dissertation writing.

**Diane Bennett Durkin** has taught critical thinking and writing at UCLA for over 30 years, publishing textbooks that merge disciplines, and helping education doctoral students understand and use writing processes to generate, organize, and communicate their ideas.

# Writing Strategies for the Education Dissertation

Diane Bennett Durkin

Routledge
Taylor & Francis Group

LONDON AND NEW YORK

First published 2021
by Routledge
2 Park Square, Milton Park, Abingdon, Oxon OX14 4RN

and by Routledge
52 Vanderbilt Avenue, New York, NY 10017

*Routledge is an imprint of the Taylor & Francis Group, an informa business*

*British Library Cataloguing-in-Publication Data*
A catalogue record for this book is available from the British Library

*Library of Congress Cataloging-in-Publication Data*
Names: Durkin, Diane Bennett, author.
Title: Writing strategies for the education dissertation / Diane Bennett Durkin.
Identifiers: LCCN 2020032315 (print) | LCCN 2020032316 (ebook) |
ISBN 9780367627034 (Hardback) | ISBN 9780367627058 (Paperback) |
ISBN 9781003110439 (eBook)
Subjects: LCSH: Dissertations, Academic–Authorship–Handbooks, manuals, etc. |
Education–Research–Methodology–Handbooks, manuals, etc. |
Proposal writing in educational research. |
Doctor of education degree–Handbooks, manuals, etc.
Classification: LCC LB2369 .D88 2021 (print) |
LCC LB2369 (ebook) | DDC 808.06/6378–dc23
LC record available at https://lccn.loc.gov/2020032315
LC ebook record available at https://lccn.loc.gov/2020032316

ISBN: 978-0-367-62703-4 (hbk)
ISBN: 978-0-367-62705-8 (pbk)
ISBN: 978-1-003-11043-9 (ebk)

Typeset in Palatino
by Newgen Publishing UK

*To Michael, my partner in life – in every project undertaken, every new craft mastered, every new adventure imagined*

# CONTENTS

# ACKNOWLEDGMENTS

First and foremost, this book needs to acknowledge the incredible support from my family – my husband, Michael, and my daughter, Celia. They believed that this book needed to be written and that I should be the one to write it.

Some key colleagues shared that belief and further encouraged me: Cindy Kratzer, Jim Stigler, and Mark Hansen were initial and long-term supporters. Along the way, others contributed to the book's progress and placement, including Mike Rose and Tina Christie, both of whom helped me at crucial junctures.

My editors at Routledge were stellar, smoothing the way and communicating well: I owe much to Hannah Shakespeare and Matthew Bickerton, who were enthusiastic and insightful from beginning to completion. They could not have been more helpful. My production team, including Ting Baker and Kawiya Bakthavatchalam, was also excellent, offering alternatives and good advice for every key decision.

Finally, I want to thank my students, who are ever on my mind. It is their work and their journey that drove this book. They have been open about their struggles, and given me access to the kinds of writing blocks they face, allowing me the chance to help future students surmount such obstacles more easily.

# INTRODUCTION

## PURPOSE

This book is a writing and rhetoric specialist's approach to producing the doctoral dissertation. It emphasizes using writing as thinking – to wrap one's mind around something new and to use rhetoric as persuasion. As a composition and rhetoric specialist in UCLA's Graduate School of Education, my advice differs from other dissertation guides. Having shepherded hundreds of Ed.D. students through the dissertation process, and taught Ph.D. writing courses, I use writing strategies, processes, barriers, and interventions to help students conceptualize and present their work. So, while the goal of this guide is similar to that of other guides, to help students finish, the advice and approach differ. And while the examples draw from education practitioner dissertations (mostly empirical studies), the advice applies to education dissertations generally.

## SLANT

Most texts on dissertation writing try to soft-peddle the process, making it seem like no big deal – all one needs are timelines, organization strategies, a standardized format, and step-by-step strategies. One text even suggests that if doctoral students write 15 minutes a day, they can finish the dissertation easily. Another calls the dissertation "a machine." The advice from these texts is meant to reassure, to simplify, and to mechanize. In reality, such advice sugarcoats the challenges, blockages, decision-making, and writing skills that characterize the creation of original research. This book takes seriously the challenges, tries to avoid mechanization, and offers ways to use writing to produce content that is new. It assumes that any creative research endeavor, by doctoral student or faculty member, is complex and multifaceted. As these endeavors are also part of a social and political setting, admittedly the advice here is tentative and context dependent.

The book focuses on the three demands that challenge new researchers the most: (1) creating the **initial proposal** (Problem Statement; Literature Review; Methodology), (2) writing up **findings** (which includes writing strategies for collecting adequate data, for analyzing data, and for presenting data), and (3) interpreting data for a meaningful **discussion** section. These all require openness, creativity, analysis, and composing skills. For methodology, the book offers some analytical writing exercises to develop the key pieces of the proposal, but leaves for other targeted texts (and for the committee Chair) advice for deciding on a specific methodology to fit specific research questions. While the book opens with writers' potential mindsets and mythologies, it strives to describe the task and processes realistically, not to reassure, mechanize or oversimplify.

The first chapter of the book discusses writers' thinking and revising processes generally, a prelude to what follows. The succeeding chapters address the key parts of the dissertation, and refer back to these processes.

In its advice on writing and persuasion, the book characterizes writers in various ways: doctoral student, student, writer, and researcher, using the indefinite "one" for general processes. It shifts between these references depending on the context. The book tries to avoid the personalized "you" (second person) because direct advice to so many different kinds of readers seems inappropriate.

# 1

# DE-MYTHOLOGIZING
# THE PROCESS
## Changing one's mindset

## 1.1 UNDERSTANDING THE TASK (PREPARING MENTALLY)

While some doctoral students have written original research papers, many come to the dissertation with little or no experience in designing a study. And students in professional programs may not have written an academic paper for ten years or more. Many doctoral students feel uncertain before the task of so large a piece of writing, with its many complex parts. Why is writing a dissertation difficult – different from writing a long class paper? For those who have always been excellent students, why do some suddenly feel overwhelmed when faced with this task?

A dissertation is more than just a difficult task. It asks students to conceptualize a new problem, evolving out of previous studies or work, and to tackle it on their own. Original work is paramount. However, the handbook advice to just "pick a topic" is naïve. Such advice assumes that students' interests and experience simply land them on a ready-made topic, which is not the case. The student's job is to add to what the research community already knows. That means that the study needs to evolve upwards out of existing research. The way forward is to read what researchers have already investigated, and look for what they say, or the writer discovers, is a possible new contribution.

That contribution does not necessarily create radical change. In fact, one might determine that a potential solution does not work; or one might discover a new way to test/confirm results. The originality could also consist of creating targeted on-the-ground change, using a new process. For instance, the researcher could recruit teachers, in an under-resourced, high crime urban high school, to implement action research; the study could involve challenging them to create lasting school interventions for their "street life" students. Despite its narrow focus, this kind of contribution requires students to do original thinking: to evaluate the conceptions of others (e.g., what are "street life" students?) and to defend their own choice of questions, conceptual framework (e.g., sense of belonging), and methods. In this endeavor, new researchers often face multiple choices, and that can be daunting.

### The difficulty serves a purpose

As doctoral students make choices to construct their studies, they gain many benefits, beyond their own study. They learn to identify the underpinnings of existing research, especially the need to align questions and methods. Through extensive reading, they see how research evolves out of previous research, creating a history, a story, of researchers' thinking. And they become more attune to the pivotal theories and assumptions that govern previous work. As a result, their own emerging work gives them insight, as both consumers and creators, into the choices researchers make as they design a study.

But new researchers don't need to feel unprepared for the task. The requirement of contribution leads many to think they need a national, headline-worthy problem, for example, "the achievement gap," "school to prison pipeline," or "secondary trauma" – and to find a whole new solution. To the contrary, intransigent problems are unlikely to be solved by a dissertation study; nor is the creation of a new theory likely to come out of a single individual's work. Rather, doctoral students need to add to what is already being researched, in a defined way. The advice here is to read according to one's interests, examine carefully what researchers say are limitations or next steps with existing research, and select a doable project. New researchers thus connect their work to the larger problems that other researchers, too, are addressing.

### Finding one's project requires digging

A useful project can be found by looking for new applications. For instance, one student applied mindset theory to urban teachers teaching third grade reading. The gap in the research was in the unique application. Early reading instruction has been studied extensively. Mindset theory has been studied extensively. But no one had combined the two, applying the theory to transforming urban teachers' practices for teaching early reading. The researcher then added another thread: how mindset theory could change how elementary teachers responded to English Language Learners' early reading difficulties. Adding an action research methodology gave the study further uniqueness: The doctoral student then participated in and recorded the teacher transformation process.

Despite its seeming narrowness, the study connects to the national problem of low reading scores – highlighting a particular theory, a particular setting, and a particular grade level. The changes in teacher practice were significant and provided ample data for Findings and Discussion chapters. The process became a professional development model for aiding other early reading teachers in urban settings. To make a contribution, the study did not require a whole new theory, just a new application – filling a gap. Dissertation writers need reminding that opening up a new field is rare.

## It can be hard to find a gap

Getting to that gap can involve some false starts. One doctoral student wanted to study students of color from low Social Economic Status (SES) communities, many of whom are first-generation students. College persistence for this group is a well-known problem. The study was thus too broad and over studied, and even choosing a particular urban neighborhood did not narrow it. The student then decided to narrow to low SES students of color who graduated from a university-assisted high school but still had college persistence problems. Now the problem stood out: Why do low SES students of color, *whose school has K-12 university support based on the latest research*, still face problems of persistence in college? Education researchers would likely be very interested in data from that study.

## 1.2 UNDERSTANDING DISSERTATION PROCESSES

Once students have a realistic notion of what comprises a "contribution," they still need help with demythologizing initial processes. What follows are some tips to lessen the initial uncertainty of engaging in original research:

## Getting used to openness and provisional drafting

The first step in writing a dissertation is banishing the undergraduate mental model of completing an assignment. An assignment has built-in assumptions about the value and approach of a topic – and assignments may limit the topic itself. Assigned work also provides a timeline and final submission guidelines appropriate to a particular course. Many of the processes are assumed in the assignment. In contrast, a dissertation asks students to choose and rationalize their topic, the approach, the timeline, and how to think about a topic. It asks for multiple drafts of a provisional nature. Those who have never carved out a study, or had to generate a process, may feel unsettled about what to expect.

But the student can embrace the openness rather than resist it. Doctoral students can tap new personal resources in setting their own timeline and goals. They benefit from entertaining multiple possible projects, trying out these projects on others, getting feedback, and spending time assessing their own processes. This is unlike any work they have likely done before, and it offers opportunities to really think about what matters to them. They could ask, broadly at first, what is the national problem that has affected them personally? What is the narrower problem, the slice of the pie, they see in their everyday life and feel capable of investigating? Then, having read extensively, what questions do they still want answered? What kind of data will help uncover answers? Who can help them find such data?

With a potential researchable problem, doctoral students might then ask further questions about themselves: When is a good thinking time to sort this out? When is the best writing time? What kind of a project person is the student? (procrastinator? perfectionist? rebel? good enough for now person?). Questions about materials and organization are also important: How does one best keep track of readings? Can Endnote or Zotero help – programs that can keep track of the articles one has read? How best store and label readings? Those unfamiliar with large projects will benefit from writing down answers to such questions, so that they can review their responses. They can also use such notes to record their thinking about where they are and the choices they are making. Having a dissertation diary of activities from each day helps students remember successful processes and emerging new ideas–insights to refer to and reflect back on.

### Learning to track one's thinking

For any project, the early thinking is going to be messy. Small notepads or recording devices might be useful, to capture unpredictable ideas. Students can also identify other doctoral candidates, with whom to share early drafts and ideas. Building good habits helps. While reading itself takes time, writers also need to summarize and evaluate articles, perhaps in extended notes; to put tags on articles for Zotero or other programs; to categorize articles by theme or potential argument; and to keep synthesizing readings (asking how articles relate to one another). Once the literature suggests a potential project, students can summarize the tentative project to share with their Chair, initiating a pattern of written give-and-take early on.

　　None of these activities is difficult, but many may be unfamiliar. This tracking of thinking and continuous note taking and other forms of writing are not like responding to a typical "assignment."

### Using the writing process itself for thinking

To further change one's mindset, one has the mantra of this book: *Writing is not the aftermath of thought, it is thought.* The advice here is to start using the writing process itself to develop initial thoughts. Even at the earliest stages, the student can write to think about possible ways of narrowing a problem. For a general problem, it helps to create a list of narrowed possibilities. If the student doesn't yet have a problem, or even a broad topic, they can first back away and read in several fields, using writing to take notes on strengths and weaknesses of the existing studies and the direction of the research. This keeps a record of one's thinking and provides practice with analyzing methodologies. Given that published studies typically identify future research needed, the student can quickly see what is already being discussed – and where others see the research going. Reading and writing about other studies has the additional benefit of exposing new researchers to the academic language and descriptors for different research areas.

　　Further uses of writing at this early stage include setting the conditions for discovering the gap in the literature – by critiquing existing studies: What questions remain unanswered? What methods would have better answered the research questions? What questions are being ignored? Notes taken while reading published studies can turn into possibilities for a new study, with the writing process itself unleashing thoughts about what one could research. The researcher might stumble across a new kind of study, perhaps in an unfamiliar field, using an unfamiliar vocabulary. This might turn into a highly innovative dissertation, a project that may have once seemed daunting because of the specialized language.

As the student uncovers a possible researchable problem, another early writing process is to list what a researcher would need to know or do to investigate a potential problem. As the list takes shape, the student may uncover a more doable project. The list may function as simple brainstorming and early planning. But it could also reveal what is a feasible project and what is not.

### Writing down divergent thoughts

A project notepad – just for the "wayward" thoughts that surface – may keep the student's thinking open and flexible. Notes may unveil something needed later on – an original purpose or an analogy too easily forgotten. At times, writers find themselves wishing they had captured a thought, as they circle back to old discarded ideas. The dissertation, as original research, poses an opportunity to act as independent researchers/writers. That means staying open and creative, and keeping a record of far-ranging thoughts.

Doctoral students often resist such seemingly inchoate, "creative" processes as writing out incipient thoughts. It is understandable that they measure as "time lost," this free-flowing writing on multiple problems, seeing it as distracting or divergent. To the contrary, writing something down itself provokes new thinking. The words on the page talk back, become an entity of their own, and stimulate new responses. When writers first set about writing, they create an internal audience, and the need to persuade, so they are already engaged in argument. Then, as they reexamine their words, they change them – remove or refine them, going beyond initial ideas. Writing a dissertation is an iterative process, and one cannot predict how one draft leads to the next.

To return to this book's premise: Writing is not just the later trappings of thought, it is the constructive act of thinking itself. And if the thoughts are messy, or unsupportable, it is good to get them down and out of one's head so that one can analyze them – reshape them, save them for later, or leave them behind. Most likely, the wayward thoughts themselves will generate new ideas, thoughts that the writer could not "think" before sitting down to write.

Divergent thinking can also be heightened by exchanges with others. When one talks to people who work in the field, either as researchers or practitioners, new perspectives open up. Questions to ask other researchers include: What are some of the under-researched questions? What questions matter? What are other researchers, boards, or organizations thinking about? Who else might have an interest in this topic? Who would benefit? Are there "clients" for such work? What information do they need or want?

Talking to people is a good way to keep moving and to find what one most cares about. Other peoples' questions and perspectives can push the writer forward.

A word about locking in: Some students decide on what they want to do, write up their project as a statement of desire ("I want to study X"), and lock in – rejecting mentors' and others' concerns. They keep trying to make the project work, despite problems such as do-ability, ethical concerns, a weak rationale, or overlap with previous research. Then, with time slipping away, they fight rewriting. The less flexible writers are early on, the more difficulty they will encounter starting again. Having several possibilities (plan A, plan B) helps. A good relief valve is also remembering that a much-cherished idea can always be resurrected after the dissertation is complete, so no great idea is lost.

## Understanding revision

Clearly, the dissertation is not a linear process, in which the student writes one paragraph after the next. Rather, the dissertation consists of continuously revisiting one's thinking. Doctoral candidates take notes and write drafts so that they can rethink their work (otherwise they can't move forward); they never really put anything "behind" them. Rather, they go over and over what they have done and thought in order to think more fully, and to ask new and better questions. This interaction with oneself means that what one writes undergoes constant revision: Everything is "placeholder" status until the final rewrite, when writers really can see what they have accomplished. They can't know what they will have when they start.

So one of the most disconcerting things about dissertation writing is the lack of finished products. As the dissertation has many requirements, the student can feel always behind. The "end" is not clearly defined. The student feels the desire to get started quickly and get sections "finished," to write them up and put them aside, to feel closer to the undefined "end." This desire is then intensified by the many dissertation handbooks – with their figures, maps, and calendars. But a quick push for certitude may lead to dead-ends – a study that has already been done, work built on false assumptions or a bias, expansive claims that no amount of data can support, or methods that don't fit the research questions.

Original research requires some uncertainty. And doctoral work requires guidance (one's Chair and others) but not absolutes. The researcher needs to write to think, to generate new and better ideas, and to think critically about what is on the page, in order to write again. In sum, getting "done" is not getting pages "finished." Indeed, the length or size of the dissertation is not at issue –it is not a "requirement." The only requirement is depth of reasoning, innovation, and contribution – defined by the research community.

## *Rethinking for depth*

That depth of reasoning is measured by how thoughtfully one responds to typical questions researchers ask of any initial research. The list is long, and what follows is not all-inclusive: Why this problem? How does the theoretical framework shape the problem? What has already been done in this area? What is the pressing need for this study? What is the rationale for the method of collecting and analyzing data? Why not other methods? Is there a plan for how findings emerge from careful analysis and synthesis of data? Will the findings be credible and trustworthy? What are the limitations to the study? Who will benefit from the findings and how? Why will these findings be important?

Such questioning extends throughout the project. It requires slow, methodical thinking and writing, reassessments of the evidence, a constant lookout for bias, and much interaction with others who are asking these same questions of their own work. These questions can serve as prompts, not judgments. In the end, it is most efficient to spend time thinking deeply about the project. (It is especially important to do a lot of upfront conceptualizing.) Writers think deeply by rereading what they have written, and by asking these questions of the text. This reflectiveness is the mindset of someone preparing for and working on a doctoral dissertation.

## *Jump-starting the writing*

Not a surprise – with an open mindset, getting started means just writing. Perhaps the writer first sets up a file, puts a working title on the first page, and then blurts stuff out (i.e. writes) about a potential problem. Maybe the writer uses project notes to do so, maybe not, but it helps to write without editing, without judging, just letting the process tap into new thinking (as suggested in Peter Elbow's foundational 1976 *Writing Without Teachers*). This process makes the writer actively search for ideas. To get the process going, the writer can ask basic, even personal, questions: Why am I interested in this topic? Are there personal experiences or a story that shapes my thinking? What actions or behaviors or artifacts do I picture in my mind when I think of this topic?

Mike Rose (*Inside Higher Ed*, April 5, 2013) suggests that one write down "the most humdrum, everyday things," including details from just watching a teacher's physical movements, gestures, tones of voice in a classroom. According to Rose, the idea "emerges from the detail and the detail grounds the idea." As an idea surfaces, gets into writing, other questions arise: Who else has written about this idea, creating research that appears exemplary? What did they have to say that resonates? Who do they cite? What do I think I know for sure about the problem? What still seems unclear, still worrisome?

If such questions don't jump-start the writing/thinking process, other writing processes can help: writing summaries of key studies – what is already known – then writing evaluations of those studies –how well they answer the research questions. That analysis might lead a new researcher to questions or hypotheses of their own. Another strategy would be to just start writing potential research questions oneself, the good and the bad. A research question focuses the student's next investigation.

There is a shapelessness to early processes. But shape is not the purpose of early brainstorming. Nobody has to read this early meandering. However, it might end up useful down the road when a writer returns to initial thoughts about the topic. Most important, loose, uncritical writing helps one think. Expectations are low. Writing is used simply to set thinking in motion.

## 1.3 DEVELOPING THE PROPOSAL – BEING READY TO REVISE

First drafts of dissertations often have typical problems, including over-generalizing, promotional language, and overinvestment. Indeed, first drafts of any writing project tend to be messy. The student needs to remain detached. As the writer settles in, and starts to write a proposal, there will likely be some false starts, untenable assumptions, or grandiose promises, all requiring revision. Back to an earlier warning – many doctoral students think that a "dissertation" must radically change researchers' previous thinking. Many then promise too much. In fact, the narrow, focused, carefully circumscribed study is much more compelling than the sweeping one, and demonstrates more clearly the research skills of the student. Writers often need cautions about how to avoid huge leaps in logic – to be careful of jumps to big claims. Seasoned researchers know that even great theoretical breakthroughs arise from detailed, focused evidence. Darwin based his theory of natural selection on the detailed study of finches on the Galapagos.

### Learning to recognize sweeping generalities

Below is an example of sweeping generalities, from an Ed.D student. This doctoral student wanted to study how to implement the eight characteristics of "high quality mathematics instruction" promoted by the National Council of Teachers of Mathematics (NCTM) at her middle school. But all eight characteristics are so broad, so sweeping, they are almost tautological; they could justify almost any instruction. The first NCTM characteristic, "establish mathematics goals to focus learning," basically says that quality math teaching is focused math teaching. But what is that? The second characteristic, "implement tasks that promote reasoning and problem solving," is equally broad and circular: Quality math teaching teaches reasoning. But what, then, is "reasoning" (given that every subject proclaims to teach reasoning of some kind)? The student needed to let go of the generalities, even though they came from an NCTM publication.

In response to feedback, the student narrowed her study. She asked how, on occasions when students failed a math problem, could teachers implement positive verbal responses; she wanted to support students' reasoning, but also to encourage alternative thinking. Comments like "I see how you got that answer … is there another way to solve that problem?" could help students see mistakes as part of solving problems. This "hum-drum," everyday example shows the researcher narrowing to a small piece of the larger problem, avoiding sweeping generalities such as those from the NCTM. The study then refocused on a wide array of modeled teacher behaviors that the researcher could observe, emptied of the all-embracing claims.

## Revising overgeneralizations

Some doctoral students may have trouble identifying when they are over-generalizing. Revising for specificity is part of honing writing. To sharpen thinking, writers seek out colleagues to propose counter examples or who question what certain terms mean. This is a natural part of focusing one's thinking.

As writers, doctoral students need to stay loose and ready to revise, welcoming questions. A great advantage of writing in the digital age is that writers can save their drafts and later see the development of their thinking. Nothing is ever lost. More important, nothing was wrong with the writer's early thinking – it was just unexamined. Sometimes even the language gets in the way of knowing what the writer is after, as in the example below.

> I want to know how an awarded civic learning program incorporates contextual/historical analysis and experiential knowledge of students of color while examining structural racism and challenging claims of colorblindness in an effort to better understand civic engagement for students of color and close the civic engagement gap.

Readers don't know what "contextual/historical analysis" means here, or what is included under "experiential knowledge"; they also do not know how these undefined concepts might intertwine with "exam-ining structural racism" and "challenging claims" (also undefined) of "colorblindness." Readers further wonder who is doing the "analyzing," the "examining" and the "challenging." The generalizations are so abstract and unconnected that we don't know what the writer means.

The doctoral student rewrote the purpose to be less sweeping:

> I want to know, what are the practices employed by award-winning high school Civics programs, including practices where teachers ask for personal histories of activism. To what extent do students of color say these practices strengthen or undermine their commitment to civic participation, including voting?

In the revision, readers know who will be reporting (students of color), what they are reporting on (specific program practices), and to what end (civic participation such as voting).

Friendly but thoughtful critiques, questions from others, and rereading the draft aloud pushed this student researcher to write more clearly, without all the jargon. What was the writer really after? How could a study of civics programs identify practices? He realized that to convince readers to "buy" his idea, he had to convince them that he knew what data he was after, from whom, through what means – and could communicate it. He accomplished this well, and the study resulted in useful findings.

## Staying clear of promotional language

Strong opinions, expressed as dictates, are not the sign of a strong dissertation. Seasoned researchers cut away all the easy, evidence-free opinions and current trendy language that creep in. This includes the editorializing and promotional writings – the "musts" and "shoulds" that come out of pre-set beliefs and biases. When defining a project, seasoned researchers let the data or other evidence speak for itself, linking carefully worded interpretations to specifics. Some advice from an old hand: Stay off the podium, leave pontificating to the Pope, and remove the bias and opinion from the project description." Press the delete key often, especially when "must" and "should" surface.

This is language to avoid:

The needs of the growing populations of racial minorities in post-secondary must be addressed.

Here is a revision that replaces "must" with data:

In 2015, 42% of all students enrolled in a degree granting post-secondary institution were non-white, compared to 16% in 1976.
(Snyder, de Brey, & Dillow, 2018)

In the community of researchers, a dissertation has little in common with an opinion or editorial. While fervent beliefs and commitments govern choices of research topics, students need to let evidence guide them. Dissertation readers look for strong reasoning, a set of views emerging from a careful assessment of data.

## Overinvestment

Wanting one's dissertation to create change is valuable, but pushing a specific change may not be. Understandably, students enter a doctoral program to create change, and they want to direct their work toward the solutions they envision. And students bring a wealth of experience to their projects that can serve to frame, detail and give meaning to the project. For instance, one student used her own experience with a learning disability (LD) to frame a project on how principals can increase LD access to mainstream classes.

However, solutions need to be closely connected to findings or results, and conceived later, with care; they are not catch-all, predetermined approaches. Solutions are not always even the purpose of a dissertation. Some projects only investigate the nature of a problem, leaving it for others to propose solutions from the data. Not uncommonly, students mistakenly jump to solutions even before they have investigated what the problem is. Overinvestment sometimes leads students to approach research backwards.

Here is an example of overinvestment: One doctoral student was invested in a statewide change at the community college level having to do with acceleration (moving students more quickly through remedial classes by putting them in credit bearing classes). He proposed that a key barrier to change was faculty intransigence: He felt that faculty claimed "academic freedom" to run their classes as they always had. Based on this assumption, he proposed investigating this barrier so that community colleges could better implement the change he supported.

This student came to the project with bias and multiple assumptions, having already assumed what the barriers were. The project eventually morphed into a multi-case study of community colleges successfully implementing this change and what constituents themselves say were the barriers to change. Those barriers turned out to be very different from the "faculty intransigence" the researcher had assumed. He had remained nimble and transformed the study so that unexpected data could surface.

*A reminder*: While a doctoral student may come to a project impassioned to justify a particular change, make a difference in a known way, or prove a theory, such a preconception has potential to bias the conduct of the study. For example, a student might ask questions of those already known to be aggrieved or ask the kind of leading questions that provoke the responses wanted. Or a student may choose participants or subjects who will say what they think the researcher wants to hear, or report behaviors that make them look good. That is not the purpose of research. Nor does the desire for a pre-specified change align with what the doctoral degree stands for.

## Countering overinvestment: the purpose of a doctoral degree

The doctoral degree qualifies one to join other researchers in the field, those able to suspend personal belief and let the evidence define what is true. Researchers need to prepare themselves to be proven wrong. For instance, if a new researcher tests a theory (a difficult task – one would need wide-scale data), it needs to be formed as a hypothesis. The researcher then clarifies what it would take to prove them wrong. When a new researcher performs open-ended qualitative research and has strong opinions, that researcher has to take extensive precautions to preserve the quality of the data. These precautions include selecting sites the researcher does not oversee, making sure that respondents do not report back what they think the interrogator wants to hear, and creating a sample or participant pool to encourage differing perspectives. None of these measures precludes caring deeply about the overall topic. And they do not preclude using personal experience to introduce, detail, and reflect back on the study, tapping into what makes the study personally meaningful.

An example of caring deeply but not over-investing follows. One student, a Latina middle school principal, cared deeply about the difficult experiences of Latina principals in training for, assuming, and maintaining their leadership roles, under a barrage of discrediting remarks and disbelief. These were experiences marking the doctoral student's own career. Rather than jumping to solutions, she decided to let a small group of principals share their own leadership stories – the tumult, self-doubt, challenges to their authority, and difficult decisions – and to let the data itself speak to the kind of leadership training needed. By prompting a mostly ignored, under researched population to tell their stories, the student kept a sharp focus, refrained from over-investment, and generated valuable findings.

## Staying detached from words

Just as the researcher stays detached from study design, the writer holds an unimpassioned relationship to words and paragraphs. If a writer creates a section that sounds impressive, but lacks clarity, protecting it might restrict working on the rest of the piece. The advice is for writers not to fall in love with their words, paragraphs, or even chapter drafts, and then try to protect them.

Having to revise does upset some students. Molding sentences into arguments takes hard work, and students don't want to face "redoing" sections. But this reluctance overlooks the writing/thinking paradigm. These students focus too much on the writing as product, which they want "done." But when writers turn their attention away from the page and discuss their ideas with colleagues, they can suddenly see where the draft obscures their ideas. In identifying the disjunction between idea and draft, most students become motivated rewriters. They let go of the inexpressive words and rewrite with a clearer sense of purpose. The earlier writings no longer reflect who the writer is and what they want out of the project.

To underscore again – this is a messy process. Writers will "read into" their written words, and feel confused when others don't get what they mean. Further, in early drafting, writers sometimes don't hear their own voice. If they start with over generalizations or circular claims, they may sound *to others* more like an editorial writer than a researcher, but *to themselves* they are conveying their passion. Or, in assuming the very thing that they need to prove, some writers may be communicating their bias, but again may accept this as the norm. The messiness comes when readers push back. Recognizing bias is a necessary step. Unless students begin by writing out their thoughts, they can't identify such weaknesses and address them. Once writers have words on the page, they can improve their work.

## 1.4 PROCESSES OF REWRITING

Along with being undaunted and staying open, what else helps in the processes of developing a proposal? Probably most important is equating writing explicitly with *rewriting*. What that means is that the writer understands something about the cognitive processes of writing. To sum up the writing process – writing is non-linear. It constantly intersects with thinking, which can move by association, along different levels of abstraction, and with greater or less focus. Writers need to write in consecutive words, but the thought behind the words is not typically consecutive. Unanticipated thoughts occur as new associations are made. And backtracking, then rewriting, is essential to going forward. Writers don't want to fight themselves in this – it would be a losing battle.

### Rereading as writing

Writers constantly reread what they write, letting the previous work release the flow of the next piece. That start-up writing might be at first a sputter, requiring lots of placeholder phrases or ideas that later need a review, so that more exacting ones can take their place. Writers can seldom just pick up where they left off, without rereading and reassessing. And even during productive writing sequences, the mind circles back, rethinks, sometimes thinks in a straight course for a while, sometimes parallel courses, sometimes halts to edit a few words, sometimes imagines some big idea for future development, sometimes simply rejects and rewrites a passage. This non-linear process is not "wrong." This is how ideas get generated and refined. Progress is organic, circular, often halting, sometimes on an expressway.

*An example*: Here is a personal example of a big structural idea suddenly intersecting my own low level editing: While revising the section on mindset, out of the blue it occurred to me that I would later need a section on voice: One hears one's voice as one rereads. So I stopped mid-sentence and wrote down a placeholder heading called "voice" for a later section. Then I went back to the original task at hand, rereading passages to move forward. The idea for voice came to me as I was editing for something else, indicating that writers may be working on several tracks at once. With this new heading, if an idea surfaces on voice, I can jump to that heading and put it down, so as not to forget it. Having the heading helped me accommodate dual tracks of thoughts, without losing my way. The "wayward" thoughts now had a legitimate place to await their time.

Given this messy, complex writing process, students often ask, what does one write (rewrite) first? How does one get into it? A suggestion: If writers have already done some early free-writes about purpose or direction, they can look back at these passages. Has the thinking changed? Does the free-write still capture the intention? Does it start up new thinking? Either way, after writers reread earlier thoughts, they can create a short proxy paragraph summarizing current rethinking of the study's outline and purpose. This provisional statement, built on earlier thinking, helps ground the next piece of writing. The new statement can be written fast, as a preliminary take, and reading it aloud, yet again, lets the writer hear the words and further assess their accuracy. At this stage, the statement could also be read to others to get reactions. Finally, it could be used to start up further writing – or simply be discarded.

## The importance of responses from others

At every juncture in proposal writing, writers need responses from others to help them revise. At some point, a writer's words become like echo chambers – it is hard to get outside them. Indeed, as suggested earlier, writers project into their words all that they know, so that the words reflect back to them those intended meanings, not necessarily what is on the page. The words seem transparently true because writers "know" what their words mean; they don't need to unpack them.

But the words likely don't convey to others the same details or fullness. Writers get wrapped up inside their own heads. So every writer needs readers. They ask colleagues: What did they take from this proposal? Where did they get confused? What meanings did they form? What questions do they have? What concrete actions, behaviors, or events did they imagine when they read the proposal? Before submitting materials to a Chair, the writer needs to insure that other students or colleagues understand the reasoning and follow the argument.

## Persistent myth of writing as a skill

To restate the book's premise in a new context: Part of students' challenges with writing can trace back to the persistent myth that writing is an aftereffect of thinking: First the writer thinks thoughts, then the writer writes them. (The academic community mostly supports this view, as context-free writing workshops and courses abound.) Writing is conceived of as a mere "skill," like learning to cook, that comes into play only after one has decided what to write (or eat). One takes out a recipe, follows it, and if one is careful, the meal is a success. Given this view, why would anyone need readers? One just needs a skills class (a diner can simply wait until the meal is cooked).

Equating writing with a skill opposes this book's key assumption, that writing not only generates thought, but is thought. Once again, the process is not a mere one-time-through skill. To the contrary, the back and forth of provisional versions – of re-reading, adding, deleting, sharpening, and connecting – is the essence of thought itself. Each time a writer returns to a draft, rereading it, that writer rethinks it – feels where it is vague, where examples are needed – where it is cumbersome, redundant, or even inexact. But because writers need to communicate, they require readers to determine if the intended message comes across. Readers can elucidate where the reasoning breaks down, where a connection is lost, where questions arise. As readers need to reconstruct the written words in their own minds, and piece together the logic, they can pinpoint where they follow easily and where they have difficulty. Writers need an outside voice to identify places that continue to require work.

## Avoiding delays: the need for readers

Below is an explanation of how counterproductive it can be to postpone writing, and how a reader or listener can help with the process, especially for the Literature Review.

Many students, trying to "think first, write second," bog down when writing their Literature Review. They read continuously, and the more they read, the more they think they have to read. Partly procrastination, partly anxiety at missing something, they fall down the proverbial "rabbit hole." These students often delay writing entirely, thinking they must first know all the research on their topic. They read and read. They assume that once they have this knowledge, the writing will just come. Maybe they make lists and notes, but they don't synthesize what they have read to form an argument.

In contrast, continuously writing about the research helps students see what is really needed (and what is not). As they begin arguing for their study, writers are forced to consolidate studies to make a point– deciding which studies to link together, which to feature at length, which to cite parenthetically, and which to ignore. The argument itself helps determine the strongest supports. Then, as writers try to communicate these points, the writing requires multiple decisions on organization, detailing, and language, decisions best approached as an ongoing process.

At the beginning of the process, readers can encourage writers to write something integrative, or at least to generate some claims related to the proposed study. When doctoral students write lists of isolated summaries, another delay tactic, they have nowhere to go. Simple reader questions such as how groups of studies either support or contradict arguments, or which studies are key to the argument, can help keep writers focused on creating an argument.

Readers as listeners are key to pushing writers to synthesize. They can simply ask writers to explain aloud how the key studies support the project. Interestingly, sluggish or blocked writers can often verbalize clearly their ideas to someone else, but then get stuck facing the computer screen. Explaining aloud not only unblocks the writing, but is also an opportunity to generate new ideas. The on-the-spot articulation helps release writers' thoughts, and these sluggish writers become both fluent and innovative. A good strategy for writers is to bring along a tape recorder when explaining to someone else their ideas (a well-known saying is, "I don't know what I think until I see what I say"). Often, writers are much more voluble and fluent when they speak to a listener. Speaking can be a form of brainstorming.

As suggested above, readers are particularly helpful reviewing (or listening to) early drafts of the Literature Review. Dissertation writers often seek to be exhaustive, describing one study after the next, list-like, but leaving to the reader to connect to a general topic. One student, studying non-academic supports for community college transfer students at research universities, wrote broadly about student engagement. The early draft revealed multiple long definitions of student engagement, categorized under different theoretical frames, and based on different methodological approaches. How does a writer synthesize this literature? Readers told the writer to choose the one he would investigate and merely reference that other models exist.

Any reader can prompt revisions with some simple questions: How do these studies argue for the project? How much background is really needed? What is the best definition and theoretical frame to go forward? How does the background lead to the main argument? What is a logical order for the arguments to follow to help keep the argument on track? Without reader response, writers might find themselves lost in the literature morass, and relying on numerous delay tactics.

## Creating a community of writers

A formal way to ensure reader response is to create a *community of writers*, a committed group of colleagues. A caveat about getting responses from others: Reader response sounds like a one-way street. Readers critique *the writer's* work. But a one-way street suggests a collision – the writer being run over by an onslaught of haughty criticism. Writers do best when they are part of a community, all of whom want response, and all of whom are supportive – a two-way or four-way street. A *community of writers* does not worry about "skill" level, which doctoral student is the "best" writer or who offers the best response. Rather, a writing community joins together those with a mutual interest in promoting each other's work.

Most important for group members is being open to giving and receiving response, and willing to commit to regular dates and times for review. Everyone's response is helpful. Divergent responses are particularly useful, as somehow the writer's language is permitting different understandings. Groups offer not just wide feedback but the sense of community. Some groups even meet for writing days, to create a writing ambiance, a mutual energy and belief.

The benefits are many. Members share drafts, experiences, inspiration, knowledge, and motivation. The community holds members accountable. Further, members bring to the table their own expanding understanding of the process. Student colleagues can explain, encourage, sympathize, and provoke. Their questions can inspire new directions. They can also identify new literature, stronger evidence, clarifications, and further rationales because they themselves are grappling with these issues. Even lacking knowledge of the topic, members can serve as simple sounding boards, explaining where they were drawn in and where they drifted off.

Despite such benefits, formal groups may need some ground rules. At times, one group member dominates the discussion and may counter or diminish others' views. Groups need to decide on norms, such as turn-taking, allowing everyone a voice, sensitivity to the writer's purpose, constructive feedback only, and reassessing group processes. While different kinds of groups exist – spontaneous or assigned – all members need to serve as honest, constructive questioners. Everyone in the group will then internalize the view that writing is really rewriting: It is not a "skill" one has or lacks.

## Gaining comfort from experience

Even with all the helpful advice, as well as guides, support, deadlines, and motivation, some writers are still hesitant to start writing. One colleague claimed that her apartment was never so clean as when she was writing her dissertation – she would do anything other than write. If students find themselves routinely reluctant to write, below are some additional reminders.

Writers will naturally become more comfortable with writing as they begin the process. The more they practice writing, the more natural it becomes. As writers choose, narrow, and justify their study, and then have to explain it over and over, the words start to come more easily. It is a bit like the way one first learned to talk: pretty hesitant and halting at first, but more fluent and expansive later on, grammatically correct without one consciously doing anything. No student sits down and writes section after section of a doctoral dissertation and then pieces them together. The process itself – guided by the Chair, supported by helpful colleagues, and normalized through simple practice – teaches the writer not to worry so much about messy drafts.

## Starting up writing

**Write:**

1 A quick paragraph describing the problem, with a key example.
2 An imagined finding from an imagined study, first stated out loud.
3 A map, as if described to a friend, of how one intends to move from broad topic to specific solvable problem.

# 2 THE **PROBLEM** STATEMENT
## Writing processes

The Problem Statement of any research proposal typically becomes the first chapter of the dissertation. It identifies the problem or question, situates that problem in relevant literature, including the theoretical framework, and states the research questions and study methods. The study's problem is the narrow researchable problem that the student argues needs to be investigated. It is supported by the literature, works that provide the problem's context (reaching from national statistics on the broad issue down to targeted, aligned studies of the narrower problem); this literature – provides evidence of the gap the study will fill. The problem is further supported by the methods, which argue for the study's do-ability.

The Problem Statement is a blueprint for the proposal as a whole. So getting it written is complex. Students can't really write it with full accuracy until they have written the other sections or chapters. That is because the Problem Statement synthesizes for the reader the key elements of the whole proposal, providing an outline of the arguments. As the rest of the proposal expands that outline, with fuller sections on the relevant literature (the Literature Review) and the methods (Methodology), the writer circles back to the Problem Statement, writing and rewriting it as the other sections of the proposal develop.

Choosing an area of interest is the first task. The doctoral student may begin with deeply felt experience (but not bias) of a problem. Contrary to the maxim "the best dissertation is the done dissertation," new researchers need to care deeply about the topic: That sense of value carries them through the years of writing and prepares them for future work in the field.

But a new researcher also needs to be realistic about the resources and time available. Those in three-year professional programs may have an especially difficult time narrowing their research to doable projects, nearby sites, and willing participants. Full time Ph.D. students in five- to seven-year programs may have more years and access, but they are also expected to carry a heavy load of theory and methods classes, teach, and possibly contribute to grant proposals. So doctoral students generally need to be flexible. A student's commitment to a problem isn't static and can emerge as the student researches, narrows and redefines the project. What follows is advice on how to remove barriers and identify an innovative, doable project, while maintaining a deep concern for a problem.

## 2.1 DEFINING A RESEARCHABLE PROBLEM: COLLECTING IDEAS, PRE-WRITING/BRAINSTORMING – BEGINNING THE WRITING PROCESS

Writing begins with brainstorming. Most students likely have an area of interest (e.g., the African-American and Latino/a school-to-prison pipeline), but not a researchable problem (e.g., urban schools lack academic mentors for *street life* students). They need a problem that can be solved empirically, research questions, and targeted data they can collect. Using research, doctoral students will need to justify the study and provide a theoretical framework to shape the work. Here are some brainstorming activities that may help define a project.

### *Finding starting points*

There are multiple ways of jump-starting a unique study. Below are just some of them.

1   One can examine statistics in reports and surveys on a topic of interest. Reading critically is a form of pre-writing. Statistics often tell a story if blocks of data are put next to one another. A unique problem may surface. For instance, one doctoral student was interested in the effects of project based learning (PBL) on the academic achievement of urban minorities. He separated out the different minorities, and noticed an anomaly in the school district's data: PBL positively affected the achievement of all school minorities, except for Latinos/as. The story had a missing part. He couldn't understand why. From the student's own teaching experience, he then hypothesized that many Latino/a students were uncertain about their English and avoided group leadership roles. The more fluent English speakers would have had a monopoly on those roles. For his project, then, the studlent built language supports and revolving leadership roles into his PBL classes. Findings revealed that the experimental Latino/a group showed the same achievement gains as other underrepresented minorities, a major finding. His study proved his hypothesis to be correct.

2   As noted earlier, ideas for a new study may also come from what other researchers explicitly say are next steps. Ideas for future research usually appear in a published study's Conclusions or Discussion section. If students immerse themselves in recent peer-reviewed studies, necessary to brainstorming, they may see new questions surfacing. Also, new researchers come to understand the conversations of a research community whose work they will extend. At some point, the student should contact these researchers and ask what work they are currently doing, and to get their reactions to a potential project. Authors, who want to know that their work is being carried forward, are typically very supportive of new researchers. A key early writing activity, then,

is writing to an author about what they are researching and matching up one's own potential interest to theirs.

3    Librarians are another resource for finding a new, researchable problem. Often, new researchers are unaware of subject headings/key words that may throw light on one's general topic area. They may also be unaware of consolidating handbooks on research, collections that synthesize current research on a topic. For instance, they might scour the handbook on *Research on Reading Comprehension*, or the *Handbook on Research of Educational Administration*. Librarians know which handbooks, which journals, what kind of subject headings, and what search engines work best for this kind of project. They can help narrow down a field quickly and create a more efficient search. A new researcher does well to become friends with the librarian who works in a targeted discipline.

4    Reference lists at the ends of studies can clarify how earlier research has influenced later research, providing key pre-writing activities. Timelines indicate direction: Who is citing whom and how far back do these citations go? Notes on this history suggest how key concerns developed. When the references from recent studies cite the same previous studies, doctoral students know that they have located the central line of research in their area. The key researchers typically cite each other, and the student comes to see who the major players are. These are the studies one wants to examine closely, and keep notes on, to see where the center of the field is going, where a potential contribution might lurk, and what shape the Literature Review might take. Doctoral students will know that they have read the key research in the field once the same names keep surfacing.

5    Another beginning point, a key brainstorming activity, is through conceptual models or theoretical frameworks. Research is embedded in such models, either explicitly or implicitly. One student interested in Critical Race Theory began with the theory and looked for unique applications. She decided to develop a program for high school principals on how to apply such theories in their leadership. Another student started with Growth Mindset Theory, which has generated studies in different subject areas and at different levels. This student chose to apply the theory to a grade level never before explored – early elementary reading – where the need for *a growth mindset* seemed unlikely. It turned out that teachers periodically applied a *fixed mindset* to children even as young as eight years old.

Using theory as a beginning point, doctoral students can choose a potential framework and then create a unique design. When they examine studies reflecting this model, they look for a gap in what has been done. Summarizing such theories is a key brainstorming activity. The student who started with Mindset Theory found that gap in the application to third grade reading instruction. She designed an action research project that trained early reading teachers to apply the theory in their responses to students' reading errors. Her ultimate goal became to improve teachers' ability to respond with a *growth mindset* to the reading errors of English Language Learners.

6    One can also begin analyzing empirical studies and let a theoretical framework surface later. Reading empirical studies can thus become a key pre-writing activity. Once students are clear about their direction, they can determine what model closely aligns with their research. This is especially true if the student is interested in policy issues. One doctoral student wanted to study how charter school decision makers adjusted to new state policies with respect to supports for Emotionally Disturbed students. As she defined her problem, she later saw that the theory of "adaptive leadership" best fit her growing interest in leader decision-making in the context of weakened state support. This framework surfaced months into the process of defining her study.

Starting points are arbitrary. Another student, studying the problem of sustaining Dual Language middle schools, struggled to situate her study. She wanted to examine successful Dual Language middle schools, whose numbers were decreasing despite state mandates for language supports. However, she lacked a theoretical frame. She finally came across the Dynamic Sustainability Framework of Chambers, Glasgow, and Strange (2013), which turned out to be a good fit for her research on sustainability. While new researchers will eventually need to be explicit about what theory governs their study, they do not need to begin with theory. At some point, however, they house their work in a theoretical frame. They likely will need to examine existing critiques of that frame to prepare for their Preliminary Orals.

### Evaluating supportive research

Honing a problem means continually evaluating pertinent articles. Some students have a tendency to believe uncritically what they see in print, reading for information and not critiquing underlying assumptions. This seems a common issue, especially with academic research. On the surface, that research may appear beyond reproach. To avoid relying on weaker studies or potentially biased reports, the new researcher first notes the reputation of the journal: Every field has its blue-chip journals whose reviewers are major researchers in the field. To assess an article, the student selects for recent date of publication, peer-review, number of times cited, and scope of researchers' work. This culling of quality research is a good start. But the student still needs to examine an individual study's methods, looking at how the research derived its findings (see below). The researcher can then select the strongest studies and scour references for additional studies of the same caliber.

To find the key research supporting a problem, a practical approach helps. As noted above, peer-reviewed articles are the coin of the realm. Google Scholar and other sources indicate this criterion. For noting the publication date and number of times each study has been cited, again Google

Scholar, EdSource, Educational Resources Information Center (ERIC), and others provide this information. New researchers can also limit their internet search to the previous ten years, thus excluding older, perhaps out-of-date articles. (Early, foundational articles surface in recent studies, and the student can work backwards to recover these.) Then, they can look for sponsorship – was the research funded by an organization with specific economic interests perhaps biasing the findings? If unsponsored, students can then skim the abstract for relevance.

With a significant body of research identified, the student can then analyze the trajectory of the research: Which are the foundational early studies and how did the research build over time? What are the most recent studies and how do they relate back (if at all) to the foundational studies?

## A critical eye

To evaluate research, the student identifies each study's weaknesses and strengths – in theoretical framework, research questions, methods, protocols, quality of data, findings, and conclusions. Is there sufficient data to support the claims made? How were the sites and subjects (if any) selected and accessed? Was there data that might have been collected but was not? What limitations to the study were noted and what others were not? Was there researcher bias to begin with? Again, notes on these key studies, especially their strengths and weaknesses, may create a path toward a study that needs to be done.

Doctoral students need to be circumspect about non peer-reviewed sources. Only articles that explicitly detail the methods of the study allow readers to assess credibility. Books by well-known researchers are useful to a point, and may reference key studies, but many such books present high-altitude opinions on a research area. Other well-known researchers may hold different opinions of the field. Such opinions cannot be cited as reasons for a study, as they do not use empirical data. Rather, new researchers need to track down the studies mentioned and examine the empirical evidence, and the methods used to produce it.

Reports require additional caution, even if they detail methods and data collected. They could be sponsored studies, to support a particular practice that the organization paying for the report wants headlined. A careful researcher looks to see what organization underwrites a cited study and what their interests might be.

## Synthesizing a body of research to hone the study

It is not enough to want to study a problem. Students at times say, I want to study something, for instance "I want to study African-American high school drop-out rates," as if the rationale were built into the desire. In contrast, for such a study the student needs data from diverse peer-reviewed journals on the effect of different variables (such as low sense of belonging, lack of career goal, weak academic supports) on drop-out rate. A critical eye might then lead the new researcher to ask, what are the key assumptions in all of these studies? What might be overlooked? Is there a gap in the research? One such student decided that African-American students themselves might have an answer to the question on dropping out, and noted that their perspective had never been examined. In the end, he chose to ask high absentee African-American students, who came to school but avoided class, why they hung out in hallways instead of going to class. This was a targeted, unstudied population with a unique voice.

## Narrowing the problem to make it doable

When doctoral students have read widely on their topic, they still need to narrow the project until it is doable, as in the study mentioned above. Here is another example of such narrowing, from national problem to doable study: While a national problem might be US students' low mathematics scores, a narrower problem might be the lack of US elementary school teachers adequately trained in mathematics. More targeted still would be how to evaluate an existing, research-based pre-service training in math for elementary school teachers. An actual doable, researchable project might then entail following 12–15 pre-service elementary teachers through their first year in-service and evaluating how often and in what context they use a specific pre-service training. The researchable problem is a small slice of the pie of the national problem. The research question becomes: *To what extent does a cohort of pre-service math teachers use their training in visual modeling in their first year of independent teaching?*

## Various ways to narrow

The above narrowing was by program, specific training, and identifiable effects. Another narrowing might be by population and intervention. One student wanted to study the low persistence rates of first generation community college students. Multiple sociological and psychological variables have been cited as causes of this low retention: family need, low college going social and cultural capital, academic under-preparedness, lower sense of belonging, and lower self-efficacy. The doctoral student narrowed the topic by looking at existing interventions, particularly for Latino/a first generation community college students. First Year Experience is one intervention that has had success in retaining first generation students. To narrow still further, the student decided to design, implement, and assess a second year experience, specifically targeting Latinos/as – a more limited population.

Narrowing can also be by type of institution and institutional relationships. Dissertations on management or leadership often revolve around relationships between organizational sectors, which can at times be conflictive. One doctoral student wanted to examine relationships characterized by long-standing conflict, with the idea of looking for successful collaborations. The student narrowed to four-year college faculty vs. administration conflicts, then narrowed again to areas where these sectors collaborated: on student retention. She continued to slice up the pie by focusing on private Jesuit colleges because although religious institutions might seem less prone to conflict, data shows they also experience this problem, only the conflict can be less obvious. She then narrowed to Jesuit college faculty and administrator collaborations formally tasked with improving student retention. This narrowing allowed for targeted data collection and detailed descriptions of collaboration within a particular context.

As new researchers narrow their studies, they need to keep notes on their thinking and rationale: For the above study, why was it appropriate to select Jesuit colleges? Why was it appropriate to choose faculty and administration as conflictive sectors? And, why did it make sense to select student retention as the collaborative effort? As the researcher wrote down her rationale for her decisions, her underlying reasoning was easy to access when her doctoral committee members asked her to defend her choices.

### A common misstep: jumping to solutions before defining the problem

Doctoral students often have experience with broad problems they want to solve, but they may also have pre-formed solutions, as noted earlier. Students need to guard against this projection. Perhaps a student wants to build an eleventh grade civics program that engages underrepresented minorities (URMs). It is not enough to say the problem is that URMs don't vote in representative numbers – such a problem could generate hundreds of solutions. Rather, the student first needs data that existing high school civics programs are *not* engaging URMs. With such data (and a researchable definition of "engagement"), the student could propose to design and assess a new program. But what if further studies identify lots of innovative programs, none with evidence of successfully recruiting and engaging URMs? What if further studies show that "engagement" for URMs differs significantly from engagement for majority students? The doctoral student may need a different kind of study.

In the case of this study, the student decided to investigate two "awarded" civics programs, to identify the perspectives of students of color, rather than jumping the gun and devising yet another program, absent underrepresented minorities' perspectives. As the problem was redefined, the solution changed. This example suggests that students need to keep reassessing the research problem – rewriting the Problem Statement as the investigation expands. It is too easy to jump to the solution.

### Determining one's research strengths

Once one has a defined problem, a key question to ask is how to use one's particular connections to gain access and to collect data. If the doctoral student is a member of a large organization (e.g., a charter school organization or a mental health organization), that student might use those connections to promote the study, and then work with the organization to collect data. After sharing their conception of the problem, the student could offer several doable projects, write them up, and ask organization members to comment. These potential respondents can provide a needed edge in that they are already vested in how this work might improve their practices. Further, the trustworthiness of their responses removes key obstacles that often affect dissertation projects. Finally, students who choose to work within a familiar setting (e.g., a charter school organization) may already have been trained in the skills needed to carry out the study.

## 2.2 IDENTIFYING TENTATIVE RESEARCH QUESTIONS

Students will find that their research questions continuously change. New researchers typically start with what they want to know, narrow it, find a doable project, and rethink the questions. But this takes multiple iterations. And with committee members, the questions can change at Preliminary Orals, and even during data collection.

### Some questions go in multiple directions

Early on, students need to avoid questions that go in multiple directions. For instance, such questions as, *Why do teachers leave the profession?* or, *How can public health systems be improved?* are too broad. In sharp contrast, the writer could revise to a more researchable question, such as *What school leadership behaviors do middle school teachers, in a high poverty urban district, say motivated them to stay beyond five years?* Narrow, yes, but the question still tackles the national problem of teacher persistence. And it is doable because the researcher ruled out confounding variables such as SES, sub-urban versus urban schools, middle grades versus upper or elementary grades, and respondents' personal motives. Most important, by narrowing to school leadership behaviors, the question directly reflects on school leaders.

Narrowing the question also solves practical problems. Such narrowing bounds the time and resources needed to do the study. For instance, 20 interviews with long-term teachers might be enough to uncover impactful leadership behaviors; or a questionnaire in a large urban district might ask retained teachers to rate pre-determined school leadership behaviors. Because the questions themselves would focus on leadership, the findings would be useful to school and district leaders hoping to retain teachers. Finally, school leadership publications would provide ready avenues for dissemination.

### Some questions are simply unclear

Some research questions are not so much broad as unclear. Below is an example of a typical first draft question, and then a later revision.

What aspects of college instructor behaviors, attitudes and interactions do under-represented minority STEM students perceive as influencing student engagement within large enrollment entry-level math and science courses?

The research question is indefinite. How can respondents agree or disagree that an "aspect" of a behavior then "influences" their "student engagement"? First, "aspect" is vague. Second, student engagement is an open-ended concept – is the researcher thinking of feelings or actions? Third, "influences" suggests a direct result, which respondents might question: If a teacher asks a question in class, does this *cause* a student to feel "engaged"? Rewritten for clarity, the question might read:

What instructor behaviors do under-represented minority STEM students, in large enrollment, entry-level math and science courses, say encouraged class discussions and discussion groups?

The question now eliminates "influences" – permitting respondents to focus on instructors' behaviors, not whether students "were influenced" or not. And "student engagement" has now been clarified to mean active class discussions.

## Bias can affect question construction

At times, unconscious bias creeps in, as in the example below:

How proficient do school psychologists feel in distinguishing between English Language Development and a Specific Learning Disability when conducting a Special Education assessment?

This question is rife with bias and ethical concerns. Readers can sense that the writer thinks that the psychologists don't feel "proficient." Yet professionals will likely resist such an admission, given that this is their job. It would be unusual for respondents to admit to a researcher that they were not proficient – especially in such weighted circumstances as assessing young children for special education placement.

A less intrusive question, with less of a negative bias, might require a different study, one that assumes not psychologists' inner sense of failure, but their willingness to sharpen their assessment skills:

According to school psychologists, to what extent does a collaborative professional development program enhance their proficiency in assessing English Language Development versus Specific Learning Disability?

This question now assumes that the psychologists are already proficient in their jobs. It also assumes that a collaborative professional development program might help that proficiency grow and that psychologists will report that growth. This student ended up with a powerful study that allowed psychologists to recognize gaps in their own training.

### Studies can also need expanding

Mostly, questions change because they need clarifying details to pinpoint what the researcher is after. But they can change because the student expanded the study, as was the case below. The following question, from a study discussed earlier, needed two parts, but the details clarify the intent:

1 What practices of awarded civic learning programs strengthen or undermine students of color commitment to civic participation? According to students of color? According to administrators and teachers?

   a *To what extent do these programs incorporate the historical and personal narratives, perceptions, and experiences of students of color?*

The question details the perspectives and program practices to be investigated. The first part leaves open the question of which practices affect civic participation; the second part hones in on practices the researcher particularly wants to target. The study ended up as two, not one, research questions.

Only rarely do research questions change because unexpected data surfaces during the course of the study, data answering a slightly different question. This event can potentially shift the study, often in a positive way.

## 2.3 REVISITING SUPPORTIVE DATA

Researchers have to continuously comb studies to ensure that their proposed project captures the problem they are trying to solve. Even after the Problem Statement is written and approved, newly surfaced data can change the project significantly – the problem description, research questions, theoretical frame, and design of the study itself. Even if the project remains essentially the same, the new data changes the context.

### How projects can shift

Two examples come to mind. In one case, a student wanted to study the experiences of visual and performing arts (VAPA) transfer students at a research institution. She wrote compellingly about how these students faced all the typical transfer student problems – low GPAs, low graduation rates, culture shock, long time-to-degree, lack of culturally responsive classes, low institutional supports – only magnified by the extra performance

requirements and lack of transfer credits for community college performance classes. However, before she submitted her problem to her chair, data
surfaced that these students' GPAs were overall higher than those of typical
transfer students, they graduated at higher rates than did typical transfer
students, the long time-to-degree was not different from that of other transfer
students (many took a year off to perform), and they had "in-house" academic supports from their various departments. The "problem" had to shift.

On deeper investigation from a pilot study, the student found more
specific data that VAPA students did very well in their performing arts
classes, but less well in their General Education classes. Data also indicated
that VAPA students did not use university support services, but rather in-
house arts supports. As a result of this digging, the student still concentrated
on time-to-degree, but this problem was particularized by VAPA students
not meeting the Mission of the research institution, remaining isolated in
their departments, and not gaining the education guaranteed by a BA from
a tier-one research institution. So the "problem" changed.

In a second example of new research surfacing, a student was
studying the lack of Dual-Language (DL) middle schools, as these were not
being sustained. (This study was mentioned earlier.) Many such schools
had ceased to exist. The student had written her Problem Statement on this
issue, proposing a case study of one "sustained" DL middle school. On further investigation, she found data showing that more middle school DL
schools existed than she had known about and that the district had planned
for six more. Given this new data, she could have changed from "sustainability" to "diffusion of innovation" and studied the decision-making of
these new schools. However, she decided to remain with her original plan
to examine sustainability, but in light of how these new emerging schools
were already planning for issues of sustainability. Interestingly, the study
morphed once again, to a single school and the complexities of even one
school negotiating conflicting values, schedules, and equities.

## 2.4 FINDING AND WORKING WITH A CHAIR

One of the most ambiguous parts of the proposal development process can
be finding and working with one's Chair and other committee members.
How does one make the best selection? How often do students communicate, ask for help (including the reading of drafts), or update their progress?
Do students rely on the Chair to find the other committee members, or
choose members themselves, which might have unknown consequences?

### Finding a Chair and committee members

Once students have identified a problem, supported it with the literature,
and generated some ideas about methods, they likely have a draft Problem
Statement, and first chapter, in hand. At this point, they may already have
discussed the project with a potential Chair. The Chair needs to be someone
who has knowledge of and interest in the project area. If the doctoral

student has not yet identified who this might be, they could scan online the research interests of various faculty members, read some of their articles, talk to other graduate students about their advising style, and create a short list of possible Chairs.

Before doctoral candidates get too far in the process, they need feedback on the originality, do-ability, timeline, and possible limitations of the project, so they need to secure a Chair as early in the process as possible. The context determines when this happens. Some Chairs want students to have a proposal before they consider a commitment. Others prefer to exchange thoughts early in the development of the project and are willing to commit to being a Chair at that time. When students have a project they can articulate, they typically send a short email to a potential Chair, recapping in a few sentences the problem and the project, and asking for a chance to share ideas and get advice. This first email is typically short and to the point. No one wants a long email from a stranger.

The first meeting may be something like a first date. It does not have to end in commitment. Both student and faculty member are seeing how well they might work together. This meeting is likely a give and take – the student presents their thoughts and the potential Chair responds, offering questions, additional sources, thoughts on the design, and questions about practicalities of performing the study. All of these questions are preliminary, and should not be taken as criticisms of the overall study. On the student's part, they may ask the potential Chair for advice on areas of uncertainty. If the conversation goes well overall, at the end of the meeting the student might ask the faculty member to become the committee Chair and for recommendations for other committee members.

Probably, the student should take the Chair's advice on other committee members. Contextual ambiguities arise when a doctoral candidate receives radically different perspectives and advice from committee members at the Preliminary Orals. While the background of some potential members might look attractive, individuals may also have a commitment to a theory or methodology that could radically change the project. The Chair's advice on members can prevent such issues from arising; however, even if issues arise, the Chair has the final word.

## Managing conflict

What follows is some advice on how to manage potentially conflicting opinions on changes that committee members want. The student first has an open discussion with the Chair about what to do. Together, they brainstorm ideas for compromise or for writing a further rationale that argues more fully for one approach over another. The student then writes an MOU that details more explicitly the changes and the rationale. The writing itself will have the most power of persuasion. If agreement is still not reached, the Chair is the one to negotiate.

*An aside:* Committee members typically are not involved in the unrolling of the study and leave to the Chair (or co-Chairs) the responsibility for the project. While the doctoral candidate may call on other members for specific expertise, the members' obligation is to provide evaluations at two key junctures – the Preliminary Orals and the Final Orals. Members are supposed to evaluate based on overall quality and not on the study's alignment with members' particular theoretical approach.

### Staying in contact with one's Chair to redefine the problem and refine the questions

Chairs are experts in the field – they help shape the study, define its parameters, and remove barriers. Once the student has a Chair who is committed to the project, it is time to start (re)writing the full proposal.

For meetings after the initial meeting, the candidate needs to come prepared – to provide a written progress report and a list of questions that need a response. Any materials for the meeting need to be sent in advance, as well as a reminder the night before. The student might also ask to tape record the meeting so as not to forget any key points. After the meeting, a note of appreciation should be sent, recapping the main points discussed, as well as next steps. This way, students make clear that they have come prepared, take in the advice, appreciate the Chair's time and expertise, and are not going to waste other people's time. The next steps might include the specific products students will produce for next time, the date they will produce them by, and the next meeting's date and time, arranged before the meeting ends.

Assuming that doctoral candidates have a project and a Chair, what follows is advice on preparing the proposal for submission to the full committee in preparation for Preliminary Orals.

## 2.5  WRITING FOR AN AUDIENCE

Dissertation writers sometimes ask, who is my audience? Is it the Chair? the committee? researchers in the field? the general public? They may have read an array of studies, some with off-putting jargon and in-group shortcuts, and may prefer a different audience. They often ask questions about informality, voice, language, and latitude in presentation.

This book advises that one's audience comprises committee members *as representatives of professional researchers in the field*. The dissertation allows entry into the work of researchers in the discipline, so it uses their language, style, conventions, and procedures. These include the expected chapters, a defense of the purpose and methods, tight alignment between questions and methods, and an objective, economical, discipline-specific language of presentation. Committee members may favor specific approaches to dissertation writing, so these may be important also.

This advice may sound constraining. But a committee is tasked with assessing these research competencies, so the student needs to clearly demonstrate them. Later in the student's career, they can take liberties with these conventions; for the dissertation, the writer needs to follow them appropriately.

### Persuasive writing

As noted earlier, when students have conceptualized a project, and engaged a Chair, they then shape their project for submission to the full committee, under the direction of the Chair. What follows is advice, as well as models for writing the needed materials. Most proposals have three sections that the student is expected to produce. These sections provide the argument for the study. At this point, writing goes beyond helping the student generate, think through, and narrow ideas. The writer focuses on communicating the project to an audience in ways that researchers expect. At this point, the writer is dominantly writing to *persuade.*

### The key persuasive sections of a dissertation proposal

As noted above, most proposals have three sections or chapters: the Problem Statement (which may be titled Introduction but includes a Problem Statement); the Literature Review; and the Methodology. The first chapter is like a mini version of all three chapters – it compresses the background/context, problem, purpose, supportive literature, and the design and methods into a succinct preview of the project. When completed, this chapter will (1) define and defend the problem, using an abbreviated synthesis of findings/results from previous studies as study context; (2) summarize the research project; (3) state the research questions; (4) identify the research design and methods, including the site(s), if any, and subjects/participants; and (5) state the purpose or benefits of the study, including who will use it and how results will be disseminated. Given such complexity, how does the student synthesize persuasively when they have not yet figured out every detail of the study?

A key suggestion is that students write out the project as *what they think they will do and why*, keeping in mind that they need to defend each of these decisions – as if readers were questioning them with alternatives. This first take will still be a placeholder draft. But the writer is now imagining the reader's response. The student is not just informing others of what they have decided to do. Rather, they are *persuading* them that each decision is the right one for this particular study. To repeat: the writer avoids saying "I want to study X" or "I would like to find out Y." This wording offers no rationale, and expresses only personal desire. Rather, one argues, "researchers need to know X in order to solve Y."

## *Opening the first chapter*

A dissertation often begins with a quick statement of purpose and brief summary of the project. This opening helps readers know, up front, what the project will entail, helping them hold key elements of the project in mind while reading the background and context. A persuasive project summary convinces readers that the argument that follows is tied to a doable project and a worthwhile purpose. Here is an example, from a study discussed earlier:

> This action research project seeks to engage ten school psychologists to address a problem within a specific school district – the overrepresentation of English Language Learners (ELL) tested and found eligible for a Specific Learning Disability (SLD).

The summary identifies the kind of project, its site and participants, and its purpose.

Most dissertations next move the reader quickly to the study's background and context. The writer asks, what do readers need to know about this problem in order to judge the study's place in the literature? For this, writers need to first present the big picture – national or international data on the problem, if available. Much national data is accessible through Google Scholar and other scholarly sites (e.g. Microsoft Academic, WorldWideScience), and includes well-documented, broad statistics, reminding readers of the larger problem; educational organizations might also have defining statistics.

This section is typically short. Readers likely already know some of these statistics, and any quarrels with them, as national problems tend to be well publicized. The writer's job is not to record all of the data and disputes, but to decide on the most reliable information and compress it. The Problem Statement can then shift to other elements of the study context. The writer needs to quickly establish common ground with readers. To persuade, the doctoral student first establishes that writer and reader have a common beginning point in credible data.

Background mostly provides the reader with studies that gradually focus the problem. This section might survey different manifestations of the problem. For instance, given middle school science underachievement, the writer could quickly discuss weak pedagogies, ineffective elementary teacher training, problematic use of science specialists, or the gender bias throughout K-12; this sketch could lead up to a focus on pre-service training needs. Or the writer could summarize the history of successful and unsuccessful interventions. This survey could then narrow to studies of a particular intervention that may require special in-service training. The writer doesn't need much discussion of each study, as this is still background. But readers want confirmation that the student has thought through what currently exists.

Selecting the central studies involves knowing what one is arguing – cutting through multiple studies to identify key findings from a few. As the historian Michael O'Malley stated in a May 26, 2019 *Atlantic* article on academic reading and writing, "We learn to read books and articles quickly, under pressure, for the key points or for what we can use. But we write as if a learned gentleman of leisure sits in a paneled study, savoring every word." In describing the research process, O'Malley continues, "academics often approach books like 'sous-chefs' gutting a fish."

## General principles for providing background

As a general principle, the proposal's context moves from wide to narrow scope, and provides readers with connections between sections. With each new section, the document ties the discussion back to the study's purpose. Eventually, the context narrows to a small number of closely aligned studies that the investigation will engage. These key studies become pivotal to the Literature Review, where they can be discussed more fully. In the Problem Statement, they provide initial arguments for the reader, defining the need for the investigation.

To help with narrowing, a logic map or outline can show how one group of studies progresses to the next in arguing for the study. Here is one example of a map, on transfer students' lack of a sense of belonging. The student proposes an empirical study on whether successful transfer students created informal friendship groups, and if they did, how these groups affected their persistence.

I **How new populations led to changes in post-secondary education in the US**
  a  Growth of community colleges
  b  New populations
  c  CA master plan
II **Increase in Community College Transfer Students (CCTS)**
  a  National data (numbers transferring)
  b  Institutional data
     i  Articulation agreements
     ii  Tracking CCTS
III **Transfer students' high drop-out rates**
  a  National data
  b  California data
IV **Transfer student special needs**
  a  Emotional support, given transfer shock
  b  Academic and financial counseling
  c  Social integration and academic integration
V **Theories of social integration and persistence to address these needs**
  a  Tinto's theories of social integration and persistence
  b  Transfer shock
  c  Sense of belonging
     i  Spending time on campus
     ii  Establishing social Nnetworks

VI **How a lack of social integration particularly affects transfer students**
  a Academic confidence issues
    i Must adapt to a new environment while transitioning to advanced coursework
    ii Anxiety about academic rigor regardless of academic preparation
  b Loneliness: due to loss of support networks: family, friends, community
  c Ineffectiveness of existing interventions
    i New environment challenges (lack of connection to new college)
    ii Orientation programs address academics and financial aid but not social integration
    iii Social networks: Why they don't always work?
VII **Known factors affecting transfer student persistence**
VIII **How successful students describe how informal social groups affect persistence**
  a As distinct from social networks
  b Potentially unique supports for transfer students

This broad-to-narrow mapping leads the reader to the proposed study. Readers would question why existing interventions are not sufficient, specifically why online or on-campus social networks do not create sense of belonging. The map leads readers to see that transfer students might have developed other kinds of friendship groups to support them on campus. The map can later be used as a framework for the Literature Review, which follows the same logic but fleshes out the argument and expands and details the supporting studies.

    Logic maps may differ depending on the kind of study the student is doing. A logic map for a policy study might look very different from that of an empirical study. It might open with a history of laws (say affirmative action bans such as California's proposition 209) that capsulize the problem. It could then tie these restrictive laws to initiatives (say admissions initiatives) that circumvent these laws. The map could then shift to supports for partnerships that could potentially improve the enrollment numbers of underrepresented minorities, at research institutions. Either at the beginning or end, the map could present a conceptual frame such as diversity management concepts and organizational culture.

### Approaches to background/context

The context persuades readers that the study emerges from previous research. What follows are some additional approaches:

  1 The background could be mostly statistics. It might offer a broad sweep of statistical data on the major problem. For instance, one might detail the disproportionate low numbers of underrepresented minorities in

graduate schools and detail existing interventions and their success rates. National statistics could point to the scope of the issue (only…% of minorities are in graduate programs, compared to percentage of their population); STEM field statistics could narrow the problem; statistical data on failed attempts to raise the low STEM numbers could underscore the need for a new approach. Other statistics could then suggest implications of this problem – loss of opportunity and income for key groups, percentage of new talent needed in key industries, projections on the numbers lost to retirement.

2　The background might provide scenarios reflecting the problem – non-English speaking parents of low-income children being shut out of school resources and information, not understanding the K-12 system, and being unable to support their children as they navigate the pipeline to college. One scenario could be a parent trying to access a middle school for information on the classes selected for her child, and hearing such responses as "her grades indicate these classes are appropriate." These scenarios might come from recent qualitative studies supplying vivid examples.

3　The background might detail a host of recent studies on a very current problem – revealing how salient this problem now is. For instance, school violence has recently garnered national attention. Current studies have refocused educators' attention on students being bullied or harassed, both in class and online. Selecting students' stories from these studies could offer a compelling way to discuss proposed research.

4　The background could trace a history, for instance the history of legal actions related to the problem. Legal judgments on the rights of language minority children have an important history in California, affecting the number and persistence of Dual Language programs.

5　The background could introduce and explain a theoretical model applied in a new way – the innovation of a proposed study. It could detail the key tenets of the theory, how the theory arose, what problem it seeks to address, and how it might apply to a new context. For instance, Critical Race Theory might be applied to a new community college mentoring model in which mentors are taught to use Counter-stories and Community Wealth to support first year Latino/a students. The background would need to explain the theory broadly, and show how it could be applied to the problems faced by first year Latino/a community college students.

Many more alternatives exist. The writer establishes credibility through the pertinence of the evidence and a depiction of a problem compelling to academic readers. This might mean highlighting recent data, identifying key researchers and any controversies that have arisen, and citing confirming studies. The background is not the place for generalities, truisms, clichés, opinions, popular ideas or pretentious jargon.

## Connecting existing research to the study

Collecting related research likely began the minute the writer started narrowing the topic. The student needs to connect these studies explicitly to the proposed study's purpose. As noted earlier, listing studies, one after the other, is not a helpful approach, either here or later in the Literature Review. Rather, the studies need to be integrated into the argument.

One begins with overall reasoning – the claims one needs in order to justify the study. The writer might summarize the whole argument first, without reference to supporting studies. Then, for each claim, the writer could select key supportive findings from the most credible studies, insert them, and detail them. If multiple studies have a similar finding, the student could put in parenthesis citations for the most credible two or three (not lists of eight). But writers need to avoid glib groupings that overgeneralize findings as well as claims of similarity that ignore major differences. If studies are nuanced, writers need to qualify what they report as a finding. And if studies reveal conflicting evidence, these discrepancies need to be reported too. Readers will question any burying of evidence.

## Describing the project itself (the full version)

With the arguments sketched out, writers face an academic audience's key question: What exactly will the study involve? Is it an intervention? An assessment of a program? An Action Research collaboration? A description of an innovation's diffusion? The project is necessarily circumscribed by the realities of a time-frame, access to data or subjects, recruitment issues, the subjects' biases or fears, the need to limit data, research expenses, the student's own role and experience, and the Chair's interest in the field. A myriad of practicalities arise.

Feasibility underlies many of these questions. The student's Chair is essential here, setting parameters and goals that the academic community will judge appropriate. Doctoral students should not be seduced by the "big" degree and its status, and equate that with a giant study. With set parameters and goals, a dissertation writer can describe the project without being ambushed by doubts, ambivalence, and uncontrolled variables.

But how detailed should the new researcher be? Writers need to describe the project as if to another researcher who does not know the study. The project typically emerges out of the literature, and reflects any "next steps" advocated. So in the back of the writer's mind should lurk the presence of readers, who will question the need for the project. Such challenges include: Why this project? What will doing X contribute? Are there any issues with collecting data for it? What about reactivity – participants saying what they think the researcher wants to hear? How does a new researcher get access to that site? How recruit participants? How code data? Will this study be replicable, and if not, does that matter?

Writers need to refine the project description throughout the early proposal writing stages.

## Writing and rewriting the research questions

The issue of research questions is so important that it requires continued guidance. So it is discussed again here. The research questions need to be clear, targeted, and answerable, without jargon – and without broad, undefined concepts. As mentioned before, students often start with generalized questions. But broad questions can become meaningless questions. The questions need to identify the variables of the study.

Here is one example of using big undefined concepts:

> To what extent do African-American students' perceptions of belonging impact their valuing of school?

This kind of question is unanswerable. Even if "perceptions of belonging" and "valuing of school" could both be operationalized into specific behaviors (not readily), those behaviors would be hard to separate from one another. It would be even more difficult to show that one set of behaviors "impacted" another. Furthermore, writers need to avoid making claims about all African-American students under all conditions.

As a writing task, the student needs to write a more defined question with clearer measures and mutually exclusive variables. But, as noted earlier, finely detailed questions may get long. Ideally, one first writes the question out fully, with all of the behaviors one has in mind – so as to clarify the empirical basis for the study, which readers demand. Later, the writer rewrites and streamlines. Here is a long version (later stripped down) to help the writer communicate what they are after:

> To what extent do high-absentee African-American urban high school students, who help create a new school mentoring program through Action Research, increase their time and effort toward their studies (as measured by time on campus, interactions with other students, work effort, interim grades, teacher reports, reported attitude toward school)?

This detailing is useful to writer and Chair – the writer circumscribes a doable study. The variables are measurable. One can measure (operationalize) "participation" by identifying how often a student shows up at AR meetings, discusses ideas, and provides suggestions for a mentoring program; these activities can be recorded. One can also measure (operationalize) a student's "time and effort" in school by investigating a student's attendance records, self-reported homework time, and teachers' reports on a student's quality of work turned in, as well as perceived attitude toward that work. This long version helps clarify what can be studied and how easily the variables can be measured.

The question can then be streamlined. The following might work:

> To what extent does African-American students' participation in creating an urban high school-based mentoring program corresponds with an increase in their time and effort for study?

This last version is still narrow and researchable, subsuming some of the details. Readers can envision the study. (Given that student grades may not be feasible to collect, a good proxy for achievement could be teachers' reports on time and effort.) From the shortened question, readers know that the population comes from a single site and that the site needs to be an urban high school. Readers also see that the variables are measurable – "participation" is measurable, as is "time and effort."

## Anticipating reader concerns

Two issues that remain are whether this study assumes what it is trying to prove and whether or not this study has already been done. The reader might wonder if the very behaviors the researcher is measuring ("time and effort") are already selected for by choosing participants who agree to "participate" in creating the intervention. The reader might also raise concerns about originality. Much research already exists on mentoring programs, especially for African-Americans.

Both concerns could be addressed if the researcher identified a unique form of participation. Participants would not necessarily be those who already devote "time and effort" to projects, who might already be considered achievers by definition. Rather, the project could recruit the most disengaged, low-achieving students, motivating them with this program as an opportunity for expression, for getting to know others, and for feeling part of the school. This thinking led to the study discussed earlier: The researcher chose "high absentee" African-American students as his population, so that recruitment would depend on low attendance records. Further, the study could not then measure what it assumes, that students will become involved, because participants themselves would generate the intervention. The researcher does not know what socio-emotional factors will play out, even while hoping for indicators of improved achievement. Thus, a study that documents such participation adds to the literature on addressing the African-American achievement gap.

## Reviewing the argument

Before deciding on possible methods, the writer can review the logic of the project, to see if it suggests specific methods. Many students jump to methods ("I have to do a qualitative study;" "grounded theory is my thing"; "mixed methods are too complex") before they have even decided on a study.

One can distill the project logic by identifying the main thread of the argument. For the study above, that full logic might be as follows:

> The achievement gap for African-American high school students remains constant, despite extensive interventions. Mentoring, which increases sense of belonging, is broadly shown to significantly reduce drop-out rates in urban schools, but not for African-Americans. This group requires other socio-emotional needs to be met, including empathy, getting along with others, and managing emotions. This project investigates whether low attendance African-American students, who create and participate in an Action Research mentoring program focused on socio-emotional needs, show an increase in time and effort in academics.

If such a logic paragraph does not come easily, the writer can explain the project aloud, in one or two minutes, to someone new to the study. This "elevator speech" helps synthesize what is important. The student thus uses talk to understand, letting the logic unfold in the process. The logic then suggests a methodological approach. For this study, which involves collaborations among a small number of students at a single site, qualitative action research seems appropriate.

## 2.6 WRITING INITIAL THOUGHTS ON DESIGN AND METHODS

For a study to be feasible (a clear concern of readers), the student needs to consider design and methods. The writer does not begin with methods, but with a problem that implies an overall approach. While choices of design and methods require a separate chapter in the proposal, they are important from the project's beginnings, evolve with the problem, and keep changing as the study is enacted. A compressed statement about proposed design and methods is typically included in the first chapter Introduction.

A large number of books exist on design and methodology. These can help the doctoral student understand and decide on appropriate methods, given the research questions. However, below are some general guidelines on how to think about one's design and methods, with some examples from completed proposal chapters. A fuller set of explanations and exercises come later in this book when the full chapter on Methodology is discussed. Assumed here is that doctoral students are taking courses in refined methodologies and have Chairs who will align the specific project with appropriate methods.

### Overview

Methods are linked to research questions. Rather than starting with what researchers would like to do (e.g. interviews, focus groups) or can envision doing (e.g. a single case study at one's site), they typically start with their research questions and the data they need in order to answer their question(s). They ask: What are the richest sources of data? What access is available to that data? Is the data composed of public records or records that may require permissions?

Researchers also consider potential problems with their data: Are any of these sources or participants likely to be biased? How well does the researcher know the participants? Would participants try to please the researcher with their responses or shade their answers to protect themselves or others? Would an anonymous survey work better? Doctoral students need to consider the nature of the data: Do the questions require in-depth answers to a few open ended questions or can they be answered better by a broad survey with a pre-set range of answers? If new researchers are looking at something as broad and variable as perceptions, what checks on participant responses can they build into the study by asking another group of respondents with different interests or positions?

These are only some of the questions that the doctoral student needs to ask when determining methods. Once again, this is not a matter of personal preference or convenience. The student's obligation is to choose the methods that will most clearly and reliably answer the questions. The choice requires a defense, as readers will most likely ask questions about methods. This book's later chapter on Methodology offers specific strategies for developing and revising questions and aligning them with methods. But much of the thinking required is outlined here.

## *Design*

The biggest question in developing the Introduction concerns the overall approach – the Design. Do the research questions indicate a qualitative, a quantitative or a mixed methods study? This question needs to be thought through carefully. If one is after depth of response – complex responses, insight into processes, unanticipated thoughts and motivations – a qualitative approach seems appropriate. If one is looking more for percentage of usage, ratings, rankings, and other numerical reports across a broad swath of respondents, one is likely going to use a quantitative approach. The research might also require a combination (mixed methods) to provide the fullest picture – both a broad swath as well as a limited probing, through interviews of a small participant pool. In such a case, the interviews might shape the survey questions, or the survey data might determine the interview questions. While mixed methods may look difficult, this design may be the best route, and prove the most rewarding. The researcher needs to remove any methodological bias and look at the study objectively.

For the Design rationale, writers need to avoid circular reasoning. For instance, students may write that they will use a qualitative design because their methods are interviews and focus groups. This begs the question: Why are they using interviews and focus groups? Rather, students need to argue for the *data* they need – why they need to know about processes, contexts, evolving thoughts, or why it is important to gain numerical ratings or values, number of times a given practice is used. Students need to persuade their reader that their Design is appropriate to their purpose and their questions.

Here is an example of an effective rationale for the Design, from a completed Methods proposal for a study discussed earlier. The research question is: How do middle schools overcome challenges to sustainability in order to maintain a successful Dual Language program?

> This study will employ a qualitative case study design in order to investigate the practices of two middle schools that have successfully sustained a Dual-Language (DL) program for at least five years. According to Creswell (2018), a qualitative approach is appropriate when there is a limited amount of research in a particular area, which is the case for DL middle school programs. A quantitative study would fail to deliver the holistic account (Yin, 2014) necessary to sustain programs in the future. I am seeking articulated, open-ended responses that include perspectives on how decisions are made, thought processes on setting priorities, opportunities for professional development, and how assessments are used to ensure sustainability of the DL program. Furthermore, the intended goal of this study is to synthesize individual perspectives into common themes, which is another hallmark of qualitative studies (Creswell, 2018). Lastly, a case study design allows the researcher to view a phenomenon or program (in this case, a Dual Language program) from many different angles, by using multiple methods of data collection and analysis to understand the phenomenon or case. These multiple methods can be used to corroborate or contradict emerging hypotheses and findings. The two case studies will enable stakeholders and future researchers to apply strategies for sustainability in middle school DL programs in real world settings (Yin, 2014). It will uncover the multiple perspectives on sustainability of stakeholders in the program. The research aims to document the programmatic and administrative structures, challenges and successes of the DL programs, and the details of the Dual Language programs' evolution, adaptation to change and improvements.

The example above justifies a qualitative case study approach to sustainability. For the qualitative choice, it stresses the need for a holistic account, including multiple perspectives, decisions, and thought processes, in a study where little data already exists. The more specific rationale for case study is fairly standard – the need for an analysis of a phenomenon from multiple angles.

The next example justifies a mixed methods study, also from a completed Methods proposal, detailing the national use of culturally responsive practices in schools' Advanced Placement Capstone courses, courses designed to improve minority students' access to and success in

Advanced Placement courses. The researcher also wanted to know how teachers who do use such practices structure their courses.

> This study will use an explanatory mixed methods approach, in which "the quantitative results … inform the types of participants to be purposefully selected for the qualitative phase and the types of questions that will be asked of the participants" (Creswell & Creswell, 2018, p. 222). This approach is necessary to integrate the strengths of both qualitative and quantitative methods. A purely quantitative approach would yield data about the types of curricula and texts AP Capstone teachers report, and the extent to which these teachers report using culturally responsive approaches to support student success. Specifically, I will survey teachers and ask them to identify from a list those factors they consider in their curriculum planning, assessment planning, selection of instructional activities, and attempts to establish classroom environments. However, such data alone would not provide rich understanding of how teachers design their courses, and their thinking in doing so.
>
> To provide this rich qualitative understanding of how teachers develop and structure their courses, this study will use the results of the initial survey to identify high use participants for follow-up qualitative investigation. I will select a sample from those teachers who indicate that they consider cultural responsiveness to be an important factor in teaching these courses. The qualitative research will explain the meaning of the responses from those teachers who indicate cultural responsiveness as a primary consideration in course planning (Merriam & Tisdell, 2016). Specifically, the interviews will uncover how teachers attempt to understand their students, and how they design learning experiences that affirm their cultural needs. Such an investigation into processes requires a more qualitative approach. However, qualitative data alone would not provide a description of the extent to which these practices are happening across the nation. Nor would a qualitative project allow for correlational analysis between other factors that may impact teachers' self-reported use of Culturally Responsive Teaching.

This explanation justifies the use of both methods because both are needed to answer the research questions (on the extent nationally of Capstone teachers who use culturally responsive practices, and how those teachers who use them structure their classes). The quantitative data is further needed to select participants for the interviews.

What follows is an early draft of a Design section for a study of executive level Latinas' journeys in overcoming barriers to achievement. The draft shows a writer struggling to use methods textbooks' rationales to support her study's qualitative design. The citations are appropriate, but abrupt and not fully applied to the particulars of the study. It was later rewritten.

> This project will use a qualitative design as the study seeks to explore and understand the journey of Latinas to UC senior positions (Creswell & Creswell, 2018). For a qualitative design, "the process of research will involve emerging questions and procedures ... data analysis inductively building from particulars to general themes, and the researcher making interpretations of the meaning of the data" (Creswell & Creswell, 2018, p. 4). As Maxwell (2013) explains, qualitative researchers try to "understand the particular context within which the participants act, and the influence that this context has on their actions" (p. 30). This study will focus on a small number of Latinas and their experiences in navigating their way to a senior position. The research will focus on the process by which events and actions take place.

This early draft tells readers little about the study but a lot about what textbook writers say qualitative studies should do. The writer needs to more fully explain what she is after and then connect these objectives to the criteria for a qualitative design. She revised her justification:

> This project will use a qualitative design, as the study seeks to explore and understand in-depth the journey of Latinas to UC senior positions. I will seek the particulars of the events, including barriers, supports, and decisions that made up their journeys, including how various people and events contributed to these Latinas' rise. As Maxwell (2013) explains, qualitative researchers try to "understand the particular context within which the participants act, and the influence that this context has on their actions" (p. 30). That context consists of UC executive searches, barriers, and low numbers of Latinas in positions of power. Also, the research will focus on the process by which events and actions take place, a criterion for qualitative design (Maxwell, 2013). Because this exploration has not been done before, I do not have pre-set interview questions, but will let questions and procedures emerge, although I will probe the role of mentors and the Latinas' reliance on cultural strengths. I will inductively build from particulars to general themes, as explained by Creswell & Creswell, 2018. This study will focus on a small number of Latinas and their experiences in navigating their way to a senior position.

This revision features the study particulars rather than general methods advice. The argument is strengthened where the writer explains the

study, with details that provide a compelling case for choosing a qualitative design.

## Site and subjects/participants

The site(s) and participants, and the numbers involved, need to be
negotiated with one's Chair. However, the researcher first develops criteria
for both. What would count as a good site for the study and why? What
characteristics must a participant or subject have in order to participate
in the study? Students need to write out the criteria in ways that relate to
the research questions. Also, they need to anticipate potential critiques of
the choice of participants. What is the likelihood of reactivity (participants
saying what they think the researcher wants to hear)? What bias might surface in the choice of a site, such as researcher bias (selecting a site one knows
will support a finding)? Strict criteria can offset such critiques.

For the African-American mentoring program, the doctoral student limits participants to those most likely to be disengaged – selected
through grades and attendance records; and the site is required to be an
under-resourced urban school with low achievement scores generally.
These criteria reduce the number of potential participants or sites whose
characteristics might confound the study.

For the sustainability study of Dual Language middle schools, the
selection criteria include administrators and teachers who on a daily basis
participate in implementing the middle school Dual Language program (or
at least have DL students in their classes). The researcher likely wants to
exclude uninvolved employees at the site who may have opinions but no
first-hand experience. Significantly for that study, now completed, English
Only teachers were included at the last minute, and provided some of
the most telling data on school sustainability. These teachers revealed the
impact of the DL program on their own classes (inequitable overload of
students), problematic schedules (figured around DL needs), and barriers
to instruction (need to adjust to DL students in their classes). This unexpected source of rich data reflects the importance of careful selection of
participants.

This student's final selection criteria, with original rationale, follows:

> Participants include the principals, assistant principals, Dual
> Language coordinators, DL and English Only (EO) teachers, and
> relevant stakeholders in each DL program. The two principals
> and two assistant principals will be selected because they have
> administrative powers over staffing, recruitment, hiring, pro-
> fessional development, and assessments. The DL coordinator at
> each school will be selected as a participant because it is unclear
> in the literature what kinds of influence they have over program-
> matic decisions. The DL teachers will be selected because they
> will provide concrete examples of curriculum and assessments
> utilized. The criteria for English Only teachers will be those

who have DL students in their classrooms and who have been teaching at the school for a minimum of 3 years.

Both DL and non-DL teachers were included because it was not clear how non-DL teachers interact with the DL program and how they think the DL program as an intervention fits into the middle school setting as a whole. The non-DL teachers proved a valuable addition to the study's participants. The doctoral student had been thoughtful about the possible participants and rationale for each group.

## Data collection methods

Again, the methods should be constructed and then negotiated with one's Chair. Students' methods courses, their textbooks written by such key methodologists as Joseph Maxwell and John Cresswell, and their Chair comprise students' key resources for choosing methods. However, the student then needs to argue for each choice in the proposal submitted for Preliminary Orals. When students first conceptualize this section, they need to identify the key methods (introducing the most important first) and how they will use each one. Each data collection method needs to be discussed in terms of answering the research questions. Why are focus groups better than interviews for asking Action Research participants about the effect of their project? Why are observations necessary to triangulate data from interviews? These are tricky questions, and require a thoughtful answer.

One way to generate the best data collection methods may be to start with the concrete data one wants to collect. A Units of Observation piece (which could later be used to develop protocols or simply go in an Appendix) includes lists all of the behaviors, documents, verbal exchanges, statistics etc. that would "count" as data–for each research question. These must be concrete, observable, identifiable data linked to research questions. The kinds of data listed could then suggest the methods that most align. Thus, the researcher starts with the concrete data, and then identifies the method that would most help to gather that data. (See example, pp. 00.) In contrast, starting with a coveted method and hoping it will produce useful data may not argue well for a method. Committee members at one's Preliminary Orals are likely to offer competing ideas about how best to gather useful data. A Units of Observation table can point one toward key methods. It starts with the data, which may not be self-evident, and then generates the method.

## Significance/public engagement/dissemination

Most dissertations require that students write a Significance section, some-times called a Public Engagement or Dissemination section, as part of their first chapter, the Introduction. This section explains the benefits of the pro-ject – its contribution, role in the literature, application. And it details how those benefits may reach those who are impacted. Typically, the section identifies who will be helped by this research and in what ways. And it details the specific methods to reach them, such as published articles, organization briefings, training programs, conferences, or site-based organizational change. Here the writer needs to persuade readers that the project is worthwhile.

### Looking forward

The Design and Methods consolidation in Chapter 1 (Introduction), as well as the full chapter on Methodology, will necessarily undergo multiple changes, especially under the guidance of one's Chair. This section will change in readiness for one's Preliminary Orals. It will also change as a result of the Orals, based on the committee's suggestions. And it will change again, once the study is completed and the writer needs to capture what actually transpired, not what was projected to transpire. The clearer and more rationalized the methods are looking forward, the more effective the student will be in rewriting it to prepare for Final Orals. For a fuller discussion of Design and Methods, Chapter 4 provides additional insights.

## Getting going on writing

**Write:**

1 A paragraph summing up the identified gap in the research.
2 A paragraph on who will benefit from the study and how.
3 A paragraph on the likely concerns, even barriers, of performing a study at an imagined site.
4 A paragraph describing three possible research questions and what kind of data each would likely require.

# 3 WRITING STRATEGIES FOR THE LITERATURE REVIEW

While some doctoral programs ask students to weave the Literature Review into the Statement of the Problem, this book assumes a separate chapter, and offers advice on how to write it. Doctoral students need to synthesize the key research in the field, and adjacent fields bearing on the problem. To reiterate a point made earlier, the Literature Review identifies a gap in the research that the student's research will fill. It is the student's job to synthesize what the research community already knows and to sharply define what it still needs to know. How to circumscribe and present that research raises key questions. The overarching question remains: "How does this body of research reviewed argue for the study at hand?"

## 3.1 RESEARCHING AND WRITING THE LITERATURE REVIEW AS AN ARGUMENT

Writers typically begin thinking about this chapter by reviewing materials they have already developed. The Problem Statement chapter, with its supportive studies, already presents key arguments. It typically funnels from broad background to existing studies, to research gaps, to the proposed study – a logic map the writer already has.

### Using what one has

*A first step*, then, is to reexamine those arguments: How strong are they? Would readers be onboard? Where would readers question the reasoning? As discussed more fully later, writers can use the Problem Statement's logic to structure the review. They can then flesh out the arguments by adding points and sub-points, other data, newer articles, and a detailing of key studies. Under each argument, the writer first brainstorms by listing the literature they already have, the studies they still need, and the studies that need further discussion. Early brainstorming can just be informal note-taking and visual mapping.

More formal early brainstorming might lead to big categories. As the Literature Review demands a full research context, the writer may need to distinguish between theoretical, policy, and empirical studies, and make clear how each group relates to the proposed research. (Most of the examples here are empirical studies housed within a theoretical frame.) Looking back at what the writer has, categorizing the studies, and identifying needed work, comprises basic planning.

## Clarifying one's theoretical framework

*A second step* might be to reexamine the theoretical framework. The Literature Review asks writers to clarify their frame of reference. What theories is the writer assuming? The theoretical framework joins together concepts underlying extensive studies on a topic. It then provides a lens for selecting and understanding data that describe a phenomenon. But has the writer chosen the best theoretical framework to support the argument?

For doctoral students, the *choice* of frameworks helps them identify key supportive studies and to construct their own investigation. For instance, adaptive leadership is a theory positing that in volatile contexts, leaders need to use strategies that help the organization shift or "adapt" in ways that maximize existing resources – appropriate for a study of policy changes. Similarly, Feminist Theory analyzes gender discrimination and explains why women experience lowered expectations and rewards – appropriate for a study of the low numbers of female principals and superintendents. As a final example, Critical Race Theory posits that white supremacy and racial power are maintained over time, and thus it explains historical injustices in law, education, politics, and other arenas – appropriate for the study of disenfranchised students of color. In the Literature Review, dissertation writers need to summarize their theoretical framework and its application to their study, defining the key concepts that make the theory apply.

With the theories identified, the writer can better select for and order the Literature Review. Two asides: First, the theoretical terminology needs to be used consistently throughout the dissertation, guiding the development of the research questions and the analysis, as well as the presentation of one's findings and conclusions. Second, the theoretical framework is not typically placed at the beginning of the Literature Review, unless one is studying the framework itself. Identifying it early in the process, however, helps organize a writer's research strategies.

## Selecting supportive studies

*A third step* in concentrating on argument is to select studies that tie back to the proposed study's purpose. Readers constantly ask about relevance. One can take notes on each study, writing a phrase (or sentence or two) on how each serves as evidence for the study. The writer keeps asking: How does the empirical data here support the need for the proposed investigation? This is a key *pre-writing* step and helps with selection.

The example below reveals a writer's initial set of notes on supportive studies, a prelude to choosing evidence that falls in line with the argument. The writer wants to study if and how Capstone Advanced Placement courses use culturally responsive pedagogies to reduce the equity gap among minority students. This is a very early outline, but shows the writer's thought process:

*Overview of the equity gap*
Extent of educational disparities, in Advanced Placement classes
One key cause: lack of cultural responsiveness (Tyrone Howard, Why Race and Culture Matter in Schools)
Arguments for Culturally Responsive Pedagogy generally, to reduce equity gap (Gay, 2018, Socioculturally focused teaching; Howard, 2003, on culturally relevant pedagogy; James Banks)
Barriers to implementing culturally responsive approaches: teacher knowledge, training, dispositions, self-efficacy, social and political context (find best studies)
AP program equity gap in participation, student success, based on type of school (low participation in high-poverty schools – Bittman et al, 2017); suburban schools slow to diversify (Kettler & Hurst, 2017)

Significance: "national curriculum" moves away from elitism (Finn & Scanlan; Hertberg-Davis & Callahan)

The list provides an initial set of notes, with key research, to serve as a starting point for further research. The notes may help the writer tie back to the major claims, as the list suggests the direction of the chapter.

In the fuller write-up, how studies tie to the claims will need to be made explicit. The writer explains how the studies support claims, and avoids generalizing them under a broad topic. It is a misstep for dissertation students to write broadly about a group of studies and then assume these references argue for the proposed research. Just because a study shares a "topic" or "theme" does not make it relevant. Readers require greater explicitness: They look for how studies' findings support the proposed research questions. So, a student's initial narrowing by argument eliminates unnecessary revision down the road. A caveat: This advice on tying back does not mean that writers should address studies one by one. A Literature Review is a synthesis, not a list.

The excerpt below shows synthesis. At times writers need to combine studies to show a general trend, and then move to more specific claims. The sentence below casts a wide net over "formal studies on the relationship between arts and health," in preparation for the writer's more specific analysis of other types of art-health partnership benefits:

Many formal studies of the relationship between the arts and health primarily centered around the therapeutic use of the arts, with a majority of published work focused on chronic conditions, anxiety, and pain management.
(Hamilton, Hinks, & Petticrew, 2003; Sonke, Pesata, Arce, Carytsas, Zemina, & Jokisch, 2014; Stegemann, Geretsegger, Quoc, Riedl, Smetana, 2019)

Less concerned with art's effect on individual health conditions, the writer combines a solid (but not exhaustive) list of key studies.

### Writing claims

*A fourth step* in concentrating on argument is to write a series of claims under which the writer will discuss certain key studies, as a way to synthesize. The claims need to relate back to the research questions, providing future guideposts to help the reader connect studies to the proposed study's aims. The earlier example on Capstone Advanced Placement courses is more notes than claims, but comes close to being an argument. The next step for this student would be writing full claims and adding more studies under each. This synthesizing of groups of articles asks the writer to move from a multiplicity of evidence to a high level of synthesis, and to provide reasons for grouping the evidence this way. The summary claims can then become headings as the writer seeks to organize the Literature Review.

Claims can keep writers focused. They help writers measure if the content is furthering the argument, and if they are explicitly using that content to support the study. Further, claims can guard against overusing or overwriting about individual studies; they help writers contain the discussion. Looking ahead, a writer can find that their claims are crucial in helping readers understand and anticipate where the argument is going.

Here is an example of a series of related claims guiding a Literature Review on an empirical study of the low numbers of Latina principals, and the barriers these women face:

1   *Latina principals are underrepresented at a time when principal instructional leadership is increasingly related to student achievement.*
2   *New research indicates how principal leadership affects student success, and how cultural responsiveness among leaders is particularly important to an increasingly diverse student body.*
3   *Existing interventions include how Latinos/as generally, and Latinas in particular, are being recruited, trained and supported.*
4   *Challenges remain – to recruiting, training, and helping Latinas persist: family, cultural bias, lack of leadership training.*
5   *We still need to know how successful Latina principals overcome barriers.*
6   *Critical Race Theory provides a theoretical frame and rationale.*

These claims help the researcher clarify what is missing from existing studies. With a structure in place, the writer can begin to compose key sections.

### 3.2 GROWING THE ARGUMENT: INITIAL STAGES

A doctoral student needs to start writing, but with a caveat in mind. The growth of the Literature Review is not typically linear, even if the final product is. New studies are found all the time during the dissertation process, right up until filing. Along the way, new categories emerge as the writer reads and rereads the argument. Further, the writer often leaves, for late in the process, an early section that might require major digging. Though often written first, the theoretical framework is typically positioned last in the Review, as a transition to the Methods chapter (mentioned upfront but detailed later). And the Introduction often gets written last, with readers in mind. So, initially, writers are free to get started with what they see most clearly. But having a tentative plan provides guidance.

## Writing with a flexible plan

When composing, dissertation writers often ask, how does one keep on track? Most importantly, the writer needs to refer back to their overall plan – how to best argue for the study and with what kind of evidence. The plan needs to be fluid – it may expand to include new sections or be cut down to exclude weaker sections. Or it may be reorganized entirely. But having a list of arguments that relate to one another helps the writer compose individual pieces without being overwhelmed by the literature: Researchers face unlimited studies that possibly *could* relate to the main argument. The writer needs a plan to select and organize the presentation.

Even with a set of arguments, the writing can become vague or wandering. Revisiting the plan as they write reminds researchers about what is important – what needs shortening and what needs expanding. For instance, it is well known that community college transfer students have difficulty persisting and graduating from four-year colleges. But reasons seem all over the map: poor academic preparation, little college knowledge, extensive remedial coursework, social-emotional reasons. These are all important variables, but they lead in widely divergent directions. If the dissertation is on social-emotional causes, how much research is needed on the other variables? How not to get lost in background data?

Rather than getting lost in the morass, writers need to cut short what is not crucial and focus on the major research; they can also use placeholder strategies, saving for later a reassessment of what is still needed. For instance, the above writer on transfer student persistence could simply describe a few key studies for each variable, to stake out the territory – but move quickly to social-emotional causes; she could also just leave the background section for later. Once the major argument is in place, writers can come back to a section and better judge what is needed. Overall, the Literature Review evolves organically. The writer's plan helps to stimulate thinking not to confine it, and the plan helps keep track of the writer's larger purpose.

A plan also helps writers be more efficient. Constant chasing down articles on a broad topic is clearly inefficient. Students need targeted searches – knowing what to argue so that they can skim, then select or discard, a host of studies. A plan of arguments helps them read abstracts quickly under each main claim. When they have accumulated targeted materials, writers might form "buckets" or categories. Even if some studies fit under more than one category, identifying the argument(s) that each study supports can help writers use the literature effectively.

### Deepening the argument when the researcher lacks studies

At times, students set about writing the Literature Review feeling dissatisfied with what research they have collected – too much well-known, broad, or old research, or too little new research related to the proposed work. After trying new search words, visiting the librarian, and plumbing recent studies for works cited, the student might search analogous work from other disciplines.

For instance, for the above example on transfer students' social-emotional needs, the writer ended up identifying sociological studies on "culture shock" (the disorientation of entering a culture foreign to one's own, usually applied to foreign travel). This research helped her argue that community college transfer students need a special "Orientation" (just as with Study Abroad students) to familiarize them with the new "culture" of a four-year college. Once the writer argued for bridging "cultures," other social and psychological arguments opened up, as well as new ethnographic methodologies: What are the "cultural" differences of four-year institutions versus community colleges? How do the students in these institutions typically differ culturally? How might these differences challenge a transfer student's sense of identity? These questions could later become the headings of a literature review–one that justifies a study of transfer student Orientations and how they meet (or do not meet) students' social-emotional needs. The study could then be based on social-integration theory. (An aside: this divergent line of investigation finally led this student to drop Orientations in order to study informal social networks.)

### Revisiting the Problem Statement

As noted earlier, writers come to this chapter with resources developed from the Problem Statement. The Problem Statement typically presents broad data used to identify the problem and to provide context for the study. One place to initiate a plan for the Literature Review is for the writer to revisit this data. Statistics are good hooks for readers. And the student has likely culled some national or state-wide data. Additional statistics can expand the data, further clarify the problem, and add nuances.

For instance, for the case studies of successful dual-language middle schools, the writer opened her Literature Review with national statistics on English Learners' (ELs) low high school graduation rates, taken from her Problem Statement. These were her only national statistics on EL achievement to justify her study, and these could have reflected a variety of causes. They needed expansion. While useful for the Problem Statement, they did not paint the full picture of EL low achievement as related to a lack of *language* supports. So, she added national data on low literacy rates for ELs, especially at the middle school level. Next, she identified further national data on the benefits of language supports for ELs, which helped her further strengthen her case. By rereading her Problem Statement, she realized that she had a lot more evidence available to deepen the context for her study.

(A caveat here about adding more national statistics: Multiple sources may not always increase readers' knowledge or may involve lengthy debates on how data were collected and analyzed. Readers expect the *writer* to choose the most credible background statistics, paint a full picture, and move on.)

Not just statistics, but key arguments can be derived from the Problem Statement. Dissertation writers often overwrite the Problem Statement, needing to convince not just themselves but their Chairs that they have a viable study. Relocating some sections from the Problem Statement to the Literature Review could improve both chapters. The revision might entail leaving only the key claims and citations in the Problem Statement, but then transporting the extended argument to the Literature Review, providing deeper analysis and synthesis of key studies.

Finally, to further use what they already has, writers might draw from their Problem Statement the *overall order of the argument* – an initial progression through the literature. The Problem Statement already embodies a funnel of arguments supporting the study, from broad to specific. This structure could underlie an initial plan for the Literature Review. The writer could derive an outline from already existing arguments, and then identify what needs to be added. New sections would likely include the theoretical framework, the chosen methodology, and newly researched applications.

### Putting a plan into action

As noted above, researchers can read and write endlessly on background material. That is why a concentrated plan can keep the writer focused on what is essential. With a sense of the whole, writers select and measure what literature is useful to their argument, judge what to value most, and make critical decisions about how best to use their time.

Writers may wonder what a concentrated plan looks like – how detailed they need to be. Here are two examples. The first is a plan for the study on AP Capstone courses (providing minority students with a culturally responsive pedagogy), a plan that emerged from the notes presented earlier.

1  *Background:* the benefits of AP classes – their role in college admissions and college success; minority students' *low rates* of taking AP courses; *benefits* for this specific group – success rates, college completion rates, student motivation.
2  *Existing supports:* classroom pedagogies; supports that already target this population; data on how *existing interventions are failing.*
3  *The intervention:* Capstone classes' theory and history – plus argument for *why culturally responsive pedagogies should work.*

4  *Gap in the research:* What we know and still need to know about existing AP Capstone course pedagogies, nationally.

5  *Theoretical frame:* culturally responsive pedagogy

The writer has lifted this logic from his Problem Statement, and it serves as an initial guide as he searches the literature in the field. It has only five categories, but these are enough to help him sift through a massive number of studies on AP courses.

Another example follows, this time on principal leadership as key to improving elementary school mathematics instruction. The writer provides a very detailed plan.

1  *Background stats:* Low math achievement over time for all levels (NAEP and other national assessments). Math low achievement at elementary levels.

2  *Diverse reasons explaining poor math achievement:* Poor teacher training/instruction; lack of development of true math understanding; emphasis on procedures and numeracy; failed models.

3  *The promise of Cognitively Guided Instruction (CGI):* Its emphasis on understanding, using students' intuitive knowledge; data on effectiveness of CGI in increasing achievement.

4  *Research problem:* The lack of CGI implementation (impediments; requirements for reform movements to take hold; need for instructional leadership).

5  *Principal leadership effectiveness studies:* Role of principal as instructional leader; impediments: administrators don't know how to support math and administrators don't know CGI.

6  *Principal trainings – limited positive results:* Some limited data show that administrator trainings can support CGI teachers.

7  *What we still need to know:* If a principal leadership seminar can help principals understand, support, and encourage use of CGI in elementary schools.

8  *Theoretical framework:* Constructivist frame that assumes the power of instructional leaders.

As with the first example, the plan reveals an argument structure, with tentative claims that might underpin each main point. The writer now has arguments that she can flesh out, and a means of judging the relevance of the extensive studies she will review. She can grow her argument in an orderly fashion, avoiding the overload that can undermine a doctoral student's progress.

These initial activities in planning the Literature Review make the next stages in the process much easier.

## 3.3  COMPOSING THE LITERATURE REVIEW

With a plan in place, students can use writing time most effectively. Writers should expect this chapter to undergo various revisions. Students initially have difficulty with synthesis – seeing how one study may require another study and how together they support or possibly dispute one's argument. Some need reminding that they cannot just cherry-pick supportive studies. Anticipated challenges include encountering studies that undermine, or at least call into question, some of the data that other studies cite. Furthermore, the methods of some studies may require analysis: On a closer look, the population may be small, the sites not representative, or the protocols inadequate. Thinking, rethinking, re-gathering, and re-conceptualizing are part of the writing process, and this means that even with a map, writers need a fluid approach to developing this chapter.

## Generating the big argument: junctures and sub points

Connecting the big arguments helps readers see main junctures. A strong argument for any study provides logical connections between big and small arguments. Below is an example from the study on informal networks for first generation transfer students. The following transition sentence connects transfer students generally, to first generation transfer students in particular:

> While culture shock applies to all transferring community college students, it is particularly challenging for first generation transfer students, as they are already breaking with family culture just by going to college.

This big connector predicts, first, broad research on transfer students' culture shock; then that it will be tied to targeted research on a narrower population, the researcher's focus. The writer next divides this narrower claim into sub points:

> First generation community college transfer students, who often live at home, face three key challenges to social integration that other transfer students do not: home conflict, work schedules, and less time on campus…

Such connections identify for the reader the specific challenges to social integration for this narrowed population; the connectors also anticipate the researcher's unique solution – social integration strategies not already sponsored by universities.

A tight organization is helpful to readers and to writers. Most of this writer's key literature needs to focus on first generation transfer students' challenges and on existing interventions. Her major questions surround her unique population: She needs to ask herself: How strong is the evidence for unique challenges? Why is "social integration" the best solution? Why do existing college support structures for social integration not suffice? Writing and revising the Literature Review needs to address such reader questions.

## *How a few key studies can underpin a proposed study*

Sometimes, one or two studies or reports carry much of the weight of the Literature Review as defense for the study. So identifying them is a critical step in developing this chapter. Students might consider first writing about how such studies argue for their project, then decide how to move the reader toward these studies. This approach might mean working backwards from the most telling research. On the other hand, the writer could place these studies upfront, returning to them throughout the Literature Review. The following paragraphs show the writer identifying, early on, two key studies as lynchpins for her study. The first is a mapping study similar to the one she proposes, identifying upfront the gaps in the research:

> The lack of available data regarding current arts in health programming limits program development, improvement, and evaluation. In an increasing field of demand, arts in healthcare administrators must decide what the costs of involvement and operation are and how to create additional value in programming without raising costs. For instance, a mapping study of arts in health programs in Florida found that 44% of organizations lacked paid administrative staff (Sonke, Helgemo, & Pesata, 2018). In addition, there is not a structured method to identify and monitor arts in health programs in the United States. Although the 2018 study helps to provide a depiction of arts in health programs in one state, it does not provide a complete data profile for arts in health programs, nor does it focus on the programming by the types of organizations providing the programming.
>
> Neither the 2018 Florida mapping study nor the 2009 State of the Field study specifically focuses on opera organizations. Established in over 108 cities in the United States and covering 88% of the 50 largest cities, these invest almost 1 trillion dollars into the overall economy annually (Opera America, 2018). Given the prominence of opera companies and their investments in healthcare settings, and with new studies demonstrating the impact of music listening on patients and service users in healthcare settings (76.8%), administrators need to create and track data within these programs; these data can be used to improve programming and management and to professionalize services to some of the most vulnerable audience members, hospital patients.
>
> (Boyce, Bungay, Munn-Giddings, & Wilson, 2018)

The writer focuses sharply on the lack of available data. She identifies the one key mapping study, similar to her own, noting the study's limitations (it is only for Florida and it lacks differentiation of arts organizations). She then discusses that key study, in combination with the one *state of the field* study, to claim that no existing study focuses on opera companies. The importance of this gap, she makes clear, comes with data on the 1 trillion dollar investment in the economy that opera companies make. These two studies, along with background data on opera company investment, clarify the need to create, track, and manage opera programming in health organizations.

### Writing the introduction: a roadmap for the reader

A fully articulated introduction is the *reader's* roadmap through a complex body of research. Its final version reflects months of research, writing and revision. The introduction might begin by reminding readers of the problem and then clearly mapping where the chapter is going and why (not unlike one's *plan* for developing the chapter). The introduction is not a list, however. Rather, it introduces and connects arguments, *persuading* readers that they will encounter an orderly presentation of research supporting the proposed study. The Introduction's most important function is to predict for the reader the major sections of the chapter according to the logic of the study. While the final draft of the Introduction is likely written after the entire Literature Review is in place, a detailed first-draft effort helps both writer and Chair understand how the work is evolving.

To develop an Introduction as itinerary, writers need to project reader concerns. (What do readers need to know first? Second? What questions are they asking? What kinds of connections are persuasive?) Writers get a sense of reader based introductions by skimming completed dissertations in the field and taking note of how each presents an itinerary for readers. While writers vary in how they present their work, they do preview for their readers what is to come. Below are paragraphs from two studies, where the writers presented straightforward roadmaps. The first is a completed roadmap, the second an itinerary that is still being rewritten.

Example 1: on creating an institution-wide faculty development program

> This review of the literature begins with a brief discussion of the history of community colleges and the shift in purpose and student demographics over time, leading to the low completion rates of students. I then show the evolution of faculty development in higher education, focusing on community colleges, and the challenges that community colleges face implementing faculty development programs that target student success. Given such challenges, I next review the evidence of effective faculty development, and follow with an explanation of the evidence that links faculty development to improved student outcomes. With student outcomes as my goal, I situate my study in the conceptual framework of the kaleidoscope convergence of bottom-up and top-down leadership (Kezar, 2012), assuming that both faculty and administrative leadership are necessary to create and sustain a widespread, institutionalized faculty development

program, nested within a collaborative culture. I will focus the conceptual frame discussion on Kezar's strategies to promote successful convergence as a lens for my data analysis.

This is a finished roadmap, central to the writer's engagement with her reader. It was likely rewritten multiple times, as the Literature Review developed, and perhaps as the student was deciding on her conceptual frame. The writer would likely have gone back to it for guidance, as she wrote. And she might also have changed it as she gathered new research. It now serves as a roadmap for the *reader*, anticipating the major arguments and tying them to the problem of low completion rates: It ends with the theoretical frame, which now logically flows from the description of the study.

Example 2: the use of mindset theory to improve teaching of EL reading

A second example also capsulizes the argument to come. But this is not a finished roadmap, and readers can identify a gap in the argument.

This review first summarizes national data on current low levels of reading achievement. It then examines data on English Learner (EL) reading achievement, largely unchanged from 2003 to 2017, despite increased resources and funding (August et al, 2006; California Department of Education, 2016). The review then summarizes reading theory and targeted interventions, which have not raised achievement scores. Given this persistent problem, I then argue for more classroom-based, collaborative teacher development programs, rooted in mindset, to address reading discrepancies. I conclude with examining how the proposed study is framed by Dweck's theory of Growth Mindset and Dewey's theory of Reflective Thinking.

In this example, the writer previews for the reader the logic of her argument: from the national problem of low reading scores, to unchanged EL reading achievement (despite interventions), to a specific collaborative teacher development program designed to "address discrepancies," to theories behind this intervention. The roadmap offers a logical progression. However, one senses a leap to "classroom-based, collaborative teacher development programs." The choice seems to come out of the blue. Readers might ask, why this particular approach when collaboration is so difficult? What other interventions might work as well? Such reader questioning may require the writer to revisit the roadmap. As the roadmap is in-process, at some point the writer will need to come back and refine this introduction.

### Getting sections written

What follows is further advice on writing processes. To reiterate, writing is messy and writers have different preferences. They can decide what section they want to write up first and at what time. Some writers feel most comfortable first writing about studies closest to their wellspring of motivation. Indeed, a researcher may have entered a doctoral program motivated to counter research contrary to experience. Starting with a section one cares most about can inspire chunks of good writing and help one plan for the rest. Most writers, however, prefer to begin with background leading up to the problem.

Writing processes that start with background, following the reader's thinking, section by section, create their own gratification. The doctoral student first writes the broad sections, then narrows, as with a funnel. The logic is very natural: Often the sentences just flow. This approach might require skipping over data one has not yet collected, leaving half-baked an argument one cannot yet make, or producing placeholder sentences for later completion. But spinning out the arguments as they follow a reader's projected thought processes keeps one targeted on persuasion.

Most important for writing is that the writer just keeps moving, writing something every day. This might mean finding a specific time and place that works. That allotted time can be used for major progress but also to write synopses of articles, comparisons between studies, a recounting of the research history, even notes to oneself. If specific times are impossible, a notepad near-by may capture fleeting ideas or make unexpected connections. Writing is thinking, and thoughts rarely stop occurring, even in one's sleep.

Writing full text, however, creates challenges of sentence structure, tone, diction, and correctness, and the temptation for doctoral students is to let everything but writing actual sentences take precedence. The best advice here is for writers to let the writing come out as close to thinking as possible, in sentence form, and not worrying about errors, awkwardness, clunkiness, disconnect, and bad phrasing. Turning off the editor can, to the contrary, make the language more natural and more attuned to thought. It is important that writers draft in consecutive prose – however tentative, provisional, or narrow in purpose. The more they practice it, the more fluent they become. When writers conclude a writing session, it helps if they jot down what the next piece of writing will be, maybe even writing the next few sentences, to jump start the next day's work.

## *How to keep being productive*

When not writing sections, doctoral students can keep doing things that move them closer to completing a section: Cross checking reference lists; tracking most recent or most cited articles; looking for repeated names; identifying new subject headings; looking for analogous research from other fields; identifying contradicting research; writing to key researchers in the field; talking to professors in aligned fields. All of these activities can involve some form of writing as thinking and can lead to new ideas and materials to discuss. Students know they have sufficient literature when all of the researchers are citing each other's works, the studies trace back to the same key research, and a convergence appears as to the theoretical frame supporting this work. The doctoral student can trace the history of major work in the field.

## 3.4 REVISING THE LITERATURE REVIEW

### *Examining and questioning the literature*

Literature Reviews typically get revised several times. First, finding key research requires time and skill. Textbooks or literature syntheses are particularly useful sources because they already select and assess key studies in specific areas. Still, some studies found early in the Literature Review process may seem to lose value over time, including textbook references. Students' sharpened analytic skills may also play a part in this reexamination. A study once thought to be a seminal work begins to look narrow – or based on questionable methods.

A newly found study, one that makes earlier pieces look extraneous, may result in a reshuffling of the Literature Review offerings. This rewriting is normal. The culling of materials, and necessary rewriting of drafts, is essential to the writing process. And the rewriting has benefits. The shift from generalized to targeted arguments helps hone one's research and writing skills. Each draft makes way for a stronger next draft.

To return to this book's theme, dissertation writers need a good attitude toward revision, especially with an extended piece such as the Literature Review. A first draft enables one to grow one's thoughts. Writing out one's arguments and evidence helps one reevaluate them, and so strengthen the case. In detailing the arguments for their study, writers come to learn what they really think about its rationale. Further, a significant piece of draft writing gives one a calling card to meet with one's Chair, where together the student and Chair can assess the literature. Most dissertation writers get used to multiple drafts, as they see their thinking develop. And early drafts are seldom read as finished products but rather as a stage in a student's thinking.

### *Reorganizing the Literature Review*

Even a good original plan of organization may undergo revision. One's first draft order may not be compelling. Or the arguments may lack tight connections and thus seem randomly ordered. In the above roadmaps, the two writers continuously tie the proposed key sections back to the problem. This tie-in came after several earlier drafts. Readers can now see how the key sections relate to each other and to each study's purpose, but the writers did not start there. After several drafts, these writers anticipated readers' questions and stated how the literature informs the study.

### *Headings for sections*

To underscore advice given earlier: Headings preview what comes next. They anticipate for the reader the next section's content, and logically connect to what came before. That means that the writer avoids one or two-word "titles" that are mere "topics" (e.g., "gaps" or "Dual Language"); rather, headings need to be closer to claims, clear parts of an argument.

The example of full headings below, featuring *training* data from opera partnerships with health organizations, shows how headings can distill the argument:

> Benefits of Arts in Healthcare; A Growing Body of Research
> The History of Arts Improving Health Outcomes
> Why Tracking Arts in Healthcare Programming is Important
> Programmatic Choices Create Different Participant Outcomes
> The Lack of Educational Training Data for Performers, Teaching Artists, and Staff
> The Necessity of Data and Evaluation for Funding and Growth

From these headings, the reader can see the logical framing of the argument for a national survey on how Opera companies design programs and train artists for their healthcare programs: From healthcare benefits of the arts comes the need to track programming nationally; tracking then reveals choices, so then comes the need for data to make those choices; data-based choices, the writer argues, can improve funding and growth potential. Readers can see how each new heading follows logically from the previous heading and connects to what is to come; the headings function like bridges.

Studies that are mostly theoretical may look different, with headings that connect parts of that theory, but still lead toward the study design. In the case below, the theory of Culturally Responsive Teaching shapes the headings:

> Persistence of Racial Achievement Gap
> How White School Leaders Negatively Impact Racial School Climate
> Teachers' Racial Erasure and Color Blind Ideologies and Micro-aggressions
> Developing Culturally Responsive School Leadership Behaviors Through Critical Self-Reflection
> How School Leaders Promote Culturally Responsive Teachers and Curricula
> Action Research for School Leader Professional Development

While these headings connect theory elements, they also lead the reader toward the study design. This will be action research, a professional development project involving White school leaders who desire training in anti-racist school ideologies. The headings provide a logical sequence for the argument: from the achievement gap, to school leaders' key role, to negative (and perhaps unconscious) ideologies, to promoting a different ideology, to the need for leader professional development.

## *Transitions*

However, headings do not substitute for in-text transitions. Writers need to be explicit about how ideas and arguments connect, and no heading can do all that work alone. Below are some in-text examples of transitions, from a proposal discussed earlier. They function like mini-bridges, often weighting one piece of information more heavily another:

> **In addition** to these known benefits [of music] for patients, a large portion of the medical community wants to improve cost effectiveness in treatments as well.
> **However,** music has been found to have benefits **far beyond** pain and anxiety management. It positively affects brain plasticity and other biologically measurable changes (Boyce et al., 2018).
> **Although** many of these decisions have already been found in clinical settings to create different patient responses, researchers do not know if opera companies track them.
> Studies have demonstrated that **even small changes** in music, such as pitch, need to be considered in music in healthcare programming, as these changes affect patient experience with statistically significant results.

These sample transitions reach backwards as well as forwards. The first offers a bridge from *known benefits* to improving costs and treatment, giving equal weight to both (*in addition*). The second bridges from known pain management to newly discovered effects on brain plasticity, weighting the second more heavily (*far beyond* known benefits). The third example contrasts clinical decision-making (not so important) with research-based decisions (more important). The fourth downshifts from general effects of music to specific effects, as from pitch (weighted through intensity, newness). Transition supports like *in addition, however,* and *although* signal this weighting.

The good news is that revising headings, and creating transitions, can generate new thought. Headings help the writer review the research and discover new ways of using empirical data. As writers add to sections, they may find opportunities for new sub-divisions, and reassess what the evidence shows. These additions may result in deepening the research base for the study. For instance, for the study above, the need to train performers, teaching artists, and staff could generate new sections on pedagogical training, necessary knowledge base (certain kinds of music affect patients differently), and effects of demographics. The writer could also begin to question required qualifications for the professional manager, who hires the artists and is responsible for programming. Such questioning could justify recommending new job requirements.

## *Tightening up the synthesis*

Writing a strong literature review involves not just expansion but also synthesis. The task is to bring articles together and distill them. Writing about groups of studies creates challenges that usually result in some revision. First drafts typically struggle to synthesize the findings from multiple studies, works with diverse purposes, populations, and methodologies. For one, synthesizing does not mean making a claim and then listing in parentheses numerous studies on the same general topic. For another, it does not mean listing studies, one after the other, and describing each one separately. Rather, the researcher analyzes a group of studies and identifies overlap or discordance among findings as these studies support (or do not support) a claim.

This grouping calls for a lot of analysis and decision-making: Specifically, the writer might decide to discount a piece of research, based on weak methods; or the writer might decide to generalize from the preponderance of like studies and communicate what they agree on (despite differences in methods or assumptions); further, the writer might decide to select one study as representative of a number of studies; also, the writer may have to decide how to acknowledge contrary findings. In sum, the writer analyzes and decides for the reader what multiple studies add up to. This task may take some rethinking, rewriting, and some guidance from peers or Chair.

*Sidenote:* One puts a study's findings in one's own words (paraphrasing), and avoids using long quotations. Only in rare cases, where the exact wording is needed, does the writer quote. In these cases, the quotations are edited down to the essentials, with a full citation including the page number. Paraphrasing is more than changing a word or two – that risks plagiarism. Rather, a paraphrase accurately restates a finding, citing the author(s) of the idea.

## *Revising the theoretical frame*

As noted above, doctoral students are asked early on in their research to identify their theoretical frame, the assumptions or theories that ground the study. As this frame undergirds the study, the writer needs to make explicit the rationale. As cited earlier, the study on low community college completion rates ended up with the following rationale: "*Because of the complexity of institutions of higher education, and the relative weakness of top-down or bottom-up leadership acting alone, the theory of kaleidoscope convergence (Kezar, 2012) drives this study.*" This student rewrote the rationale several times before making it fit well with her study.

Below is a longer example of a writer arguing for distributed leadership as a theoretical frame for a study identifying Community College strategies and leadership styles used to reverse enrollment declines:

> A leadership model that facilitates the development of relationships and trust is distributed leadership ... In his foundational work describing distributive leadership, Spillane (2006) identifies its specific qualities useful as a tool to evaluate leadership in practice ... Distributive Leadership assumes that a single actor does not possess the skill, knowledge or capacity to perform all or even a majority of leadership activities necessary in an organization ... Because California community college enrollment management occurs within the campus environment, which is largely defined by participatory governance, it is appropriate that this investigation use distributed leadership as a lens to analyze enrollment management practices and the implementation of related strategies.

Both examples show an explicit rationale for the choice of lenses, requiring several iterations. For the first writer, the complexity itself of higher education required a theory of complexity. For the second writer, a panoply of possible theories required arguments for his choice.

### Concluding the Literature Review

At the end of the Literature Review, writers typically sum up the bodies of research supporting their study. As these bodies of research typically change, so does the Conclusion. Furthermore, as this last section often leads directly into the Methods chapter, it often introduces the methods that support the design (case study, action research, mixed-methods, grounded theory). The writer's Conclusion typically awaits the writing of the Methods chapter for it to take final form.

## Getting going on writing

**Write:**

1　A paragraph synthesizing three to four key articles related to the proposed study.
2　A paragraph stating three major arguments the chosen literature makes to support the study.
3　A paragraph summing up one's theoretical frame.

# 4 WRITING THE METHODS CHAPTER, GETTING PAST PRELIMINARY ORALS, AND GETTING STARTED

The Methods chapter of the proposal is critical to one's study and develops in concert with one's Chair. The Problem Statement already identified prospective methods (see advice above), and, as noted earlier, there are a plethora of textbooks to help a new researcher refine them. But discussions with one's Chair are what help fully align those methods with the specific research questions and the specific data the researcher wants to collect. This alignment is crucial in preparing for Preliminary Orals.

The Preliminary Orals will then likely change or refine the methods further. Members of the Committee will offer varying suggestions for the most useful methods, and changes often lie with data collection methods. These may be added to, changed, or cut – to make the study more efficient or even doable. Committee members may then ask for a Memorandum of Understanding – a list of the agreed-upon changes in methods. Finally, once the study is completed, writers revise again: The study's real-time unfolding requires a researcher to state what they actually did. This final revision is governed by the need to make the study steps replicable, and the findings valid or trustworthy. It tends to be very detailed – so others can trust in the findings and potentially follow the steps outlined.

## 4.1 WRITING STRATEGIES FOR METHODS CHAPTER PIECES

A number of writing strategies can help the writer generate key pieces when proposing methods. These strategies help one create sections of the proposed Methods chapter, which later can be woven together under the direction of the Chair. This book offers a range of such tasks – required pieces or arguments needed in the chapter; however, these tasks are not a linear plan for the chapter. To discuss these pieces, this chapter draws examples from several students' Methodology chapters at the proposal stage, to show what students produced at this juncture.

### Summarizing the objective

It can be useful for writers to briefly remind the reader of the study problem, objective, and research questions, so that upfront the reader can quickly tie the methods to the specifics of the questions, and the questions back to the objective. Every choice involving methodology needs to be rationalized in terms of research questions and objectives, so this upfront summary needs tight connections.

Here is an example of a tightly summarized problem, objective and questions:

> As noted earlier, colleges have tried various approaches to providing housing for transgender students, most often gender neutral housing. However, these options have not well accommodated transgender students (Bilodeau, 2009; Pryor, Taub, & Hart, 2016).
>
> I will use sense of belonging to examine students' experience in gender-neutral housing. Sense of belonging is influenced by how students perceive college policies (Garvey, Sanders, & Flint, 2017; Vaccaro & Newman, 2017). I will examine how the different college policies may interact with students' sense of belonging on campus. To gain a fuller picture, I will also examine implementation from the perspective of the college administrators who put the program into practice.
>
> 1. What are students' perceptions of gender neutral housing policies on their campus? How do these perceptions interact with their sense of belonging?
> 2. How do liberal arts college administrators describe their decision-making process when implementing and developing their gender neutral housing policies on their campus?

The quick summary here is closely reflected in the writer's research questions.

## Arguing for the design

A second upfront piece is an extended rationale for the choice of design. Is this going to be a qualitative, quantitative or mixed design study? The researcher likely already has a short version of this in the Problem Statement. But a thoughtful, well-articulated rationale is needed here.

The wording of the research questions is key to this section. Is the researcher asking open-ended questions about perceptions, experiences, reflections, exchanges, processes, descriptions, or narratives, where unforeseeable responses may emerge from these questions? Typically, such questions require a qualitative approach. In contrast, is the researcher asking for preselected effects, measurements, ratings, scores, percentages, or degree of acceptance or approval, where data fit along a predetermined spectrum? Such questions typically indicate a quantitative study. For design, writers need to explain what they are after, so that the design fits the objective. Then, the questions need to be worded so that they will produce answers to the questions that then meet the objectives.

Here is an example of a doctoral student providing a rationale for his proposed design. The writer identifies the unique capabilities of qualitative research and applies those to the study's objective, which is to investigate successful enrollment stabilization practices at three community colleges.

> Qualitative research is uniquely suited to understand processes, including the people, actions, and events that influence them (Maxwell, 2013). Nearly everything on college campuses is shaped by the specific context of the individual campus. Variations between campuses can include differences in faculty cultures; in relationships between faculty, staff and administrators; available resources; and other elements. What works on one campus, may fail dismally at another. Qualitative case studies will support a close examination of the contexts at the individual sites and how these contexts influenced the success of the enrollment strategies. A distinctive feature of qualitative studies is their ability to access the perspectives of the participants. Understanding how participants make meaning of what has occurred on their campuses and how their perspectives influence their attitudes and behaviors will provide a nuanced view; the distinctions this will provide are needed as college campuses have multiple constituent groups with oftentimes opposing cultures, values, and goals. While quantitative methods, such as a survey, could certainly generate data on the enrollment strategies and leadership practices used by the colleges, a qualitative approach is better suited to these research questions because qualitative methods support the discovery of unidentified and unforeseen factors. This is particularly important for this study, as it may be that colleges are utilizing similar enrollment strategies that result in different outcomes. This qualitative study seeks to understand the reasons this occurs.

The writer's rationale makes the choice of a qualitative design fit the objective of the study – to look at enrollment stabilizing processes. Because these processes are tied to a unique context and are reflected in the perceptions, events and actions of participants, the study calls for open-ended qualitative methods.

An argument for a quantitative design is very different because the researcher is looking for usage, ratings, priorities, correlations, etc. The student writing the rationale below wanted to know about a correlation between preselected, measurable variables: What relationship, if any, exists between under-represented minority (URM) faculty service workload (range, time spent, level of burden) and their intent to remain in or depart from their respective careers? The researcher explained what was sought but also reasons for this unique choice of methods:

**Design rationale**

Faculty retention research has produced significant qualitative data on both service work and the career trajectories of URM faculty. As this study seeks to add to existent URM faculty retention research, it will follow a quantitative approach, which will provide measurable data and thus an opportunity to reveal a potential correlation between two distinct variables: service work and career intentions. A quantitative method is best suited to determine whether a relationship exists between these two variables, but will also allow for analysis and desegregation of data to reveal statistical significance of the independent variables (Creswell, 2014). Further, the measurable data provided by a quantitative method will be generalizable to the nation's URM faculty population, at large.

The writer justifies the design in terms of what is missing from existing research, then the need for correlation between variables, and the benefit of disaggregation of data to identify significance. These are recognized rationales for a quantitative approach.

A rationale for mixed methods needs to argue for both methods, but it also needs to connect them. The following rationale proposes a mixed methods study on the use, nationally, of mixed-reality simulation as a means of teacher trainings, as well as leaders' perceptions of the effectiveness of its use.

I propose an explanatory sequential mixed methods research design. This design involves collecting quantitative data in the first phase of the study and then using those results to build on the second, qualitative phase (Creswell & Creswell, 2018). For my research, the quantitative results will "inform the types of participants to be purposefully selected for the qualitative phase" (Creswell & Creswell, 2018, p. 222). As such, the survey data – specifically information on the length of time the [simulation] program [for teacher training] has used the technology, the frequency of simulation usage, and the size of the student population exposed to the technology, will serve to inform who is chosen for the qualitative population sample – those leaders whose programs that have the most prolific use of simulation being selected for interviews.

A quantitative design is appropriate to answer the "in what ways" framed research question and sub-question involving [national] simulation use as it includes analysis of scale, percentages, frequencies, and degrees of use. A qualitative design will then deeply investigate the perceptions and opinions of leaders of simulation. Thus, an explanatory sequential mixed-methods study is an appropriate method to examine the current use of simulation nationally as well as gain a deeper understanding of how the technology is being utilized, led, and diffused. As this study aims to incorporate users from all U.S. institutions of higher education currently using simulation, a purely qualitative study could not adequately capture its breadth. Similarly, a solely quantitative design could not thoroughly describe the perceptions of simulation leaders related to the research questions.

The writer justifies this approach by relating the methods back to the research questions, justifying the need for both quantitative and qualitative methods as providing both the breadth of usage and the depth of leaders' perceptions. The quantitative data also supports the selection criteria (the most usage) for appropriate "leaders" to interview.

## Identifying Units of Analysis and Units of Observation

A brainstorming technique to pinpoint data collection and analysis may derive from the proposed Design. First, one identifies Units of Analysis – the category of data one seeks. For the above qualitative proposal, it is "processes." This doctoral student wants to know how each community college responded to the problem of unstable enrollment, how each college chose strategies, and how strategies were implemented. So the basic Unit of Analysis is processes. But what counts as a process? The researcher still needs to identify Units of Observation. These might comprise the concrete events or decisions underlying a process. The student listed as many possibilities as he could think of, so that he knew what he was after, but he left the possibilities open ended. Some processes included changes to class scheduling and enhancing student support programs.

A writer can create a table for processes, which links each *process* to a research question, to Units of Observation (data one could collect), and to the data collection method appropriate to them. Or one can generate and simply list each:

Research question: How do single community college districts on *stabilization* respond to enrollment challenges?

For processes, examples of Units of Observation might include:

- Changes to class scheduling processes (interviews and documents)
- Conversion of non-enhanced noncredit offerings to enhanced noncredit (interviews and documents)
- Encourage part-time students to enroll full-time (interviews)
- Enhance student support programs, for example, tutoring and counseling (interviews)
- Implement time blocks for class scheduling (documents)
- Increase in adult education offerings (documents)
- Increase in high-demand class offerings (those class offerings that enrollment data demonstrate that there are not a sufficient number of offerings to meet student demand) (interviews and documents)
- Increase in dual enrollment courses (courses offered in area high schools, taught by the college's faculty) (interviews and documents)

- Increase in noncredit offerings (documents)
- Increase in online offerings (documents).

Having brainstormed these Units of Observation (or collected data), the writer can see that he needs two data collection methods – interviews and document analysis. With such data in mind, the writer can anticipate the kind of analysis he will need, likely combining data sources to answer his research question.

As a writing strategy, such an exercise helps the researcher further detail the design section and also to outline data collection and analysis sections. It serves as a check on the consistency between a research question, design, method, and data sought. If the Units of Observation did not fit the research question, were too broad to answer it, or did not fit the method (e.g., were measurable with a Likert scale or were yes/no answers), this study would lack alignment. But once aligned, the Units of Observation can generate interview questions or suggest probes to produce rich data; they can also become possible coding strategies for analyzing data. If the student used a table to brainstorm these connections, it would likely go in an Appendix, as a confirmation of the writer's analytical processes.

### Defending one's site

Another writing piece, essential to this chapter, involves creating a persuasive rationale for one's site(s). While tips were provided for the Problem Statement, here the writer needs not just a summary but detailed anchoring of the particular site to the study's objectives. Why would only this site, or type of site, work to meet the study's objective? What follows is an example of a set of criteria for site selection from the above study proposal:

> Multi-campus districts are able to balance full time equivalent student (FTES) shortfalls at one of their colleges with FTES increases at other colleges within the district. Since FTES reporting occurs at the district level, this balancing act is obscured in the 320 Reports. For these reasons, I will focus on single college districts. A purposeful selection approach will be utilized to select the final sites. Site(s) will be selected from those single college districts that received stability funding and were able to restore their pre-stabilization FTES levels in subsequent years. I will limit the colleges to those that lost and regained at least five percent of their FTES. Five percent was selected as a threshold to exclude those colleges that missed their FTES targets by a marginal amount.

Here, the writer explains his reasoning, anticipating possible concerns. He restricts possible study sites to single college districts to counter the critique that multi-campus districts can "balance" their enrollment, thus obviating the need for stabilizing them. Further, purposeful selection enables him to select from those sites that received stability funding and were then successful in restoring enrollment levels. The writer narrows even more, limiting sites to those that regained at least 5 percent, again to offset a potential criticism. For this section, it is important to connect the "restrictions" on the researcher's site selection to the study's objectives.

## Defending the choice of participants or sample

As with defending a site, the doctoral student needs to fully defend the selection of participants or sample: What are the criteria for inclusion in the study? What concerns made the student limit the participants in this way? How do these criteria exclude those who would not contribute to the study? What is the aim that underlies each requirement? The above proposed study on stabilizing community college enrollment addresses these issues, and again ties them to the study "aim":

> To select study participants, I will employ a purposeful sampling approach with the aim of securing interviewees that are knowledgeable about enrollment management strategies, processes, and leadership at their site. It is important to note that it can be commonplace for many faculty and staff members and some administrators to perform their duties, while being largely unaware of enrollment management issues. For this reason, I will aim to interview the administrator who leads enrollment management at the district, other administrators who participate in enrollment management, faculty leaders, classified staff leaders, and those who serve on enrollment management committees. I include faculty and classified staff leaders because they are more likely than regular faculty to be aware of enrollment management issues because of their greater involvement in college participatory governance. Interviewing faculty, classified staff, and administrators will allow for comparison of the perceptions among the different employee types. It may be necessary to use snowball sampling to identify participants that are knowledgeable about enrollment management at each site because involvement in enrollment management can vary from site to site.

The writer foregrounds his study's "aim." He seeks knowledgeable participants because he is looking for leadership practices, requiring those with knowledge of the issue. He also needs to justify asking "different employee types." While he is not clear why comparisons between these types are important, he acknowledges that he will make use of those different perspectives.

## Recruitment

In defending participant selection, students need to defend their strategy for recruiting participants and keeping them. New researchers' major worry is that they recruit too few participants or that participants leave the study, mid-way. They need to describe how they will recruit them, what incentives or motivations they will offer, and why these participants are likely to respond to these incentives. Participants may also be reluctant if they sense they could experience exposure, retaliation, or damage to their reputation or that of the institution. Or they may simply not understand the time commitment. But if a student has already received numerous preliminary commitments, reviewers feel more assured. Still, students need to explain back-up plans.

A recruitment plan also describes any site accommodations, especially if these are for time and/or resources. For instance, the researcher might be asking teachers to take away from instructional time or add to their workload after school. Given such concerns, the writer discusses what accommodations are offered, when and where participation will take place, and why these choices suit the participants' and the organizations' needs. An example follows from a study on exclusionary practices at an affluent high school; it interweaves selection and recruitment, without need for accommodations. Clarity of information and rewards seem appropriate for recruitment.

> I announced my project to upper school students at an assembly in September 2015. I then held an information session for interested students, which provided more detail about the project and the time commitment. I provided a one-page application that collected students' names, grade level, information about their objective and subjective SES (see appendix).
>
> I selected student participants using stratified non-random sampling so that the group was relatively equally balanced with regards to SES, even though the community itself is predominantly affluent. This reduced the likelihood that lower SES students would feel outnumbered, as they are in the broader school environment, and therefore made them more likely to speak openly about their experience and ideas. I also selected only students in tenth, eleventh, or twelfth grade because ninth graders would likely not have sufficient knowledge about the upper school culture and may not have the intellectual capacity or maturity for participatory action research. I aimed for a relatively even number of students from each of the three grades as well as a balance between boys and girls.
>
> I informed selected participants via email and provided them with consent forms. I sent an informational packet home with student participants, providing parents with an overview of the project, the time commitment, and a consent form, which they signed and returned. All participants received a $25 Amazon gift card, and I encouraged students to include their action research work on college applications. They did not

receive class credit, but they could treat their participation as they would membership in a school club or service project.

While the researcher did not specify what she would do if she did not recruit enough participants, the incentives appear significant and are well detailed.

## Describing data collection methods

Another key section is a complete description and rationale for each data collection method (or "strategy of inquiry"), summarized in the Problem Statement. Each method needs to be tied to the research question(s). The writer explains why each method is necessary, what type(s) of data are to be collected (perhaps drawing from the Units of Observation chart), what documents the researcher needs (if this is a method) and why. If the researcher chooses a focus group over interviews, the rationale then explains why an exchange of ideas among participants outweighs individual perspectives.

Below is another section from the enrollment management study, describing a key proposed method – interviews:

> All of the interviews will be semi-structured and will consist of questions about the enrollment strategies the college used to improve enrollment, the processes for implementing the strategies, and the leadership approach used in realizing enrollment improvements. I use semi-structured interviews because I need to understand the relationship between leadership styles, types of processes, and success of the strategy. To accomplish this, I will ask interviewees about specific strategies known to have an effect, for example, outreach and recruitment or use of efficiency targets in the scheduling process. Furthermore, I will ask specific questions to assess the degree to which distributive leadership was used, what other leadership approaches were used, and the perceived effect of leadership on enrollment efforts. For example, I will probe whether an authoritative or participatory leadership style was responsible for the success or failure of the enrollment strategies. Interviews will last approximately 60 minutes and be conducted at the college site in the offices of the interviewees or in a neutral location, such as a conference room. The dialogues will be recorded on a digital audio recorder and an iPhone for back-up.

The rationale is tied to the research questions, which focus on processes, approach, and strategies. By highlighting processes, the writer justifies *interviews* as the key method; also, a sensitive topic such as leadership styles lends itself to individual perspectives. More specifically, the writer clarifies the need for *semi-structured* interviews by arguing that he needs probes to understand connections between processes, leadership approach [with measures described elsewhere], and strategy success. As the reader can see, this is a complex argument.

## Writing protocols (avoiding inadequate data)

As part of a description of methods, writers develop and describe their protocols. A protocol is the list of questions (including survey questions), moves, back-up questions, probes, facilitations, explanations, directions, or actions to observe that the doctoral student intends to use to gather the needed data. For each method, writers need specifics about what they will do or ask. Too often, doctoral students have compelling reasons for their study's objectives, design, and methods, but have written rough, generalized protocols. These then produce weak, generalized, commonsense, or predictable data that leave students with little to write about.

First, the new researcher needs to tie each protocol question or observation to a research question. What data will the protocol question produce? The researcher can also try out the protocols on friends or colleagues. Or more rigorously, they can perform a pilot study. Key questions from these trials include the following: How do the respondents interpret the questions? What does the data gathered allow the writer to say? Is there anything surprising here? Does the data clearly answer the questions? Responses to such queries may help dissertation writers decide to test different versions of the protocols to see which garners responses that target the objectives.

## Ensuring access

Another key argument to include in this chapter is a credible access plan – access to data as well as to a site. Many organizations that have already collected data may not want to share it with a new researcher. Potential study sites may also be leery of having researchers investigating their environments or probing their employees. If one aims to explain a site's failure or fix a problem – a reminder of problematic leadership – the doctoral student may not gain access. Also, leadership can change quickly, leaving the student without permission to carry out the study.

When doctoral students write up their access plans, they explain in their proposals all connections or guarantees for gaining access (who they have contacted, what ties they have to the site, why the site leader would permit this study). Most researchers obtain a Memorandum of Understanding (MOU) from site leaders to ensure that the access remains in place. It is commonsense that students proposing to study "successful" sites overcoming a key barrier are more likely to gain access than students proposing to study sites experiencing failure.

An example follows, from the same researcher, recounting what he did to gain access:

Through the president at my current college, I was put in contact with the vice president of instruction at the selected site,
Western Community College (a pseudonym). He and I met and
discussed the study. He agreed that the college would participate and offered to help facilitate the interviews.

Here, the college was interested in the study. The college president made
the contact. Further, the leadership helped with data collection. Some sites
or leaders may not be so amenable. They may be working on their own
analyzes or wish to keep certain documents, not publicly held, out of the
public eye.

Another example comes from a high school site, where school violence was a problem. The researcher found support from this school, despite the topic:

The principal of Lascaux gave me access to the school. I met with
the principal to discuss this project prior to beginning and he
was enthusiastic to participate. He and his administration want
to know the answers to this project's research questions. The
students' Humanities teacher gave me access to the classroom in
which much of the work was accomplished. After presenting my
research questions and goals to a faculty meeting, this teacher
approached me and offered to work with me. Throughout the
project my partnership with him was critical to maintaining the
integrity of the PAR [Participatory Action Research] and the PAR
process.

This student found a site already primed for work on school violence.
Administrators paved the way for a presentation at a faculty meeting,
leading to a key commitment from a teacher.

With quantitative studies, students worry more about response rates.
The researcher may need access to heads of organizations – leaders who
can encourage members to fill out questionnaires or who can provide membership directories to widen the pool. They might have to be creative and
place themselves where they can personally ask for a response. Finally, doctoral students need to identify contingency plans for every identified risk to
obtaining access or response.

## Writing the plan for analyzing data

Methods chapters require a plan for analyzing data. If the study is quantitative, the student knows what kind of data they will have and how they will
analyze it, aided by systematic approaches such as SSRI. This plan is already
determined by the Problem Statement and needed approval of one's Chair.
For a qualitative study, however, the plan is likely to be more hypothetical, as the doctoral student has not yet performed the study and does not

know what data will surface. So the plan can be somewhat general. It can say the researcher will code, index, or label for themes, for example, consistent behaviors, attitudes or ideas – reflecting probes from one's protocol. The plan can say the researcher will look for patterns and connections, and then use these to answer the research questions. It might also note that the researcher will analyze one set of data to determine themes that will be used to shape a different protocol.

For qualitative methods, students likely need to assure the reader that they will read and reread the data, coding it and recoding it for accuracy and significance. They can offer first and second cycles for coding, depending on the study. These might include a first-take placeholder coding strategy, a descriptive set of categories, simultaneous coding, coding for elements of the theory, or simple coding by emerging themes. For coding by theory elements, the student can also specify how the theory or frame helps devise provisional codes. Included in the plan is a detailing of the kinds of data the researcher is targeting (again, the student can select from the Units of Observation). The protocols are already good indicators of how the data will be used to answer the research questions, so the student can revisit them.

Numerous standard types of analysis exist, such as content analysis (reoccurring topics that appear in speech, documents, or behaviors), discourse analysis (speech that occurs in everyday conversations, within a specific social context), or narrative analysis (stories that one constructs from narratives, field notes, interviews). A data analysis plan can anticipate possible ways to analyze data, even though these may change once the data has been collected. While data analysis for quantitative studies typically follows a projected plan, it is different for qualitative studies.

Irrespective of the proposed plan, for a qualitative study the key to data analysis is to immerse oneself in the data so that patterns can emerge or insights surface. This is an unpredictable process. A newly perceived pattern may lead the researcher to follow up on a new strand of data. Categories may surface that the researcher has not anticipated, forming new themes. Emergent themes may also suggest the need to collapse categories or form new ones. The process of writing about a theme may lead the writer to see some data in a new light.

The insights from this complex process will eventually form the basis of the Findings chapter and offer an array of presentation possibilities. Whatever plan the student proposes for data analysis, it may not turn out to be what they actually do when analyzing findings.

What follows is an example of the proposed data analysis method for a mixed-methods study, in this case the national study on culturally responsive practices used in Advanced Placement Capstone courses. The student includes the projected coding categories, as to how he will analyze the data. He has yet to write how he will integrate survey data with more probing interview data.

> I will analyze survey data first via descriptive statistics to describe
> the sample data set in terms of teacher characteristics and school

demographics. I will also provide descriptive statistics for the key variables and constructs my survey measures: instructional planning, assessment and planning practices. These statistics will include measures of central tendency such as mean scores, and mode, frequency of certain responses, range and distribution of responses to questions. Providing these statistics will allow for clear observation of trends and patterns within responses.

To measure associations between these variables, I will perform a multiple regression analysis with the overall cultural responsiveness score as the outcome variable (Huck, 2012). A multiple regression analysis will allow me to predict the extent to which certain explanatory variables contribute to teachers' overall score on cultural responsiveness. These explanatory variables will include teacher age, gender, years teaching, ethnicity, and primary content area. They will also include demographics about school context: school size, school location, school type (public, private, charter, magnet, etc.), percentage of students on free and reduced lunch, and student ethnicity demographics. Teachers scoring in the highest quartile for self-reported use of culturally responsive practices will be categorized into a separate list, from which I will draw my sample for interviews.

Interviews will be transcribed and coded for the following themes, using the Culturally Responsive Instruction Observation Protocol (2017) as a starting point. These interviews will provide illustrative qualitative data about what teachers who self-report the highest levels of cultural responsiveness on the initial survey actually do in their classroom. Per the definition of explanatory mixed methods, these data will help explain the significance and meaning of the survey results (Creswell & Creswell, 2018). These results will shed light on some practices that other teachers who self-report high levels of cultural responsiveness may be using in their classrooms, as well as practices that other teaches who report low levels of cultural responsiveness may not be using.

| Coding Categories for Interviews |
| --- |
| **Assessment practices:** *Formative assessment practices are used that provide information throughout the lesson on individual student understanding, Students are able to demonstrate their learning in a variety of ways, Authentic assessments are used frequently to determine students' competence in both language and content, Students have opportunities for self-assessment.* |
| **Instructional practices:** *Instruction is contextualized in students' lives, experiences, and individual abilities, Students engage in active, hands-on, meaningful learning tasks, including inquiry-based learning, The teacher focuses on developing students' academic language, The teacher uses instructional techniques that scaffold student learning, Students have choices based upon their experiences, interests and strengths* |

| Coding Categories for Interviews |
|---|
| **Discourse:** *The teacher promotes active student engagement through discourse practices, The teacher promotes equitable and culturally sustaining discourse practices, The teacher provides structures that promote academic conversation, The teacher provides opportunities for students to develop linguistic competence* |
| **Critical consciousness:** *The curriculum and planned learning experiences provide opportunities for the inclusion of issues important to the classroom, school and community. The curriculum and planned learning experiences incorporate opportunities to confront negative stereotypes and biases. The curriculum and planned learning experiences integrate and provide opportunities for the expression of diverse perspectives.* |

This level of detail helps answer projected reader questions and increases the credibility of the study. Having initial coding categories that align with the survey and interview questions assures a targeted study and findings that will answer the proposed research questions. As this is a projected data analysis method, it will likely undergo revisions after Preliminary Orals and again after the candidate completes the analysis.

## Ethical issues

Ethical issues arise when there is a possibility of coercion, role ambiguity, invasion of privacy, loss of income, or other harm done to individuals or organizations. When the researcher works with children, these issues are particularly sensitive. The Methodology chapter needs to confront any possible ethical issue and offer a description of how to protect from harm those involved in the study. For this section, students need to consider: How freely the participants feel to join or depart from the study; how students will protect the anonymity of each participant; and what the researcher's role is with respect to power or possible coercion (does the researcher have any supervisory role over participants?). The researcher also asks: Is there a potential that participation could negatively affect that person's employment conditions? Could there be retaliation? At the beginning of a study, students should be aware that research institutions have an Internal Review Board (IRB), which reviews all proposals for ethical issues. Doctoral students need to contact members early in the proposal process to identify potential conflicts.

An example of ethical concerns comes from the study of low socioeconomic students reporting feelings of exclusion at an affluent school in an Action Research study designed to identify exclusionary acts and make the student body aware.

> Ethical considerations with action research are substantial, particularly when the topic is socioeconomic class and privilege and the project involves students. To ensure the wellbeing of participants, I maintained strict confidentiality throughout the process and used pseudonyms for the site and all participants in this manuscript. In addition to gaining informed consent,

I discussed confidentiality norms at the first AR team meeting. I devoted a significant portion of that first meeting to discussions of avoiding judgment, speaking honestly, and building a respectful environment within the group.

I also collected data through electronic journals to ensure confidentiality and privacy. Any information collected by participants and shared with the team did not leave the group. I closely monitored the AR process to ensure that participants were emotionally safe, particularly low SES students who may have felt vulnerable discussing their experience. In fact, higher SES students tended to express the most discomfort and guilt throughout the process, and I occasionally followed up with individual students after reading their journals; such conversations helped to make students feel more comfortable and encourage continued participation.

In a study rife with ethical issues, the researcher took extensive precautions to ensure protections.

## Credibility and Trustworthiness

Issues of credibility (how does one know that the findings are true and accurate?) and trustworthiness (to what extent could the study be repeated or be reanalyzed by other researchers and have the findings remain consistent?) are key concerns of qualitative research, and the writer needs to discuss them. One of the ways to ensure credibility is to triangulate the data across methods. This means that the researcher uses multiple data sources to ensure that the data from one source is confirmed (or not confirmed) by other sources. Another way to confirm accuracy is for the researcher to recheck with participants to see if the write-up has accurately portrayed their responses or actions. This checking ensures that researcher bias does not creep in. The student can also field test protocols, use standardized coding procedures to offset bias, and provide rich descriptions and quotes to support findings. For trustworthiness, the doctoral student needs to clearly detail the process of deriving interpretations and findings from the data.

One key concern for qualitative work is that responses from participants may reflect social desirability – wanting to give the response that makes the respondent sound like a good citizen. The respondents may also wish to please the researcher, thus biasing their report. In proposing a study, doctoral students need to strategize ways to guard against such slanting of the data, including keeping responses anonymous, underscoring the need for accurate data, asking respondents for concrete examples, and reiterating the goal of the study.

Social desirability is a form of reactivity, participants adjusting their behavior or their response through interactions with the researcher. Beyond wanting to appear the good citizen, participants may change their responses to conform to the study's purpose, the researcher's assumptions, or to the simple condition of being observed or questioned.

Another potential loss of credibility comes with coding inaccuracies. To ensure coding accuracy, one strategy is to have another researcher recode the data, and review the findings for consistency.

The example below, from the same study on class-based exclusion at an affluent school, offers and responds to numerous threats to credibility and trustworthiness.

> The greatest threat to credibility for this project was reactivity. Participants knew the goals of the project and could have skewed their responses, particularly in the post interviews, to indicate a positive change through the process. To address this credibility threat, I triangulated my data collection methods. In addition to interviews, I used participants' journals, team meeting observations, and a questionnaire to provide a more complete picture of the extent to which the action research process changes participants' attitudes. The pre- and post-intervention questionnaire provided useful quantitative data about changes in participants' views and attitudes, which I used to support or complicate findings from interview data.
>
> Another threat to credibility was my own bias and the small sample size. I carefully documented the entire process through consistent data collection methods and used systematic data analysis to avoid inserting my own bias. I sought member checks to ensure that I was accurately interpreting my data, and I had peers review some of my interview transcripts to check for accuracy in my own coding and categorizing. My coding aligned with that of peer reviewers.
>
> The small sample size is a typical feature of action research; to some extent, findings from action research are inevitably limited in their generalizability, as the AR process is unique to the particular participants and setting. However, my sample selection process insured that there was at least internal generalizability (that is, participants' experience was likely similar to how other participants from within the same site would engage in the same process). Detailed data collection through interviews, journals, surveys, and observation, as well as a careful documentation of every step of the process, also allowed for the action research process to be replicated at a similar school, possibly with similar results.

The researcher covers numerous concerns about credibility, including reactivity, personal bias, and a small sample size, responding to each with consistent data collection methods and multiple data sources.

## *Validity and reliability*

For quantitative studies, there are instruments with metrics to measure validity and reliability. Validity is the extent to which the instrument measures what it is supposed to measure. For instance, would a Likert scale of 1–5 for "sense of belonging" work to determine students' true sense of belonging when in a particular housing option? Reliability is the degree to which one can achieve consistent results, when repeating the study using that measurement tool. A reliable instrument that achieves the same results time after time may still not be a valid instrument, namely a good measurement for the intended question. The instrument for the above question might reliably achieve the same results, but not measure "sense of belonging" accurately. The student's Chair will have reviewed instruments to check for validity and reliability.

## 4.2 ORDERING THE PIECES

Once separate pieces supporting the proposed methodology are developed, the writer next orders and presents these pieces, weaving them together and eliminating any repetition. The writer can look at models from other dissertations. But the sections for the Methods chapter typically follow a logical order. The sections move from broad to narrow, building from problem and objective to design (approach), to methods that support the approach, to issues that arise out these choices. The logic makes sense from a reader's perspective. The headings support this movement, with some variability among approaches.

## *Different headings for quantitative vs. qualitative studies*

While both approaches use similar headings (such as population/sample, data collection, data analysis, findings/results, credibility/reliability, and discussion), quantitative studies vary in requiring specific detailing under data collection and data analysis. The data, if pre-existing, needs to be described: Where did it come from? How robust is it? If not pre-existing, the writer clarifies the methods of collecting that data.

For both possibilities, the writer needs to detail the variables measured and the instrument to be used. These issues might appear as *sub-headings*. Also, as the analysis was chosen in advance, the writer clarifies what the analysis entails and why it was chosen. If a statistical analysis is used, which one and why? Again, this information might require a *sub-heading*. In contrast, qualitative research has more latitude in sub-headings and these depend on the challenges of each study. For both approaches, writers can use these headings and sub-headings to order their writing, checking to see if they have positioned explanations in the most logical place. One common oversight is to repeat information in various places.

## Readers' expectations

For the chapter as a whole, readers likely expect upfront a short recap of study objectives and the research questions. Research questions govern the project, so they typically come at the beginning. Readers then want to know the broad research design, with key rationale – the big picture first – for how the student decided on the overall approach; readers look critically at whether or not the chosen approach makes sense, given the research questions. This section transitions to the explicit methods – with an eye to how methods fit design and relate back to the questions. Writers need to make the tie-in explicit.

The detailing of methods likely begins with descriptions of the site and participants, with justifications that align with study objectives. These pieces are upfront because readers first ask who? and where? – to put themselves in the context of the study. As thoughtful readers, they also want to know the limiting characteristics of who can be involved and where the study might take place. Readers also question how the student is gaining site access and adequate numbers of participants: What are the incentives? How does the researcher overcome participant barriers?

Once readers understand the limiting characteristics of site and population, they can better process how the writer envisions specific data collection and analysis methods, which typically come next. The possibilities for *data collection*, as noted earlier, include interviews, focus groups, documents, surveys, and observations (the protocols can go in an Appendix). Readers question how each chosen data source contributes and how it interacts with the other data sources: The writer thus needs to persuade the reader that collecting this data will answer the research questions.

For *data analysis* methods, the next piece in a logical sequence, readers have diverse expectations. For quantitative studies, readers expect one to name and explain the instrument, citing its use elsewhere for similar studies or how one has created or modified an instrument. They ask: Is this the best instrument for this study? For qualitative studies, readers may ask for a range of possibilities and strategies for analysis, a tentative (but logical) analysis plan, or one that is developed in the process of data collection. To weave these sections together, writers connect by anticipating readers' questions and concerns.

## Ordering the other pieces

Other pieces require a logical order as well, but commonsense helps here. If readers endorse data collection and analysis arguments, they still will have questions about the data itself. So transitioning to trustworthiness and credibility, or validity and reliability, seems logical – the quality of the data surpasses all other considerations. More general issues can be pushed to the end – for instance, ethical issues and role management issues. Readers assume that the study would never have gone forward without these critical concerns being addressed. So readers look for a report on the writer's early thought: Will the data be collected ethically? Does the researcher's role undermine the data (too inexperienced or too chummy with the participants)?

Overall, readers look at all of the researcher's choices and rationales and analyze them against other possibilities – to assess if the choices seem adequate, appropriate, ethical, and doable.

## 4.3 PREPARING FOR THE PRELIMINARY ORALS AND STARTING THE STUDY

### Recursive rereading and rewriting

Before submitting the proposal to their Chair, writers need to take a step back and reassess all three chapters of their proposal. They loop back, verify, redo. The chapters were often written in pieces, so what do the pieces look like as a whole? This reviewing is known as recursion, a high-level mental review that repositions all of the parts as they weave into a larger whole. At a very minimum, it means making research questions consistent across all of the chapters, aligning methods with those questions, eliminating redundant arguments and information, and fitting the pieces together. More challenging, recursion means reanalyzing how readers take in the study's overall purpose and design. This overview may identify which arguments need to be compressed and which expanded. Thus, recursion may spark adjustments in length, depth, content, and presentation so that the proposal functions as a whole, not a pastiche of parts.

When writers are satisfied that their proposal functions as a whole, they are ready to submit it to their Chair. The Chair may then see the work differently, raise questions, and ask for revisions. This *re-seeing* is part of the process (of *revision*), and serves to strengthen the work even more. No writer can *see* what the reader sees, and having expert eyes view the work differently allows writers to better communicate with readers.

### Practical steps

Once a Chair has approved a proposal, and given permission to set an orals date, a number of practical steps lie ahead. First, the proposal needs to be sent to all committee members. Second, some form of date management like doodle needs to be sent out, with dates starting two weeks from the time the proposal was sent out. The student needs to allow multiple time alternatives as well, offering half hour increment changes (e.g., Tuesday, 2–4 p.m.; 2:30–4:30 p.m.; 3:00–4:00 p.m., etc.), as faculty members have very different teaching schedules. Third, a short presentation, possibly with power point, needs to be prepared, with special attention to the methods.

A good way to open the presentation is with a brief personal history featuring the student's commitment to the study – and how it evolved. It helps to use the personal voice, heightened with a few photographs or biographical examples. Then the candidate can transition to the study's objective, the research questions, a few key studies situating the study, the study's theoretical framework, and the research methods. This presentation of the study requires synthesis, a key writing skill. The writer extracts the important elements and connects them. It might help for the candidate to practice an *elevator speech* to a community of writers, to get used to synthesizing and connecting. The student can also write out various *abstracts* of the study, to see which works best. Writing and speaking both help the student present cogently.

### The Preliminary Orals' purpose

Even though the Preliminary Orals' purpose is to insure quality, it is seldom an *exam*. It typically unfolds like a conversation, in a collaborative attempt to sharpen the research questions and to streamline the research process. Committee members also keep an eye on how the work will contribute to the field, and may offer numerous suggestions.

The doctoral candidate may not even complete the entire presentation before this conversation starts up. The student has one (and maybe a backup?) recording device to capture the free-flowing talk. Typically, faculty members interrupt the presentation and ask questions – meant to clarify or present alternatives – because their primary role is to help strengthen the study. While such questions may feel like critiques, and candidates may feel put on the spot, these are typically open-ended questions of genuine inquiry. No set answers precede them. And new suggestions that surface will likely strengthen and simplify the study, not radically change it.

This exchange is fodder for new thought and writing, an opportunity to dialogue in ways writers could not dialogue with themselves. The faculty–student interactions offer invention strategies for further writing, insight into audience concerns, and a language that may be more precise than in the proposal draft. In transcribing the recordings, the student may find that through dialogue, the study became clearer, more precise, more targeted, and more doable. Listening to the emerging language (the student's and the faculty's) may also help the writer better distill what the proposal sought to capture. With a transcription in hand, the student can take notes on each part of the exchange, as it sparks new thoughts that add, clarify, or refine what is already there. Most students find the Preliminary Orals to *prime the pump*, and leave wanting to write down what they see as new insights and direction.

A Preliminary Orals can, however, sometimes present a bumpy ride. At times, one committee member may have a very divergent view of a needed change. This may be upsetting to the student, who is not prepared for managing disputes. But while all committee members oversee quality, they also typically trust the Chair's judgment. Ultimately, it is the Chair's job to identify all needed changes, and these get detailed at the end of the Orals.

Usually the Preliminary Orals results in changes. The student is asked to write a Memorandum of Understanding (MOU) to the Chair, and possibly the committee, to insure that everyone is on the same page with respect to what changes are needed. This is another reason why a recording device (plus backup) is essential, as the student needs to respond to the suggestions of the committee. If competing or confusing suggestions have surfaced, again it is up to the Chair to decide what is essential to the revision. Usually, the candidate and the Chair remain after the Orals to discuss and document what those changes will be. The student's MOU, then, is fairly straightforward. It lists or outlines the major changes. It is an agreement between the student and the committee, with the Chair as arbiter, an agreement that clarifies what will be done next.

A word about the student's role: The Orals presents the first opportunity to present oneself as a researcher among other researchers, not as a student taking a *test*. The student is a rising expert in a field, and is typically treated as one. The Orals also presents an opportunity to learn from other experts, who are focused solely on this study for a few hours of this special day. The student can ask the committee members questions and seek their advice, especially on methods. Of particular importance to probe are the protocols. Here, new researchers often do not have the experience to predict the mishaps of overly long or vaguely worded protocols. The candidate can make use of this occasion to ask direct questions about these critical instruments or about any other concern looking ahead to the study's unfolding.

### The Internal Review Board: before getting started

Once having passed the Preliminary Orals, written the MOU, and made changes to the proposal, the student needs to submit to the Internal Review Board (IRB) so that board members can review the study for potential threats to subjects. Most review boards are very detailed in their instructions, so doctoral students need to follow these instructions to the letter. Likely, there will be several submissions before completing this process. While waiting for approval, however, students can use their time well to move forward. Most important is identifying materials, dates, sites, and possible participants/subjects for the beginning of the study. Furthermore, continuing to pilot the protocols can provide new insight, with subjects or participants not in the study, in case there are lingering issues with wording. Finally, students can continue to expand their Literature Review, as new studies surface.

With IRB approval, the study begins. It is important to keep notes on study events, decisions made, participants' involvement, unexpected events, the student's thinking at the time, the Chair's suggestions, what the student did in response, a timeline, and the general unrolling of data collection. A dissertation notebook is key. All of these notes may be important when writing up findings. They become part of the methods revision, once the study is complete, and may even become part of the findings themselves.

## Getting going on writing

**Write:**

1 A paragraph on the key data collection method (anticipating Preliminary Orals).
2 A paragraph on how two data sources might actually support or contradict each other in a particular case (anticipating Preliminary Orals).
3 A paragraph on one's personal commitment to the topic (as a lead-in for Preliminary Orals).
4 A draft of several protocol questions, which the writer pilot tests and then revises.

# 5

# COLLECTING AND ANALYZING DATA, THEN WRITING UP RESULTS AND FINDINGS

## 5.1 OVERVIEW OF QUANTITATIVE VS. QUALITATIVE APPROACHES

### Quantitative approach

Quantitative and qualitative studies differ in how results and findings get produced. With quantitative research, the researcher has already accomplished the upfront tasks of setting up the study – identifying the hypothesis, means testing the hypothesis, and developing the protocols. Once the protocols are developed and tested, data collection and analysis remain unchanged. Codes are typically decided *a priori*, set by the theoretical frame. The results then confirm or do not confirm the hypothesis. For these reasons, the presentation of quantitative results typically follows a set organization, related to the research questions. Tables and figures fill in the data. Even the layout of these visuals may be in place before the researcher collects data.

There is still some leeway in presentation, once the data is collected. The writer may decide on more or fewer figures, how to combine data to use fewer tables and figures, and how to introduce each visual related to a research question. Further, the writer has some room in deciding which trends, comparisons, or frequencies to call attention to, after presenting a table or figure. In a Results chapter, writers present data that has been analyzed by a preset procedure. What follows in the next section, then, are mostly issues related to qualitative data collection and analysis, where findings emerge and where writers discover how to write about them.

### Qualitative study challenges

With qualitative research, ambiguities in collecting and analyzing data create challenges for new researchers. There is no set course. And the process can be unpredictable. When upsets occur, for instance a site refuses access, researchers need to have back-up plans, including other possible sites. They also need a willingness to adjust protocols as they go along, to ensure that the data is concrete, detailed, and directed at the research questions. Further, multiple types of data might be needed, to ensure enough data to answer the research questions. No collection is perfect, nor does any adjustment totally fix a problem. But new researchers need to make changes where needed and write about what actually happened – as these events help readers understand how findings were derived.

Findings don't just get written. Typically, they reflect multiple activities: recording, transcribing, note taking, assessing, analyzing data through coding or other means, extracting essential data, identifying themes, combining themes into larger findings, deciding on presentation strategies, and then producing multiple drafts. The big activity is inductively conceptualizing the key findings or claims, which emerge from the data, not from any preconceptions.

A note of caution: A finding is not an interpretation, which the writer reserves for the Discussion chapter; and it is far from an opinion, what readers expect to find in the Opinion section of a newspaper. Rather, a finding is an empirically derived statement that consolidates factual events or conversations. It starts with an objective compilation of data into categories: The researcher first codes all the data (using emerging or pre-set codes, such as use of a certain word or response); the codes are then used to create groups of coded data; these become themes.

Granted, low-level inference underlies this sorting and choice of themes, but the focus is on patterns not meaning. Based on these themes (or other categories), the researcher derives the findings. A finding, then, is a summary statement or claim responding to a research question and supported by themes derived from coding. While the writer might choose a table to show a spread of response, typically a series of representative quotes alone do the job. Some of these processes involved in data collection and analysis are discussed below. Others are guided by advice from the Chair.

## 5.2  ASSESSING PROCESSES

Writers of qualitative research assess their processes as they collect and analyze data. It is an ongoing process. They may adjust data collection to obtain a better result: Students assess where the richest strands of data are surfacing. They ask, what in the protocol is generating the richest information? What spontaneous follow-up questions or probes unleashed interviewee response? What data looks to be particularly important? What unanticipated data is surfacing and does it require follow up? Weak data can also require strategic change: How can an interviewer, for example, prevent an overload of generalities, misunderstandings, or guarded, unresponsive answers? Such assessment is important to ensure quality data but also because researchers record their processes, including any shifts they make. Records of researchers' in-process modifications sharpen a study's methods and deepen the trustworthiness of the findings.

As noted earlier, for quantitative studies, the major work begins in advance of data collection. Researchers develop the instrument to reflect their theoretical frame; this instrument is set to produce quantifiable data (nominal or ordinal). The questionnaire is thus typically precoded, reflecting expected answers, although open-ended questions may require post coding. As to processes, quantitative researchers field test the instruments, to see if they are producing the desired information – this step ensures that the instruments measure what they are designed to measure. In addition, before data collection, researchers develop plans to ensure a high response rate, and create backup plans. These plans may require in-process assessment. Overall, with so much upfront design, quantitative research requires fewer open processes in writing up results than for qualitative studies.

## Looking ahead: example of a data analysis

Explaining the process of data collection and analysis will be important for final versions of the Methodology chapter as well as for the Findings chapter. But, as noted earlier, students cannot fully describe this process until after they actually do it. Below is an example of what one doctoral student wrote about her processes, once she had analyzed the data:

> The process by which I analyzed data includes the extent to which I combed and re-combed data for supporting evidence, as well as counter evidence. For the supporting evidence, I continuously checked the data to align the data with the theme. Each participant was represented under each theme. If the participant did not mention the theme, their cell was left blank. Further, I distinguished counter evidence within each cell. I then developed further codes to categorize the kinds of evidence for and against each theme and assigned these a working title. When I wrote the analysis of data for each emergent theme, I checked to see that I did not over represent any one participant.

When asked in her Final Orals to detail further, the candidate reported that she used Quirkos to place references into bubbles; these bubbles then visually identified what groupings she might make. Rather than using a highlighter, she explained that she chose Quirkos to help her code and then identify emergent themes. (Other data analysis technologies include NVivo, Provalis, Research Text Analytics, MAXQDA, with different tools useful for different tasks such as transcription analysis, discourse analysis, and content analysis.) The student's explicit detailing was compelling.

This depiction, after the fact, of the candidate's process reassures readers that the data was analyzed with care. It describes how the codes were derived, how the themes were developed, and how the findings were checked. However, the researcher still struggled with processes before this final retrospection. Some of the issues with data collection for qualitative studies are detailed below.

### How well are the protocols producing useful data?

Before the qualitative researcher gets to analysis, things can go awry. As the researcher collects data, it helps to assess the efficacy of the initial data collection. Is the data adequate? Is it too general or too reflective of idiosyncratic individuals? Is the researcher hearing only well-known truisms? Do the interview or focus group questions require rewording (with the Chair's general approval) to produce more telling data? The student might increase the quality of the data with some minor changes to wording, to the order of questions, or to the explanation to participants as to the study's intent. Further, the researcher's role in administering the protocol can affect response. Do participants seem withholding, reacting to the researcher? What are they experiencing during the interview or study events? The researcher might ask respondents to write anonymous feedback to help overcome such barriers.

The wording of questions often needs adjusting, even in the midst of data collection. Students often ask if they can still make such changes, once the study has started, because this change might trigger an Internal Review Board (IRB) review. The answer is that the wording can be changed without IRB approval, as long as the intent has not changed. If the protocol's wording is ineffective in eliciting the intended data, then the questions need revision. This situation sparks a note of caution: Before the study begins, students need to write and rewrite their questions, trying them out until they have removed all ambiguity and they are consistently getting responses that answer the research questions. They also need to reexamine the responses as the study unfolds.

If the questions seem accurately worded but the data still appears inadequate, the researcher can also add additional subjects or revisit interviewees to ask clarifying questions. For such additions, the student keeps notes on changes. But there is no need to record oversights – unless they affect findings. However, a researcher cannot introduce a new method without IRB approval; even for such a case, the IRB can quickly approve an amendment – if the intent, site, and participants stay the same and the safeguards remain in place.

### What if some participants have stopped "participating" or if the response rate is low?

These are confounding issues. If the researcher has thought through the "recruitment" section in the Methodology chapter, this possibility has surfaced. That chapter identified motivations, incentives, accommodations, and follow-up plans to recruit and retain participants or respondents. However, the proposal probably did not detail contingency plans. Having back-up participants or respondents, names of others who might be used for the study, or starting with more participants than needed – these are all contingency plans. Chairs can help with establishing the bottom line for the study to be viable. The student can then work backwards – to create a large margin for study erosion and to create strong motivators for participants and respondents. How this is accomplished depends on the study. The student's Chair can offer further suggestions.

## When does the student begin analyzing data?

Doctoral students often ask when can they start to analyze data. For quantitative data, the researcher waits until all of the survey or other quantitative data has been collected. For qualitative data, it is possible to analyze as one proceeds. For an action research study, the researcher needs to continuously analyze data in order to follow the Plan, Act, Analyze, Reflect cycle – the cycle requires analysis as one goes, especially because participants are themselves creating agendas and questions and helping to analyze data. For mixed methods studies, interviews from qualitative studies can produce data that helps the researcher decide on survey questions. Or answers to survey questions can help the researcher narrow interview questions or identify interview participants.

With most qualitative studies, ideas pop up during data collection. The researcher notices patterns, formulates possible codes, themes, and findings, and may write them down – early on. These patterns are not fixed in stone – just early thoughts. While textbooks often describe the research process in linear terms, in reality the student is continuously generating ideas about potential groupings, meanings, or significance. Initial insights can be invaluable later on. While the writer delays formal writings on meaning, it is still possible to record such insights. Informal notes can be retrieved later. For this stage, however, during the recording of final interviews, focus groups, or observations, the student begins to analyze systematically and factually, according to the plan in the Methodology chapter.

## Keeping track of the data

Researchers have various ways of keeping track of their data, and starting initial coding. What follows are some of the strategies students have noted: Students have color-coded pages of transcripts by particular wording or response; they have used an analytic software tool to visually identify patterns in texts; also, a simple word search of the documents has proved helpful, once key words surfaced in transcripts; for longer phrases, students have also created a spread sheet, filling in categories; finally, old fashioned Post-its have worked, with careful labeling.

Using a separate file for big picture data may be a good idea. First, even in the midst of methodically collecting data, researchers look for surprising or uniquely informative data, which they note for later selection and detailing. When they encounter such data, they place it in a file and quickly label it, predicting what it might indicate. Conversely, weaker or generalized data might be combined under a broad category, eliminated, or put into a simple table. Such initial sorting lays the groundwork for telling the bigger story, and later for discussing implications.

## *Analyzing qualitative data: the process begins with formal coding*

As a researcher collects qualitative data, they code data, and formally record the process. For emerging, ground up coding, without pre-existing codes, this means finding similar occurrences, wordings, viewpoints, or behaviors across participants or incidents. The researcher then labels collections of data that fall together into patterns (buckets or categories), distinct from other patterns. These might be large tentative categories. Although the patterns will be relevant to the research questions, the researcher does not necessarily start coding explicitly by research question. Rather, they analyze for commonalities, then label or code these regularities, then recode for more refined or specific codes (in line-by-line coding one might code everything), and then systematically develop the codes into emergent themes. The latter typically reflect the research questions.

This inductive process is often based in thematic analysis. For example, identified patterns of *safe* or *neutral* locations on a high school campus are codes. Sub codes might include *specific geographical locations* with respect to administrative offices; also, they could include *types of student populations* that congregate there. The researcher can then develop such codes into themes – for instance, the scarcity and location of campus safe places, for particular groups. Each emergent theme represents a low-level form of inference, transparent to readers who may question how these themes were derived.

While categorizing low-level data may uncover new themes, some studies require coding data that immediately connects to the research questions. *A priori* codes might be needed. For instance, if a researcher wanted rich descriptions of how teachers responded in an emergency such as an earthquake, they might code for *known teacher behaviors*, already described in the literature. These include asking students to duck under the desk or to move away from windows. However, data might reveal teachers rushing students out of the classroom or simply getting under a desk themselves. This unanticipated data might lead the researcher to contrast codes on known appropriate behaviors (from *a priori* codes) with new codes of actual emergency behaviors. The *a priori* codes were needed to highlight the unanticipated data on injuries resulting from desks moving away from students and from non-structural elements (students getting hit with falling computers or toppling file cabinets). Themes might then emerge about this contrast, including teacher awareness of classroom hazards. This *a priori* combined with inductive coding could lead to a finding that teachers had only partial awareness of types of classroom hazards in their everyday environment. Down the road, the writer could recommend additional training in emergency response.

The process of coding presents some ambiguity. Some data might be coded for more than one category or be read as both supportive and contradictory. For instance, a code for teacher directives to get under the desk but not hold onto it supports teacher awareness but also disputes it (the desk can move). The researcher might also have too many codes or too few. Or the researcher might have a code that has too little data for significance, for instance a single teacher out of 20 who runs out of the classroom during the earthquake. Despite such quandaries, conscientious coding assures readers of the empirical basis for the doctoral student's findings.

In sum, the qualitative researcher, if using an inductive approach, does not rely on pre-existing codes, but lets the patterns that surface in the data determine the codes. While the researcher may have a pre-existing conceptual frame, such as distributed leadership or Critical Race Theory, the data is not adjusted to only fit that frame. Rather, patterns of data may shift while data is collected, and some patterns may lose importance, thus changing the emerging themes. Key here is that the themes reflect an *inductive* process of openly recording patterns through coding, identifying new codes, determining the most prevalent codes, and finally combining or collapsing codes to identify themes that then answer the research questions. A theoretical framework can be applied as one assigns data to codes, and later as one collapses codes into themes.

## 5.3 WRITING THE FINDINGS CHAPTER

### From codes to initial writing

A way to get started drafting is to write about the codes as they take form. The writer can begin by identifying a tentative code and then find data that supports it; rereading that data may help the categories gel.

Here is one alumni's recollection of her early writing processes:

> I started by taking one "code" and finding the quotes, then writing … then editing, then going on to another code. I also outlined my path through findings to map what I was hoping to demonstrate. The more I read and listened to the words, the more they started to fall into categories. I tried to write succinct statements for findings and prove my finding – what is the story I want to tell?

This writer recollects that she merged the processes of writing and coding. For each code, writing involved multiple processes of finding quotes, writing, and editing. She did this for each code, then went on to the next code. And for each, she challenged herself to write a "succinct statement" that functioned as a kind of heading. Along the way, she used writing to outline (and recollect) her "path."

Early notes and writings provide the materials for initial drafts. While still forming a code, the writer can be selecting primary evidence (e.g., representative quotes, observations, documents), then going back to reformulate the code, based on that evidence. In seeking the best evidence, the writer looks for the richest, most concrete, compelling data, prioritized by relevance. Selection is important – the writer does not want to swamp the reader with evidence. A researcher does not use every compelling quote, observation or document, just because collecting each was hard. In particular, the writer chooses quotes that *represent* a group's response; and each quote should be edited down to the essential words (using ellipses for deleted words). Readers want *sufficient* evidence, not all the evidence.

When the doctoral student sits down to write the Findings chapter, this early writing, note taking, and selection can support evidence-based findings tied to the research questions.

*A caveat here:* In deriving and writing about Findings, doctoral students need to have in mind later revisions to their Methods chapter, as their coding represents what they actually did, not what they proposed to do. In their revision, writers tell the story of their analytic processes so that readers can follow and assess these processes. Specifically, a writer might unfurl how the literature provoked an alertness and pre-disposition to analyze certain clusters of data under a pre-existing code (using a deductive method for coding). They could then recount how they remained open, by not asking narrow questions, which would have limited data to these pre-set codes; they could note how they looked for counter or qualifying evidence. The story might then shift to how a writer's personal experiences spurred them to probe more deeply into the surprising or qualifying data. Finally, the story could conclude with how newly surfaced codes became themes – namely, how certain codes related to one another to form a bigger picture. Dissertation writers often think that the messy process of analyzing data should remain under cover, obscured, cleaned up, when in reality readers most of all want to know how findings were derived.

### The role of the Chair

Dissertation writers will receive different levels of guidance during data collection and drafting the Findings chapter. Faced with perhaps mountains of data ("so many words" one student moaned), even beautifully coded data, the student still has to start writing a draft. What are the key findings? What is the overall order and presentation? How does the writer interweave the different data sources? If the writer can identify a strategy, and outline the chapter, with notes on how data supports major points, they can ask to meet with the Chair. Before they get too far, students want to have a critical discussion of the data and how best to present it. This conversation could then lead to a better plan for writing this chapter.

### Upfront strategies

The Findings chapter is the heart and soul of the dissertation. How the writer organizes the presentation matters. Does the writer trace an evolution? Divide by theme? Answer in order of individual research questions or combine them? Or categorize by importance to intended clients or users?

These questions relate to an overriding question: What does it mean to "tell the story"? Such decisions turn on purpose and significance. The writer looks for the key themes – and the data that most vividly conveys them. Researchers generally look for the big surprises, or what they and others can most learn from the study, given this purpose. The writer does not have to report all the findings nor all of the data.

Even with a storyline and major themes, writers grapple with what comes first and how much to say. They often question, should they include upfront more about context and data gathering processes? Should they recount procedures, going back to Methods? Further, do they return to site and participants, as these details become prominent in the study's unfolding? Sometimes, even basic questions are stumbling blocks: How avoid overgeneralizing? What inferences step over the line into interpretation?

Many dissertation writers have little experience presenting data. How does the writer fairly represent a spectrum of variations? The question of what to include leads to the question, how does the writer integrate contradictory voices, and is this required for every finding? Presentation means distilling for readers the essence of the study. In selecting material, writers envision a reader and ask, what does that reader need to know?

A few upfront strategies may help. One strategy is to reread the Problem Statement and Methodology chapters, to renew the researcher's sense of purpose. Doctoral students in the midst of sorting and analyzing data tend to lose sight of why they did the study in the first place and what it is they promised to do. Rereading helps writers rethink their central purpose and contribution. As they reread, they can take notes on what jumps out as important in what they promised readers. Rereading is a form of writing.

A second strategy is to make two short lists: one, what the research community knew before the study; two, what the research community will know after they read the completed study. These can be focal points for both the Findings and Discussion chapters. For instance, the student studying the challenges of sustaining a middle school Dual Language (DL) program opened her study with "a day in the life of" a Dual Language school, described from vivid observations; she then divided up subsequent findings into "already known challenges" (difficulty scheduling, low funding, unequal access) and "surprising findings" (hours of extra preparation time for DL teachers; burdens of extra students for English Only teachers). The division prompted key writings for this chapter.

A third strategy is to use writing to anticipate possible reader response. The writer starts with a one-page synthesis of key findings, from the point of view of what the study adds, then follows up with alternative roadmaps (in paragraph form) of how the chapter might unfold. Each placeholder roadmap introduces the reader to what follows in a different way. The writer then rereads and compares the different approaches to assess which appears to work better for the particular study. Writers can try out these roadmaps on peers (one's *community of writers*) to get reader response. This writing is not wasted but helps researchers assume the reader's perspective—which they often overlook in writing up findings.

## Openings

To stress again, there is no single way to open the Findings chapter, either quantitative or qualitative. Quantitative studies, however, are more direct in answering the research questions and may take them up one by one. The study's questions and methods can be quickly summarized. Qualitative and mixed methods studies have more variation. Most studies, however, remind the reader upfront of the study's purpose and data sources, preview the order of presentation, and summarize key findings.

Here is one example. The following Action Research study examined the lack of school support for street-life oriented boys, and designed an intervention. The research questions dealt with the content and process of the research team, and the opening not only consolidates this purpose but it also synthesizes the study's findings.

> This chapter begins with a brief review of the action research process. I then present findings aligned with the two major aspects of this study—content and process. "Acknowledging the façade" explains the core content produced by the team's three months of action research. This content includes the iden-tification of a worrying limitation in the school's promise to support street-life oriented boys as well as a revealing misper-ception among participants about the challenges faced by street-life oriented boys. "Leading together" describes the process by which this group of teachers became a community of practice that explored the difficult topic of street-life orientation at their school site. With minimal guidance or direction, the participants developed their own democratic process of inquiry and grew into a community whose collaboration was reported to be more worthwhile and effective than the other forms of collaboration at their school site.

This opening offers readers a tightly knit synopsis of the study's purpose and its findings as well as a roadmap to help them anticipate the following sections.

For qualitative studies, because researchers synthesize and order data for the reader, writers do well to present, first, any big, surprising, signifi-cant findings, irrespective of the order of the research questions. For one, the research questions themselves may overlap or intertwine. For another, different research questions may produce different quality and quantity of data. By opening with the key findings, writers provide readers with the big picture first. That picture reflects the study's purpose. Readers ask of any study as a whole, is the purpose of the study being met? What is the story here? What is the major take-away? What is new here? How writers answer these questions slants readers' take on the entire Findings chapter. Writers need to assess evidence, codes, and themes with a clear picture of how findings support study purpose.

## Describing the context

As with any story, unraveling the researcher's findings begins with context. The context sets the stage. In telling the story, the writer may want to start with description: the setting, the participants, the program, and the behaviors or intervention. A barebones description of sites and participants may already be in the Methodology chapter, to establish selection criteria for the study. But concrete sensory details beyond these criteria may place the reader fully in the study environment. Here is an example of a richly descriptive opening to a case study of a professional learning community– at a school that is at risk for Program Improvement status:

> When a visitor steps onto an elementary school campus, his initial impressions are likely to register the routine and familiar aspects of public schools: the sight of students hurrying into classrooms, the sound of bells signaling the end of recess and even the nostalgic aroma of school cafeteria fare. With repeated visits, careful observations and purposeful interactions with the staff, a school's unique culture emerges from the mundane. This case study begins with a description of Ocean View Elementary School's culture, as gleaned from teacher interviews, survey data, observations, and a review of school documents.

The writer opens this Findings chapter with rich description of elementary school environments. These sounds, smells, and images prepare the reader for the important details of the particular site analyzed. This opening also identifies the multiple data sources the researcher uses to paint the picture.

## Using interview data to describe the context

Description is a key tool for telling the story. Writing up the first theme on the elementary school's culture, the researcher for the above study lets teacher interview data describe the site:

> When asked, "What makes Ocean View unique?" teachers responded without hesitation, "We're so small." Teachers also described the local community served by Ocean View as a small, "laid back" neighborhood. Ocean View teachers referred not only to the small student body, but the fact that there were just thirteen regular classroom teachers on staff. Margaret's remarks were typical. "I think the thing that stands out, and what I really like, is the school size … it's like a village … I mean you see each other, and even at staff meetings you don't feel like you can get lost."

The teachers' own words thus create the picture, and the researcher keeps an objective stance. She later notes the prevalence of such comments and their tenor: *"Most Ocean View teachers viewed the school's small size as an asset in developing professional relationships. Francis related, 'Because we're a small school, it helps a lot especially in cross-grade collaboration… .'"* Here the researcher does not offer interpretation, just a record. Her inference stays close to the teachers' descriptive data *("most … teachers viewed … small size as an asset").* She avoids significance or judgment. She is also careful to integrate more than one data source: As these portraits derive solely from teacher interviews, the writer interweaves her own observational data as well. A later comment reads: *"Ocean View teachers also noted the informal atmosphere at the school … The school building itself reflected this ambiance of informality. The architecture was visually attractive, and described by some as 'whimsical.'"* Here, the researcher triangulates data, checking what teachers describe against what she observes. As noted earlier, when one triangulates data, one uses additional data sources to create a full picture of the setting or phenomenon; and one also has the opportunity to confirm or to call into question that data.

### Ensuring that descriptive data does not bury evidence

This researcher did call into question some of her developing story line. She conscientiously included contrary descriptions, refusing to cherry-pick only responses that support her theme. Her caveat reads as follows:

> In relationship to professional learning community, however, informality and small size did not always add up to collaborative practice. Some teachers in both upper and lower grades described a lack of collaboration among grade level teams. Sharon, for example, shared: "… You'd think that when you have only two classes per grade that you'd be working intimately together and doing the same thing, but … that's not the case. We kind of do our own thing."

Here, the writer judiciously selected a quotation that describes the paradox of small size not leading to collaboration. While she noted the range of teachers who felt similarly, she did not need to quote each one.

### The temptation of too much evidence

With description, the temptation may be to multiply quotations, exactly what each respondent said. Writers may believe that one's argument gets stronger with each supporting quotation – but that is not the case. Redundancy actually weakens the argument. And long quotations are tiresome – they take the reader's attention away from the researcher's purpose. For the study above, the writer chose only one of the quotations she might have used, and made it speak for many participants. This allowed her to edit the quote, integrate it into her story, and name the groups it represented – choices that sharpened her point.

## Eliminating weak evidence

At times, the researcher collects weak or ancillary evidence that does not answer the research questions. This data can be eliminated. For instance, one researcher asked his participants to define a key concept to be investigated, in this case *sense of belonging*, and received circular, vague, or contradictory definitions. While this wide range of definitions might seem interesting, the researcher had no practical use for this data. The writer can reconsider whether participants' range of definitions can make a difference to practice.

The writer needs criteria as to what to keep. In sum, students keep findings that are consistently supported from the data, that solidly answer a research question, that are compelling to a client or to readers, that are consistent with or challenge findings from other studies, and that pass the "so what?" test. These findings help solve a problem or inform a policy or add new understanding. As said before, not all findings are equally compelling. The writer goes for depth rather than breadth. Some research questions generate more significant findings, even surprising findings, so the writer then devotes more time and pages to answering one question over another.

## Summarizing the key themes

In telling a story, writers typically summarize their key themes upfront, the themes that underlie the findings. Such a summary might tell readers how the stated themes were derived, what the data sources were, how the themes relate to each other, and how they support the findings that answer the research questions. This foregrounding assures readers of the credibility of the study and makes the ensuing story easy to follow.

The example below offers a summary of one researcher's themes, helping readers anticipate the unfolding of the chapter. This was an Action Research study, described before, focused on students determining the causes of class-based exclusion at their elite private high school. The writer summarizes her two key themes early on:

> "Making the invisible visible" describes the team's discoveries, recommendations, and changes in thinking around the subtle, cultural forms of exclusion based on SES. Over the course of the research, participants developed an "SES" lens they previously did not have, which allowed them to see SES in the culture where they had not seen it before. "The experience gap" explains how the team worked to understand and address the more tangible, visible ways that Hamilton students have access to different activities and experiences based on SES. Participants increasingly understood ways the school could shrink the experience gap between wealthy and non-wealthy students, whereas prior to the research they saw such a gap as inevitable.

Here the writer chooses two strong metaphors to convey her themes and make her major findings clear: "making the invisible visible" and "the experience gap." Upfront, readers have two overriding themes to guide them through the data. These derive from action research student data. Students at this school investigated class-based exclusion, recommended solutions, and implemented changes to school culture. The story of their actions follows this timeline, not the order of research questions. As the writer forewarned readers that she was intertwining her research questions, readers can then focus on this story.

## 5.4 ORGANIZATION STRATEGIES

As noted earlier, the researcher's obligation is to present *significant* findings. One's selection and organization of findings reflect one's implicit judgments of significance. Selection means that the writer has latitude in how much and in what order to present. What follows are some examples of organization strategies. These suggest the wide variety of choices doctoral students make in adjusting their presentations to their study type and findings.

### *Latitude in organization*

For quantitative studies, the organization of data typically follows the research questions. But visuals can be organized to enhance an underlying story: One study asked, how are classroom simulations replacing required pre-service field hours, given the crisis-level need for new teachers? The researcher anticipated providing charts over time to show the slow diffusion of this innovation through major schools of education in the U.S. An effective addition to this story might be visuals that contrast education's slow response to innovation with nursing schools' immediate and full-blown adoption, over the same period of time.

An example of latitude in organization for qualitative studies is revealed in a study of the life histories of 12 Latina professors. Using Sarah Lawrence-Lightfoot's method of portraiture, the doctoral student first presented several key themes, drawing data from all 12 women. But she then selected three richly detailed portraits and presented them as individual stories. The decision not to portray each participant equally was made because presenting all 12 created problems of length and overlap. Instead, she decided to first present common themes. Then, she chose three representative stories, each selected for representing a different place on a continuum.

Other kinds of organization choice include combining numerous themes (say, ten themes) into a small number of umbrella themes, then subdividing them. A research question on causes of low attendance rates for African-American high school boys, as perceived by the boys, may spawn a host of themes. Readers need the writer to help them absorb the data. Listing ten themes, all of equal weight, will dull the impact of all of them. Instead, the writer prioritized the themes, connecting them back to the research question. He stayed flexible, which is important: A writer can invent two or three different ways to prioritize themes and weigh the advantages of each.

## *A caution*

One caution about latitude, however, arises when writers think to use data from each data collection method to present separately. For instance, the writer might think to first present data from interviews, then from a survey, then from observations, then from documents. However, unless the writer requires the data from one collection method to shape the next, or has another purposeful reason for separating the data by method, this may be the least effective way to present data. It can lead to overlapping points and a weakening of the study's findings. Typically, the purpose of different data collection methods is to synthesize different perspectives and provide a check on one's findings. The findings then emerge from all of the data sets together, referenced as the writer proceeds – as good checks on inferences.

## 5.5 REVISING DRAFTS OF FINDINGS

Despite good planning and advice from the Chair, first drafts are usually rough drafts. Once in a while, they are significantly off base. Three descriptions of such off-base drafts follow. One example is of a student whose "themes" for her Action Research study comprised the known stages of Action Research (plan, do, check, act). While the writer had many quotes from each of these stages, she had not coded the data to come up with emergent themes. She needed to reanalyze her data. In a second case, a student had coded for themes, but had few supporting quotes, and those were taken mostly from one data source. He had paid little attention to his processes and he did not triangulate his data, so his Chair was skeptical of the themes. (Researcher bias was a possibility.) In a third situation, a doctoral student wrote at such a high level of generalization that readers sensed she was *asking* for belief in her findings not *proving* her claims.

Although these doctoral students felt they had endured a "setback" when required to rework, each had made progress toward the next draft. In the next stage, they reviewed their data, analyzed and reanalyzed it, identified themes, trends, or results, and then came up with new findings and a new organization. The chapter was much improved. Such revisions are common. Writers need to distinguish for readers what is already known from what is newly discovered. Readers want to know up front about significant or surprising findings, what the big take-away is, before they invest time in the rest. Once doctoral students have rethought key findings, and have a new order of presentation, they can ask the Chair for another review of the work. The ensuing guidance can lead them to analyze more effectively and to select more telling quotes, observations, documents, or other data to tell the story.

In qualitative research, the story is especially important for readers. One of the best ways to see if the story takes hold is to read it aloud. How consistent is it? How detailed and compelling is the evidence? Another way to measure is to ask colleagues to read the chapter. Does the narrative answer the research questions and provide new perspectives? Is the researcher's initial purpose clear? Do the chosen events, descriptions, and narratives convey the main points? What do readers say they learned from the findings? What do they say they still want to know? The writer might consider ending this chapter with a telling summary of what was learned.

## 5.6  USING REVISION TO DEEPEN THE ANALYSIS OF ONE'S EVIDENCE

### Analyzing the data more fully

It is not just the story that may need revision. One may have the story, but lack a powerful analysis. The evidence may indeed be rich, but the surrounding discussion may seem weak.

Revising a draft often includes thinking more deeply about the evidence. The researcher needs to ask how the evidence reveals what they say it does. Writers often skip over this analysis – making a general claim and then merely citing a quote or other evidence and leaving it for the reader to infer. They may feel hesitant to analyze, thinking they will overstep into interpretation. As a result, they often let rich data go unexplored.

In the draft below, the writer claims that school principals with special education training helped teachers create equal access for special education students. But she offers too little analysis of the rich quote she offers, either in her lead-in or her follow up.

> As discussed previously, Action Research school leaders, with Special Ed. training, acknowledged that in creating and implementing inclusive practices, they had a "leg up." Given credibility from years of experience as a special education teacher, program specialist, and student advocate, they quickly made progress with their staff. In a post-workshop interview, Brenda shared:
>
> > Oh, I definitely had an advantage. Being able to lead staff while, just having that knowledge base to where they'll come to me and ask me questions because they know my background, is huge. But also them trusting me enough to know that what I'm saying is accurate and not just made up. I was able to support them and even shift their perspective on things. To hear them even change and how they talk about a certain situation or a child … I know that's my influence.

An interesting quote, but the writer offers little analysis. The prefacing only states that experienced principals had "a leg up" and "made progress" with their teachers, a weak framing of a rich quote. Also, the *"Brenda shares"* lead-in offers no guidance on what Brenda is about to share. With no follow-up analysis, readers do not learn what the evidence shows.

Questioning her evidence, the writer later asked: what kind of "leg up" does the quote actually reveal? For one, she noted these trained principals promoted a change in both teacher behaviors and attitudes, so the writer led with this. After the quote, the writer noted changes in specific staff behaviors (e.g., they *"come to me …"*) as well as language (*"how they talk about … a child"*), leading to a change in attitudes (*"trusting me"*). This quote is packed with rich data, which the writer later brought to light.

An additional example from this same early draft further demonstrates the need for targeted analysis. In the following example, the writer identifies "messaging" as one of six key practices principals use to inspire special education inclusion. The excerpt below offers a powerful quote that lacks sufficient commentary.

> Although the district was influential, team members also stated that messaging had to start with them. It was essential that staff understood that inclusion originated with the principal, not some district mandate. Anna elaborated:
>
> > I've never told my staff that it's the district wanting me to do this. Or parents pushing for this. Otherwise, it would get brushed off. I believe in this, so you should too.

The framing is wordy and broad. It misses the participant's fervent voice of personal responsibility (*"I've never told my staff that it's the district wanting me to do this…"; "I believe in this so you should too"*). Later, the writer framed the quote as school principals' *personal commitment* to producing the message. Here is a sharper revision:

> Principals insisted that they needed to embody the message – it had to start with them, not some district mandate. Anna in particular stressed the need for personal commitment:
>
> > I've never told my staff that it's the district wanting me to do this. Or parents pushing for this. Otherwise, it would get brushed off. I believe in this, so you should too.
>
> Anna persuades staff and parents through her personal belief, not through abstract mandates. She would not have her beliefs "brushed off" as impersonal messages.

In the revision, early framing and later commentary deepen the analysis. The writer has sharpened the contrast between incentives for inclusion – personal and lived vs. abstract and external. And the sharper verbs ("insisted," "stressed") tell us how deeply these principals felt about their messages.

## Tying data explicitly to the research questions

The need for deeper analysis can have another motive – to tie data explicitly to the research questions. Typically, writers believe this connection is obvious. However, readers need to know exactly how data relates to a specific question; and readers want writers to explain any inconsistencies if they surface. In making these connections, and explaining inconsistent data, writers often generate new insight.

Below is a draft from the case study on how successful Dual Language (DL) middle schools sustain their programs and maintain equity for their DL students. The researcher investigated programmatic and curricular challenges. In this draft, the writer decided first to give readers a basic idea of what a Dual Language day looked like, so that readers understood the challenges to equity. While accurate and detailed, the description needed to tie explicitly to a research question.

> Sunnyville Middle enrolls 625 students. Within the school, there is a Dual Language Spanish program and a DL Mandarin program. The day begins for Dual Language teachers an hour before their colleagues. They prepare for their students who arrive for a "zero period" that begins at 7:30 a.m., which is an extra early period before the start of the normal six-period day. Teachers arrive up to ninety minutes before the start of "zero" period to prepare. The three Mandarin DL instructors (sixth, seventh and eighth) plan their day as a group, discuss students and curricula, as do the three Spanish DL instructors.
>
> There are three kinds of classes a Sunnyville DL student might be in for zero period: Physical Education, their language arts course in the target language, or their DL content course. For the content course, Spanish DL students take Social Studies (6th grade) or History (7th and 8th) in Spanish while Mandarin students have a Chinese culture course in Mandarin. Zero period runs from 7:30 a.m. to 8:22 a.m. Zero period PE is the only time that DL Mandarin and DL Spanish students will take a period together without any English Only students.
>
> The English Only students, meanwhile, arrive at school by 8 a.m. for their Breakfast in the Classroom (BIC) and Sustained Silent Reading (SSR), a 22 minute period where they receive free breakfast from the school and read. Public announcements are also made during this time. Period 1 begins for both EO and DL students at 8:22 a.m.

This is granular, detailed data; it helps readers see how the day unfolds. However, it lacks an overarching claim connected to Dual Language equity. When questioned, the writer noted how she wanted to show the complexity of maintaining equity for DL students, in both scheduling and curriculum.

So, she then revised this section to open with this claim. As a result, her descriptive data unveiled the equity challenges of locked-in courses and timeframes, prompted by complexities of scheduling. The next draft more sharply defined the inequities.

Interestingly, this analysis raised additional questions. The data only inconsistently supports DL inequities. The English Only (EO) students arrive later than the DL students, likely missing a content-based, zero-period class. And readers know from earlier data that DL students show higher achievement scores than EO students. This reverse inequity for students seems a surprising finding. Another surprising inequity arose from this data, this time for teachers. DL teachers are working longer hours than non-DL teachers, arriving at work 90 minutes before the start of zero period, thus at 6:00 a.m., to plan the day. This over commitment likely benefits DL students but exploits their teachers. Unfortunately, this later point had been swept under the carpet, as the researcher was not investigating teacher inequities. However, she used this data later, to discuss school sustainability overall. Analyzing inconsistent data led the researcher to new insight.

## Distinguishing analysis from interpretation

A few words about analysis here, and why writers may be confused by it. Doctoral students are told to avoid interpreting their findings – to hold off their views until their Discussion chapter. This dictum is easy to follow in a quantitative study, where the analysis is preset, and the findings are numerical. Qualitative researchers, however, are more concerned about interjecting bias into a "finding." So, they may present data by itself, leaving the reader to analyze it.

While important to guard against *reading into* qualitative data, a researcher's analysis of data lies at the heart of the study. And analysis differs from interpretation. When researchers analyze, they break down and reassemble data into parts. The researcher then highlights certain groupings for the reader. For instance, in one of the examples above, the writer identified data distinguishing district mandates from personal appeals. The writer then analyzed this contrast to infer that change came from examples of personal, lived beliefs rather than impersonal dicta. The data support this inference, so this contrast illustrates analysis, not reading in.

But to caution again, analysis is more than finding useful categories to explain cherry-picked pieces of evidence. The categories need to explain all salient elements of a quote or other evidence, because ignoring data is another form of bias. For instance, ignoring the tone of a principal's comment such as *"Are you going to partner with me to make sure that this kid doesn't go down that path"* would be to ignore the pressure this principal places on her teaching staff. This demanding tone is consistent with *"I believe in this so you should too"* (cited above). The researcher may need to add a comment on *how* the principal swayed teachers, even if this qualification goes against her desired storyline.

New researchers are right to be concerned about interpretation creeping in, however. There is a fine line between analysis and interpretation. One's categories might be devised to support a pre-held "meaning." Or the categories themselves might be subjective or value laden. So, researchers need to check themselves. Most helpful might be creating a three-tiered chart that labels evidence, analysis, and interpretation as three separate categories, all of them under a particular research question. And one could ask others to reanalyze the evidence to check for consistency.

## 5.7 WRITING HEADINGS TO ORGANIZE FINDINGS FOR READERS

Headings reflect for readers the larger movement of the Findings chapter, structuring the presentation. Headings may be written as writing guides as the writer develops the chapter, but in final form they serve as critical signposts for the reader. The sample headings below are drawn from the completed action research project supporting street-life oriented boys, discussed earlier. These headings communicate to readers the chapter's overall structure. To clarify the logic, the headings have been streamlined and adjusted. In outline form, they offer the two research questions, the two major themes related to those questions (on content and process of the collaboration), five key findings under those themes, and subheadings stated in participants' own voices.

*RQ 1*: *What are the key principles and components of an intervention program for supporting the success of street-life oriented boys?*

*Theme*: *Acknowledging the Façade*

> *Finding #1* (*RQ 1 – principles and components*): *Participants identified an unanticipated and disquieting absence of support for the school's street-life oriented boys.*
>
>> *"Everyone thinks [Mass Mentoring Partnership] is the solution and it's not designed for that"*
>>
>> *"We don't seem to have any program that's directed specifically at these kids"*
>>
>> *"Teachers don't refer [students to support systems]"*
>
> *Finding #2* (*RQ 1 – principles and components*): *Participants grew in their understanding of street-life oriented boys and the challenges they face in their pursuit of education.*
>
>> *"I wasn't expecting this"* [*real-life videos of street-life youth boasting of drugs, sexual exploits, and violence; and data on 383 crime incidents in one month in city of the study*]

*RQ 2*: *What is the process by which a group of teachers in a community of practice design an intervention program for street-life oriented boys?*

*Theme*: *Leading together*

*Finding #3* (RQ2 – Process): *Participants created a teacher-driven collaborative process*

"*There was a freedom to direct*"

"*We didn't really allow anyone to not participate*"

*Finding #4* (RQ2 – Process): *Establishing a sense of community and trust enabled participants to work through disagreements and share accountability.*

"*It was more egalitarian than I expected*"

"*We're going to talk it all out*"

*Finding #5* (RQ2 – Process): *Participants felt that this action research project was more effective than other Whitman collaboration and that it more closely reflected their ideas about what teacher collaboration should look like.*

"*I felt like I was fully involved and engaged*"

"*It didn't feel like some sort of top-down thing*"

"*It is an issue that clearly has been here for a long time*"

"*When do we get the group together again?*"

For this qualitative study, the outline of headings above moves the reader from the research questions to the two major themes. Under each theme appear several key findings. And under each finding are subheadings (written in participants' own words) that gather up and organize the data. The headings thus help the reader navigate through the complex relationships between data, findings, and research questions. This example of headings reveals the benefits of a final check on how headings are guiding readers. In the course of writing, writers may have shifted headings; or they may have used proxy headings to produce further writing. A final stage is for the writer to review the logic of their headings – to ensure that the headings encapsulate for the reader the data discussed, and that the headings relate the data to the research questions.

## Getting going on writing

**Write:**

1  A paragraph describing what stands out as most significant among the findings.
2  A paragraph describing what appears most surprising among the findings.
3  Two different paragraphs opening the Findings chapter.
4  A proxy list of imagined findings, in outline form.

# 6
## WRITING **UP** THE
# DISCUSSION
## Conclusions and recommendations

The Discussion chapter is where the researcher can comment, interpret, recommend, reflect, judge, draw implications, conclude, and generally make meaning of the findings. Whereas the Findings chapter reports data and patterns of data, enabling readers to interpret for themselves, the Discussion chapter is about how researchers interpret the data. Here, the researcher's expertise in the data, choice of significance, and ultimate purpose all drive the discussion. Whereas a personal voice is muted in the previous chapters, it finds expression here. Writers choose what to concentrate on, why certain findings matter, how to present significance, and how best to engage readers.

## 6.1 AN OVERVIEW OF SIGNIFICANCE

A number of broad questions tie to significance. What follows are just some of the things to write about: First, how does the study support, extend, or contradict previous studies of this problem? The writer needs to clarify the study's contribution, so tying findings to previous research is critical. Second, if the study confirms other studies, why is this confirmation significant? Or if one's hypothesis is refuted, why could this be so and why important? Third, what are the recommendations that are generated from these findings?

Recommendations need to be tied explicitly to the findings and be doable, not just "pie in the sky" suggestions. So, fourth, who benefits from this study? Did the participants benefit and in what ways? Are there clients who will benefit? If so, how can they use these findings? More broadly, how can these findings be used in similar sites or contexts, or be helpful to other groups such as administrators or policy makers?

Fifth, what are the limitations of the study – those known beforehand considered delimiting (exploratory nature, time constraints, number of participants, type of methodology, etc.) and those limitations discovered later (participants drop out or do not finish, survey response is low)? Every study has limitations, and the researcher is obligated to discuss them. At times, these limitations become justifications for future study.

Sixth, what future research or tests follow from this study, including other ways of studying the problem? Seventh, what personal meanings does the study have? All of these questions probe the significance of the study, and the writer can use these to generate ideas.

Several concerns arise from this freedom to discuss the research. Some writers, students and faculty alike, overreach with the data, making more of it than is there, pushing the data to make unwarranted recommendations. Less commonly, writers can be overly careful in discussing study limitations, thus undermining their findings and encouraging readers to dismiss the study. Finally, some writers create a jarring, pontificating voice that irritates readers and erodes the objectivity of the study.

Guidelines include the researcher tying recommendations closely to a specific finding, so as to maintain objectivity. Another is remembering that interpretations require referencing the data collected, so that readers see the line of reasoning. Typically, the student's committee or peers will catch any overreach or underplaying of significance: "Where do you get that?" they might ask. "So what?" is a more abrupt repost. "What is the story here?" is a gentler check. All writers need such checks, faculty and students alike. Especially important is selecting one's community of writers, peers who are not timid when commenting on each other's work.

## 6.2 BRAINSTORMING: USING WRITING TO GENERATE IDEAS

A number of systematic brainstorming activities help the writer get started. While the suggestions above define some broad questions, the list below includes writing strategies that help the writer tie the dissertation chapters together.

1 The dissertation writer revisits the Problem Statement chapter and does a quick write: What are the big educational issues pictured here? To visualize, writers can create bubbles of ideas from the Problem Statement, ideas that overlap or intersect. They can then take notes on whether these ideas and intersections have changed, given the data that has surfaced. Sometimes a metaphor can describe the overall relation of the study to the big issues (for instance, seeing a school as "the Ellis Island of Los Angeles, where newcomers first encounter the culture"). The writer asks, does the metaphor stay consistent? How much of the story does it explain?

2 The writer revisits the Literature Review: What did the findings add to what researchers already know? How does the study change the direction of the research? How do the study's findings reflect the theory that generated the research? Quick writes on such questions record such overview thinking.

3 The writer revisits the Methodology chapter: What was the process like? What did the researcher learn along the way? What does the journey itself communicate? At some point, did the study change? Why was that? Revisiting notes on the process may lead to telling depictions. The writer can rewrite those notes as an introduction to this chapter.

4 The writer reflects on the Findings chapter: Of the findings, which were the most significant? Why? Which were the most surprising? It helps to write these out.

5  At some point, the student considers public engagement: How will this study reach the people who need to know about (and implement) this work? The student can consider several audiences (policy, administrative, research based) and write two or three drafts on the study's impact, meant for different audiences.

In addition to revisiting previous chapters and quick composing, writers of the Discussion can use even more concrete brainstorming activities to put words together. Early Discussion chapter writing needs to begin somewhere. Some processes that might jumpstart writing follow:

1  The writer creates a storyboard of the Findings chapter – what the study involved, its purpose, how it unfolded, how events shaped the findings. Then the writer reshapes this story, filling in significance as the writing develops.
2  The writer selects key quotes not already used and comments on their larger significance. These help generate ideas about the big picture.
3  The writer begins with a reflection: What surfaced that was not expected? Then, working backwards, the researcher tells the story of how the work ended up in this unexpected place.
4  Surprising findings can generate unanticipated implications. The writer describes how a key finding changed their thinking. This might include new applications, new research directions, and new priorities.
5  The writer stands back from the whole process and writes for ten minutes just on significance, letting what comes to mind flow onto the page.

## 6.3 OPENING THE DISCUSSION CHAPTER

The formal opening of the Discussion chapter is where a dissertation writer can make a powerful statement on significance that pulls the reader in. It may be written last. But this opening is where the writer's voice most strongly surfaces. The writer has latitude in describing the problem anew (perhaps from an aerial view), in suggesting the study's prominence in the literature, in indicating the project's reach, or in unveiling a personal history and commitment to the problem. With the luxury of retrospection, the writer can reassess the study's unfolding, and can newly present the study's worth to readers.

### A strong personal voice

A language of sharp contrasts can heighten this sense of immediate significance. The example below, on how participant action research can ameliorate school violence (featured earlier) powerfully engages readers:

Rich or poor. Urban, suburban, rural. Public or private. Large or small. None of these factors determine whether a school will, sometimes or often, confront violence in its culture. The problem of school violence and the negative culture it creates is endemic. Students inhabit schools along with teachers and other adults, but the student culture of the school is the majority culture. They determine what life will be like on campus for everyone. Adults can exert an influence on this culture, but absent a long-term plan for cultural change that is at least partly owned by students and which is empowered by their voice, adults cannot control it. For decades data from government and private sources have shown persistent patterns of low-grade student-to-student (and in severe cases, student-to-teacher) violence on school campuses across the country – bullying, name-calling, taunts and jeers that sometimes escalate into physical violence and disorder. But not always. Most of the time, these poorly understood or invisible factors are sufficient to make life miserable for significant percentages of students at school. Students are powerless to change their school culture unless they understand it. This study demonstrates one way in which students might come to better understand their school culture and, so empowered, help change it …

My study offers a community a potentially transformative series of tools and approaches to gather data about itself and then to use that data to effect change. For seven weeks, a cohort of students and I at Lascaux Middle School, a typical middle school in the Los Angeles Unified School District (LAUSD), used mapmaking, photography and focused, data-driven discussion to learn how Lascaux functioned as a place of violence and cultural conflict.

This writer's voice rings out in the series of opposing adjectives, signaling the sweep of the speaker's dismissal of previous research foci. He deftly gathers up and rejects decades of studies limited to school adults, and insists that only studies that involve the students themselves have any hope of changing a school culture. In doing so, he redefines the problem for research. The violence lies in factors that are "poorly understood or invisible." It is an effective move, and places this study at the forefront of research on school violence.

### Using personal experience

Another writer (also featured earlier) opens her Discussion chapter of a mixed-methods study with forceful personal experiences and commitment – and a strong personal voice. She casts herself as a "witness" to the negative impact on Emotionally Disturbed (ED) students of a shift in state policy that eliminated mandatory professional support for ED students.

This study arose out of my own personal and professional experiences working with students who have mental health or social-emotional needs. These needs created barriers to success for these students in the schooling environment. Typically, these students end up in special education identified as students with ED. In my career, I have had the opportunity to work in non-public/private schools, traditional urban school districts, and the Option 3 charter school community. In my current role as a special education decision-maker, I have had increased exposure to the impact of policy on schools, high-level decision-making, and leading an organization through change – all with the focus of ensuring marginalized students with disabilities are supported in their educational endeavors. Over the course of my career, I have witnessed the shift in policy from AB-3632 to AB-114, and I am interested in how the loss of mandatory interagency collaboration impacts a school's ability to meet the needs of students with ED. I am also fascinated by the unique experiences of Option 3 charter school decision-makers regarding this policy. Lastly, I have interest in leadership styles and the role of adaptive leadership in responding to this policy specifically, and educational policy more broadly. For this study, I engaged with Option 3 charter school decision-makers to explore and describe how they responded to AB-114 and how adaptive leadership organizational viewpoints manifested. After the analysis of data, a few key findings surfaced.

This is highly personalized writing. While the writer still references the bureaucratic jargon of losing *mandatory interagency collaboration*, she brings to life the real people and experiences this bureaucratic shift affects. Her own professional experiences sharpen her credibility. She is especially convincing in describing her *exposure*, her *witnessing*, her *interest*, her *fascination*, and her *engagement*.

### Using the literature for contrast

Other chapter openings explicitly reference the literature and the findings, with personal experience conveyed in terms of the study findings. A first paragraph can quickly convey this intention:

In this study, I sought to discover how a high school–college collaboration could better prepare students [with disabilities] by influencing them to attend college and seek disability services to persist while attending. Student data show promise in some components of the program, and proved wrong many of my assumptions based on the literature and my personal experience. The collaboration process itself highlighted crucial institutional factors for educators to successfully implement such programs given disparate legal systems governing secondary and postsecondary education. Insights from this study provide

new perspective on commonly held beliefs in transition literature, and offer guidance for educators wishing to collaborate to
make college a reality for students with disabilities.

The opening keeps the reader's focus firmly on the data. It predicts a judi-
cious weighing of program elements of a high school–college collaboration, based on student data. Readers can further expect that institutional
factors will surface, contrary to expectations. The opening contrasts this
finding with both the literature and the researcher's personal experience.
Readers can anticipate that recommendations will follow closely from
surprising data.

In a final example, the Discussion chapter below opens with a quote
and builds on it, questioning previous research pretenses to objectivity
when studying privilege. The writer focuses on the collaborative inquiry
itself, which forms the base of the researcher's contribution. She distills her
study's contribution to the changes in thinking of the participants themselves as they helped to change the culture of an elite school.

Reflecting on the study of privilege, Peggy McIntosh (2012)
writes, "Traditional 'objective' research techniques will not
work to excavate the workings of a phenomenon we were carefully taught not to recognize within ourselves and our cultural
systems" (p. 204). My study used collaborative inquiry to understand and develop solutions to address class-based exclusion
at an affluent private school; the team's recommendations can
inform initiatives to foster belonging at similar school sites. This
study builds on others that have explored the problem but not
offered detailed solutions. Perhaps the greatest contribution of
the study is the demonstrated changes in thinking of participants
themselves. Such shifts point to collaborative inquiry as a way to
disrupt privilege and ultimately increase belonging by changing
the culture of elite schools.

The contrasts in this introduction are implied more than explicit: traditional "objective" (surface) research gives way to needed in-depth
explorations; explicit findings concerning privilege are less telling than
findings about the research method itself; previous studies reveal the
problem but offer no solutions. Contrastive openings like this typically lead
into a summary of the chapter's contents.

### Road maps

Openings typically also preview for the reader the contents of the chapter.
The writer on privilege above provides a road map for her readers:

This chapter first discusses implications of the team's
recommendations for increasing belonging for lower SES

students at affluent schools. The causes of class-based exclusion identified by the team largely align with what we already know about the lower SES student experience at elite schools. But few schools have taken meaningful steps to address the problem. The recommendations that emerged from this study can therefore inform practice. Next I discuss my study's most important finding: the shift in participants' thinking. Participants came to see through collaborative inquiry the subtle forms of class-based exclusion in the school culture. They developed an "SES lens" that most did not possess before the research process.

Collaborative inquiry itself is the key recommendation of my study. Such methods offer a way to expose and disrupt privileged norms that exclude lower SES students from elite school cultures. Few studies have explored participatory action research to develop privilege consciousness and sensitivity to micro-aggressions. I conclude the chapter by discussing the study's limitations and directions for future research.

This example identifies how the recommendations emerged from the findings. It also demonstrates the writer shifting from general causes of class-based exclusion to the "most important finding." The writer feels free to feature her method, participatory action research, as itself most likely to develop "privilege consciousness and sensitivity to micro-aggressions." Of note here, the road map does not just list findings, but moves readers toward the key finding about the process itself.

## 6.4 AFTER THE OPENING, WHAT IS MOST WORTH DISCUSSING?

### Discussing a significant finding

In the Discussion chapter, most writers summarize rather than list the key findings for the reader, but only the ones that will be discussed. Readers do not want a simple repetition of findings from the previous chapter. Also, the writer can order these findings by significance rather than study design or question order. Typically, only findings that directly answer the research questions will be discussed. Criteria for significance might include: What did I most learn? What are my most solid findings? What surprised me the most? Which findings impact the widest groups? Which findings relate directly back to previous research, confirming or disconfirming? Once the writer has prioritized and selected key findings, the task then is to convey this significance in an impactful way.

Below is an interpretive paragraph from the above study on school violence. The study used mapmaking, photography, and data-driven student discussions to reveal a school's cultural conflicts. The paragraph below describes a key finding about how mapmaking unveiled the depths of students' experience of conflict:

The mapmaking exercise showed that students have a deep and personal relationship with their school as a physical place. It has sociocultural as well as physical contours. Both of these contours influence how students live their day-to-day life on campus and affect how they see themselves, how they form relationships, and how they value their education. Previous research suggested that students would be able to map their school from a safety perspective and from an ethnic perspective. As I reported in chapter 4, it was only when these two maps were aggregated that the true story of the school's culture began to emerge. Uncomfortable realities of submerged racism, unacknowledged hurt, and seething anger were all there from the start of the project. They only revealed themselves when the maps showed the students what they anecdotally and intuitively knew but would not acknowledge.

Here, in reporting on a single crucial finding, the writer explains the significance of the mapmaking for uncovering the school's hidden culture – students' painful day-to-day realities *unacknowledged* by themselves or by the literature. Their "true story" emerges when the methods of the study allow students' maps to converge. These findings, the writer tells us, have an effect not only on the students themselves but also on the school and the community. The findings extend previous research, which was limited to students mapping their school only from separate safety and ethnic perspectives.

### Offering recommendations

Significance can also take the form of recommended actions. Here are several general criteria for recommendations: First, recommendations need to flow from specific findings. It is important to avoid sweeping calls to action. A list of multiple possibilities has a shotgun effect – without a particular target. More importantly, readers wonder how multiple actions would be feasible.

Second, each recommendation needs to be carefully examined before being suggested. For example, recommending that *all* experienced principals be placed in program improvement schools seems an overreaction to current program inequities. In contrast, recommending that experienced principals rotate between high-achieving and program improvement schools might appear more feasible, given the stigma attached to certain placements. As recommendations offer a long-awaited opportunity to argue for change, they need to appear doable, beneficial, and tied to data. Further, if one has already built support for one's recommendations, the study's significance appears greater.

### Cautions

Claims of significance require objectivity, concern for ethics, and some restraint. A researcher avoids overgeneralizing benefits or import from the results of a survey, especially if the researcher's numbers are not statistically significant. For qualitative studies, the researcher ensures that conclusions spring from the participants, sites, and conditions of the study, not from the student's intent or bias. As to ethics, any downsides to findings – potential harm to participants, subjects, or users – are noted.

While the writer's voice surfaces in this chapter, restraint creates credibility. Researchers can offer possible implications for other contexts and groups, but offer them tentatively. Researchers need to remain close to their data, avoiding large claims from small, exploratory studies. And, as noted earlier, they need to remind readers of study limitations. Most Discussion chapters restate what was actually found and link these findings to next steps, new questions, and needed additional information.

## 6.5 STRUCTURES FOR THE DISCUSSION CHAPTER

There is no one template for organizing a Discussion chapter. The organization of the chapter aims to persuade readers of the big picture – the story of this research as it evolved out of previous research. Writers and readers have a common interest – the impact of new knowledge and a road toward needed change. How one achieves those ends can take many forms. And while the organization typically emerges as the writer tells the story, what follows are a few broad patterns that doctoral students have used to convey those impacts and recommendations. These orderings may spark some ideas. They are not meant as templates.

**Mixed methods study**

Findings highlights (especially surprises)
Value of the study to various groups
Limitations
Further research
Implications
Recommendations for policy and practice
Final thoughts

**An action research study**

Overview of the findings
Returning to the major themes
Implications
The road ahead (next steps)
Limitations
Lingering questions
Conclusion

**Qualitative case study**

Introduction
Revisiting of one's role
Discussion of key findings – cross-case analysis
Limitations of the study

Recommendations for practice
**Qualitative – life history**

Introduction
Analysis and summary of findings (the people, programs)
Implications for research and theory
Implications for policy and practice
Limitations
Recommendations for future research

**Quantitative – survey**

Introduction
Discussion/interpretation of results (tied to literature)
Limitations of the study
Conclusions: ideas on implementation; recommendations for
        future study
Final thoughts

The above categories reflect different doctoral studies with different approaches. They are not the only choices, nor should they become one's outline – making writers think they only need to fill in under each heading. But the categories give writers a sense of how other students have ordered this chapter.

## 6.6 WHERE DOES THEORY FIT?

As noted before, dissertations are embedded in a theoretical frame, one that governs the study's objectives, research questions, and methodology. In the Discussion chapter, the writer revisits that frame, which is likely detailed in the Literature Review. The question lingers for the reader: How does that frame inform the conclusions? For a quantitative investigation, the theory likely helps narrow one's conclusions to the variables being studied. For a qualitative study, the theory helps explain and interpret behaviors. In both cases, returning to the theory helps writers describe how they understand findings.

### Using theory to frame recommendations

As all studies are embedded in theory, writers likely will return to theory to situate their recommendations. An example follows from the study cited earlier on how autonomous (Option 3) charter schools adapt their leadership to a key change in policy related to ED students (AB-3632 to AB- 114). The theory governing the study is *adaptive leadership*, which refers to leaders' actions, as they support others in responding to change. The excerpt below offers a recommendation to *individual* decision makers, based on the theory of adaptive leadership.

For individual decision-makers, especially those within the Option 3 charter community, this study posits that when one intentionally incorporates adaptive leadership viewpoints in planning for change (such as shifts in policy), one may learn to identify personal gaps in knowledge. As leaders become aware of adaptive traits, they can use them as tools to strengthen policy understanding. As both the literature and this study show, adaptive viewpoints help leaders create a structure for change where one may not currently exist. Utilizing this theory as a tool may allow leaders to build their capacity around policy intent and implementation (Buck, Morsink, Griffin, Hines, & Lenk, 1992).

The researcher uses adaptive leadership theory to recommend to leaders some positive actions governed by "adaptive traits" – in the face of a disheartening reduction in support for ED students. The theory suggests that when leaders identify personal gaps in knowledge and establish a "structure for change," they adapt better to policy changes affecting how they serve their most vulnerable students.

### Reiterating and foregrounding theory

Another example also foregrounds theory. The researcher makes the theory of anti-racist identity the core and upfront purpose of her action research project. Her Discussion chapter then relies on anti-racist White identity theory to address participant change and to argue for improving pre-service administrator preparation. Before introducing her conclusions, the researcher opens with the theory and its challenges:

> Embarking on a journey of anti-racist identity development is painful. This work requires a support network consisting of a skilled facilitator and peers who can hold up a mirror. Although the facilitator and pre-existing group relationships created a unique dynamic affecting group culture, the findings from this study have implications for improving pre-service administrator preparation programs.

For this study, the theory preceded the investigation: Participants signed up for the project because they believed in White racial identity theory, and the researcher charted their response by referring to specifics of the theory. The writer's conclusions require a repetition of key theory components:

> A positive White racial identity is internalized and manifests in a "lived commitment to anti-racist activity, ongoing self-examination and increased interpersonal effectiveness in multiracial settings." The individual belongs to a network of

allies that work to promote understanding and acceptance of diversity.

(Lawrence & Tatum, 1997, pp. 2–3)

For this writer, the theory and study are inextricably intertwined – for the Problem Statement, Literature Review, Methods, and Findings, as well as for the Discussion chapter. This means that for her conclusions, the writer reviews key components of the theory and explicitly ties the findings and implications to that theory.

## 6.7 WHAT ABOUT LIMITATIONS?

The Discussion chapter presents the opportunity to explain study limitations. Limitations are typically not admissions of fault or regret, just the necessary conditions of time, resources, and unanticipated or uncontrollable events. Writers that openly identify these limitations preclude readers' criticism. It is important to distinguish limitations the researcher accepts going into the study (delimitations) from those unanticipated, uncontrolled events that surface later (limitations). What follows is an example from the school violence study detailing some key delimitations, most of which the writer knew in advance but get discussed broadly as limitations. Although the writer might have gone further, he admits enough to convince readers he is aware of the limited nature of his study:

> Every study has limitations. This one is no different. The limitations of this study take nothing essential away from its findings …
>
> There is little doubt that I would have developed a deeper understanding of Lascaux Middle School if the study were based on multiple rounds of action research, rather than just one. Highly effective Participatory Action Research (PAR) is based on long-term engagement, with a research team at a site. Undoubtedly, my student team would have continued developing their skills had we done more action research cycles. To their credit, they came a great distance in seven weeks …
>
> While the ethnic balance of the PAR team was broadly representative of the student body, it was not all encompassing. There were ethnic groups (small, but present) at Lascaux that were not represented in the PAR group. Furthermore, the PAR team was derived from a subset of the magnet population at Lascaux. Though the study team was not "honors magnet," it was also not part of the school's general population …

The writer discusses the delimitations on study time and representativeness of participants. These are issues the researcher knew going in. Other weaknesses, most likely in data collection, likely surfaced later, though he did not divulge these. But the writer's awareness of study constraints confirms the truly exploratory nature of the study.

A second example, from the study on community college enrollment management, also explains limitations as mostly known constraints. But the researcher translates these limitations into opportunities for further investigations. The writer details limitations stemming from perceptual data, scale, design, and transferability.

> Though care was taken in the design and execution of this study, limitations do exist. These limitations do not compromise the validity of the findings; rather, they point to opportunities for further investigation. I describe these important considerations in this section.
>
> One limitation of this study was that it primarily relied on participants' perceptions and memories of the examined phenomenon. Observing the phenomenon as it unfolded would have been beneficial. I could have interviewed participants as the events occurred and observed the phenomenon directly. Interviewing multiple people to confirm responses and conducting document analysis helped to address this limitation.
>
> The study is also somewhat limited as a result of its scale. Eleven of the 15 interview participants were employed in the academic division of the college. Four were employed in the remaining divisions, including student services and business services. Although this breakdown is similar to the representation on the Enrollment Management Committee – where 30 of the 49 members were from the academic division of the college – in a larger scale study, broader representation from more areas of the college would incorporate more perspectives.
>
> The site for this study was selected in part because it had increased FTES generation from the academic years 2013–2014 to 2016–2017, a time of system-wide enrollment declines. Colleges that were able to buck the national trend of shrinking enrollments during this time may have been able to do so because of enrollment management leadership, the focus of this study.
>
> This study revealed the challenges that WCC encountered in regard to enrollment management leadership, suggesting that its enrollment growth from 2013–14 to 2016–17 occurred in spite of the leadership around enrollment management. A limitation of this study is that it was not designed to identify the reasons why the growth occurred. This is an opportunity for further investigation.
>
> Finally, transferability of the findings is dependent upon context, which is limited to the CCC system. Furthermore, the transferability of the findings is limited due to the unique

internal contextual factors at WCC. When I began this study, I could neither anticipate that the college leadership employed top-down leadership nor that faculty members were in the process of resisting it. While this unique internal culture does limit the transferability of the findings, it also points to implications for further research.

The researcher covers a wide array of limitations, including an unexpected finding that limits transferability. The inclusiveness vividly depicts for readers the main concerns going into the study.

## 6.8 REFLECTION OR FINAL THOUGHTS

As any dissertation is a personal journey, students can end their study with personal reflections about the meaning of their work. A student likely began the study with a purpose that arose from personal experience. At the end of the dissertation, the writer might review the journey, expressing how the research originated, why it is so important personally, what the student originally expected from it, how expectations changed over the course of the study, what was learned, and what, finally, the study means on a personal level.

An example follows, from the study on policy change around Emotional Disturbance:

> This study enabled me to engage with three areas about which I am passionate: special education, educational leadership, and policy. Early in my career, I became aware of the distinct struggles of students with ED, and this study offered insight into how policy, educational leadership, and special education intersect. It highlights the need for a shared construct of knowledge building across all levels of educational authority: from the individual decision-maker up to the policymakers (and back down again). They share responsibility for continually building knowledge and making connections to ensure that students get what they need.
>
> This research has ignited an interest for me in how educational institutions can be both managed through and provided flexibility by local legislation. The mix of accountability and flexibility in Option 3 charter decision-makers offered an appropriate population from which to collect data on Adaptive Leadership and policy change. I have agreed to share my findings with the Option 3 community as my target audience, but also reach out to those who can influence policy. I plan to promote my conclusions through the California Charter School Association (CCSA) and the National Center for Special Education in Charter Schools (NCSECS). This research should not stop here,

since locally Option 3 charter schools grow in number each year, and research on the impact of the shift in policy from AB-114 is still developing, and nationally students with ED continue to struggle. The work of dedicated educators is inspiring, and I am prepared to promote both research and policy to increase positive outcomes for vulnerable students.

Such a personal reflection charts the history of the researcher's original passions, her learning, and her intended future actions. The arc it creates is a compelling conclusion to years of deep thinking and writing, and it shows an increased commitment and expertise in advocating for vulnerable students.

## Getting going on writing

**Write:**

1 A paragraph summing up the study's key addition to previous research.
2 A paragraph on what could have been tightened up, extended, or revised.
3 A paragraph on the personal significance of the study.

# 7

# REVISING
# THE DISSERTATION
# AS A WHOLE

A student writes a dissertation in evolving sections, recycling back through various iterations, with an ever-changing sense of the "whole." This means that the writer needs to review the work as a complete document, and go back and make it flow logically and consistently – as if one had written the pieces in a smooth and seamless process. Of course, this has not been so. But readers need to proceed through the work as if the process were smooth. In this recursive process, the writer reviews the completed work from beginning to end, for logical unfolding and persuasiveness as well as for voice and sentence clarity. Some suggestions follow.

## 7.1 REVISING FOR ACCURACY, CONSISTENCY, AND PERSUASIVENESS

### Returning to the Problem Statement and Methods

Once doctoral students complete their Discussion chapter, they need to review the entire dissertation for accuracy and consistency. Significant time has passed since the study was proposed. On review, the Problem Statement may require modifications in conceptual frame, emphasis, and information. Over the course of the study, the student's thinking changes – the image of the whole dissertation may have shifted. Writers need to check if the study's original purpose and justification fit with what they actually did and with their later description of outcomes and benefits. Writers also need to check if the early framing of the problem – theoretical, statistical, historical – is consonant with later framing in the Findings and Discussion chapters. Any summary of Methods in the Problem Statement needs to match the fuller Methods chapter, and both need to be rewritten to state what the study actually did, not what it proposed to do. After the writer takes notes on where to best tie together these parts, they can rewrite sections of the Problem Statement and Methods to make them consistent with later chapters.

It is not just consistency, but also persuasive power that writers assess. Looking back at the Problem Statement, the writer likely thinks of new persuasive tools – how better to convince readers, from the beginning, of the need for the study. What do readers really need to know upfront? Is the problem accurately described? Does the researcher now have stronger evidence to justify the study? How can the writer better connect to the interests, knowledge, and concerns of readers? With the experience of conducting the study behind them, doctoral students can write more persuasively about the evidence for doing the study.

Rereading (sometimes aloud) helps. Writers can find inspiration for the first chapter in rereading the Discussion chapter, as it may generate a fresher Statement of the Problem. They can also reread their Methods, checking for internal alignment of problem, questions, design, and methods; this helps with correcting any early misstatements, and justifying choices (e.g., site and participants) more cogently. When writers revisit their Methods chapter, they typically see ways they can improve the detailing, sharpen wording, and tie data collection and analysis methods more closely to findings. Details engage readers more fully in the essential research processes.

As noted earlier, writers are required to revise their methods to state what they actually did (now in the past tense). In doing so, they likely create a more compelling case for their work. Easy revisions might be changing "what?" wording of questions to "how?" or "to what extent?" questions – to fit how data was actually collected and recorded. More subtle changes might include revealing the researcher's improvised recruiting practices that required ingenuity and creativity. Readers are engaged by such unanticipated necessities as waiting outside classrooms to target participants. However, not every unanticipated event is of equal import. Luckily, most challenges are not that important, and don't need reporting. Students are not under orders to discuss what did not work smoothly unless those attempts determined what finally did work.

### Returning to the Literature Review

The Literature Review typically calls for a final revision. New studies likely have surfaced, and some old studies seem less relevant; the arguments themselves may need sharpening. Furthermore, the theory driving the study may require more explanation. As the Discussion chapter often refers back to the literature – to show how the project advances knowledge – writers reappraise the Literature Review: Does it accurately describe the studies that become important in the Discussion? Has any contrary evidence emerged that the researcher needs to report, both in the Literature Review and in the Discussion? Does the Literature Review lead readers to the methods that the researcher actually used in the study?

Questions about newly discovered literature often arise. One doctoral student recently asked: If a study surfaced that she has decided to use in her *analysis* of already collected data, should she place it in the Literature Review? The response is that any research or method used in the data analysis needs to "precede" that analysis – to be part of the literature generating this method. The fact that she found the study *after* she had collected her data did not matter. She needed to describe it in her Literature Review and also in her Methods chapter in order to explain and defend the way she analyzed data. Readers need to see the student's data analysis as deriving from a justified method. The actual order of discovery of this method is not important.

More subtly, another student wanted to know if he could use newly surfaced studies to better explain his own findings – but not put these studies in his Literature Review because he had "discovered" these studies later. The response is, again, that if new studies help readers present findings, then these "new" studies need to be placed in the Literature Review, as if the writer had known about them all along. The writer may not have anticipated this method of explanation, but he has to write about it as if he had. The new studies are being used as a tool. However, if the writer's "explaining" is really "interpreting," then the whole section belongs in the Discussion chapter: The new literature, used to interpret, does not need to go in the Literature Review.

New literature often comes to light in the process of interpreting findings. This literature can be added as the writer conceptualizes the final chapter. While far-ranging studies can offer broad new perspectives, more tightly connected studies can help the writer interpret, draw implications, offer recommendations, define limitations, or suggest next steps. Given that this literature was not essential to designing and performing the study, it can remain solely part of the Discussion chapter.

## Returning to the Findings and Discussion chapters

Broad revisions for overall consistency come first. The Findings and Discussion chapters need to be related to each other and to earlier chapters. The writer asks: Do all the chapters accurately reflect the research questions? Are the chapters consistent in their depiction of the study's purpose, methods, context, and findings? Especially important, does the Findings chapter explicitly meet the objectives of the study, provide the information promised, and add to the research in the way envisioned? The writer reviews these broad questions first.

Then, the writer looks for specific intersections between the final two chapters: Given key findings, do claims in the Discussion chapter evolve out of and tie back to those findings? Does the Discussion chapter discuss whether or not the findings fully answer the research questions, and why they do or do not? Have the study's limitations been accurately stated in the Discussion chapter, and reflect how readers might have responded to the findings?

Finally, the writer revisits the Findings chapter for the most persuasive, specific evidence. During revision, doctoral students look for better ways to present. As a start, they can ask, have they overlooked any in-process data that could be included? For example, dissertation notes, in-process thinking, and memos to oneself, can be re-examined. Often, students discount this data, thinking that it is irrelevant or too commonplace for inclusion. But these notes may be relevant to how the methods unfolded, and the findings emerged – supplying the quotidian routines and experiences of the research process itself. These added details can reveal the complexity and depth of the research as it took place.

Quantitative and some mixed methods studies may promote some rethinking about when and how to use tables and figures. If the writer cannot explain the data in a few sentences, a table may improve the presentation. The writer thus compresses and visualizes relationships that would take paragraphs to explain. The table should be easy to read, from top to bottom, and offer identified columns. However, the writer still needs to title the figure (italics), later describe key points (not repeat the information), and give attribution, if the table was adapted from others' work. Tables help readers synthesize key evidence, but too many tables turn them away from the writing.

Augmenting specific evidence can also mean new selections or deletions. Long quotes get tiresome, but a series of well-selected, edited, and poignant quotes, or observed actions, vivifies a scene. One doctoral student, writing about findings from her participant action research study, added some powerful revelations. These revealed school psychologists reassessing how they distinguished a student with a learning disability from an English language learner (ELL).

> It took me some time to realize that I have no problem adjusting test administration to a student with Autism because I know they might have language difficulties, yet I couldn't see how that change was acceptable for ELL students. I'm embarrassed by my resistance, yet thankful my colleagues kept pushing the topic.
>
> This makes me feel the same as when I test a student for traumatic brain injury – I do it so infrequently I don't realize what I don't know.

The admissions, introspective and self-revealing, tell a powerful story of participant reflection and change. By substituting these haunting self-appraisals for more generic evidence of "change," the writer captures the import of the study's findings. This psychologist realized that she may have been inaccurately assessing ELL students as needing special education classes.

## 7.2 REVISING FOR VOICE

In revising for accuracy, consistency, and persuasiveness, writers reread their words and sentences. If read aloud, those words create a distinctive voice – what the writer sounds like. The voice may sound formal and distant or direct and immediate. It may sound crisp, strong, and confident in one place, and long-winded, imprecise, and unsure in another. Reading aloud is an opportunity to revise for voice. The writer hears the words in context, and becomes conscious of the wording, emphasis, patterns of short and long sentences, and connections – all the ways a writer "talks" to a reader. This listening to one's words directs attention to voice.

A consistent and assured voice encourages reader identification. While credible evidence broadly unites academic writers and readers, the choice of language and language structures actualizes their sense of common belief. To heighten their voice, academic writers choose wording and syntax that are clear, economical, and easy to absorb. They build their sentences into paragraphs that are logically connected and move the reader forward.

By reading aloud, writers can hear where the writing is off-putting, or simply circular: Then, with some helpful strategies, they can learn to reconstruct the syntax, cut the overlap, replace inexact words, reduce prepositions, create emphasis, and tie pieces together – and as a result strengthen their voice. When readers identify with the writer's voice, they are taking in the argument. What follows are some analyses of what makes sentences obscure and roundabout, and then some advice on how to make them clear and economical.

Getting rid of clutter is essential. Recognizing where the clutter comes from is the first step.

## Clarity

Excessive wordiness, generic language, jargon, repetition, and convoluted syntax all indicate that the writing is cluttered and unclear. Often, the writer is mimicking the language of published articles that have a lot of jargon and that use an abstract, objectified style. Below is such a sentence from a study abstract:

> We examined the predictive value and interplay of elementary school students' understanding of the control-of-variables strategy, a domain-general experimentation skill, and their prior content knowledge for subsequent conceptual knowledge acquisition and conceptual change.

The jargon piles up – "predictive value," "interplay … of students' understanding," "domain-general experimentation skill," "prior content knowledge," "subsequent conceptual knowledge acquisition," "conceptual change." The language pushes readers away. All of the potential *verbs* (predict, understand, control, experiment, conceive, acquire) have been objectified into *nouns* (understanding, experimentation, acquisition) or adjectives (predictive, control-of-variable, domain-general, conceptual). When imitated, this style is particularly off-putting. It is considered a "noun style" – where entities not actions accrue.

A noun style often promotes convoluted syntax and clutter. In the above sentence, the simple subject-verb opening ("We examined") is then completed with an object phrase that is 34 words long. Most of this object phrase consists of nouns and noun phrases but is further tangled up in clumps of hyphenated nouns serving as adjectives ("domain-general experimentation skill"). This is not a reader-friendly style.

A noun style aligns with other clarity issues that style books decry. It links to the overuse of the passive voice ("was discovered" not "Darwin discovered"); doubling of passive verbs to cover one's bases ("was examined and analyzed") so that readers don't know which or how; overuse of generic active verbs ("have," "said," "do" "make," "give," "get"), so the verbal information remains generic; reliance on "to be" verbs ("is," "are," "were" "will be," etc.), so there is *no* verbal information, just an equation; and using nouns as one's verb ("he will transition," "she will optimize"), so the sentence action still feels like a "thing" not an "act." A noun style also typically eschews the personal voice.

While the personal voice can appear in qualitative research, it is typically absent from much quantitative research in the social sciences. Researchers and their concrete actions and subjectivities stay out of the picture. This exclusion may result in formulas such as "was studied," "were described," and "will be calculated." The doer of the action remains unspecified. Such writing is not so much wrong as it is incomplete, unclear, and sometimes misleading. Readers do not know who performed the action, and in what context. The action itself stays generic, so it is not fully realized. And the wording misleads, because someone did or does perform an action and readers don't know who did it, or what exactly it was.

In sum, readers respond better to a verb style than a noun style. Verbs are the crux of the sentence. Active verbs convey more, a point made clear with qualitative data, where the verbs are often rife with information ("teachers reflected," "the principal intoned," "the superintendent contradicted"). However, active verbs can lose their advantage if they are reduced to the same generalized choice. For instance, if one writes, "Joanna said" and continues with "Peter said," and then "Michael said," one has eliminated nuances from the interviews – the tenor of the statement. If one writes, instead, that Joanna "whispered" but "Peter exclaimed," while "Michael admonished," one is still reporting objectively – but readers know a lot more about the interviewees' positions and attitudes. Verbs carry significant information. And they are crucial to one's voice.

### Highlighting verbs over nouns

Revision strategies that focus on the verb can resurrect voice. To revise for verbs over static nouns, the writer can locate the key active verb and rework the rest of the sentence around it, cutting out extraneous phrasing. If a key active verb is absent, the writer may find it underlying a noun or noun phrase; if not, the writer can introduce a new verb. Strong verbs sum up the action of the sentence. They are the sentence fulcrum, allowing the writer to work backwards (asking who performed the action) and then forwards, asking who or what received the action.

Below is an analysis and then revision of an Abstract from a published study – illustrating a writing style typical of some strands of academic research. A revision for active verbs can provide a way around the passive-voice sentences that sound more like a machine than a human voice:

Associations between attachment security, assessed as a secure base script (SBS), and teachers' social competence ratings were examined in two samples (one from the Midwest region and the other from the Southern region of the United States). Consistent with previous reports, significant associations between domains were obtained in both samples and after combining the two samples. R = .33, p<.001. The associations remained significant when child sex, age, and verbal intelligence were controlled.

Here, the passive voice ("assessed," "were examined," "were obtained," "after combining," "were controlled") dominates the writing. Human beings engaged in research are not in the picture. While quantitative studies may favor this style *because* it erases the researchers, the sentences remain difficult to process. The actions need untangling.

A revision that reinstates the researchers clarifies the action (though not the technical language):

Researchers examined associations between children's attachment security (measured by a secure base script) and teachers' social competence. They drew two samples from the Midwest and from the Southern U.S. Consistent with previous studies, the researchers found significant associations in both samples, and with both samples combined (r = .33, p < .001), even when they controlled for children's sex, age, and verbal intelligence.

While the academic jargon still narrows the audience, the sentences are comprehensible. They have consistent subjects (the researchers) that are placed next to active verbs ("examined," "used," "found" "controlled"). Even without technical knowledge, the reader can understand the overall meaning. And real people are talking about their work.

For their own writing, doctoral students can become conscious of their voice, learning how to resurrect key active verbs hidden in adjectives or nouns. They need to transform a noun style into a verb style. What follows is a student's original version of a mostly passive sentence:

Since charter school decision-makers have more flexibility in how they build their programs, variety is found in hiring practices and in the development of supports and services to meet the social-emotional needs of students when compared to LAUSD.

Here, the passive "variety is found" diverts the reader from the main point. The writer needed to find her key verb and align it with her subject; then she can transform the many noun phrases into verbs. The revision reads:

Unlike LAUSD, charter schools can build their own programs, so they can hire more flexibly, and develop supports and services to meet students' social-emotional needs.

The active verbs "build," "hire," and "develop" now pop out. The key verb "build" comes early in the sentence, after the writer eliminated much of the clutter of the long introductory clause. Better yet, "build" comes right after its subject, "charter schools" (decision-makers is redundant). The other new active verbs, "hire" and "develop," had been hiding in the adjective "hiring" and in the noun "development." The adjective and noun had downplayed the action. Further, the revision eliminates the passives ("variety is found," "when compared to …").

When a writer disinters the active verbs, other parts of the sentence take shape. The revision now frontloads for the reader the contrastive structure of the sentence ("Unlike LAUSD") rather than tacking it on to the end of the sentence with a passive comparison ("when compared to LAUSD"). This repositioning helps the reader use the contrast to better anticipate the sentence meaning. Further, whereas the unedited version jars readers with its six prepositional phrases, the revised version has none. Overall, the edited version flows smoothly from subject to active verbs, and the unedited version does not.

## Wordiness: the need for economy

No writer is exempt from wordiness. Writing means producing words and not all words are equal. Wordiness comes in a plethora of forms: strings of prepositional phrases, overlap, attempts at clarifications ("to be clear," "in other words"), redundancy, circular claims, intensifiers, hortatory remarks, asides, straying from the point, overlapping examples, unnecessary detailing, overusing lists of definitions, academic jargon, and probably a host more. All writers need to cut once they have a substantial text. Not to take this time marks a writer as unprofessional – unserious about the work.

The approach here to economy addresses sentences not paragraphs. Few dissertation guidebooks ever look at sentences, and fewer still at economy because they leave that to the "style" books – as if economy were a cosmetic concern. This text takes economy seriously as an issue of accurate communication – of eliminating the slippage that occurs when both writer and reader are a bit vague about meaning.

Revising for economy applies to all writing practices. Once writers identify the main verbal action, they can revise most other parts of their sentences too, as in the sentences above. This is an enterprise worth the effort. The additional examples below also come from doctoral students' writing. The first example is already a short sentence, but still wordy and unclear:

> The potential contribution to school engagement of research on student experience has not been fulfilled.

The tacked on passive verb at the end is a giveaway. The sentence directs readers to a "potential" – a vague subject – that "has not been fulfilled,"– a vague and passive action. But the real action hides in the noun "contribution." When one asks, what could "contribute" to what, the sentence almost rewrites itself:

> Student experience could contribute to research on school engagement.

Here is a clear, economical subject-verb-complement sentence: 15 words down to nine. Readers understand what the action is, who or what is doing it, and what receives the action. Phrases like "the potential … has not been fulfilled" just got in the way.

Another sentence by a doctoral student further reveals how economy creates clarity.

> Additional knowledge to be gained from this project is obtaining a better understanding of faculty instruction of the co-requisite courses and what changes in pedagogy will be implemented to work with what used to be remedial students who are now enrolled in higher level math courses.

The giveaway lies in the weak main verb "is." The sentence has a long subject phrase (eight words) on one side of "is" and an exceptionally long complement phrase (37 words) on the other side. The sentence identifies no actors, only passive receivers ("remedial students") and several vague, overlapping, passive actions (knowledge "gained," understanding "obtained").

Strategies for economy typically start with the main verb. But barring a dominant action, a writer can also focus on sentence subject, and then reconstruct the action. As this writer is describing her project, she needs to place "project" in the subject position, then ask what the project will *do*. This simple strategy helps writers cut away at extraneous words. Here is the revised sentence, with economical subject and verb – and 46 words down to 26:

> This project will identify the best pedagogies for teaching the co-requisite courses, for students once labeled remedial but now enrolled in credit bearing math courses.

Sentence kingpins, specifically main verbs and main subjects, offer an incisive way to revise for economy.

## Other strategies for economy

Sentence wordiness can take other forms. What follows are some common examples of different forms of wordiness, and some sentences and phrases that need cutting.

1 Writers often use *too many* verbs or verbals and thus diffuse the action:

> Evolution in the way giftedness is presently defined creates opportunities for students who demonstrate high intellectual ability and talent to develop into adults with outstanding capabilities.

In this sentence, too many actions, explicit or implied, overlap: "evolving," "defining," "creating opportunities," "demonstrating," "developing." The various events in the sentence blur its meaning. The key doer of the action gets lost: The gifted students, who already have "high intellectual ability and talent," are achieving "outstanding capabilities" – what they already have.

The revision below removes the blurred actions, subordinates background information, removes overlap, and highlights the main subject and verb. One action remains from six:

> Given new definitions of giftedness, students with high intellectual talent can now develop their capabilities.

The revision keeps readers focused on the students, reduces "new definitions" to background information, and highlights the key action – students can "develop" their capabilities. Further, 26 words are edited down to 15.

2 Similarly, writers often use overlapping verbs or verb phrases, possibly for sentence rhythm, but the phrases often add little:

> Nonetheless, given these challenges, the high school stakeholders endeavored to engage and implement effective strategies and succeeded in establishing a relationship with the community college.

The dual infinitives "to engage and implement" offer rhythm but no additional content. Likewise, the parallel main verbs "endeavored" and "succeeded" can be eliminated, with "established" now the main verb. Rewritten, the sentence reads:

> Despite these challenges, the high school stakeholders implemented strategies that established a relationship with the community college.

The overlapping verbs have disappeared, and 25 words are reduced to 18.

3 Writers at times judge "importance" or proclaim a theory's "critical nature," but they may simply be avoiding content – editorializing rather than explaining.

> Taking into consideration the evolving components of ethical leadership and underlying assumptions about the theory

is important to understanding how ethical leadership can be practiced.

Here, the writer lets "is important" substitute for content, while generating extra words (and a dangling modifier): The writer leaves out *who* is "taking into consideration" these "components" and who is "understanding" how to practice ethical leadership. A revision needs to fill in the doer(s), while eliminating the empty phrases. A revision reads:

> Leaders need to consider the assumptions and evolution of ethical leadership in order to practice it.

Without the empty judgment, the sentence appears more objective. What's more, the writer has removed the overlap and other unnecessary words that were substituting for content. The revised sentence now clarifies who performs the action and why. Furthermore, 25 words came down to 16.

When writers judge for readers, they add unnecessary words and undermine objectivity: examples include "striking" findings, "exhaustive" data, "conclusive" evidence. Readers need to judge for themselves from the evidence.

4  Writers at times rely on intensifiers – other empty words that can undermine writers' objectivity. Examples include "very," "strongly," "highly," "extremely" – adverbs that contribute no new information, only an intensity of voice. Readers interpret these words as the writer *insisting* without evidence.

5  Other common empty structures include sentences with artificial subjects ("there is," "there are," "it is apparent that …"). These dummy or artificial phrases add words and slow down the reading. Strings of prepositional phrases also slow readers down with empty words, as do formulaic, empty openers like "another factor in this … is …" or "another research study that deals with retention is …").

Wordiness diffuses meaning because it distracts, undercuts key words, eliminates emphasis, and undermines voice. It slows readers down, loosens the connections between sentences, and allows ambiguity to creep in. Reducing wordiness is not just a cosmetic re-facing, relegated to the surface skills of one's editor. Rather, it is part of the essential task of creating meaning.

## 7.3 REVISING FOR FLOW (COHERENCE)

Flow consists of the movement between sentences, how they cohere into paragraphs. Although some writers prefer short punctuated sentences, and others prefer longer, more subordinated sentences, *all* writers need to connect sentences to move the reader forward. Various cohesion devices can support flow, though used for their own sake, they can be mind-numbing.

One misused linguistic device, often promoted in textbooks, is to repeat a key phrase, as below:

> An essay requires a thesis statement. The thesis statement states the writer's key argument. The thesis statement also creates a structure for the argument.

While "thesis statement" is repeated in all three sentences, and the second sentence neatly collects it from the end of the first sentence, the three sentences go nowhere. Cohesion devices can break apart and then obscure a simple claim, in this case, better written as: *An essay's thesis statement structures the argument.*

Other cohesion devices, again purely linguistic supports, include parallelism, transitions, and organizers. These also support flow but do not create it. Parallelism likens or contrasts two passages by putting them in similar syntax (*We are typically examining the needs of systems and processes when we should be measuring the needs of individuals and communities*). Transitions deliberately connect by using words that predict a specific relationship (*in contrast, similarly, in addition, however, moreover, nevertheless*). Organizers connect by time or by priority – *first, second third*; or *next, afterwards, finally.* While organizers convey relationships, they are not sufficient to make the sentences cohere.

While such devices help, coherence requires underlying connections of logic and evidence. For instance, the standard connector "in contrast" must lead to mutually exclusive ideas, not just different ideas. Similarly, the much used "in addition" and "also" should not be used as all-purpose glue, but require a logically related idea. What's more, connectors that form a list or offer a timeframe need to have a logical purpose for this ordering, for instance the unfolding, over a period of time, of an action research project.

### Academic coherence: logic and evidence

In academic writing, coherence typically means the movement from general claim to example – or from general claim to result, explanation, or implication of claim. Whatever the movement, all of the standard connectors must serve a larger connectedness.

The example below illustrates how the logical moves from claim to example to details about the example help move the reader forward, without the need for standard connectors to heighten these moves:

> The team's research revealed the subtle, daily comments and actions in the Hamilton culture that celebrated affluence and ignored, dismissed, or disparaged lower SES students. Observation data included comments such as: "There are two standards of rich, Hamilton rich, and what regular people think of as rich"; and "Having a Birkin bag is like the ultimate life goal. That's when you know you've made it"… The team

logged 25 distinct comments or moments from November to mid-December 2015, averaging almost one observed moment per school day. Observation data fell into three categories: disparaging lower SES norms; showing off status symbols; and displaying ignorance or unawareness of lower SES students' experiences.

Here, one sees a logical shift from overall claim – "subtle, daily comments" that celebrate affluence – to examples – "having a Birkin bag is like the ultimate life goal." The writer then shifts to information about the scope of the examples – "The team logged 25 distinct comments … from November to December, 2015." These shifts from general claim to specific examples, then to specific numbers, moves the reader forward, creating coherence through logic.

Coherence is further heightened by the continuity of sentence subjects. The writer repeatedly references the research team's work: "The team's research revealed …," "Observational data included …," "The team logged …" This writer did not need to use connecting devices such as "also," "for example," or "furthermore" – the continuity of sentence subjects supported the logic of the sentence shifts.

## Looking out for false coherence

To sum up, the big strategies for enhancing the flow of ideas include shifting from claim to example, explanation, or result; emphasizing key ideas by subordinating lesser ideas; and using consistent subjects to keep paragraph coherence. The standard connectors ("however," "in addition," "furthermore," etc.) can help by supporting the paragraph logic, but can't replace it. What follows is a list of suggestions for double-checking one's choice of standard connectors and suggesting the use of other coherence strategies:

1 Identify every use of "also" or "in addition" between sentences and see if this all-purpose connector can be replaced with a content-based connection. State explicitly the relation between the two ideas. If the two ideas are not equally weighted (lists convey an even weighting), make sure the follow-on idea explains, shows a result, gives an example, or offers further meaning.

2 Look closely at new paragraph openers. Instead of using "another" idea, flaw, intervention, study, etc. as the connection, state the relationship between the major claims of consecutive paragraphs. Rewrite the first sentence of every new paragraph so that this sentence explicitly connects the new paragraph's main idea to the main point of the entire previous paragraph. Even if the connection is already good, it can likely be made better. Readers use these first sentences as guides through the paragraph, so these signpost sentences need to be explicit.

3 Refine all sentence-to-sentence connections where the direction of the argument changes. Look carefully at such connectors as "nevertheless,"

"yet," "thus," "however," "conversely," to see if they correctly signal the intended change of thought. Ask others if they follow the signals. Make sure the contrast is sharp.

4  Look at the sequence of subjects from one sentence to the next to see if the paragraph is still discussing the same subject. Look for "leaps." Where needed, add sentences to connect the thought. Ask others if they think all of the sentences contribute to the main point.

5  Writers often use "this" to refer back to a previous idea – a weak connecting device. As an indefinite reference, "this" can ambiguously refer back to a specific concept or to a whole passage. Identify every floating "this" (indefinite reference) and add what "this" refers to.

6  Add or rework headings to better guide the reader. Headings help the reader by making key content-based connections – previewing what is to come. They enhance coherence by predicting the big arguments.

The above suggestions provide a rubric for double-checking the connectedness of one's writing.

## 7.4  EDITING USING ALL THE RESOURCES OF THE LANGUAGE

Dissertation writing can appear stodgy and uniform, but it does not have to be. Writers have more linguistic resources at hand than they realize, and key resources can create emphasis and relative importance.

### *Punctuation*

Starting with the basics, all writers have punctuation tools that allow them to move parts of a sentence around, compress or expand, emphasize, or downplay. Included here are the semi-colon, the colon, the dash, and the subordinating comma – all used to shape the larger sentence elements.

*Independent clauses* (which can stand alone as a sentence) are punctuated in different ways. Which punctuation mark one chooses to end an independent clause depends on intended meaning and effect: Does the writer want a full stop to the sentence (a period)? a stop that still ties two independent sentences together (a semi-colon)? a stop with a *specific* link that reads "as follows" (the colon)? or no stop but a glide into another more important phrase or clause (a dash)? These choices affect meaning.

The example below uses the colon to say "as follows" or "in this way":

In Halliday's model, the fierce competition over private education drives a sort of "arms race": Students bear the burdens of increasing expectations and growing workloads in order to ensure that their own education retains its luster.

The colon, which translates into "as follows," leads to the explanation of "arms race." While colons can connect two full sentences, they typically connect one independent clause to a list, example, clarification, or quotation; the follow-on material does not have to be a complete sentence. In contrast, the semi-colon ties two complete sentences together, giving them equal weight, as in the example below.

> Emotional Intelligence determines daily behaviors with uncontrolled or controlled emotions; these emotions affect students' learning styles and, once recognized, can help improve their Emotional Intelligence.

The two complete sentences are closely related, and equally weighted – connection that the writer signals with a semi-colon instead of a period.

The dash offers a different ending to a sentence. The same writer created an independent clause, which could stand alone as a sentence, then used a dash to add new, clarifying information:

> This neglect of emotional supports leads to the prevalence of the problem – increasing numbers of K-8 students with emotional and academic needs.

The dash tells the reader that the add-on information at the end is especially important – a comma or even a colon would have lessened that significance.

*Dependent clauses*, separated from independent clauses, are punctuated by commas. Writers find it useful to turn some independent clauses into subordinated or dependent clauses (which cannot stand alone as a sentence), and relocate them as a sentence opening or closing. Placed as a sentence opener, the now dependent clause provides background or contextual information; placed as a sentence ending, it can clarify or qualify its details completing the sentence (it then bears the sentence emphasis). To create dependent clauses, writers use *subordinate conjunctions*, including "although," "while," "after," "as," "as long as," "because," "before," "even if," "once," "since," and "now that."

Typically, introductory dependent clauses are marked off from the independent clause with a comma: *"Although California is taking steps to reduce remediation at community colleges, the state has not targeted the needs of specific groups."* Here, the dependent clause opener provides background information; this information is deemphasized. In contrast, the independent clause that ends the sentence carries the emphasis – its independence and sentence position give it added weight.

However, when dependent clauses are placed at the end of a sentence, they are not read as just background information; they now significantly qualify or refine the meaning of independent clauses: *"California has not targeted the needs of specific groups, although it is taking steps to reduce remediation at community colleges."* Placed at the end, the dependent clause here adds key information, gaining the sentence emphasis by its placement.

Punctuation choices to mark off phrases, the smaller sentence parts, offer additional choices for communicating significance. If one encloses a phrase in parentheses, one signals that the information is of least importance; the writer is creating an aside. If one flanks the phrase with commas, the phrase is still part of the main sentence but is downplayed. If one places dashes around the phrase, it becomes an emphatic qualification – the dashes make readers pay attention, as in the following:

> Researchers Mueller and Dweck (1998) tested to see if praising different causes of good performance – as due to either smartness or to effort – might have different impacts on students' resilience after a setback.

Within the dashes above lies the key contrast – an impact due to either "smartness or effort." The dashes tell the reader that this distinction is essential.

### Placing sentence elements: smoothing out the movement forward

To recap: Writers create emphasis through punctuation and through subordination, but also through placement of information, as suggested above. Information included in introductory clauses or phrases typically lacks the emphasis of information appearing at the end of sentences, where readers complete the idea. So, writers usually put background information up front, leaving for the ends of sentences the major claims or key information. But how do writers balance and smooth out the move from background to main clause?

When a writer opens with a dependent clause, that information needs to be streamlined, so readers can move smoothly to the main clause. Linguists discuss this strategy as putting "old" information in sentence beginnings ("old" in that it is linked to previous sentences and has now become background) to help readers then take in the "new" information in sentence endings.

The example below shows old information placed upfront and minimized to smooth the reader's path to the new information in the main clause, and to the qualifier that ends the sentence:

> When international students expand their social network, they increase their self-esteem, sense of satisfaction, and mental health, leading to higher rates of persistence and retention.

In terms of content, the reader moves smoothly from short background, to main claim (clause), to final import of the claim, with the emphasis placed on new information at the sentence end.

A similar sentence from the same student shows how a long upfront dependent clause can impede the reader's path and undermine final emphasis:

By understanding and developing sensitivity to the different dimensions of acculturative stress and the impact of social relationships on the management of such stress, college faculty and administrators can better support the international population and enhance their institution's rate of retention (Abe et al., 1998; Andrade, 2009; Constantine et al., 2004; Misra et al., 2003).

Readers get lost in the introductory ideas (old information) before getting to the main claim (new information) in the independent clause. Too much background material can undermine emphasis because readers cannot hold so much information in mind while waiting for the new information at the end.

A streamlining of the introductory material helps the reader get to the main idea:

By understanding how social relationships help students manage acculturative stress, college faculty and administrators can better support international students and retain them.

With this reduction, readers now move readily from the background to the main point. The revision cut the sentence from 41 words to 22; and prepositions went from 6 to 0. Writers need to help readers through such sentences.

## Word choice as a key resource

It seems appropriate that this book on writing concludes with a section on word choice, as words underlie all writers' choices.

*Metaphors.* First, a few words about the metaphoric nature of language, even dissertation language. Images infuse our understanding and foster our attitudes. For instance, the word "infuse" suggests being steeped, soaked, saturated. That word affects readers differently than, say, "shape" or "impact." Even in their "objective" chapter on findings, writers can exploit images: For instance, a participant who "announces" something is different from a participant who "reports" something. Furthermore, images permeate one's Discussion chapter, which highlights significance. For instance, the image in the following sentence provokes an anthropological view of schools: *Students inhabit schools along with teachers and other adults, but the student culture of the school is the majority culture.* The image helps us see a school as a small city/state. It promotes identification with students and makes us sympathize with the everyday "misery" of their life at school. An earlier image of the school, with its "low-grade" threats of violence, proffers the image of disease, working further on readers' sympathies.

*Jargon.* On the other side of the coin, writers can weaken reader identification by using extensive jargon. Granted, for their dissertations, writers require a vocabulary to describe their study in a specialized field. However, they need a vocabulary that also communicates. The advice here is that the writer stay alert to jargon: to distinguish between technical language meant to narrow and clarify, and language meant to signal in-group credentials. When writers employ technical language without context or definition, readers question the writer's actual understanding. An academic audience requires one to communicate accurately a study's purpose, rationale, procedures, and achievement.

Doctoral students typically do not intend to create barriers. For this reason, they need to ask non-technical friends to read their writing and identify where the language proves impenetrable or even just difficult.

*Hindrances and help in subject and verb choices.* In seeking clarity, writers attend to the words that count the most. Clearly, one's subjects and verbs have the most power to focus readers' attention.

One's choice of sentence *subjects* might seem pre-determined, as such a choice depends on one's topic. However, different levels of abstraction affect clarity. In addressing abstract concepts, writers often make these concepts the subjects of their sentences; then they complete the sentence with other abstract concepts, blocking meaning. The following sentences illustrate a common problem:

> Supervision can positively impact teacher growth.
> Coordination can positively impact leadership.
> The supervision process plays a powerful role in developing and nurturing a teacher's instructional capacity, which can contribute to students' academic success.

In each sentence, one abstraction (the sentence subject) is said to affect another abstraction (the sentence object). All of these concepts remain at the same level of abstraction, so readers have no clear idea of what the writer means.

When subjects are more concrete, the sentences become clearer. The first sentence above can be revised: *When principals observe teachers' classrooms, they can positively impact teachers' growth.* The subject of the action is now clear. The second sentence above can also be revised: *When a principal meets with teachers, their leadership deepens.* Again, the subject of the action is clear.

*Improving verb choices.* Creating more concrete subjects can spark one's choice of verbs. Writers can entertain a plethora of choices. Strong consolidating verbs not only reduce clutter but also communicate more information. What follows is a list of active verbs found in social science research, listed here to provide alternatives to the standard, generic verbs writers overuse – "have," "is," "get," – and the ubiquitous "impacts," "plays a role," "addresses," and "affects." A rough categorization follows:

> *Verbs about what researchers do:* claim, aver, asseverate, announce, stress, highlight, state, reflect, uncover, emphasize, underscore, remind, imply, suggest, indicate, announce, pronounce, detail, present, unfold,

consider, show, reveal, take into account, tell, disclose, acknowledge, admit, affirm, report, declare, divulge, evince, designate.

*Verbs about research activities*: examine, investigate, study, compare, explore, describe, review, report, probe, scrutinize, analyze, consider, evaluate, assess.

*Verbs about what the research accomplished:* found, uncovered, demonstrated, reported, reviewed, established, identified, noted, evaluated, determined.

*Verbs about subjects' or participants' actions:* responded, reflected, confirmed, iterated, described, detailed, announced, specified, stated, declared, divulged, identified, reported, remarked, noted, observed, said, conveyed, replied, revealed, emphasized, stressed.

*Verbs about findings:* indicated, designated, determined, marked, showed, revealed, affirmed, reviewed, substantiated, supported, presented, underscored, confirmed, identified, disclosed, unveiled, displayed, uncovered, offered.

*Verbs about implications:* suggests, implies, recommends, reveals, shows, entails, connotes, points to, intimates, signifies, predicts

These choices (sometimes overlapping) are listed above to promote a sense of choice. There are multitudes of others that may be even more consolidating. Writers adjust their words to refine for accuracy, simplicity, and powerfulness. While individual word choices may not be the first revision made, in the end the dissertation comes down to the words one uses.

*Final words.* The dissertation process is designed to imbue doctoral students with a sense of their own resources. Their writing and revising taps these resources – as they internalize strategies and sensitivities. Revision, at every stage, prompts new thinking and new language. Over the course of producing their work, writers may change their attitude toward the complexity of composing: They may even welcome the nonlinear, unpredictable course of writing as thinking; at the end of the road, they can see that where they started and where they ended up are radically different. No set of structures could have predicted this outcome – writers have had to trust the process. With dissertation in hand, doctoral students may better appreciate how their contribution has depended on this intensive honing of thought through revision.

Printed in Great Britain
by Amazon

37423374R00090

Following the Money

# Following the Money

## The inside story of accounting's first mega-merger

Samuel A. Cypert

## amacom

AMERICAN MANAGEMENT ASSOCIATION

This book is available at a special discount when ordered in bulk quantities. For information, contact Special Sales Department, AMACOM, a division of American Management Association, 135 West 50th Street, New York, NY 10020.

This publication is designed to provide accurate and authoritative information in regard to the subject matter covered. It is sold with the understanding that the publisher is not engaged in rendering legal, accounting, or other professional service. If legal advice or other expert assistance is required, the services of a competent professional person should be sought.

Library of Congress Cataloging-in-Publication Data

Cypert, Samuel A.
    Following the money : the inside story of accounting's first mega
-merger / by Samuel A. Cypert.
        p.    cm.
    Includes index.
    ISBN 0-8144-5002-4
    1. Klynveld Peat Marwick Goerdeler--History.  2. Peat Marwick
International--History.  3. Klynveld, Main, Goerdeler (Firm)-
-History.  4. Accounting firms--Reorganization--History.
    5. Consolidation and merger of corporations--History.   I. Title.
HF5611.C97   1991
338.8'361657--dc20                                                90-1200
                                                                     CIP

Printing Number
10 9 8 7 6 5 4 3 2 1

To the men and women of KPMG.

# Contents

# Preface

Writing a book was described by Sir Winston Churchill as a great adventure that begins as an amusement but eventually becomes a tyrant; F. Scott Fitzgerald compared the process to swimming underwater while holding your breath; and Edward Everett Tanner characterized writing a book as no harder work than digging ditches. My own observation is that while the views expressed by such noted authors are probably correct, the willingness to undertake such an onerous task is most likely the manifestation of a rather advanced form of insanity. It isn't perfectly clear to me, however, whether writing a book causes insanity or whether only a slightly daft person would take on the task.

The process I knew well, having written other books, and my own experience has been corroborated by authors I have known over the years. No one I know likes to write. It is a lonely, miserable, wrenching form of self-torture. On the other hand, every writer likes to "have written." We like the part where we wear our tweed jackets and wax wise at cocktail parties about the insight we brought to this or that story. If we didn't truly believe that we could contribute in a small way to the understanding and appreciation of a particular topic, all those lonely months of being chained to a keyboard would definitely not be worth the effort.

This book about a major and fascinating event in business

history was the brainchild of Ron Ashworth, the vice chairman of marketing and specialized industries for the U.S. practice of KPMG. A man not given to rash decisions, he read another of my books before proposing the idea of a book about our firm's merger. I didn't even have to think about the answer (which no doubt confirms the insanity observation) before responding in the affirmative. I believed then, as now, that I was given a rare opportunity to see up close the innermost workings of the world's largest professional services firm.

Ashworth helped develop the idea and sell it, and he provided encouragement and support when it was sorely needed throughout the entire process of selling, researching, and writing the book. Early on he arranged a meeting with the international marketing committee, for whom we outlined the idea. After some discussion, chairman Colin Sharman (United Kingdom), international director of marketing and communications Clarence Schmitz (on secondment from the U.S. practice, now managing partner of the Los Angeles office), and committee members Anthony Kewin (Australia), Kees van Tilburg (the Netherlands), and Dieter Lotz (West Germany) agreed to endorse the idea and present it to their respective chairmen.

One of the early supporters of the project was Caspar Broeksma, the newly merged firm's first executive partner, whose job in my view required every gram of his world-class diplomatic skills. He, too, helped sell the idea, arranged difficult meetings, patched up misunderstandings, and helped locate "nonexistent" information.

The initial reception from the chairmen was cautious. They recognized that for the book to have any appeal, it would have to tell the complete story, including—as the expression goes—the good, the bad, and the ugly. In those early days following the merger, the firms were just learning to coexist, and no one wanted to reopen old wounds. It was a delicate situation.

For my part, I figured this was the greatest challenge and biggest risk of my career. My assignment was to reconcile the interests of the national firms involved in the merger, the publisher, and the reader in a way that would result in a book that I would be proud to tell the world I had written. I wasn't at all sure it could be done.

My skepticism began to erode in the first meetings with KPMG (and U.S. firm) chairman Larry Horner. The list of people he suggested I interview included the merger's supporters, as I expected, but it also included its opponents. After I had spent some time with four of the principal architects of the merger—Horner, U.K. senior partner Jim Butler, German chairman Hans Havermann, and Netherlands senior partner Johan Steenmeijer—I was decidedly more optimistic. Perhaps it had something to do with their being auditors, whose professional careers are devoted to truth and fairness; they were candid, forthright, and committed to telling the entire story. They referred me to more supporters and opponents.

They also treated me with warmth and kindness. Horner always found time to talk to me when I needed his perspective, and he steered me through the diplomatic and cultural minefields. He was helpful and understanding even when I woke him with a phone call on a Saturday morning after he had flown home to New York on the red-eye from the West Coast.

Butler furnished a car and driver when pressing schedules made it difficult to make connections in London. And he and Hubert Thompson, senior regional partner for the U.K. firm's northwest practice, waited for me at Manchester Airport to give me a lift to the U.K. marketing conference, where I was to interview several partners.

Steenmeijer found time for me in New York, Amsterdam, and Helsinki. He also arranged for me to meet many Dutch partners who were enormously helpful in piecing together a very complicated story. I was particularly impressed with his straightforward approach to life. He is a man who says what he thinks. I like that in a person.

Havermann told me his story, introduced me to Reinhard Goerdeler, and even found the time and energy to speak to me by telephone from an inn in Germany's Black Forest, where he was recuperating from a rather serious illness. He is one of those good-natured people who somehow seem to always make you feel better for having talked to them.

I began to fully appreciate the opportunity I had been given after a delightful visit to Düsseldorf to interview Havermann and Goerdeler. Upon the conclusion of the interviews I planned to take the train to Koblenz, where I would meet Karl Graf zu Eltz, my counterpart in the German firm, who had invited me to spend the night at Burg Eltz, a 120-room castle that had been in his family for 900 years. When he learned of my destination, Goerdeler insisted on giving me a lift in his automobile. As our driver sped along the Autobahn, the gregarious Dr. Goerdeler pointed out the sights, described the postwar reconstruction period, and breathed life into German history for me. Later I learned what an important role his family had played in that history—and at what cost.

I will always remember fondly a great dinner in London with Graham Corbett, former chairman of PMI's Continental European Firm. One of the first to support the idea of a merger in Europe, he opted out after it was completed. Despite his disagreement with some of the terms of the merger and some of the people involved in it, he was ever the gentleman in describing those differences. He was delightful company and an articulate spokesman for an alternative viewpoint.

I regret that I never had the opportunity to meet former Australian senior partner Geoff Kelleher, who died suddenly during the research phase of the book. If the esteem in which he was held by his colleagues—including his successor George Bennett—is any indicator, he was a fine man and a true professional. Bennett, too, carved out time in a very busy schedule to talk to me in three different locations around the globe.

I saved retired KPMG chairman Jim Brown for last. I had worked with him on a couple of projects when he was PMI chairman and knew him to be a wonderful storyteller. I expected that he could fill in any blanks. He did so magnificently. We started over morning coffee at Canada's national office in Toronto, worked through lunch, took a break for another interview, and resumed over dinner. The transcript of his interview was several hundred pages long; throughout the writing of the book, when I desperately needed a key piece of information late on Saturday or early Sunday, I found it in Brown's transcript.

For several months I was a fixture at KPMG conferences. Wherever they were held, I was likely to be there, huddled in a corner with a tape recorder and a KPMG partner. The interviews were a challenge for the transcribers. They had to deal with countless accents, occasional colorful language, and background noise that included doors and gates slamming, airplanes droning, air conditioners humming, ice cubes tinkling, and plates and teacups clattering. On at least two occasions, through some electronic quirk, the tape recorder picked up transmissions from a local radio station and a police broadcast. Such things prompted the transcribers to offer some colorful comments of their own.

I will never forget the many kindnesses extended to me by KPMG partners and employees around the world and the great respect I developed for people who rose to the occasion when presented with a once-in-a-lifetime opportunity to do something no one else had ever done. I hope I've done justice to their story.

Samuel A. Cypert

# Acknowledgments

Although there is usually only one author's name on the book jacket, many people contribute to the creation of most nonfiction books. This one is no exception. In addition to the firm's leaders, many former and present KPMG partners and others in the profession consented to be interviewed—some more than once—answered endless telephone and telefax queries, and reviewed the manuscript before the book was published. As with most writing, decisions about what to omit were far more difficult than questions about what should be included. Hundreds of people participated in the events leading up to the merger, during the negotiations, and after the merger's conclusion. It simply was not possible to include all their stories. Nevertheless, all the information provided was useful in ensuring accuracy and completeness and in allowing me to exercise an informed editorial prerogative.

The author gratefully acknowledges the contributions of the following:

John Adcock, Giuseppe Angiolini, Ronald Ashworth, Robert Beecher, George Bennett, Lee Berton, Arnaud Bertrand, Paul Boschma, Caspar Broeksma, James Brown, James Butler, Graham Corbett, Robert Dillon, Jr., Dickin Drew, Katja Elväng, James Emerson, Reinhard Goerdeler, Sir John Grenside, Stephen Harlan, Hans Havermann, Larry Horner, Michel Janicaud,

Harald Kessler, Anthony Kewin, Ole Klette, Dieter Lotz, Alan McLintock, William Morrison, Caj Nackstad, Walter O'Connor, John Palmer, Robert Piard, Rae Scanlan, Clarence Schmitz, Gunther Schultz, Colin Sharman, Michael Speer, Johan Steenmeijer, John Thompson, Kees van Tilburg, Jan Uiterlinden, David Vaughan, and Ross Walker.

In addition, there were a good number of people who helped with logistics and schedules and who collected data, information, and photographs—usually on short notice. These included Vera Boesten, Lize Bos, Heda Chazen, Karl Graf zu Eltz, Monique de Graaf, Karen Hadeler, Eve Jacob, Robert Meade, Helen Pappas, and Timothy Roberts.

A note of thanks goes to the U.S. firm's communications professionals who handled production and design and offered good advice about the approach, style, and content: Norel Blundo, Donna Bonavita, Patrick Fisher, Suzann Futral, Ruth Langfelder, Sandra Levin, Lynn McClelland, Carol Selhorn, Claudia Stepke, and Robert Strozier.

Finally, the author especially appreciates the assistance of Denise Weber, who handled most of the typing and secretarial chores; editor Nancy Adriance, without whose help the book would not have been finished; John Higgins, who used his public relations skills to reconcile the interests of the firm and the publisher; Stephen Dietrich, who offered good counsel about how to make the book as appealing as possible; and AMACOM editors Myles Thompson and Eva Weiss, who challenged some closely held assumptions in the interest of producing a better book.

# Introduction

The once placid world of accounting firms was profoundly shaken in the spring and summer of 1989 as, in rapid succession, members of the Big Eight announced intentions to merge with each other.

Ernst & Whinney would combine with Arthur Young to form Ernst & Young, a firm that would replace KPMG as the world's largest professional services firm. KPMG, the speculation went, would retaliate by merging with Coopers & Lybrand. Deloitte Haskins & Sells would merge with Touche Ross; Price Waterhouse, the bluest of the blue bloods, announced it was courting the profession's street fighter—Arthur Andersen. The Big Eight became the Big Seven, which gave way to the Big Six and then fell to Five and Four before finally climbing back to Six and settling.

Things changed so quickly that industry observer James Emerson dumped the title of his trade paper, the *Big Eight Review,* in favor of *Emerson's Professional Services Review.* Rumors swirled through the profession—denied by one firm one day only to be confirmed by another the next.

Much of the difficulty in staying on course and presenting a united front to the media and the public lay in the organizational design of the firms themselves.

Unlike most other billion-dollar organizations, Big Eight

accounting firms are usually partnerships. To be sure, each may have thousands of partners and tens of thousands of employees, but they are, nevertheless, partnerships. To complicate the equation, many are composed of national partnerships. The leaders of the international firms may agree to merge, but it is still up to the national leaders of individual firms to decide whether they want to go along. The degree of difficulty in persuading them depends in large part on their cultures. Decentralized firms, accustomed to making their own decisions, may be perennially stubborn while centralized organizations, used to taking direction from the top, may fall into line more quickly. But the firms' partners are independent thinkers who have made careers of advising others—they are professionals who keep their own counsel.

It was precisely this attitude that led Ernst & Young's Canadian affiliate to KPMG's door two years after it left the fold and caused Deloitte Haskins & Sells' British and Dutch affiliates to defect to Coopers & Lybrand.

Most of the mergers were driven by the perceived need for an expanded global presence. *BusinessWeek* observed, "The firms with the urge to merge aren't intimidated. . . . They only see the success of KPMG Peat Marwick, where revenues have grown 44 percent, to $3.9 billion, since the 1986 merger of Peat Marwick International with Klynveld Main Goerdeler."[1]

But KPMG's experience was anything but smooth sailing. The first attempt at a merger ended in failure, and when a deal was finally stitched together, it was an agonizingly slow and painful process. In country after country the deal threatened to fall apart, held together at times only by the sheer will of its proponents.

It was a logical fit. KMG's deeply rooted continental European culture and traditions were a perfect counterbalance to PMI's Anglo-Saxon heritage. Together, they would be a formidable, global powerhouse.

---

1. David Greising, "The New Numbers Game in Accounting: A Pressing Need to Cut Costs Is Driving Six of the Big Eight to Pair Up," *BusinessWeek,* 24 July 1989, 20.

But when the deal threatened to collapse from its own weight, it was the chemistry between the five architects of the KPMG merger that held it together. That same chemistry paved the way for moving forward through the consolidation and growth that followed.

The formation of the world's largest professional services firm began with a phone call from Larry Horner, the popular chairman of PMI's U.S. firm, to Hans Havermann, the gregarious chairman of KMG's German firm.

The duo agreed that the merger was something that should happen and proposed a meeting to see if it could be arranged. They agreed to meet for dinner in Paris. They had known each other casually and professionally, and they genuinely liked each other.

Horner was different from most Americans. He understood and respected European traditions; he had in the past served as managing partner of PMI's German firm, and he has many European friends. Over dinner, Havermann and Horner spoke candidly about a merger and the difficult challenges it posed, but both agreed it was something that had to be pursued.

They gradually widened the inner circle to include the affable Englishman P. James Butler, then senior-partner-elect of PMI's U.K. firm; Johan Steenmeijer, the likable but tough head of KMG's Dutch firm; and James Brown, the highly respected former leader of PMI's Canadian firm.

The difficulties encountered in the mergers and attempted mergers that followed underscore the complexity of combining a collection of fiercely independent individual professionals from wildly varying cultural and firm backgrounds into one cohesive whole.

The accounting world had changed enormously in the thirty or so years the five had worked in it. It was no longer a "gentlemen's profession" where differences were settled civilly behind closed doors and client lists and firm revenues (or any numbers that might be used to "back into" them) were as carefully guarded as the most valuable trade secrets. The accounting world of the late 1980s was intensely competitive, a reflection of the profession's maturity, worldwide mergers and acquisitions of companies generally, and deregulation in the United States. From the accounting firms' point of view, every corporate merger meant the elimination of an audit. Growth would not come easily.

Ironically, it was Price Waterhouse—the firm that twice failed to consummate a merger amid much publicity—that set the juggernaut in motion. When its late-1984 attempt to get together with Deloitte Haskins & Sells fell apart at the eleventh hour, other large accounting firms began to consider seriously the merits of such a global capability.

The inside story of the KMG/PMI merger is a fascinating one, filled with all the drama and pathos of careers made and careers ruined by a force that, once unleashed, was unstoppable. But the merger is only the beginning of the story. The complexities of the deal and the lessons learned by the players in this high drama apply to anyone whose business life has been touched by a merger—or an attempted one. This is that story.

# Chapter One

# Following the Money

Wherever the money goes, accountants are sure to follow. The earliest accounting firms in the United States were established in the nineteenth century to look after the interests of foreign investors concerned about the risky fledgling economy. British investors in particular saw cause for concern, partly because of lingering recollections of America's Revolutionary War and also because of the nature of the businesses developing in the robust new country. In those days, foreign investment was concentrated primarily in real estate, railroads, and fire insurance companies, all considered extremely speculative under the circumstances.

Despite a reputation for being highly ethical and conservative, the first U.S. accountants were sometimes colorful characters. When John Barrow of Barrow, Wade, Guthrie & Co.[1] died in New York in 1886, he was succeeded by his assistant, Oscar Morton, who apparently decided there was little benefit to his being in partnership with the British founder of the firm, Edwin Guthrie.

---

1. Barrow, Wade, Guthrie & Co., America's first public accounting firm, was founded in 1883 and merged into Peat, Marwick, Mitchell & Co. in 1950.

When Guthrie and his assistants showed up at the New York office of the firm a few months after Barrow's death, Morton slapped a padlock on the door and refused to let them in.[2]

When Guthrie demanded to be allowed to examine the partnership books, Morton called the cops. Guthrie retaliated with a lawsuit that he eventually won, and the court-appointed receiver divided up the assets of the fractured partnership. Morton left the firm, and a trusted Guthrie partner took over the business.

Scotsman James Marwick opened his doors in New York in 1895 and quickly established a tradition of fierce independence that would characterize his firm and the profession. The corporate treasurer of his very first client, a mortgage company with deposit agencies in Scotland, refused to provide documentation for an audit of the company's balance sheet. Other company officials eventually prevailed on the treasurer to reveal the documents, and Marwick soon discovered the cause of the client's resistance. Some securities had been overvalued by about $350,000 and were being carried at cost despite a sharp drop in their market value.

The client refused to revalue the securities, and Marwick eventually appeared before the board of directors to plead his case. When the directors declined to accept Marwick's recommendation, he wrote in his audit report that not only had he pointed out the excessive overvaluation to the directors, but they had refused to do anything about it. When he presented his report, the directors reconsidered and unanimously voted to revalue the securities. Instead of firing him as auditor (as Marwick feared), many of the directors sent work to him. They admired his guts and integrity.

Those traits served him well in another early engagement. Marwick was retained to review the operations of the Fitchburg Railroad of Boston, whose directors were eager to dispel rumors of rebates and other questionable practices. The directors were delighted with the work, but Marwick created quite a stir at the

---

2. T. A. Wise, *Peat, Marwick, Mitchell & Co.—85 Years* (New York: Peat, Marwick, Mitchell & Co., 1982), 2.

company. Ten days into the audit, the internal auditor committed suicide, and the president of the company dropped dead—presumably of a heart attack—the day after Marwick presented him with the audit report. Ever precise, Marwick noted in his records that the president failed to keep an appointment with him for that morning. The directors reappointed Marwick to perform the annual audit, an engagement he continued for years.

It was during the railroad review that Marwick met Simpson Roger Mitchell, also a Scots immigrant, who ran his family's textile factory in Fitchburg, Mass. When tariff reform ruined the Mitchell operation in the United States, young Mitchell was faced with either seeking a new venture in America or returning to Scotland.

Marwick's enthusiasm about prospects for the accounting profession apparently caught Mitchell's fancy. Although he was not a chartered accountant, Mitchell was vice president and treasurer of the family business and had a good deal of business savvy. He and Marwick quickly saw the mutual benefit of joining forces.

Marwick needed a solid partner. The business had grown so much he couldn't handle it alone and continue to maintain his high standards. The two canny Scotsmen began another tradition that would long endure in the U.S. accounting profession: the inside man and the outside man.

Marwick inspired confidence in clients and liked fieldwork; Mitchell preferred supervising the office work. They were a perfect fit. They opened an office on Nassau Street in New York City on Monday morning, August 2, 1897, under the name Marwick, Mitchell & Co.

The early days of the U.S. accounting profession also set the stage for other traditions—some cordial, some antagonistic—that would characterize the profession for the next several decades. In the early professional accounting societies, American members rankled under the domination of English and Scots accountants, who considered their training and education superior to that of the

Americans. The Canadians didn't like Americans much either, preferring to deal with English accountants. The city of Winnipeg even went so far as to tell Marwick that it didn't want American accountants auditing its books and that all staff members assigned to the engagement should be British.

Competitors seized opportunities to discredit other firms with the professional societies; because of one such altercation, Marwick for years had a running feud with the predecessor of the American Institute of Certified Public Accountants.

Business prospered, despite the civilized brawling that went on as the new firms tried to outmaneuver each other. As the railroads opened up the country, accountants followed their clients, protecting their new investments. By 1910 Marwick, Mitchell & Co. boasted offices in New York, Minneapolis, Chicago, Pittsburgh, Philadelphia, Kansas City, Washington, D.C., New Orleans, Boston, and Milwaukee.

On the other side of the Atlantic, continental European financiers who provided much of the funding for the American railroads were more than a little worried about their investments. Rumors swirled and newspaper articles trumpeted stories about the excesses of American railroad barons.

After more than two decades of wheeling and dealing, graft, bribery, and corruption, "The bubble finally burst during the summer of 1872 in a scandal gigantic enough to match the stakes the railroad barons had played for."[3] The scandal came to light through the infighting of officials of the Union Pacific Railroad.

When two Union Pacific officials were unable to resolve their differences, their bickering spilled into the courtroom. What the courts—and eventually the U.S. Congress and the public—found was shocking. Close to $23 million couldn't be accounted for. Stock in the company had been given to congressmen at virtually no charge, and the scandal eventually reached the highest levels of

3. *The Railroaders,* by the editors of Time-Life Books with text by Keith Wheeler (New York: Time Inc., 1973), 78.

the U.S. government.

Indeed, much of the blame for precipitating the great financial panic of 1873 could be laid at the feet of the railroad barons.

The country and the railroads eventually recovered, but by 1890 German investors had had enough. A group of German bankers—headed by the large, prestigious Deutsche Bank—and some private bankers from Frankfurt got together to form Deutsche Treuhand-Gesellschaft (loosely translated as German Trust Company), or DTG, as it has since been known, to provide an independent opinion of the financial conditions of the railroads in which they were invested. German investors sought some sort of structure to ensure that the bonds they owned would be protected. DTG's charter was eventually expanded to include looking after the rights of all bondholders.

The combined efforts of the investors and the outcry from the American public following the railroad scandals led to a cleanup of the industry. In short order German investors were reassured, and Deutsche Bank shareholders saw no need for DTG to continue to focus on American railroads.

By the turn of the century, the bank had redirected DTG—its auditing subsidiary—to take advantage of the great opportunities it saw in Europe. Companies were expanding outside their national borders, their stocks were being traded on exchanges in financial centers in other countries, and outside auditors were needed to verify managements' reports. In addition, since universally accepted worldwide accounting standards did not exist—and still don't—a great deal of trust was placed in the public accountants; much depended on their reports.

In addition to auditing managements' financial reports, DTG accountants helped troubled companies with *umstrukturierung*— that is, reorientation, restructuring, reconstruction, Chapter 11 reorganization. By the early 1900s DTG had overcome much of the business community's initial opposition to an auditing approach based on Anglo-American practices and procedures. By

1907 the firm had more than 400 clients, including some of Germany's most prestigious companies, and was already thinking internationally.

DTG had also established itself as a firm with uncompromising standards. In an early annual report, the firm served notice that it would not bend on the issues of quality and independence, saying, "Restricting the scope of an audit merely in order to enable a reduction to be made in the fee is most inappropriate; where, in one case or another, such a suggestion has been made to the company, it has preferred not to accept the assignment."

Germany's neighbors to the west, meanwhile, were also laying the accounting profession's foundation. In fact, one of the oldest financial centers is Amsterdam, home of the world's first stock exchange, founded in 1602. At first, it was not a place for trading shares or other financial instruments; traders exchanged goods, making it literally a "stock" exchange.[4]

The city's founding date is a little less precise, but historians know that people lived there as early as 1225. The name of the city—Amestelledamme, which translates to "dam in the Amstel (river)"—first appeared in a written document in 1275.

Trade came naturally to the Dutch, an industrious people who literally created the country by draining marshland and building dikes to keep out the sea. The bustling capital city could not exist solely on crops and dairy products produced in the surrounding countryside, so it was natural that the Dutch would turn to the sea as a source of income from both the fishing industry and trade with other countries.

The Dutch thrived as traders and over time moved from active trading to investment. Foreign enterprises, particularly the English South Sea Company, princes, governments, and even the Bank of England, borrowed extensively in the republic.[5] By 1790 it was estimated that some 1,500 million guilders (the word *billion*

4. Renee Kistemaker and Roelof van Gelder, *Amsterdam* (New York: Abbeville Press, 1982), 90.
5. Kistemaker and Van Gelder, *Amsterdam*, 183–184.

didn't exist in the Dutch language at the time) were invested abroad.

There was an active market in Amsterdam for bills of exchange and letters of credit, a new financing instrument developed around 1700 for importers and exporters. Abuses followed, unethical entrepreneurs bilked the public, and crises in credit and confidence caused authorities to halt trading briefly; there were bankruptcies for many, and a few got rich, but there was little if any long-term effect on the "traders of the wind," as the locals dubbed the brokers of the day.

Amsterdam was a free and open city. The country welcomed immigrants, and Dutch businessmen traded with foreigners both on the stock exchange and abroad. The Dutch were very tolerant of other religious views and customs that didn't affect them directly. They financed guns and butter for friends and enemies alike; after all, politics was politics, and business was business.

It was against this colorful tapestry of history that Piet Klynveld opened a small accountancy practice in Amsterdam in 1917. Others involved in emerging businesses shared Klynveld's entrepreneurial spirit, and he became their accountant and grew with them.

Klynveld adapted quickly to the changing economy, offering new services that his rapidly growing clients—and client list— demanded. He established a strong working relationship with an independent tax law firm, Meijburg & Co., and hired bright young accountants capable of serving the ambitious companies that would become the business leaders of Holland and the world.

One such accountant was Jaap Kraayenhof, who became senior partner of the Dutch firm upon Klynveld's retirement. Under Kraayenhof's dynamic leadership, Klynveld Kraayenhof & Co. (KKC) developed its specialized industry approach, offering a full range of services to the banking and export industries. Fiercely independent, Kraayenhof inspired the same trait in his partners and employees. Rather than seek alliances with other accounting firms to serve Dutch clients whose operations were rapidly encircling the globe, KKC followed its clients to major financial centers in Europe and South America, eventually establishing an international network of offices that stretched from Antwerp to Argentina.

Holland's Scottish neighbors were likewise making their mark on the fledgling accounting profession. In the early days of the profession in Scotland, it was relatively easy to declare oneself an accountant and go into business, which may account for the seemingly large numbers of Scottish accountants both at home and abroad. H. Woolf, in his *Short History of Accountants and Accountancy* (1912), said, "A great deal of accountant's work was formerly in Scotland performed by solicitors (attorneys), and it is not uncommon to find the legal term 'writer' and the designation of 'accountant' applied to one and the same person. Scottish merchants were also sometimes spoken of as 'accountants,' and we also meet with instances of the latter term being used to designate those who were really teachers of bookkeeping."[6]

One such Scots accountant was Thomson McLintock, a young man of Irish descent whose ancestors reportedly went to Scotland on a cattle boat. He hung out his shingle in Glasgow in 1877 at the age of twenty-six. Despite his lack of formal accounting training, young McLintock was admitted as an associate member of the Institute of Chartered Accountants in England and Wales in 1880 at the time of its incorporation by royal charter.

Three Scottish societies of accountants were in place at the time, and, as seems typical in any formative business or profession, there was considerable bickering and infighting among the separate groups. And outsiders claimed the societies were too restrictive in their membership and created unfair competition. It wasn't until 1951 that the three societies combined to form The Institute of Chartered Accountants of Scotland.

---

6. Rex Winsbury, *Thomson McLintock & Co.—The First Hundred Years* (London: Thomson McLintock & Co., 1977), 12.

Like his Dutch, German, and American counterparts, McLintock followed his clients' investments. Thomson McLintock was a family business; four generations would work in it before it became part of the KPMG family. McLintock took advantage of business opportunities wherever they appeared. His daughter, Jean, married Norman Sinclair of Robert Sinclair & Co., tobacco merchants of Newcastle Upon Tyne; the company's accounts and the family's financial affairs were handled by the McLintock firm.

Another daughter, Mary, married William Fraser, who was to become the first Lord Strathalmond and who was manager of Pumpherston Oil Company at the time McLintock was a director and chairman of that company. This was to become a very important connection since Pumpherston developed, via Scottish Shale Oil, into a part of British Petroleum Company.

McLintock, though an austere, proper Victorian accountant, preferred practicality to theory. He was called upon to sell the assets of a failed grocery business, but instead of dumping the inventory at discounted prices—as was the custom at the time—he opened the store, rolled up his sleeves, and sold groceries. Creditors were so pleased with McLintock's performance (and their higher-than-expected return) that when any were involved in other bankruptcies, they insisted he be named trustee.

The McLintock name became well known and respected in the United Kingdom, and by 1910 Thomson McLintock had achieved such success that he was able to delegate much of the day-to-day operation of the firm to his sons. The firm's reputation attracted as clients a variety of Scottish companies and U.K. companies that grew into major groups, such as Associated British Foods, ICI, and Grand Metropolitan. As these clients grew and expanded their operations, Thomson McLintock followed. By the early 1960s it was apparent that the firm would have to "go international" if it was to keep pace with its clients.

In London, meanwhile, another Scottish "accountant" set out

to make his mark in the world. Actually, William Barclay Peat, like many of his contemporaries, wasn't an accountant at all when he began in the profession. The son of James Peat and Margaret Barclay (of the banking family), W. B. Peat studied law in Scotland and upon graduation from Montrose Academy became an indentured apprentice to a lawyer in Montrose. Records indicate he apparently never qualified for the bar, and he moved to London in 1870 at the age of seventeen. This was an unusual move at the time since Scots law didn't apply in England. No one knows why he made the move or why he decided to shift from law to accounting.

Nevertheless, he apparently used some family connections to get an interview with a prominent accounting firm in London, where he secured a position as a junior accounting clerk. Young Peat rose rapidly through the ranks. He earned the respect of his clients and the senior partner of the firm. Five years after joining the firm, Peat journeyed to Middlesbrough to investigate the financial affairs of the municipality. Ever alert to opportunity, he quickly spotted potential in the iron and steel business there, and he sought permission to open an office.

At twenty-four years of age, he was made a partner in the firm and put in charge of its Middlesbrough office. The retirement and death of the firm's senior partners put Peat in a difficult spot in 1891. To keep the firm alive, he would have to move to London, assume responsibility for the debts of the partnership, and take over the leadership of the firm. Peat visited the firm's creditors, promising them that if they would give him the time and support he needed, he would pay off the firm's debts. They did, and he did.

His integrity and honesty were traits that would pay dividends years later. One of the firm's creditors was an investment banker who was a trusted adviser to King Edward VII. When the monarch asked for a recommendation for a good and reliable accountant to handle the accounts of the Privy Purse, the investment banker sent him to Peat, who handled it "with such discretion that few knew the identity of the auditor of the Privy Purse."[7]

Peat was so discreet, in fact, that when called as a witness in an early-1900s lawsuit in New York, he declined to identify his clients or reveal why he had been knighted. He testified that he was the chartered accountant for some ten banks and twice as many railroads in England and that his firm had twenty-five offices around the world. When asked why he had been knighted, Peat replied, "They just went along and did it."

W. B. Peat met James Marwick aboard a luxury liner during an Atlantic crossing in 1911. Peat was traveling to the United States on business; Marwick was returning to the home office to report on the opening of an office in Paris and on negotiations with another accounting firm to serve as its representative in America. The two Scots knew of each other, but it isn't certain whether they had actually met before this time. In any event, they liked each other, and before the journey was over had struck a deal to merge.

The agreement would help Peat's firm expand into America and strengthen Marwick's operations in the United Kingdom. Both expected the relationship to help them expand on the European continent. They inked the agreement on October 1, 1911.

The accounting profession's pioneers had established an underpinning of traditions that would endure well into the next century. In addition to their integrity, discretion, and hard work, turn-of-the-century accountants also established a tradition of pushing out frontiers and looking after the financial interests of their clients as they boldly explored new worlds. The foundation firmly in place, Peat, Marwick, Mitchell & Co. went on to expand into a multimillion-dollar organization through a series of mergers with firms throughout the world.

It seemed logical to Larry D. Horner in 1984, when he assumed the chairmanship of Peat, Marwick, Mitchell & Co. in the United States, that the firm should look to the world's shifting financial centers for growth and—in the tradition of the profession—follow

---

7. Wise, *Peat, Marwick, Mitchell & Co.—85 Years*, 15–16.

the money. Horner had a unique perspective for an American. He was raised in the Midwest, worked on both coasts, served as senior partner for the firm's operations in West Germany, married a German, and traveled the world. His vision for the global organization he would one day head was a business without borders—a collection of strong national firms, each firmly grounded in its own country but linked by people and technology and each with a commitment to its own firm and the international organization.

Peat Marwick International (PMI) had, for more than a decade, studied the implications of a rapidly changing world. Its long-range planning committee, under the chairmanship of Gordon Cowperthwaite, issued a report in March 1977 that recommended studying national and international socioeconomic trends in order to "have a chance of anticipating change rather than being surprised by it."

The report also stated, "We need to give intense thought to the shape and structure of the international firm—how best to look national locally and multinational everywhere else. We need to focus on our geographical coverage and the responsiveness of our own structure to change in geographical groupings around the world. The crisis of public confidence in the accounting profession, certainly in the United States and the United Kingdom, means that the firm needs to take a major initiative in establishing its own leadership role independently of the standing of the profession as a whole. If we neglect any of the foregoing, or regard them as of secondary importance, our competitors are likely to remind us—too late."

The committee's words proved to be prophetic. By the late 1980s the U.S. Department of Commerce, which studies such things, reported that direct investment in the United States had ballooned 5,000 percent in the previous quarter century. U.S. multinationals, which in the mid-1970s accounted for half the world's direct investment, were at 40 percent and dropping fast a decade and a half later, not because American companies had slowed investment activity, but because European and Japanese companies increased theirs. The pie just got bigger.

Across the Atlantic, the top partners of Deutsche Treuhand-Gesellschaft (Reinhard Goerdeler and Hans Havermann) and of Klynveld Kraayenhof & Co. (Geert Timmer, Jan Uiterlinden, and Johan Steenmeijer) and other KMG leaders were headed in the same direction. The formation of KMG (Klynveld Main Goerdeler) was a major event on the world accounting scene in 1979. In an unprecedented international grouping, DTG, KKC, and several other large national accounting firms joined to form an international firm that would be preeminent in Europe.

KMG, comparable in size to the Anglo-American Big Eight, was the result of a collection of prestigious national names. Big Eight firms, on the other hand, gained their size through the coming together of large British and U.S. firms that expanded through the world either by opening their own offices or linking with leading local firms.

In the mid-1980s KMG engaged the respected strategic consulting firm of McKinsey & Co. to gaze into its crystal ball and predict KMG's future. Specifically, KMG leadership was interested in its prospects for "going it alone" in an increasingly global economy.

McKinsey team members met with KMG leaders and studied the situation for three or four months. What they found was a loosely knit collection of national firms held together primarily through a *verein,* a Swiss not-for-profit entity whose primary asset was the KMG logotype, which it licensed to national practices for their use. These practices were so fiercely independent, in fact, that the largest accounting firm headquartered outside the United States did not have a formal international business plan. That had to change, McKinsey believed, if KMG planned to continue as a major player in the global arena.

McKinsey specifically noted the need for KMG to enhance its

image in the U.S. financial community. Their interviews during the course of the engagement led McKinsey to conclude that Wall Street investment bankers often steered international clients wishing to raise financing away from Main Hurdman, KMG's U.S. affiliate.

The consultants recommended that KMG form a small, high-caliber team of partners (possibly including a European partner) to improve relations with Wall Street. The team would be in charge of sales and marketing for international Securities and Exchange Commission work and should, with the support of senior partners of the firm, launch an intensive, targeted marketing program focused on key investment banks and institutional investors as well as others who influence purchasers of accounting services, such as large commercial banks and law firms.

Partners in the national firms interpreted the recommendations to mean a larger contribution to a central budget, but in general they seemed willing to accept such an assessment for the greater good of the firm.

It appeared that despite differences in organizational structure and operating philosophies, KMG—with its strong European presence and traditions—and PMI—with its Anglo-American roots and strength—were pursuing the same strategy: following the money.

# Chapter Two

# Failed Negotiations

The year 1984 was a milestone in the accounting profession. It was the first time two major accounting firms attempted a mega-merger. Their efforts to vault over the competition sparked a battle for supremacy that inspired one wag to note that 1984 was the year the profession officially traded its gentlemen's evening gloves for boxing gloves.

The accounting industry had become increasingly competitive since being effectively deregulated in the late 1970s. The Federal Trade Commission put pressure on the American Institute of Certified Public Accountants, which removed prohibitions against advertising and direct solicitation. Accounting firms flexed their newfound marketing muscles by dabbling in advertising and mounting active and sometimes aggressive public relations and direct marketing campaigns.

In truth, accounting partners had already become very good salespeople. They might not have recognized the terminology, but they knew how to identify and qualify prospects, generate sales leads, and make effective sales presentations. They belonged to all the right clubs, mixed with the right people, and had incomes already well into the six figures at an age when their contemporaries in other lines of business were just beginning to make their marks.

The allure of marketing gradually faded. Well-capitalized firms in the Big Eight could quickly check each other's moves; no one firm was really prepared to significantly outspend the others, and the firms learned quickly they could burn a lot of money with an aggressive advertising campaign. The new marketing freedom, while offering important advantages, wasn't the high-octane fuel that would propel the firms to dizzying heights. Growth would still be slow and laborious.

With mergers and acquisitions going on among large corporations, the pool of potential new clients was shrinking. When one Fortune 500 company acquired another, the net effect to accounting firms was the loss of an audit and the fees it generated. Big Eight accounting firms, heretofore interested mostly in public companies—the bluer the chip, the better—turned their attention to smaller and emerging companies that had been served by local or regional accounting firms. Young audit partners dreamed of discovering the next Polaroid or Xerox. The tale of the partner who was invited to Edwin Land's home one Sunday afternoon to discuss his revolutionary photographic process and the accounting and consulting needs of his company became part of the professional lore about how to be the sole-source supplier of services to growth companies. The firms and the profession studied trend analysis and developed techniques for identifying startup companies with the best chances for rapid growth. They targeted companies on a variety of lists: *Forbes'* "Up and Comers," *Inc.*'s "100," and the NASDAQ (National Association of Securities Dealers Automated Quotations) "100 Growth Companies" and "100 Profit Companies." Accounting partners developed relationships with bankers, lawyers, venture capitalists, and any other referral source imaginable.

The bubble didn't exactly burst; rather, it drifted away. From the early 1980s—when high technology industries matured—to the late 1980s—when junk bonds lost their seductive charm—the world changed. Middle market clients still account for a huge percentage of KPMG's business, and the firm has thousands of professionals dedicated to serving middle market companies. But such practices now more realistically expect the slow, steady growth that characterizes more mature industries. By the late 1980s the middle market's "go-go" days met reality, but back in 1984 the market's stars shone brightly. "It is in the middle market that the 'great bulk of demand' for new services exists," John A. Thompson, chairman of KMG's U.S. affiliate, Main Hurdman, told the *New York Times* in 1984.[1]

Thompson's comments were aimed at putting into perspective an event that had just rocked the profession: Price Waterhouse, the fourth largest U.S. firm, and Deloitte Haskins & Sells, the eighth largest, announced that they planned to merge. Mergers were a regular occurrence, but this one was different. PW/DH&S would be a worldwide partnership of 50,000 people with revenues of almost $2 billion. The size of the proposed firm frightened smaller competitors and concerned regulators. Most of the accounting profession was stunned by the news; Rep. John D. Dingell, Jr. (D-Mich.), head of the Oversight and Investigations Subcommittee of the House Committee on Energy and Commerce, called for an antitrust review of the merger and scheduled hearings on the accounting profession.

What irritated the other large accounting firms—PMI and KMG in particular—was that PW and DH&S had apparently beaten them out of the gate. For several years PMI and KMG had independently studied the futures of their firms and the potential for exactly such a mega-merger. To have competitors get the jump

---

1. Gary Klott, "Merger Moves in Accounting," *New York Times*, 3 October 1984, D1.

on them was annoying.

To the great relief of many in the profession (some PW and DH&S partners among them), the deal fell apart less than three months after it was announced. The chairmen of the two firms' international organizations said in a joint statement that "the merger discussions were terminated largely because mutually acceptable arrangements could not be established in certain countries."

In a "Stop Press" insert expanding on the two firms' problems, the *International Accounting Bulletin* (IAB) speculated, "The U.K. practice of Price Waterhouse is strongly rumored to be in the forefront of those rebelling against the proposals, which were first mooted at the highest levels of the firms in the U.S. 'It was, and always was, a very difficult thing to do,' a PW London partner said. 'There were doubts about whether it was possible right from the start.' "

IAB went on to say that Australia also was "tipped to have vetoed the merger," but that the United States, where the merger "would have made the most strategic sense, is believed to have supported the proposals."[2]

The failure of PW and DH&S to consummate a merger served as an ominous warning to others about the difficulties of combining large, culturally diverse professional services organizations. But it also brought home the realization that the world was changing rapidly. Firms that had been cautiously exploring merger opportunities realized time had become a luxury. Merger efforts had to be speeded up.

KMG knew it had problems. Its organization worked well in countries where national firms were strong, but little centralized management and authority gave few options to the firm's international leaders when major problems arose. KMG's U.S. affiliate, Main Hurdman, was particularly weak compared with its compet-

---

2. "Price Waterhouse/Deloitte Haskins & Sells Merger Scrapped," *International Accounting Bulletin* (December 1984), "Stop Press" insert.

itors. Main Hurdman's clients were primarily midsize, although it did boast the giant Union Carbide and CPC International in the United States and could point to such blue bloods as Philips, Daimler-Benz, BMW, Grumman, and Pfizer, which KMG's European firms numbered among their clients. Yet, with a ninth-place ranking in the United States, revenues of $234 million, and 86 offices that averaged 35 professionals each, Main Hurdman was scarcely able to impress the giant multinationals.

KMG's leadership had for some time explored its options. The ferocity of U.S. competition precluded taking large market shares away from other firms, so about the only route to substantial growth was through mergers and acquisitions. Main Hurdman was no stranger to mergers, having been built through a merger, most notably between Main Lafrentz and Hurdman and Cranstoun. Only recently the firm had failed in an attempt to merge with Alexander Grant & Co., the tenth largest firm in the United States. Main Hurdman was in a position that required decisive action.

In addition, clients outside the United States were restless and were pressing for better U.S. representation. And in the wave of litigation that swept the accounting profession, Main Hurdman had more than its share of lawsuits. Several problems in California had brought on a rash of inquiries by state officials, and although it wasn't widely known in the profession, Main Hurdman had problems with the Securities and Exchange Commission regarding the firm's audits of the First National Bank of Midland, Texas, and Houston-based Time Energy Systems.[3] Main Hurdman needed a merger, and KMG's leadership let it be known in the profession that it was available.

According to Lee Berton, the reporter who covers accounting for the*Wall Street Journal,* "KMG Main Hurdman has been discussing a possible merger with every major accounting firm

---

3. Eric N. Berg, "S.E.C. Assails Main Hurdman," *New York Times* , 26 March 1987, D5.

except Arthur Young & Co. and Price Waterhouse over the past year. And [accounting profession officials] say that a marriage for KMG Main Hurdman may be more a necessity than a convenience."

"KMG Main Hurdman must boost its U.S. marketing clout or it could be left in the lurch as competition continues to increase among U.S. accounting firms," said James C. Emerson, publisher of the *Big Eight Review* (now known as *Emerson's Professional Services Review)*, an accounting firm newsletter based in Bellevue, Wash.

Added Berton, "While all eight major firms generate at least half their revenue in the U.S., KMG Main Hurdman's international organization, Klynveld Main Goerdeler, based in the Netherlands, gets only 23% of its revenue here."[4]

Industry sources speculated that Main Hurdman's slow growth rate, coupled with aggressive competitors snapping at its heels, was posing big problems for the firm, not only because it was losing ground to competitors, but also because international executives were unhappy with Main Hurdman's performance.

Not true, said Campbell E. Corfe, director of international services of Main Hurdman. "We're growing very rapidly in the U.S., with some of our strengths in health care, government services and small business," Corfe told the *Wall Street Journal's* Berton. Corfe noted that over the previous two months the firm gained as clients Healthtext, Inc., Raymond International Inc., Ronson Co., and New York City, adding, "We have extremely strong marketing positions in some of the Midwest and Mid-Atlantic states." Said Berton, "But officials at other U.S. accounting firms say that top executives of Klynveld Main Goerdeler in Europe are unhappy that KMG Main Hurdman doesn't have a stronger U.S. marketing position."[5]

While some KMG European partners were troubled about Main

---

4. Lee Berton, "KMG Main Hurdman's Merger Interest May Portend a Marriage of Necessity," *Wall Street Journal*, 24 September 1985, 1.

5. Ibid.

Hurdman's competitive position relative to the Big Eight in the United States, similar problems were beginning to surface in Japan. For several years prior to the 1985 merger discussions, Seichi Nishitani, executive partner of Sanwa Audit Corporation, KMG's member firm in Japan, and Anthony Kewin, KMG's regional chairman, had pursued merger opportunities with several Japanese firms in an attempt to bolster the firm's presence in that country. Most of those discussions were fruitless because of KMG's weakness in the U.S. market, which the Japanese considered essential to the success of any worldwide merger. When they learned of a potential KMG/PMI merger, Nishitani and his firm voiced their enthusiastic support.

When the combination failed to materialize, Sanwa found itself in a difficult position. For some time the Japanese Ministry of Finance had been attempting to reorganize the country's accounting profession into five strong firms and had been actively encouraging mergers between Japanese accounting firms. Nishitani worried that if he could not get Sanwa involved in one of the merger discussions, his firm would be left out in the cold. It would not become one of the Big Five. As 1985 drew to a close, Sanwa notified KMG that it was in merger discussions with Tohmatsu Awoki & Co. The seriousness of the situation was not lost on KMG and figured prominently in its deliberations as the firm considered its options. (Sanwa and Tohmatsu announced their intention to merge in April of the following year with an effective date of October 1, 1986.)

In other parts of eastern Asia, KMG worked closely with the SGV Group, which, with 3,500 people, was the largest accounting and consulting firm in Asia. The goodwill between the two firms was originally based on a close personal relationship between KMG chairman Reinhard Goerdeler and international executive Jan Uiterlinden and SGV founder Washington SyCip. The relationship was so strong, in fact, that Kewin, KMG's senior representative in the region, attended SGV's executive committee meetings.

It was an important connection. SyCip was a charismatic leader who was well known in the profession, and his contacts in industry ensured that most of the accounting work in the region was performed by SGV regardless of which firm did the parent company work. Many of the Big Eight were represented in one country or another by SGV. The firm had a strong—many said preeminent—market position in several Asian countries, including Thailand, Malaysia, Singapore, the Philippines, Korea, Hong Kong, Taiwan, and Indonesia.

Shock waves from the Price Waterhouse and Deloitte Haskins & Sells merger talks reached around the accounting world, and many of the larger firms seized the opportunity to take a run at SGV. Eventually, most SGV firms joined Arthur Andersen, but Malaysia and Korea joined DH&S, and Hong Kong stayed with KMG. The fracturing of SGV in 1985, however, required KMG to change almost all of its national practices in the region. It was another series of events that had a profound influence on the KMG leadership.

Nobody knew for sure at the time what would happen, but critics and supporters alike acknowledged that a KMG/PMI alliance made good sense. In virtually every location where KMG was strong, PMI was weak, and vice versa. The synergy would be remarkable. There were problems, of course. Compensation was an issue. PMI partners were better paid than their KMG counterparts in several countries, and in the United States partner-to-staff ratios (the formula that firms use to determine their effectiveness in delegating work to the lowest possible level without affecting quality and an indicator of management costs) were seriously out of balance. Peat Marwick's ratio was 1 partner for every 7.9 staff members, while the ratio for Main Hurdman was 1 partner for every 5.7 staff members. Main Hurdman's cost of doing business was considerably higher and profits commensurately lower.

These were not insurmountable problems, PMI leaders

believed. While PMI may not have been quite as eager for a merger as KMG, it nevertheless needed to strengthen its European presence. Since the 1970s PMI's senior partners had studied their options, and they were generally divided between those who believed it might be possible to meet growth goals in Europe by aggressive practice development (a dwindling minority) and those who saw a merger as the only viable option.

PMI particularly wished to expand its presence in West Germany, where it already had good people and strong leadership but needed to grow beyond a business base largely composed of German affiliates of U.S.-headquartered companies. In large measure, PMI's German operation, like many of its Continental firms, was viewed by most Germans as Americanized.

During the 1970s, before the founding of KMG, PMI was principally interested in acquiring or merging with two German firms: Deutsche Treuhand-Gesellschaft (DTG) and Treuarbeit, by any measure the two largest firms in West Germany. Both were corporations, as was the custom of the country. DTG had been founded by the large Deutsche Bank, which still owned some stock in it; Treuarbeit was totally owned by agencies of the German government and various German states.

Through a professional society known as the International Federation of Accountants (IFAC), several PMI partners had met Goerdeler, president of the group and chairman of DTG; both he and DTG international contact partner Hans Havermann were approached to test their interest in a PMI/DTG combination. Meanwhile, several other PMI partners began sending out feelers to their contacts at Treuarbeit.

Although a merger with either would be a major coup in West Germany, second-largest DTG seemed to be the better firm. PMI had a strong contact with Havermann through Joe Cummings, PMI's international contact partner and deputy chairman of the U.S. firm from 1972 until 1978. Havermann and Cummings had served together on the International Accounting Standards Committee and had talked at times about the possibility of some sort of combination. Treuarbeit also had a lot going for it. For one, Treuarbeit audited Volkswagen, which was experiencing phenomenal marketing success in the United States at the time.

PMI pursued both firms on and off throughout the 1970s. And Larry Horner, during his tenure as managing partner of the German firm, had secured approval to engineer a merger. By June 1976 outgoing Continental European Firm senior partner William Mecklenburg and his successor, P. Graham Corbett, agreed that a merger was necessary in West Germany. In the ten preceding years, German industrial companies had grown significantly and had become important investors in the United States, South America, the Middle East, and central Africa. PMI senior partners were convinced that even if PMI were successful in securing a few large German companies as clients (a highly unlikely possibility), the firm would draw the ire of professional societies and regulators alike. The clients themselves would be under enormous pressure from German-headquartered firms to deal with German accounting firms. A full and complete merger seemed the preferable course.

PMI stepped up its activities. Canadian senior partner Gordon Cowperthwaite and U.S. senior partner Walter Hanson flew to West Germany in August 1976 to meet with Goerdeler of DTG and Karl Heinz-Forster of Treuarbeit. The meetings went well with both firms, but much later, over dinner in London with Cummings, Havermann got the impression that Hanson had unilaterally made the decision to cut a deal with Treuarbeit. The allure of Volkswagen was too strong.

Despite great optimism at the outset, by March of the following year PMI's hopes for a full merger had been reduced to a working agreement with Treuarbeit that appointed PMI as the sole representative of the German firm in North America. The announcement of the agreement carried a small note of hope, promising that this was "an interim understanding until such time as the parties are in a position to enter into a broader agreement affecting other parts of the world."

The PMI/Treuarbeit agreement eventually fell apart, and DTG went on to become a founding member of KMG on September 1, 1979.

Despite a rather rocky start, by the mid-1980s KMG had consolidated its operations and was once again thinking about options for expansion. The Price Waterhouse/Deloitte Haskins & Sells situation provided a sense of urgency. In September 1984 KMG had scheduled its annual meeting in Copenhagen. The resort's amenities and location—described as "marvelous" by the attendees—matched the tenor of the meeting. The five-year-old affiliation was working well, people were happy, and the mood was decidedly upbeat. Not even the gloomy weather could dampen the spirits of KMG partners gathered to socialize and exchange business leads and tips with their fellow partners from around the world.

In the executive committee meetings, however, the mood was a little more restrained. Chairman Goerdeler told the assembled group, "The accounting profession is now being led by Price Waterhouse and Deloitte Haskins & Sells, much as a conductor leads an orchestra. We are being managed by events. We must take charge of our own affairs." Havermann spoke up. "If we don't assume an active posture, if we don't start contacting other international accounting firms to discuss merger opportunities, we may well find ourselves standing on the platform after the last train has left."

By the end of the conference, KMG leaders had concluded that the timing was right to consider a merger. They would go out and contact their friends in other accounting firms to test their receptiveness. Word spread quickly; several senior PMI partners reported KMG contacts.

PMI's Cowperthwaite succeeded KMG's Goerdeler as chairman of the IFAC. They had gotten to know each other well through their involvement in the IFAC and would often stay in each other's homes when travel schedules permitted. Despite their cordial relationship, the KMG/PMI contact was made rather indirectly. At an IFAC meeting in the Philippines, Cowperthwaite was approached by a KMG partner from the United Kingdom whom he knew slightly. They exchanged pleasantries; during their short conversation, the British partner let Cowperthwaite know that if PMI were interested, KMG might be "ripe to consider a merger." Cowperthwaite promptly phoned Stanley Klion, executive vice chairman of PMI, who in turn notified Corbett in Continental European Firm (CEF) headquarters.

In October 1984, a little more than a month after KMG's annual meeting in Copenhagen, PMI's U.S. partners held their annual meeting in Florida at the Boca Raton Hotel and Club. In keeping with tradition, several international partners were invited; the firm also used the occasion to schedule meetings of its U.S. board of directors and the PMI executive committee. The people were already there, so it made good business sense, though it did generate a certain amount of pressure on the senior partners who were required to attend marathon meetings.

The schedule was even more hectic than usual since politics was the order of the day in the States. A new chairman and deputy chairman would be elected at that meeting. There had been three candidates for chairman—Horner, far western regional vice chairman; Dudley C. Mecum, New York office managing partner; and Donald R. Sloan, deputy chairman. After a primary campaign of sorts, the board chose Horner as its candidate —who then chose Robert W. Beecher as his deputy chairman—and the two ran unopposed. Beecher, a lanky Bostonian with a calculator-like facility with numbers, was northeast regional vice chairman. (In accounting partnerships, senior partners who run unsuccessfully for chairman typically resign. Mecum went on to become director and group vice president of Combustion Engineering, Inc., in Connecticut. Sloan became a private investor, acquiring two companies: C. B. Forms, a printing company in Missouri, and Telacast, Inc., a Texas company that provides point-of-sale advertising.)

At the PMI executive committee meeting following the election, much of the discussion centered on merger talk in the profession. There was a good deal of speculation and concern about the Price Waterhouse and Deloitte Haskins & Sells merger discussions. At that point, the outcome was anyone's guess. Among the group, it was pretty widely known that KMG had already been approached by many of the Big Eight. Corbett, head of the CEF, was particularly concerned. "If KMG gets together with Arthur Andersen, which is already very successful in Europe, the combination will absolutely slaughter the rest of us."

That night in the bar a spirited discussion took place among the PMI senior partners, and most agreed the merger should not be pursued. The next day, in the cold light of day, Horner used his formidable persuasion skills to bring them around. They would explore merger possibilities.

By the end of the meeting, it had been agreed that Corbett would contact KMG executive partner Paul Boschma at his Amsterdam headquarters. They knew each other reasonably well and liked each other. Never one to waste time in idle speculation, Corbett phoned Boschma and asked for a "purely exploratory session" to see if there might be interest on either part in pursuing a merger. They scheduled a dinner in Amsterdam for mid-November.

Things went well—far better, in fact, than either had hoped. Early in the discussion they realized the two firms fit extraordinarily well, both geographically and by specialized industry practices. PMI was very strong in banking and finance. KMG firms, particularly the Dutch and German, were strong in manufacturing with clients like Philips, Siemens, BMW, and Daimler-Benz.

There were tremendous opportunities for the firms to refer work to one another. The Philips work alone was enough to get PMI's attention.

Corbett and Boschma frankly discussed the situation in continental Europe. Both recognized the problems inherent in trying to combine the PMI organization—which encompassed the whole of continental Europe and in which all partners participated in the profits—and the KMG organization, which was divided along national borders. The deal would not work if it appeared to either firm that it was being taken over by the other. They would create an entirely new firm—one that would be neither KMG nor PMI—with a completely new international structure that would draw upon the considerable, but different, strengths of each.

They also agreed that if the structure was going to work, it would need to assume the attributes of a professional partnership. This approach could be a bit sticky at KMG, which had several important national practices organized as corporations, but dinner went well, the brandy was good, and the mood was jocular. By the time they bid good-night to each other, Corbett recalled, "We really believed we'd invented the world."

Each reported back to his executive committee on their singular success. Both believed the firms should begin serious negotiations.

A major meeting between representatives of the two firms was scheduled for January 5, 1985, at the Ritz Hotel in Paris. By this time, a code name had been given to the project. It was dubbed Smith-Brown, with KMG known as Smith, PMI as Brown. Remembering which was which was made slightly easier by the fact that PMI's chairman-elect was James R. Brown, senior partner of the Canadian firm. The code name wasn't selected to coincide with Brown's surname; it was sheer happenstance, but it did, nevertheless, help keep things straight in confusing meetings.

Eight representatives of each firm attended the Paris meeting, which was hosted by Corbett. The representatives were (from

KMG) Reinhard Goerdeler, chairman of KMG; John Thompson, president of KMG and chairman and CEO of the U.S. firm; Paul Boschma, international executive of KMG; Hans Havermann, international contact partner of the German firm; Anthony Kewin, international partner of the Australian firm; William Morrison, executive partner of the U.K. firm; John Palmer, executive partner of the Canadian firm; Johan Steenmeijer, chairman of the Dutch firm's executive committee; (and from PMI) Thomas Holton, chairman of PMI; Larry Horner, chairman and CEO of the U.S. firm; Sir John Grenside, senior partner of the U.K. firm and former chairman of PMI; James Brown, chairman of the executive committee of the Canadian firm; Geoff Kelleher, senior partner of the Australian firm; Dieter Lotz, senior partner of the German firm; P. James Butler, deputy chairman of the U.K. firm; and Stanley Klion, PMI's executive vice chairman.

PMI had scheduled a meeting for December 7, 1984, in London to discuss some of the sensitive issues the firm needed to address before the joint meeting with KMG. The firm's leaders knew one of the touchiest subjects would be the situation in continental Europe. The CEF partners resented what they called "reactionary reluctance" on the part of the international firm to allow them equal standing in PMI. Because other national practices had invested significantly in the CEF before it became profitable, the investors (primarily the U.S. and U.K. firms) expected a reasonable return on this investment. CEF partners thought they had contributed enough.

The situation was complicated by the fact that senior partner Corbett's management style, in keeping with the tradition of the CEF, was to heavily involve the partners in all major decisions. It was a democracy in a situation that called for a benevolent dictatorship.

Corbett tried to put the CEF partners' feelings in perspective for the PMI leaders:

A desire to see a return on investment is understandable on the part of those who made the investment, but by now I believe they ought to be fully satisfied. The majority of the current recipients have made no financial contribution to the Continental European Firm. We clearly need to have a source of funding for new ventures or for practices in financial difficulties. The historical accident that lands many (but by no means all) of these issues on the plates of the U.S. and/or U.K. firms is no substitute for an effective PMI structure that recognizes the responsibility that *all* PMI partners have for such activities. The time is past for us to continue to hide behind formulas about "contractual arrangements among member firms." PMI has a vital interest in ensuring that historical structures do not hinder future development. The U.S. and U.K. firms are uniquely able to show real leadership in demonstrating that they understand this. Why don't we seize the opportunity to make dynamic and farsighted changes for the future, rather than apply iodine to the wounds left over from the past?

Despite Corbett's impassioned plea, many of the issues remained unresolved as the January 5, 1985, meeting date drew near. Both firms, despite their separate interests, turned their attention to the joint meeting agenda. Neither side wanted to appear to be trying to dominate the meeting, yet each wished to make sure the important issues were discussed. It was a delicate situation that required circulating several drafts of the agenda before it was finally published. It was ambitious in its scope. Topics to be covered were:

- *Strategic objectives,* including geographic coverage, national/"supernational" image, service capability, growth, and profitability.

- *Image and culture-related issues.* Smith's side (KMG) was particularly interested in national identity and the name of the merged firm; Brown (PMI) was concerned with worldwide professional standards. Both wished to discuss operating autonomy, international identity, and the organizational structure of the merged firm.

- *Business issues,* including expected reaction from clients, the business and financial communities, and governmental and regulatory authorities; internal reactions from partners and staff; personnel issues; and synergistic opportunities (referrals, complementary skills and resources, and new business development opportunities). Also of interest were potential client losses from conflicts of interest, disaffection, forms of association (total integration versus corporate agreements), whether structures should be the same in every country, immediate implementation versus a step-by-step approach, recognition that total integration would effectively call for the absorption of the less powerful by the more powerful firm in each country and the implications thereof, international financing, and the possible need for an international fund for problem areas.

- *Information needs,* including the timing for items requested; national operating information, such as numbers of partners and staff, chargeable hours, and fee volume; nature of ownership interests, including equity (if any) held by nonpartners; partner income; client profiles; and client lists.

- *Other matters.* The last point on the agenda was to make arrangements for further discussions and who would be involved in them, deadlines, reporting relationships, and the process for identifying and focusing on major problem areas.

The agenda remained in flux until the meeting date. When the participants arrived at the hotel, they received a memo from Corbett about details of the meeting along with the revised agenda. The meeting would be held in the Psyche Room on the ground floor of the hotel with a buffet dinner for the two groups in the Louis XV Room. Day one would be primarily a *tour d'hori- zon* of why the firms were interested in the discussions, the bene- fits that each saw in such an association, and the internal and external reactions that needed to be taken into account in consid- ering such a merger. The first evening would be structured to allow each group time to reflect separately on the matters dis- cussed that day.

Things had progressed to where more information was needed; operating statistics arrived by courier, and the final agenda included new information needs such as professional literature, standards of professional performance, retirement ages, pension rights and funding, pending litigation, and professional indemnity insurance arrangements. The agenda concluded with a footnote that "all of these items are likely to be needed for global discus- sions in a later stage, as will detailed financial information for those responsible for working out details on a country-by-country basis."

Nothing was left to chance. Even dinner seating arrangements had been made in advance to make sure each participant had an opportunity to socialize with his counterpart from the other firm.

By all accounts the meeting progressed remarkably smoothly. The agenda was handled with dispatch, a joint steering committee was appointed by the group to oversee the process, task forces were assigned to further study major issues, and the meeting concluded amid high optimism.

Areas requiring further study centered primarily on compensa- tion issues, the organizational structure and management of the firm (continental Europe in particular), international auditing standards, partner protection, and, of course, what the new firm would be named.

Over the next several months, task forces met, studied their options, and reported back to the joint steering committee. The deeper they looked, the more the merger made sense. KMG had some very strong national firms, while PMI was effective in coordinating client services internationally; both had a strong audit base; PMI's tax and consulting practices would fit nicely with KMG, especially considering PMI's ambitious expansion plans for Europe; the matchup of specialized industry skills was very appealing, with PMI's strength in the financial sector and KMG's manufacturing and insurance strengths; and the combined resources and strengths of the firms in developing and implementing strategies and plans throughout the whole of Europe made good business sense.

Yet despite the obvious strategic fit of the two organizations and the general agreement of the participants that the merger made sense, nagging problems persisted. First, for the merger to work, PMI's CEF would have to be dissolved and integrated into the KMG national firms. This would have a decidedly detrimental effect on the incomes and career plans of PMI partners. Second, disparity between incomes was a problem in some national practices, but it was generally conceded that the problems could be worked out over time. If adjustments were made during the four or five years after the merger, equality could be achieved relatively painlessly. Then there was the issue of the name. None of the negotiators could seem to find a suitable compromise, and neither would yield completely to the other.

KMG officials invited PMI to send a small contingent to its international partners' meeting in San Francisco, which preceded a major joint negotiating session slated to be held in Amsterdam in September 1985. Chairman Holton and chairman-elect Brown represented PMI. A meeting was arranged with Goerdeler, KMG chairman; Boschma, KMG international executive; Geert Timmer, senior partner of Klynveld Kraayenhof, KMG's Dutch firm; and Steenmeijer, chairman of the Dutch firm's executive committee.

It was a very difficult meeting. Timmer had for years been the client service partner for Royal Dutch Shell, which was jointly audited with Price Waterhouse and Ernst & Whinney. Brown and Holton got the distinct impression that Timmer believed that if there were to be any merger, it would be between KMG and PW, a firm for which he had a great deal of respect.

Whether it was a negotiating strategy, a reflection of his fondness for PW, or just his personality, Timmer came across to Holton and Brown as extremely tough and stubborn. Holton, a rangy, quick-tempered Texan accustomed to the respect his office afforded, became angry. Brown marveled at Holton's uncharacteristic restraint; he half thought that at any moment Holton might leap to his feet and pitch the recalcitrant Timmer through the thirty-fourth-floor window.

The issues weren't any different from the ones around since talks began; it was Timmer's inflexible, demanding manner of presenting them that annoyed Holton. The name was a big question mark. Both firms were proud of their heritage, and KMG was particularly sensitive because problems about what to call the firm had almost scuttled KMG before it was fully formed a few years earlier. Timmer insisted on KMG Peat Marwick; that was unacceptable to PMI partners, who not only refused to part with tradition, but also feared that their clients would view the merger as a takeover of the larger merger partner by the smaller one. They suggested Peat Marwick KMG.

Timmer was emphatic, Brown recalled later. Said Timmer, "KMG Peat Marwick. There is no other way to put it. Those are the facts of life. Besides, it's more efficient and euphonious. Anyway, what firm would want Peat Marwick in front of its name?"

Organizational structure was an ongoing concern, particularly in the United Kingdom and continental Europe, which would require massive changes for either PMI or KMG. Since Thomson McLintock, KMG's U.K. firm, had recently moved from several regional partnerships to a national one, PMI's U.K. firm considered its regional structure essential. Neither wished to change.

International standards were also a problem. PMI's U.K. firm insisted that a single audit manual with one set of worldwide standards was imperative. This was a problem in several countries, most notably in France, where KMG's firm saw such a requirement as onerous. The firm considered several possibilities, including having one set of standards for national work and another for international engagements; an acceptable compromise seemed impossible.

Then there was the question of who would be the boss. Timmer insisted that the first chairman should come from KMG's ranks, and he initially demanded a majority on the board of directors. Eventually, he offered a "compromise" position. KMG would accept equality on the board—on the condition that the Dutch firm have veto power. It was almost more than Holton could stand.

By the time the Amsterdam meeting rolled around in September, it was apparent there was a great deal to be done, despite the fact that most of the task forces had completed their work and presented generally favorable recommendations. The participants didn't seem to have violent objections to the deal; it was more of a nagging feeling that something wasn't quite right. KMG had been talking to several other Big Eight firms and had not yet agreed that PMI was the best alternative. KMG leaders weren't even sure a Big Eight merger was the best alternative. Many believed the "go-it-alone" strategy that McKinsey recommended was the answer.

PMI was still struggling with issues revolving around the name, international auditing standards, partner-to-staff ratios, and the organizational problems in the United Kingdom and continental

Europe. Though both firms hoped for the best, it was difficult to be optimistic as the Amsterdam meeting approached.

To exacerbate an already difficult situation, word was beginning to leak out. Despite the commitment to secrecy on the part of the negotiators, it was virtually impossible to keep the lid on indefinitely, given the expanding number of participants. The *New York Times* broke the story in its September 21, 1985, late city edition. Spokesman Dallas Kersey, Peat Marwick's director of communications, first denied the reports, according to the newspaper account, "but later acknowledged that 'We've had discussions with other accounting firms.' Pressed about reports from inside Main Hurdman of merger discussions with Peat Marwick, Mr. Kersey said, 'I'm telling you that, not only are we not engaged, but that we just met at the bar—and we've done that before with many other firms.' " The article quoted sources as saying merger talks had been under way for several weeks and speculated that the firms had even gone so far as to exchange written documents. The news traveled quickly around the world. Within two days, the story was published in virtually every country in which the firms practiced.

The Amsterdam meeting got off to an ominous start. With only the most senior partners from each firm attending the meeting, everyone knew a minor inconvenience in arrangements would quickly escalate into a major problem. Careful attention was given to the most minute details; everything was checked and rechecked. Despite the best efforts of the planners, a major faux pas occurred when one of the most traditional, most conservative, and most senior PMI partners arrived. In contrast to his KMG counterpart's luxurious accommodations, the PMI partner's were spartan. As the hotel staff scurried about trying to rectify the situation, the PMI partner groused to his associates. "If they can't even get the hotel accommodations right, what makes us think they know how to run an accounting firm?"

The glare of the media, along with questions from partners and employees who had not been involved in the negotiations, ratcheted up the pressure. The ultimate breakdown of the discussions seemed to center on what most agreed was an ancillary issue: the name of the new organization. In fact, the name became the rallying cry around which any dissatisfaction could be wrapped. It was an emotional issue and an unarguable point. There seemed to be no answer.

Despite frantic last-minute attempts to avoid jettisoning the merger over such a trivial disagreement, the talks went into a rapid tailspin from which they never recovered. Just four days later, the *New York Times* published the obituary of the talks. "Preliminary merger talks between Peat Marwick, the nation's second largest accounting firm, and KMG Main Hurdman, the ninth largest, were terminated yesterday after three days of negotiations in Amsterdam between officials of the firms' international organizations. In a joint statement, the firms said, 'The complexities involved in bringing about such a combination have led the representatives of both organizations to conclude that these discussions should not be pursued further.' "[6]

The participants left Amsterdam to face the music with their partners and clients and to ponder the question, "What went wrong?"

Horner was especially disappointed, but as he reflected on the events, his disappointment gradually turned to resolve. If he ever got another opportunity such as this, he would make sure it was handled differently. First, he would keep the group smaller. It was too difficult to accommodate all the special interests represented by a large group. Second, he would approach future merger discussions with the assumption that a merger could be done, that problems could be overcome. They would deal with the major points of the merger, sign the deal, and then work out the details.

---

6. Gary Klott, "Marwick Ends Hurdman Talks," *New York Times*, 25 September 1985, D5.

Finally, a merger this complex would require strong leadership to keep the talks from stalling around issues that could be resolved later. Leaders would have to make tough decisions and live with the consequences. Horner would get a chance to revive this merger and set it aright.

# Chapter Three

# The Players

Scores of people contributed to the making of KPMG—starting with the failed negotiations of 1985 and then throughout the successful negotiations of 1986 and subsequent consolidation of the two firms. Through it all, however, five men emerged as prime movers of the merger—leaders willing to take the inherent calculated risks and able to persuade their partners to join them.

The five became good friends as they shaped their dream and created the world's largest professional services organization. They disagreed on occasion as they strove to maintain the delicate balance between the interests of the national firms and the greater good of the entire organization. But they never lost sight of their goal.

So immersed were they in the challenges of the merger that everything else took second place. Intercontinental trips were so frequent they joked about buying their own Concorde, and phone calls at two in the morning were commonplace. Larry Horner even had a telefax machine installed in the study adjoining his bedroom so as to keep up with communications between countries.

Through it all, the five knew they were doing something worthwhile. Time alone will reveal the magnitude of the changes they wrought in their own firm, in the accounting profession, and in the world of business. The prime movers were Horner of the United States, Hans Havermann of West Germany, Jim Butler of the United Kingdom, Johan Steenmeijer of the Netherlands, and Jim Brown of Canada.

### Larry Horner

Larry Horner is a true visionary, though his style belies the stereotype. He is as sophisticated and urbane as the CEO of a large multinational firm is expected to be; at the same time he comes across as a big, warm, friendly person, someone people enjoy being around. He can work a room like a politician, and by the time he's finished he will have met almost everyone and will remember most of their names.

Walter O'Connor, former PMI international vice chairman and now director of the masters in taxation program and professor of accounting at Fordham University in New York, recalls the time he arranged for Horner to meet some Japanese accountants from a firm with which PMI had an interest in merging. It was at a U.S. partners' meeting in Boca Raton, Fla., and O'Connor was worried that Horner might be distracted by the demands of the meeting and make a poor impression. O'Connor recalled:

> He was incredible—like an athlete who turns on the adrenaline at just the right moment. He positioned himself correctly in the photos, got all the names right—despite his not speaking Japanese—had separate photos taken outside, and just happened to have with him some Peat Marwick golf covers that at the right moment he presented to our guests.

Somebody had to have prepared him, but I don't know who or how. He really dazzled them. As I shook my head in amazement, he looked at me as if to say, "You bozo, did you really think I was going to flunk this? I know what's going on in Japan. Now let's get on to the next problem." It was vintage Horner.

Horner is not a man consumed by minutiae, as is sometimes the case with those in a business where attention to detail is tantamount to success. He is a big-picture guy in the extreme. He may toss out several ideas that would have a major impact and would require millions to fund and legions to staff. Those are not his problems. Once he's given someone the destination, it's up to that person to figure out how to get there and occasionally let him know how the trip is going. It's a management style that empowers the motivated and strikes fear in the timid.

Although he is genuinely friendly most of the time, he can move from cordial through annoyed to angry with breathtaking speed when he feels unfairly challenged, focusing on detractors with an intensity that withers even the most iron willed. The storms pass as quickly as they arise, but they leave a lasting impression.

Horner was born in 1934 in Marquette, Kansas, to parents who mixed kindness with discipline and believed in basic values, hard work, and naming their children what they planned to call them. His name is Larry, not Lawrence. He earned his degree in 1956 at the University of Kansas, which in a 1989 alumni profile of him wrote, "Horner once extolled the opportunities available in accounting particularly 'for those lucky enough to have attended the University of Kansas.' But the objective view reveals the School's good fortune in being able to count among its alumni talented individuals of Larry Horner's caliber."

Horner played semipro baseball prior to attending the university and football for a couple of years during college. To his sports experiences he attributes his competitiveness in business development as well as his ability to function both as a team player and as its captain when the situation requires.

Upon graduation he joined the Kansas City office of Peat, Marwick, Mitchell & Co., where he paid his dues like the thousands of staff accountants who had gone before him. He worked his way up through the ranks quickly and was admitted to the partnership after eight years. He served as a partner in Kansas City until 1970, when his "people skills" attracted the attention of the firm's leaders.

From 1970 until 1974 Horner served as managing partner of the firm's German practice, based in Frankfurt. It was there that he developed a reputation for client service and practice development and began to lay the international foundation that would prepare him for future leadership roles.

When his overseas assignment was completed, Horner returned to the United States as managing partner of the Miami office, a position he held until 1977. He then transferred to Los Angeles, where he held the post of managing partner for two years until he was appointed vice chairman of the firm's western region.

In 1984 he was elected chairman of Peat, Marwick, Mitchell & Co., and in 1988 he became chairman of KPMG, a position he held in tandem with his responsibilities as CEO of the U.S. firm.

Horner is not a green-eyeshade accountant. He thinks as much about the business and strategic implications of a situation as he does its accounting ramifications. Moving with equal skill through the upper echelons of civic, professional, and business organizations, Horner counts among his friends many of America's top corporate executives and serves on boards of charities and cultural organizations with the leading CEOs of U.S. business.

He is a member of numerous prestigious business, civic, professional, and philanthropic organizations. Horner has three sons and two daughters. He and his wife, Inge, have homes in New York City and on the north shore of Long Island.

## Hans Havermann

Like most leaders of substance, Professor Dr. Hans Havermann is a man who spends far more time looking ahead than dwelling on history. He doesn't like to waste time worrying about things he can do nothing about, preferring instead to direct his considerable energy toward things that matter.

Havermann is a pleasant, polite man who goes out of his way to be courteous to others, but he is not given to idle chatter. He likes to get the business done, then socialize—rather than the other way around. He is at once a stern, no-nonsense professor and a kind, compassionate mentor who inspires his partners and staff to ever-higher levels of achievement.

His days start early. By eight o'clock most mornings Havermann's Düsseldorf office is already abuzz with activity as his first appointments begin. If he is not lunching with clients, potential clients, or other civic and business contacts, he may pause only briefly to eat a sandwich at his desk before plunging into his hectic afternoon schedule. If there is no social engagement or preparation for a lecture at the University of Cologne, evenings may be spent quietly at home with his wife, Marei (the couple has three daughters). Havermann is a gracious host and an accomplished pianist who often delights party guests with his extensive repertoire. His musical skill places him atop many guest lists.

His entertainment experience enables him to adapt quickly to the role at hand. He often compared the merger to a play. There was a good plot, the script had been cleverly written, and it was up to the actors to ensure a good performance. He never failed to perform flawlessly as he convinced audiences around the world of the benefits of the combination of KMG and PMI.

Havermann could speak persuasively about the benefits of a merger from firsthand experience. He joined KMG's German firm through its acquisition of his smaller firm and rose to the challenges the new firm presented. He understood very well the delicate alliances that had to be forged to succeed in a new environment and was determined to ensure that people at every level were presented with the opportunity to succeed. After that, it was up to them to live up to their potential.

Havermann also learned well the diplomatic skills necessary to maneuver in the upper echelons of management. As Reinhard Goerdeler's second in command before assuming the top spot himself, Havermann traveled the world representing his firm, but still had to get the work done back home.

Although his modesty would preclude his saying so himself, Havermann had a good deal of influence in building KMG. He and Jan Uiterlinden spent several months in 1979 traveling through Europe and other continents, attempting to piece together the firm that wouldn't coalesce in late 1978. They met with the managing partners of the founding firms several times over a six-month period, patiently identifying the problems and developing solutions to be written and circulated in discussion drafts. Working through the diverse languages and cultures was unparalleled training for the challenges they would face in the years ahead.

Havermann's official title is chairman of the managing board of directors of Deutsche Treuhand-Gesellschaft, KPMG's German firm, which is now by far the largest in the country. Accompanying the title is responsibility for the management of the firm's far-flung operations and its key client relationships.

Havermann was born in 1930 in Marl/Recklinghausen. After his graduation from the University of Cologne and his appointment as *wirtschaftsprufer* (the German equivalent of a British chartered accountant or a U.S. certified public accountant), he was active in the profession nationally and internationally, in addition to maintaining his firm and community responsibilities. He served as a member of *hauptfachausschuss* (accounting principles committee) of the German Institute, serving as president of the institute from 1976 to 1978 and as chairman of the institute's international relations committee from 1976 until he stepped down in 1989.

He has distinguished himself in service to the profession in other capacities as well, serving as the German delegate of the Union Européen des Experts Comptables Economiques et Financiers (UEC) and of the Groupe d'Etudes des Experts Comptables (CEE). Havermann headed up a committee to merge the two groups into the Fédération Experts Comptables Européen (FEE) and was asked to serve as the new organization's first chairman, a position he declined because of his increased responsibilities at KPMG. He also served as a member of the Group of Experts on International Standards of Accounting and Reporting of the United Nations Commission on Transnational Corporations.

For many years Havermann has been active in the International Federation of Accountants (IFAC) and has served as the German delegate on the International Accounting Standards Committee. He also served on the IFAC Council and its planning committee.

He has held the prestigious post of special adviser to the European Community and the Organization for Economic Cooperation and Development (OECD). In addition to serving as a lecturer at his alma mater, Havermann is editor in chief of the German professional journal *Die Wirtschaftspruefung*.

### Jim Butler

In a 1988 *Accountancy Age* profile of KPMG's firm in the United Kingdom, writer Nick Speechly characterized KPMG Peat Marwick McLintock as the gentle giant among the Big Eight—a firm that is confident, but not unduly aggressive; competitive, but not ruthless. It is a description that could just as easily be applied to the U.K. firm's senior partner, Percy James Butler. An avuncular man, he is outgoing yet discreet, and you immediately know he is truly interested in what you have to say and that whatever you say will be kept between the two of you. No doubt these traits have served him well in his career in public accounting. Sound advice, a pleasant personality, and discretion go a long way in inspiring client confidence.

Those attributes were also essential to the success of the merger. As PMI's Continental European Firm began to run amok, it often fell to Butler to meet with the protagonists in the various dramas in an attempt to work out a compromise. Sometimes it worked, and sometimes it didn't, but Butler almost always received high marks for his efforts. No one is universally liked or always able to reach agreement on every issue in a large, highly competitive organization, but those are the problems that go with the territory, Butler figures.

He is a strong proponent of the partnership system and the committee structure that governs it. As senior partner, he sees one of his principal roles as being someone who provides a launchpad for ideas. He opines:

> As senior partner, I serve as chairman of several key committees. In that capacity my job is to lead, not simply to react to the ideas and suggestions of others or be an arbitrator of ideas or disputes between the partners. If I do my job well, I can identify goals and provide an environment in which each partner and employee can make a contribution toward reaching our overall goals. The mark of a good leader is to be able to persuade others to align their personal goals with those of the organization. When that happens, the results can be phenomenal.

Butler earned his spurs at the side of Sir John Grenside, senior partner of the U.K. firm from 1977 until 1986. Born March 15, 1929, Butler joined the firm as an articled clerk in 1952 after graduating with an honors degree in mathematics from Marlborough College and Clare College, Cambridge. He qualified with honors as a chartered accountant in 1955 and became a fellow of the Institute of Chartered Accountants in England and Wales. He was named an associate partner of the London practice in 1965, a time when British law limited the size of partnerships to twenty. The law was changed not long afterward, and in 1967 Butler was admitted as the twenty-first full partner of the London practice. He became a member of the general partnership (equivalent to the board) in 1971 and became senior London regional partner in 1981. Butler became deputy senior partner of the U.K. firm in 1985 and on July 1, 1986, assumed the top post—serving there through the merger, until he became senior partner of KPMG Peat Marwick McLintock on April 1, 1987, when the merger became official.

Butler has held a number of leadership positions in the international organization, serving on the PMI international council from 1978 to 1986 and on the PMI planning committee from 1974 to 1983. He became a founding member of the KPMG executive committee at its inception in 1987 and serves as a member of the KPMG European board. He has served at various times as liaison partner with PMI practices in the United States and central and southern Africa.

Although his management responsibilities limit his involvement in the details of an engagement, he continues to work with clients, many of which he has served for years. He is the advisory and client service partner for several of the U.K. firm's leading clients, including Adwest, APV, Lex, Lonrho, Nestlé Rothschilds, and Vickers. In addition, he makes himself available to meet frequent requests for the senior partner's involvement in other client engagements.

Although he is modest about his achievements, Butler is also very involved in British business affairs. He has been a government-appointed director of the Mersey Docks and Harbour Company since 1972, becoming deputy chairman in 1987. In 1981 he was appointed a commander of the Order of the British Empire for his services to Mersey Docks and was the same year appointed by the secretary of state for transport as a member of the Serpell Committee on British Rail. He holds a number of distinguished posts in the banking community, including an appointment by the Chancellor of the Exchequer to a panel of accountants and solicitors available to hear appeals under section 11 of the Banking Act of 1979.

Butler is equally active in civic affairs. He serves as a member of the finance task force on inner cities and is a trustee of Winchester Cathedral Trust. He is chairman of the cathedral's appeal committee, which recently launched a £7 million (US$11.5 million) fund-raising effort. He serves as an officer, fellow, or director of numerous social and civic organizations.

Such demands leave little time for fun and frivolity. Butler usually begins his days early in the morning, a habit he picked up studying for exams at the university, and his workdays often stretch into the evening. He does occasionally find time for a bridge game with friends and Margaret, his wife since 1954. His favorite hobby, though, is overseeing his 500-acre farm near Winchester, where he spends most weekends. He may have to plow through a briefcase of reading material while there, but the farm is home to the Butlers and the social center for their three grown children and many friends. It is there he finds the peace and solitude necessary to relax, reflect, and recharge himself.

### Johan Steenmeijer

Johan Steenmeijer is a tough, stubborn Dutchman and proud of it. After the first ill-fated attempt at a merger, Steenmeijer decided he would never again negotiate out of desperation. KMG would make its organization stronger, and it would negotiate from that position of strength. His firm would be an equal partner in a merger; on this point he would not yield. It was a point that sometimes put him at odds with other leaders in the international firm despite the nearly unanimous support he enjoyed from his partners. Steenmeijer held his ground, and by the time the merger was completed, he had won the respect of KMG and PMI leaders alike for his determination.

Steenmeijer comes across as a no-nonsense, slightly gruff businessman who doesn't want to waste a lot of time on formalities. He wants to lay out the objectives and then get on with achieving them. He is polite to the point of being deferential at times, but there is never any misunderstanding about where the conversation is going. It is going where he directs it.

Once past the tough exterior, one finds a proud leader who cares a great deal about his people and encourages them to be their best. If someone shows an interest in an idea, Steenmeijer will give him or her the opportunity to develop it. Like Butler, he attempts to involve his partners in all major decisions that affect the firm. In merger negotiations, he could act decisively because he already knew he had the full support of his partners. And like a careful poker player, he revealed only what was necessary at the time.

Steenmeijer does his homework, preferring to have the facts in hand and the alternatives considered before he meets with anyone. Before discussing a subject, he has very likely considered every possibility, determined his objective, and decided on a course of action.

Born in 1933, Steenmeijer grew up amid the fears of World War II, the war itself, and the following reconstruction. He understands the importance of tenacity and fierce independence in surviving and prospering. Like other senior members of Klynveld Kraayenhof & Co. (KKC), he is something of an iconoclast who enjoyed sparring with the "eight big Anglo-American accountancy firms," and he takes no small measure of pride in the role KMG played in changing the face of the profession.

During the merger negotiations, Steenmeijer struck up an especially good working relationship with PMI chairman Brown. The two seemed to have an immediate chemistry, perhaps because of the natural affinity the Canadians and Dutch have for each other (the Dutch crown princess waited out World War II in Canada) or maybe because the success Havermann and Horner had in working together dictated that Brown and Steenmeijer would collaborate on other areas of the merger. In any event, the two often talked at great length about solutions to merger problems. It wasn't unusual for Brown to phone Steenmeijer at home on Sunday evening to talk for a couple of hours about the ramifications of a particular decision.

Steenmeijer makes known his displeasure. When KMG's Canadian firm announced its plans to join Ernst & Whinney after talks broke down with PMI, it was Steenmeijer who angrily pointed out to the Canadians that they were violating their agreement with KMG and reneging on their commitment to the other firms. In 1989, when Thorne Riddell senior partner John Palmer phoned KPMG Canadian senior partner Ross Walker to discuss the possibility of leaving E&W to join KPMG, he said, "I'm carrying some baggage, particularly with Johan. If that baggage is serious enough, you may want to tell me to keep on going down the street."

At the 1989 KPMG international partners' conference in New York, the first acquaintance Palmer saw was Steenmeijer. Palmer recalled, "I arrived for the conference on Saturday night and was due to go to Larry Horner's for dinner. I had just checked into the hotel and gotten on the elevator, and there was Johan. His jaw dropped, but he was very gracious. As it turned out we were both spending the evening at Larry's. Afterward, we adjourned to the bar with our wives and were there until about two in the morning. We had a marvelous time. It was a kind of homecoming, and a great way to begin again."

Steenmeijer earned a degree in economics from the University of Groningen in 1959 and joined KKC in 1960. He qualified as a registered accountant in 1964 and was elected to the partnership in 1971. He became a member of the executive committee in 1982 and its chairman a year later.

In addition to his KKC responsibilities, Steenmeijer also had a leadership role in KMG's international firm. He became a member of the central management committee in 1985 and served in that role until KMG merged with PMI in 1986. He then became a founding member of the KPMG executive committee, a post he still holds today. In 1989 he was named chairman of the KPMG European board.

Steenmeijer's other professional distinctions include serving as associate professor of auditing at the State University, Groningen, from 1974 to 1979 and as vice president of the Dutch Institute of Registered Accountants from 1980 to 1981. He served as a member of the institute's council from 1979 to 1982. He is also a member of the Foundation Amsterdam Gateway to Continental Europe, an organization promoting Amsterdam as one of Europe's leading financial centers.

Steenmeijer is very active in the Dutch business community and numbers among his friends many key business leaders. Under his leadership, KKC changed from a highly respected, conservative firm to a dynamic market leader. According to a 1988 survey, 66 percent of business decision makers with large companies consider KPMG to be the market leader in accountancy; Moret—the Arthur Young affiliate—was second, with 15 percent.

Steenmeijer has two daughters and one son and lives in Noordwijk (between Amsterdam and The Hague) with his wife, Agnes.

## Jim Brown

In an organization owned by its partners—who elect the chairman of their firm—political acumen is an essential trait for those who aspire to leadership positions. Technical skills are a must, of course, but in an environment where everyone is technically competent, the ability to work with others can separate the successful from the merely ambitious.

Whether James R. Brown was born with good political instincts or developed them, his ability to lead others led him to the top of his profession. Ask anyone who knows Brown to describe him and inevitably the words *nice, personable, honest, intelligent, diplomatic,* and *principled* are used. Someone totally honest may also say he is slightly disorganized and manages people better than paper.

His communications skills are formidable, no doubt a combination of a keen interest in the subject, native ability, education, and experience. He is a prodigious storyteller despite the fact that he has trained himself to forget details—his way of keeping client business confidential. He studies problems, works out solutions, and then promptly forgets the specifics. He likes people, though, and can spend hours in conversation about business, politics, or another of his many interests. He has an uncanny ability to make the person he is talking to think that he or she is the most important person in the world.

Born in Kingston, Ontario, in 1925, Brown always had to work a little longer and try a little harder than everyone else. His right hand is missing and has been since birth. He doesn't talk about it and long ago learned to compensate. One of his many amazing characteristics is that he does most things better with one hand than the average person does with two. He plays good golf, sails, plays tennis, skis cross-country, and is so deft with a knife and fork that if not paying close attention one might not notice he is doing everything single-handedly.

His communications ability and his penchant for hard work often surfaced in committee work with PMI. He would attend all-day meetings and then retire to his room to draft reports or proposals for review the next day. He often followed the same practice during the merger negotiations. Said KPMG Canadian senior partner Walker:

> Jim was chairman at the time we were negotiating the merger, which was very fortuitous. He is one of the bright-

est people I've worked with—almost too bright at times because he challenges you with so many things that it slows the process. You're prepared for him to ask you twenty questions, and when he asks you twenty-five, you have to stop and get answers to the other five. He's a good listener, and he can get several people's views and combine them in a document that won't offend any of them. He loves to put pen to paper and get things done. In fact, he wrote a very large part of the Canadian Income Tax Act. If a key member of the group had a problem with part of the merger agreement, for example, Jim would come up with another draft the next morning. He's not just a scribe; he's a determined man with a view, but he has the innate ability to listen to people, hear what they're really saying, take some notes, synthesize the views, and come back with something that is acceptable to everyone.

Brown marked many firsts during his forty-year career with the firm. Two of the most significant were his elections as the first Canadian chairman of PMI and as the first chairman of KPMG. He joined the firm's Vancouver office in 1947 after graduating from the University of British Columbia with a degree in business communication. In 1955 he transferred to Prince George, where he was elected to the partnership the same year. Two years later he transferred to Toronto and was soon asked to head the tax department. He moved to Montreal in 1960.

For seven years the firm lent Brown to the federal government in Ottawa, where he served from 1964 to 1965 as senior tax adviser to the Department of Finance. In 1965 he was named assistant deputy minister of tax policy in the Department of Finance, a post he held until he rejoined the firm in 1971 in its Montreal office. He served as managing partner of the Montreal office from 1973 until 1980, when he was elected senior partner of PMI's Canadian firm.

Brown maintained the friendships he established during his years of government service and the respect he earned from political leaders. When national elections were called in 1984, he was personally recruited to run for the parliamentary seat to represent Etobicoke-Center by the Liberal party candidate for prime minister, John Turner ("I'm one of the few liberals in KPMG," Brown jokes). Both Canadian law and firm policy required him to resign in order to run for political office. Walker was elected to succeed him.

When the Liberal party was defeated by Brian Mulroney and the Conservatives, Walker invited Brown back into the firm as chairman of the executive committee, a position he held until he was named PMI chairman in 1985.

Brown served as chairman of the federal legislation committee of the Canadian Institute of Chartered Accountants and held several other important professional positions during his career. In 1988 he retired in a blaze of glory as his colleagues honored his achievements while his wife, Ruth, and four children watched with pride.

The Canadian firm published this tribute: "Through his unfailing dedication to the firm and his obvious love of his work, Jim has achieved a level of excellence which few will attain. From a fledgling graduate in 1947, he methodically moved through the ranks to head the largest accounting organization in the world. He has grown to be one of the most respected leaders in the accounting profession and will go down in Peat Marwick's history as one of the foremost architects of the world's largest accounting firm."

# Chapter Four

# Cultural Influences

Like many organizations (and individuals), the combined firm's greatest strengths were its greatest weaknesses. KMG's roots reached deeply into the European countries that spawned its founders; PMI drew on its proud Anglo-Saxon heritage. Each had its own separate and distinct culture that attracted employees, partners, and clients who shared the same basic values and reinforced its beliefs.

Because of these strong corporate cultures, KMG had over the years acquired a distinguished list of continental European-headquartered firms, while PMI's notable clients were based predominantly in the English-speaking countries. Each, of course, served clients in the other's domain, but in Europe, for example, PMI tended to serve the European subsidiaries of companies based in the United States, Canada, and the United Kingdom, while KMG did the reverse for its continental European clients.

Even their organizational structures were very different. PMI's Continental European Firm (CEF) was a single partnership in which the partners participated in a single profit pool. KMG, on the other hand, was an organization of national firms bound by an international agreement. The Dutch ran the firm in the Netherlands, the Germans ran Germany, and the partners in each country shared only in the profits of that country's operations. If, in the KMG culture, a German firm client needed assistance in the Netherlands, the work was referred to the Dutch firm in return for a fee. At PMI, this was an alien concept since continental Europe was all one firm.

With so many cultural influences at work, it seemed at times an impossible task to merge them. Each of the firms had not only a primary culture, but also subcultures within the organizations. PMI's CEF was a reflection of the entire organization, but it was unique in many ways. KMG was European to the core; its American firm—Main Hurdman—had adapted to European ways.

In a philosophical sense, KMG had accomplished what generations of kings, princes, statesmen, and politicians had been unable to do: It had unified Europe. It is a curious anomaly of history that businesses can find a way to transcend national borders while governments can't.

Few would argue that a united Europe makes sense. Luigi Barzini opens *The Europeans* with this observation:

> There are so many simple and obvious reasons why the venerable and illustrious countries occupying the jagged western rump of Asia, occasionally pecking at each other like irritable hens or quarreling with the United States, should form what the Americans (who, by their very nature, have never been satisfied with mere perfection) would call a 'more perfect union,' and why they should do it immediately, today, tomorrow morning at the latest without wasting one more hour or waiting for one more windy and inconclusive meeting of experts, that only a few fanatics are left who bother to exalt or mock the idea.

There is, to begin with, one irrational emotional reason, which should not be entirely disregarded. . . . It could be called 'the European Dream.' It is many centuries old. Dante described, in *De Monarchia*, the vague hope of seeing the Continent pacified under one sovereign. It was proposed as a cure-all by great princes, emperors, statesmen, thinkers, poets, and starry-eyed idealists down the centuries. Nothing ever came of it, yet it never died. . . . Aristide Briand, the French foreign minister, solemnly proposed the creation of the United States of Europe to the League of Nations on September 5, 1929. . . . It was duly entrusted to a committee and was heard of no more.[1]

KMG's vehicle for achieving economic cooperation among its national practices was to form a mini–trading bloc, an approach similar to the one now being taken by the European Community. National firms were encouraged to maintain their national identities not only because it made good business sense, but to help each other with international work. For example, the large, West German–based multinationals using KMG's German firm would have a bona fide German accounting firm. It had practiced in Germany since 1890 and was as German as sauerbraten. But it, like other members of the KMG family, was part of an international organization that knew no boundaries.

Although some KMG leaders favored the merger, some preferred the "go-it-alone" strategy. The firm had gained a good deal of recognition, particularly in Europe, as an alternative to the Big Eight, and many thought things should continue as they were.

Although it was a prime topic of discussion, the McKinsey report probably did little to dissuade those who saw a merger as the only viable option. It did, however, provide a rallying point for those who opposed it. The study influenced KMG leaders as they

---

1. Luigi Barzini, *The Europeans* (New York: Simon and Schuster, 1983), 11. (This excellent book on the Europeans is excerpted on several occasions in this book.)

considered their options, both during the unsuccessful merger attempt in 1985 and during the one that finally worked a year later.

McKinsey recognized KMG's strength in Europe and noted that

> outside the United States—and principally, perhaps, in Europe—many large clients continue to value an accounting organization with strong roots in the local country, with a European weight that more than balances the power of the U.S. member firm. KMG thus represents the only alternative comparable in overall strength to the U.S.-dominated Big 8 firms.
>
> KMG is indeed the largest international organization outside the United States—and number 4 worldwide. A "go-it-alone" strategy should therefore be built on the theme of KMG as the premier international accounting organization.
>
> KMG's European client roster is unmatched by any of the Big 8 both at the Fortune 500 level and in overall depth, providing a source of attraction to those very Wall Street investment bankers who today know little about KMG.
>
> KMG's combined size and financial strength are greater than often realized—because KMG people often compare KMG central spending with worldwide expenditures by Big 8 firms. When making more appropriate comparisons, KMG and its member firms collectively will be seen to have somewhat more comparable spending levels in some areas where there formerly appeared to be extremely large differences (e.g., training, computerized auditing).

Despite a rather optimistic opening, McKinsey went on to point out that substantial changes would be required if KMG decided to remain independent. First, the central budget would have to be increased, and national practices would have to make a much stronger commitment to making KMG work. The report stated:

Objectively speaking, the challenge facing KMG does not seem to be an insurmountable task. However, it is not possible for an outsider to make a fact-based analytical evaluation—on the basis of such a brief exposure—as to whether this organization, these member firms, and these people in leadership positions will be able to carry out such a major program. At present, the skepticism throughout KMG may in itself be the most difficult obstacle for a "go-it-alone" strategy. Thus, each member firm must make an assessment of these intangibles to determine whether independent development would seem preferable to a merger with a Big 8 firm.

McKinsey went on to recommend specific changes needed to make KMG effective on an independent basis. The first step would be to strengthen shared values by increasing funding for the international organization, strengthening central management and increasing its authority, and requiring the application of international standards for any client with potential referral value. Second, Main Hurdman would have to strengthen its image in the U.S. financial community. To do so would require an extensive effort that would include forming a sales and marketing team for international Securities and Exchange Commission work composed of top Main Hurdman partners, with representation from the leading European firms. In addition, the U.S. firm would have to strengthen its expertise in specialized industries (particularly in banking and insurance) and improve its depth of experience and geographic coverage by bringing in and subsidizing management talent and expertise in key U.S. cities and by discounting fees to secure a broader client base.

Besides suggesting expanded coverage in the United States, McKinsey advised KMG to beef up its operations in high-priority markets, including Japan, eastern Asia, and Italy. Further, McKinsey recommended that KMG strengthen its capabilities in new audit technology, international tax, management advisory services, practice development, and training in order to fully service its international clients. There was, of course, a price tag attached. McKinsey estimated the firm would need about $15 million to begin funding the recommended initiatives.

KMG did not have an operational or practice unit. Legally organized as a Swiss *verein* (association) based in Zurich, KMG's primary function was to license the use of the name and service mark to national practices and "to provide the means through its national practices to administer and coordinate professional services of the highest quality in the areas of auditing, accounting, taxation, management consulting, and other related activities in the international field."

KMG had three classes of membership. Category I members were required to sign an International Cooperation Agreement that required them to "use their best endeavors" to persuade clients to use the services provided by national practices or representatives in other countries, to provide management and technical people to support the international organization, and to place expatriate partners or managers in other countries "to ensure that clients are provided the combined expertise of expatriates and nationals of their countries of operation." In return for those commitments, Category I national practices were assured representation on the various committees and international-firm governing bodies and the right to vote on all major issues affecting the firm.

Category II firms had exclusive use of the KMG name and logo in their respective countries in conducting international work, and they were required to identify themselves as KMG national practices. In return, they agreed to render professional services for KMG clients in their countries unless special circumstances (such as conflict of interest) prohibited them from serving such clients. In accordance with KMG's general practices, national practices would receive referral fees for work they sent to other national practices, and they would be compensated for work they performed for KMG clients in their countries at an agreed-upon rate. Category II firms had some limited participation (along with KMG expatriates) on local management committees, but not on regional or central management bodies of the firm. They could attend KMG regional and general meetings only as nonvoting observers, as long as they paid their own travel expenses. Category II firms weren't required to contribute to central and regional administration costs.

Category III, or representative firms, could conduct work for KMG, but had few rights in the organization. They could refer to themselves as KMG representative firms on their own firm stationery, but were not allowed to use the KMG logo or sign the firm's name in the conduct of work for clients. They were expected to be KMG's exclusive representative and not to "hold themselves out to be associated with any other international firm or organization that renders auditing, accounting, and related services, unless otherwise approved by the central management committee in exceptional cases."

Although its national practices were in many cases as old as the profession itself in their home countries, KMG was itself a young organization at the time the firm began extending merger feelers to Big Eight accounting firms. The international association of accounting firms, as it called itself, came into being in September 1979 with nine founding members:

- Deutsche Treuhand-Gesellschaft (West Germany)

- Fides Revision (Switzerland)

- Fiduciaire de France (France)

- Hungerford Hancock & Offner (Australia)

- Revisionsfirmaet C. Jespersen (Denmark)

• Klynveld Kraayenhof & Co. (the Netherlands)

• Main Hurdman (United States)

• Thomson McLintock & Co. (United Kingdom)

• Thorne Riddell (Canada)

Two additional firms were admitted to membership in 1980:

• Alex. Aiken & Carter (South Africa)

• Reynolds Cooper McCarron (Ireland)

A profile of the firm distributed at the time of the merger painted this glowing portrait of KMG:

> Founded in 1979 by leading, long-established national firms in nine key countries, Klynveld Main Goerdeler has grown rapidly to become one of the world's largest accounting and business advisory practices, offering a balanced range of professional services through 57 nationally-based member and representative firms active in 73 countries throughout the industrialized and developing world.
>
> KMG has 2,827 partners and 23,372 staff operating in 435 offices.
>
> All KMG national firms are professional leaders in their home countries. Each has been selected on the basis of national status, reputation, stability, and international competence.
>
> Worldwide, KMG firms are coordinated and administered through a Central Management Committee, an International Executive Office, and regional management structures. A proven international quality control system ensures that KMG firms work to the highest professional

standards, applying state-of-the-art procedures and techniques.

In addition to accounting and auditing services, KMG offers consultancy services in areas including national and international taxation, management information and data processing systems, financial reorganization, and access to international capital markets. Clients also benefit from KMG's role as a leader in the development and application of EDP (electronic data processing) techniques. For the year ended March 31, 1986, KMG reported revenues totaling $1.044 billion and 26.3 million client service hours.

Public relations hype aside, when KMG and PMI began discussions in late 1984, there were major differences between the two firms in the way they organized and managed themselves and in the professional standards they followed—attributes that were inextricable parts of their corporate cultures.

To KMG partners, some PMI partners seemed unnecessarily concerned about professional standards and quality control. PMI, on the other hand, fretted that KMG worried too much about organizational and representation issues. Regulations governing KMG's international agreement devoted far more space to general meetings, organizational issues, and requirements for membership in KMG than they did to international standards. In addition, KMG had two sets of standards: one for international work, which was in accordance with KMG's international audit manual, and another for national work that should be "in accordance with standards that are at least equal to those generally accepted as best practice in their respective countries." PMI partners unfamiliar with European practices worried that the net result of what they perceived as a double standard would be lower-quality work.

PMI was also concerned about what appeared to be KMG's loose affiliation of national practices. Its international cooperation agreement, the foundation document for the organization, allowed national practices to withdraw from the organization for any reason, so long as they gave the central management committee at least twelve months' notice. The committee would even allow less notice under certain circumstances. Such an arrangement didn't appear very permanent to PMI partners, who were accustomed to more binding relationships.

Like some of the KMG founding firms, PMI could trace its origins to the beginnings of the profession. In the United Kingdom, William B. Peat entered the accounting business in 1870 and had helped shape the development of the profession in his country. James Marwick opened his office in New York in 1895, joined forces with Simpson Roger Mitchell in 1897, and merged with Peat in 1911. In fact, a firm that merged into Peat Marwick in 1950 could point with pride to the fact that it was America's first accounting firm; it had been in business since 1883.

In contrast to KMG's national firms, which didn't link up internationally until the late twentieth century, PMI grew as a tightly knit family of firms. It merged with others, acquired smaller firms, and expanded geographically and added new services in response to client needs. The firm had an active international exchange program; promising partners, managers, and staff people were sent abroad to learn something of the firm's international operations, and expatriates from other countries were housed in U.K. and U.S. offices to work with clients from their home countries. Where PMI didn't have an established office, the firm formed representative arrangements with local firms and, in some isolated instances, with Big Eight competitors. Such firms agreed to respect PMI's client arrangements, audited to PMI standards, and reported audit results to PMI management. Occasionally, they referred work to each other.

PMI's public relations profile at the time of the merger read like this:

Peat Marwick International is the umbrella partnership of

all PMI firms established to provide for a commonality of approach while recognizing the individuality of each member firm. The origins of the firm trace back to the firm of Marwick & Mitchell, founded in the U.S. in 1897, and William B. Peat & Co., an English firm established in 1870. The two were merged in 1911.

Over the succeeding 75 years the firm continued to grow through strategic mergers, and today PMI has 2,733 partners and principals and 28,300 staff operating in 342 offices in 90 countries. For its fiscal year ended June 30, 1986, PMI reported revenues of $1.665 billion and 34.6 million chargeable hours.

PMI is an umbrella partnership with every partner a signatory. The firm is governed by a council of 32 senior partners and an advisory committee of 11 members. The council oversees a number of committees, including specialized industry committees (energy, banking, insurance, and high technology); professional practice committees (audit, tax, and management consulting); and practice development, ethics, and personnel.

These committees have overseen the development of important projects to enhance the quality of services delivered to PMI clients. Chief among these are the creation of one audit standard for use throughout the world; the design and implementation of a computerized support system to handle many of the routine, mechanical aspects of an audit, thereby improving the efficiency and the quality of the audit; and the opening of important markets, such as the Republic of China.

Notwithstanding the public relations rhetoric about its global expansion, PMI was primarily an Anglo-Saxon firm in the eyes of KMG and most other strong national firms in the countries in which PMI practiced. Even when the firm did have senior partners who were natives of the countries in which they operated, they tended to be anglicized, since the bulk of their business was composed of work conducted for the foreign subsidiaries of companies based in the United States or the United Kingdom.

Europeans, as a general rule, have trouble understanding Anglos. The British seem to have an uncanny ability to build empires, be they economic or political—a trait that has spawned jealousy and imitation throughout recorded history. But to Europeans, the British appear aloof. In fact, the British seem to have trouble deciding whether or not they are a part of Europe. When one asks a Briton, "any Briton, point blank, 'Are you European?'" author Luigi Barzini says, "the answer is always, 'European? Did you say European? Er, er'—a long thoughtful pause in which all other continents are mentally evoked and regretfully discarded—'Yes, of course, I'm European.' This admission is pronounced without pride and with resignation. . . . In a way, Britain still sees itself as the sceptered isle, cut from the Continent by divine will. If God had wanted to tie it to the rest of Europe, He would evidently not have dug the Channel."

Barzini capsulizes the views of many Europeans, as well, when he describes Americans—the second half of the Anglo duo—as "baffling."

> What actually causes uneasiness and dismay (occasionally verging on panic) among Europeans is not only the obvious fact that the United States is big, rich, powerful, and incredibly productive, or that Americans occasionally tend to shift preferences, political opinions, tastes, and hopes en masse at the same time, often unexpectedly, so much . . . that they seem not always to be exactly aware of their country's actual size, of its strength, and its influence. They occasionally underestimate the effect of their actions or words or they overestimate it optimistically with disappointing

results. They do not seem always to be able to control, harness, and direct their awesome power. The consequences of some of their moves are in fact sometimes as surprising and shocking to them as to the rest of the world.[2]

As with most Big Eight firms, PMI had invested heavily in Europe, particularly during the postwar reconstruction period. The primary investors, the United States and the United Kingdom, had sent money, technology, and people at a time when it was sorely needed. PMI's Continental European Firm (CEF) had prospered, and the U.S. and U.K. firms expected to participate in the profits of the firm they had helped build. It was an idea that—in concept—was fine with the CEF partners.

The problem lay in the definition of "reasonable." By the late 1970s and early 1980s, CEF partners figured the debt had been paid in full. They chafed under U.S. and U.K. firms' members on their board of directors and resented having to share their profits with them. In their view, most of the CEF's recent success had been the result of their own hard work. And the foreign partners who had invested in building the CEF after the war had long since recouped their investments, made respectable profits, and retired from the firm. It wasn't fair, CEF partners thought, that they should have to continue to pay every generation of partners that followed.

In spite of the dispute with PMI about the European firm's contribution to the enrichment of U.S. and U.K. partners, CEF partners weren't so sure that disbanding their firm and folding it into KMG's national firms was the best option. Then there was the question of the secrecy that surrounded the merger discussions. CEF senior partner P. Graham Corbett particularly disliked keeping his partners in the dark about the negotiations. It conflicted with his management style and his personal beliefs. He had always made it a point to keep his partners informed about all matters

2. Barzini, *The Europeans,* 59, 64–65, 252.

that significantly affected their firm. Corbett made it clear at the January 1985 meeting with KMG that he was participating with the understanding that they were only "holding the bridge for three or four weeks before they would be able to tell everyone what was going on." It was the beginning of a running conflict with other PMI leaders about how much to disclose to the partners. Corbett felt that he was betraying his own partners and going behind their backs in considering the most important decision the CEF had ever faced.

Corbett and five others—three each from PMI and KMG—formed the joint task force responsible for evaluating professional standards. Their mission was to determine if a gap existed between standards applied by the firms and to identify national practices from either side that might have difficulty harmonizing standards. They traded audit manuals, met, and sent out questionnaires.

By the July deadline, the group had concluded that the audit manuals that set the standards for the quality of work performed (statistical sample size of transactions verified, adequate documentation, planning, computer audit programs, attendance at physical inventories, internal control evaluation, and other audit processes and procedures) were broadly consistent. KMG had already begun studying the standards of its national practices and had queried many of them about how long it would take to achieve uniform standards.

KMG's Paul Boschma was especially concerned about the standards issue. A Dutch accountant who began his career with a small Amsterdam accounting firm that merged with Klynveld Kraayenhof, Boschma had worked his way up to the position of executive chairman of KMG's international organization. He understood fully the difficulty of reconciling standards in the various countries and the patience it would require.

You can't change the world in one big blow. You must

realize the difference is that PMI in Europe mainly lives on referred work. When you have to deliver audit reports to U.S. and U.K. organizations, the standards must be very high. It is a very different story when you are issuing a local report in some countries.

Those standards need to be upgraded, but it takes time and time and time. You can't all of a sudden impose international standards on all the work being done by all the different firms. Various cultures have diverse opinions about what an audit certificate really means in different circumstances.

Boschma thought PMI, especially Corbett, went too far in questioning people about their audit methods and in insisting on a strict international standard. "You are being too tough about these things," he cautioned Corbett.

Boschma was also troubled by an early draft memorandum of understanding recommending that in case the merger couldn't be consummated in three problem countries—Singapore, New Zealand, and Ireland—the PMI firms would join the merged firm, and the KMG firms would be excluded. "This is not right," he said, "that they should be excluded in the first place. If there are problems that can't be overcome, fine, but this is a dictate. As chairman, I will not go along with it. If this is the mentality they have, I say, 'Tell Peat Marwick to go to hell.'"

The European continent, the task force concluded, had its problem countries as well—France and Switzerland. The KMG firm in Switzerland estimated that its larger engagements were pretty much in compliance with KMG audit manual standards and that if a transition period were required, it would be only two to three years. Small and midsize companies, on the other hand, were a major problem. It would probably never be possible to harmonize standards. The market simply wouldn't permit fees to be raised to accommodate the time required to audit at the higher standard.

In France it would take more time for the KMG firm to close the standards gap. The KMG firm in France, Fiduciaire de France, followed KMG standards for larger organizations' audits, but for traditional French statutory audits *(commissariat)* of small and midsize companies, considerably less time would be spent. France could be a problem.

Corbett had no illusions about how difficult the merger might be. He recalled later:

> We always knew it would be incredibly difficult for the CEF because all of us understood that the achievement of this wide objective internationally was inevitably going to be painful. But none of us had the remotest concept of how difficult it was going to be; otherwise, I'm not sure we would have attempted it. Nevertheless, we knew going in that we were the guys who were going to finish up between the grinding stones, to some extent or another. Obviously, the expectation was that we would have some voice, ultimately, as to whether the deal was done or not. I guess we were pretty naive. But nevertheless, I believed it, and I managed to persuade my partners that this was the case.

By the summer of 1985, Corbett was very troubled by the fact that the secrecy agreement precluded him from advising his partners, but he did take comfort in the fact that most of the major players on the Continent (from both organizations) had agreed on the major concepts behind the merger. The terms of their agreement dealt with the partnership concept, opportunities for individuals, and the idea of a pan-European structure, among other things. It was signed by the senior partners of the national firms with the understanding that they would review it with their own partners.

Corbett regarded it as a major triumph. He reasoned that if the news leaked out, he could at least present his partners with a piece of paper reassuring them that he had been negotiating in their best interests and that he had secured for them a strong voice in the shape of the new organization. If there would be problems, Corbett anticipated them in the United Kingdom, not in continental Europe. KMG Thomson McLintock senior partners didn't trust PMI's U.K. firm, Corbett thought, and he expected problems with the difference in partner-to-staff ratios. As the summer of 1985 drew to a close, however, things seemed to take a turn for the better. Corbett began to believe real progress was going to be made.

Nevertheless, he felt he had to let his partners know what was happening. He told Larry Horner and John Grenside, "Look, I have a CEF partners' meeting at the end of September. There is no way on God's green earth that I can walk into that meeting and tell them for the first time what we've been up to for the last nine months. The roof will come down on our heads.

"I have no confidence whatever that I can hold the ensuing holocaust. This is going to be an absolute catastrophe. I can't wait any longer. I'm going to notify my partners," Corbett declared. On September 15 he sent a memo to his partners advising them that the Firm had been in negotiations with KMG since the beginning of the year.

The timing of the meetings was difficult from Corbett's point of view. Three hours after the meeting with KMG in Amsterdam he would be on his feet before the CEF partners. The only good thing about it was that he expected to deliver the good news that PMI had agreed in principle to merge with KMG.

Of course, it didn't work out that way. The discussions fell apart, the talks were terminated, and Corbett had to face his partners, who were boiling with rage. One irate partner summed it up: "Look, bloody Graham Corbett. You've been with us for some ten or twelve years, developing us as a partnership, telling us how important the concept of partnership is. Then when you have a really important decision, you treat us as though we were office boys!"

"I agree with every damn word you're saying," Corbett said. "If I were in your shoes, I would be saying exactly the same thing." It was an unpleasant meeting.

In an ironic twist of fate, it was at the same meeting that the process for selecting Corbett's successor would begin. Corbett had been reelected twice; his three terms would end in 1987. According to the partnership agreement, he could not run again.

The usual practice was for a senior national partner to run for the position; several months would be allowed for a smooth transition. Corbett would handle the day-to-day operations to give the incoming CEF senior partner time to think about some long-term objectives. Harald Kessler, senior partner of the Dutch and Scandanavian firms, won the decision. Kessler was the only candidate for the post whose campaign platform included support for a mega-merger, an issue that he recalls "was very much on the partners' minds at the time."

Shortly after the election, rumors began buzzing about some sort of discussions being resumed with KMG. Partners from all over the Continent phoned Corbett to check their validity. Corbett touched base with Horner and Jim Butler, who gave him vague reassurances that there was no truth to the rumor. On July 10, 1986, another partner phoned to inquire. His knowledge was so detailed and so precise that Corbett decided he could no longer accept the notion that nothing was happening.

He phoned PMI chairman Jim Brown at his home in Canada. "Jim," he said, "I've just received some information that I simply don't know how to respond to. What's going on?"

"Can I phone you back tomorrow?" Brown asked.

True to his word, Brown phoned the next day with the whole story. Corbett couldn't recall a time in his life when he'd been angrier. Later, he recalled, "I couldn't believe these guys were playing ducks and drakes with my firm without my knowing about it. At that moment I found myself in the shoes that my partners had been wearing the previous September."

Corbett called together the CEF partnership board for a tempestuous meeting. After much heated discussion, the partners resigned themselves to the fact that the merger was going to happen whether they liked it or not. They could only decide if they wanted to participate. "We've got to play this really carefully," Corbett said. "It's no good just standing by and watching it happen. We've got the interests of our partners to look after, and it is not clear that they are going to be well served by our embarking on a major campaign to pull this pack of cards down. If this merger is going to go ahead anyway, we'd better sort out how we want to see ourselves. Do we want to be part of it, or don't we want to be a part of it?"

A PMI council meeting was scheduled for early August, just a few days after the CEF partnership board meeting; Corbett, convinced that it was in his partners' best interest, asked his partners to empower him to advise the council that the CEF was prepared to participate in the discussions. They refused. He did manage to dissuade them from forbidding him even to attend the meeting by agreeing to read a statement at the meeting asserting that he was there without any authority from the partnership board, but that they knew he was there and that he was there with their consent. "Beyond that," Corbett asserted, "I have no authority to commit them to anything."

Corbett wanted PMI leaders to know how he and his partners felt. The CEF partners believed PMI had committed to conditions that the partners would find unacceptable and felt they had been the bargaining chip.

More stormy meetings followed. By the time the memorandum of understanding was signed in August of 1986, the CEF had reluctantly agreed to participate in the merger discussions, but each meeting was preceded by a tense negotiating session with the CEF board outlining the conditions under which a vote would be held. Corbett was annoyed with Horner and Butler's seeming unwillingness to accept the democratic nature of the CEF. Corbett's view of the situation was that his nonresident American and British partners simply could not believe it was necessary to go through such a tedious exercise. He thought they had little, if any, understanding of the complexities involved in pulling together a multinational firm with West Germans, Dutchmen, Italians, and Frenchmen—those for whom the very concept of a partnership was alien. Corbett felt he had a lot of himself invested in the democratic nature of the firm, and he was unwilling to compromise it.

Horner and Butler's frustrations were multiplied by the ire directed at them by a small but very vocal group of CEF partners who were angry about everything from nonresident participation in their affairs up to and including every detail of the merger negotiations. The CEF soon moved from dissention and disarray to open revolt. France, Switzerland, Spain, and West Germany threatened to self-destruct, as Corbett struggled to hold it together. Butler became increasingly impatient.

Finally, in exasperation, he asked Corbett, "What the hell difference does it make if the CEF blows apart? It's practically fallen apart already."

"It matters ultimately, Jim," Corbett responded, "because we lose everything we've got together and because you and the U.S. firm are going to have to pick up all the bits and pay for the damages, and they will be horrific. We had better make certain that doesn't happen."

As the January 1, 1987, merger date drew nearer, pressure on the CEF intensified. Partners scrambled to protect their own interests, in some cases at the expense of the firm and their partners. Things were chaotic as the CEF prepared for its December 1986 meeting. By this time, Corbett was convinced that—however miserable the choice—the only thing that would protect the partners' interests would be to push forward with the merger.

Before the meeting, he spoke long and frankly with Horner and

Butler. "I believe I can come out of this with something short of a vote of the partnership insisting that all discussion stop. But it's going to be very difficult. We will only do it by being prepared not just to accept, but actually sponsor from the leadership of the CEF, some resolutions that will be extremely critical of the way the firm has handled the whole thing. Otherwise, the partners will almost certainly refuse me a mandate to sign the merger agreement. Frankly, I don't mind if I sign the merger agreement or not, but I think that if I push for approval to sign the agreement, what I am likely to get is a resolution passed to stop all discussion."

Corbett focused on a strategy of warding off resolutions calling for total withdrawal from negotiations. There were six resolutions raised from the floor. Each was defeated in its turn, though Corbett was soundly criticized later for the order in which he accepted and dealt with the resolutions. In the end, he got what he wanted. The partners wouldn't empower him to sign the merger agreement, but they did not require the CEF to withdraw.

Corbett spent the next week attempting to whip up support from senior partners of PMI's national firms not in the CEF for postponing the signing of the merger agreement. In a passionate memo to them, he outlined all the reasons he favored postponement and asked for their help. Some expressed sympathy, but when the vote was cast, the merger carried the day. The only votes against the merger were the two representatives from continental Europe. After the anguished meeting, several of the senior partners approached Corbett to express their condolences and to try to explain their actions. Corbett accepted their explanations stoically. They had done what they had to do.

There was one more order of business for the CEF. At a meeting in March 1987, it met to authorize the national firms to complete their negotiations and to disband the CEF. It became effective June 30, 1987, the end of the fiscal year.

As he reflected on the tumultuous events of the previous year and a half, Corbett felt that he had done a remarkable job of meeting his objectives against a background of very unhappy partners in the midst of the greatest crisis of their careers. He later reflected:

> *I expect, though, that my partners will say, "Okay, he did a great job in terms of his objectives, but he started off with the wrong objectives, and what a helluva pity. It's too bad that he didn't get his sights pointed in the right direction at the beginning."*
>
> *I understand why they say that; I really do. But I still believe I was right.*

# Chapter Five

# The Catalyst

Perhaps no one was more distressed about the failed negotiations of 1985 than John Palmer, executive partner of Thorne Riddell, KMG's Canadian firm. Palmer had participated in the merger discussions from beginning to end and was optimistic about prospects in Canada. Auditing requirements in Canada generally require financial institutions to have two outside auditors; given Thorne's position as the largest accounting firm in Canada and PMI's strength in the financial community, it was inevitable that the two firms would work together on audits and review each other's work. The general feeling among Thorne partners was that the PMI culture and style were very similar to their own. Both firms were partnerships in the truest sense: Both were very democratic, were very open, and encouraged the flow of ideas and initiatives from the bottom up and from the top down. It wasn't strictly top-down management.

In addition, Palmer had a good working relationship with Jim Brown, senior partner of PMI's Canadian firm. They respected each other as competitors and cooperated on joint audits, and they ran across one another at social and charitable functions and at professional meetings. Palmer and Brown both believed a merger between their organizations could be accomplished quickly and efficiently. Whatever happened in the rest of the world, Canada would progress smoothly. In fact, Brown and Palmer were so sure of a deal that they concluded early on that Brown should focus his attention on other parts of the world where there were problems.

As KMG explored both its merger options and the "go-it-alone" strategy, Palmer and his partners became increasingly convinced that a merger was essential for the Canadian firm. It was generally felt that the level of U.S. expertise and resources—to be tapped by other national practices—was inadequate. The Canadians found themselves having to learn more and more about U.S. taxation and other specialized areas of practice with which they were unfamiliar, and they felt they lacked the expertise on U.S. matters to serve their clients adequately. They couldn't devote the time to learning U.S. accounting practices while simultaneously serving Canadian clients. Palmer and his partners went on record early in support of a merger with PMI.

During the two-day meeting in Paris in January 1985, Palmer tried to identify potential stumbling blocks to an international merger. PMI's British firm seemed concerned about a single worldwide audit process and believed it was essential to develop one quickly. This was a problem for KMG's French firm, which had a different process in accordance with French law and custom; its partners felt an audit approach acceptable to the British would be far too labor-intensive and therefore too expensive to adopt in France. The group discussed alternatives. Perhaps there could be one standard for domestic work and another for international work. This was a sticking point as far as PMI was concerned.

There were other issues, such as compensation and the structure and management of the new organization, but Palmer's take on the meeting was that getting to a set of international standards acceptable to all the firms would be one of the most difficult hurdles to overcome.

Palmer also sensed some cultural differences. One of the best examples was the debate over whether to issue a press release from Paris announcing that the two firms were holding preliminary discussions. Descriptive language was a problem. After all, when did preliminary discussions become negotiations? Was it, as Alice (of *Alice in Wonderland)* said, "The words say what I mean for them to say, or at least mean what I say"? Or could the group agree on a more precise definition? PMI finally decided it wanted to issue a press release.

The business press in the United Kingdom is particularly aggressive and devotes a good deal more news space to accounting firms than does the press in most countries; reporters are always hungry for news, speculation, or anything else that might make a good story. And in the United States there was Lee Berton, who covered accounting for the *Wall Street Journal.* He always seemed to have a source somewhere willing to leak a big story. This certainly qualified; after the Price Waterhouse/Deloitte Haskins & Sells fiasco, a merger between the second and ninth largest U.S. firms would be big news.

KMG, on the other hand, preferred to close ranks, stress the importance of internal discipline, and keep a lid on the story—in other words, no press release. Actually, KMG representatives were less opposed to a press release than they appeared. They were responding to what they thought were PMI's ulterior motives. They were concerned that if news got out, pressure on them would be increased to consummate a merger that would result in a takeover. KMG had no plans to be taken over by anyone. Any merger would be a merger of equals.

Palmer understood. "We Canadians know very well the fear of being taken over by the giant next door," he told his KMG associates. But he knew it would not be easy to dispel KMG's fear that, despite friendly assurances to the contrary, PMI's real intention was to dress its takeover ambitions in the clothing of a merger.

An additional difficulty, it seemed to Palmer, was that Geert Timmer, the senior partner of the Dutch firm, was really interested only in Price Waterhouse as a merger partner. When the PW and Deloitte Haskins & Sells deal fell through in 1984, Timmer raised with KMG executives the possibility of a KMG and PW merger. As late as the summer of 1985, Timmer and other KMG leaders met with PW officials to see if a deal could be worked out.

In July PW unequivocally said no. The breakdown of discussions with DH&S had apparently been very draining for PW partners, and they had no desire to pursue discussions with anyone for a couple of years. Further, they had recently brought the German firm Treuarbeit into the PW orbit. KMG's Deutsche Treuhand-Gesellschaft thought it would have difficulty merging with Treuarbeit because of its partial ownership by the German government. Much to Timmer's disappointment, PW ceased to be an option.

As far as Palmer and other members of the KMG executive committee were concerned, the PW affair was another option eliminated. But the Dutch weren't quite ready to capitulate. There was still the question of the hidden Anglo agenda—a takeover. The Dutch were justifiably proud of their history and what they had built, and Palmer understood their trepidation. Nevertheless, because of his good relationship with Brown and his own judgment, he believed PMI was sincere about making the firm a more global organization with representation from all major economic sectors. He and other leaders spent the summer of 1985 hammering out international partnership agreements that ensured substantial European influence so that the new firm would not be dominated by the English and the Americans.

Palmer's friendship with Brown helped smooth the cultural differences. They compared notes about the progress of international negotiations, searching for ways to overcome problems.

Palmer told Brown of the concerns voiced by KMG's British and Dutch firms; Brown explained PMI's position. Both tried to use that knowledge to keep the talks moving forward. Despite their sincere best efforts, the talks stalled.

Many of the problems, Palmer believed, were brought about by miscommunication as thorny issues passed between cultures and languages. Signals that one group thought were perfectly innocuous were interpreted by another to mean something dastardly. Part of the misinterpretation might have been intentional—Palmer couldn't tell for sure—but one thing was certain: There was ample misunderstanding. KMG leaders tended to believe the worst interpretation of PMI's actions; Palmer could do little to convince them otherwise, and his influence was diminished by his early public support for the merger. His credibility as an impartial interpreter of events was strained.

The level of apprehension was articulated at the KMG conference in San Francisco just prior to the "final" negotiating session in Amsterdam in September 1985. One of the participants said angrily, "They are putting up smoke screens and giving us a few beads and small trinkets to appease us, but what they plan to do is take us over. KMG people—those in continental Europe in particular—will be swallowed up by the Anglo-Saxons."

Though the Canadians didn't particularly share this point of view, there apparently was some justification for such an opinion. Some of the senior PMI partners *did* seem inflexible. The firm had a proud heritage; it had only recently adopted a new worldwide identity system and wasn't ready to part with it. From the perspective of a potential merger partner, it was difficult to sort out who had the most influence—the moderates, who seemed genuinely to want a merger of equals, or the radicals, who wanted only to conquer the world.

It seemed to Palmer that what the Americans and British viewed as Timmer's Dutch stubbornness and inflexibility was his way of trying to provoke them to reveal themselves as the hard-nosed, aggressive Yanks and Brits they really were. It was a classic case of culture clash.

The negotiating style of the Europeans and the Anglo-Saxons seemed vastly different. Most Anglo-Saxons generally start the negotiating process with an opening position that is some distance away from their final position. They see the negotiating process as a series of moves in which one finds a compromise position somewhere between the opening and "will-not-budge" positions. The Dutch, on the other hand, are generally more direct in their views and take a no-nonsense approach, preferring not to waste a lot of time in discussion. As a result, it appeared to the Anglo-Saxons that the Dutch would stake out a position early in the game and then hunker down and remain immovable.

This was the cultural influence at work, Palmer thought. The British and the Americans expected the other side to be giving. The Dutch had nothing left to give. Had either side understood the other's position early in the game—and played by the same rules—most of the problems could have been avoided. Instead, a tense, negative atmosphere resulted.

Palmer didn't attend the meeting in Amsterdam. He stayed in Canada while his partner, Bill Goodlet, chairman of Thorne Riddell's policy group, went to Amsterdam. Goodlet reported back to the Canadian firm about the late-night meetings, the continuing negative interpretation of events, and the final break. He believed, given the emotions and attitudes of the participants, that it was very unlikely there could ever be a merger between PMI and KMG. After the negotiations broke down, Palmer met privately with Hans Havermann, John Thompson, and other KMG leaders in an attempt to understand where they thought the firm was going and to try to determine if the possibility of a merger with PMI was still alive.

It was his impression that Havermann alone thought there might still be a possibility of a KMG/PMI merger. Havermann had established a good working relationship with Larry Horner, and he believed they could reestablish communications after the participants had time to bind their wounds and reposition themselves for further discussions. Others, particularly the Dutch, were still suspicious about PMI's motives and still concerned about a takeover.

Palmer also thought the McKinsey "go-it-alone" plan might have influenced several national practices' willingness to continue merger discussions. KMG had even committed additional funds to its international budget to fund some of the initiatives McKinsey recommended.

The Canadians were disappointed at the merger's failure, but not altogether surprised. It left almost a feeling of foreboding. The Canadians had helped formulate the initial "go-it-alone" strategy—indeed, one of the founding principles of KMG had been to offer clients an alternative to the Big Eight—but Palmer and his partners had long since lost confidence in such an option. They simply had encountered too many problems in the United States. Large Canadian clients listed on the New York and American stock exchanges found that Main Hurdman wasn't well recognized on Wall Street, and they were being pushed by underwriters to go to Big Eight firms with the depth of resources and recognition KMG did not possess. Such pressures convinced the Canadians that spending another $15 million on the McKinsey initiatives wouldn't solve the problem. It was simply too large to be overcome by anything other than a Big Eight merger. "Going it alone" wasn't an option for Thorne Riddell. There were good ideas in the McKinsey study, the Canadians believed, but they were Band-Aids.™ They would not stop the bleeding.

Palmer and his partners spent the months of October and November 1985 studying their options. It seemed unlikely that a resolution of the differences with PMI would be forthcoming. In the longer term, the possibilities were real; for the short term, prospects were doubtful.

Palmer knew that Havermann was very much in favor of renewing negotiations and would be attempting to establish a dialogue with Horner. Palmer had only met Horner for the first time at the Paris meetings, but he immediately recognized him as "a powerful guy who could get things done." The Thorne Riddell partners knew that with movers like Havermann and Horner, there was a possibility of success. However, they still doubted the possibility of getting the two firms' Dutch and British contingents together. If a merger did happen, it would take a very long time—time the Canadians didn't have.

Thorne's need for better coverage in the States was urgent. Major clients, which had been appeased throughout 1985 by knowledge of the potential merger, were getting restless. When news of the failed merger attempts broke in September of that year, clients began telling Palmer and his partners that their solution was no longer working. Some clients said that as much as they liked the service in Canada, if they couldn't get comparable service in other countries—particularly the United States—they would have to change auditors. The large multinationals needed a full-service firm that could provide audit, tax, and consulting services at a consistent level of quality around the world.

"We stand to lose the upper end of our client base," Palmer told his partners. "These clients not only produce a lot of tax and consulting work for us, they are also the foundation of our reputation. Because we have them, others come to us. We cannot afford to jeopardize these relationships."

The Canadians began to review their options. They assembled data on all the Big Eight firms in Canada and asked questions. One possibility was to arrange a unilateral merger with PMI; after all, they knew all the right people. But they were convinced PMI wouldn't consider a merger in one country unless it was part of an international initiative. Besides, such inquiries might tip their hand before they were ready.

Of the other major firms, Ernst & Whinney seemed the next best choice. E&W had a strong international presence and was the number-three firm in the United States. The Canadian affiliate of E&W was not large, so Thorne Riddell would be important to the firm; the Thorne partners also liked E&W's entrepreneurial spirit. They were slightly troubled by their potential partner's weakness in continental Europe, but on balance, a merger seemed a good option. It would be a good, easy fit in Canada, and E&W's excellent position in the United States filled Thorne's immediate needs. Thorne would seek a merger with E&W.

Palmer paid a call on PMI's Brown. Because of their friendship, Palmer felt he owed it to Brown to tell him as much as he could. During the meeting, Palmer reviewed with Brown the major obstacles he saw to accomplishing a KMG/PMI merger, laying out a "road map" of problems and his view of how they could be solved. Palmer knew his friend well enough to know that he had already talked to many people involved in the merger process and "already had lots of road maps," but Palmer wanted to express his views anyway.

Next, Palmer told Brown he was very pessimistic about the way the discussions were going. Although he could not tell Brown directly about his plans, he wanted Brown to understand—in hindsight, when he read the news—why Thorne had merged with another firm.

Finally, Palmer said, "We have talked enough and should suspend discussions from this point on." Brown was clearly puzzled by the last message, but Palmer was insistent. Although he strongly disliked not being able to reveal the truth to his friend, the Thorne CEO thought it inappropriate to discuss a merger with PMI if Thorne was beginning exploratory talks with E&W.

By February 1986 the Thorne partners were in discussions with E&W. By early April both sides had pretty much concluded they could make a deal. Though nothing had been formalized, partners had gotten to know each other's style of dealing with problems. By the end of April, Palmer felt comfortable with E&W. He presented the idea to the Thorne Riddell policy group (similar to a board of directors) and asked for authorization to enter into formal negotiations with E&W. The request was granted.

The tough decision had been made, but Palmer knew his problems were far from over. He still faced the difficult task of telling his friends and associates at KMG that he was leaving the fold and going to a competitor. The first stop was New York for a meeting with Thompson, a good friend and chairman of Main Hurdman. Thompson was disappointed by the decision, but not totally surprised. The U.S. coverage had been an issue for some time, and Thompson didn't feel he could go too far in trying to dissuade his friend without appearing self-serving. Thompson warned Palmer to move slowly and wished him well.

The response was spirited on April 23 when Palmer delivered the message to Paul Boschma in Amsterdam, particularly when he laid out the timetable. Thorne planned to negotiate the deal during the rest of April and May, present the package to the partners for approval at the end of May, and make the merger effective August 1, 1986. After his initial surprise, Boschma urged Palmer to slow down and reconsider his plan. Boschma promised he would reconsider a Big Eight merger and help solve Thorne's problem in the United States.

As Boschma received the news in Amsterdam, Havermann, Johan Steenmeijer, and their partners Fred Janssen and Ruud Koedijk were meeting in Schleiden, West Germany, to discuss a possible merger with PMI. Extremely upset, Boschma phoned the four, interrupting their meeting to discuss the issue. After a hurried telephone conversation, Steenmeijer and Havermann caught the next flight to Amsterdam to meet with Boschma and Palmer.

Palmer was direct. "We have thought through the issues," he said, "and we're serious about going forward. While we haven't closed our minds to your suggestion, we have worked with KMG for more than a year to make something happen. Essentially, we have lost faith in KMG's ability to deliver and in our ability to influence KMG. Our position is very vulnerable; our risk of major client loss is imminent. We must do something; we cannot wait any longer."

It was a long flight home for Palmer. He was exhausted, but unable to relax. As he replayed the events of the preceding days in his mind, he was convinced more than ever that he and his partners were doing the right thing. They had studied their options carefully and considered all the avenues open to them; they had protected confidences, yet been truthful with everyone involved. His conscience was clear.

Palmer's experiences had dramatically underscored the key decision facing leaders involved in a merger. One alternative is to resolve all the details before the merger is approved. The other choice is to deal with the merger at a high level—resolve some of the overriding issues and then leave it to the merged firm to work out the details. Palmer would take the high road with E&W.

Despite the tensions that Thorne's potential defection created, KMG leaders tried to save the relationship. The weekend following their meeting with Palmer in Amsterdam, Havermann and Steenmeijer went to Toronto to meet with the executive committee of the Canadian firm. They left Toronto encouraged; Steenmeijer later described the mood as "rather optimistic about future developments."

Their optimism, however, was short-lived. Not long after the meeting, KMG received word that again things were not going well in Canada. This time it was Bill Morrison, managing partner of KMG's U.K. firm, who went to Toronto. His meeting with Thorne Riddell's Goodlet was unsuccessful.

On May 10 a KMG delegation consisting of Boschma, Morrison, Steenmeijer, and Thompson met with Thorne's full policy group. At the special meeting, they told the Thorne partners that they had reviewed KMG's position and had decided to try to revive merger discussions with PMI. Upon careful examination, in the harsh light of logic, they were quite optimistic that problems that seemed insurmountable the previous September could be overcome. KMG had an aggressive timetable that matched this optimism. The duo asked the Thorne partners to suspend negotiations with the still-unnamed Big Eight firm in Canada to give them the opportunity to see what could be accomplished with PMI.

For hours after the presentation, the policy group debated. KMG's request certainly seemed reasonable. Steenmeijer and others were very optimistic; perhaps it could work. After weighing the pluses and minuses, the negatives tipped the scale. The Canadians didn't doubt the sincerity of the people involved, but it was difficult to gauge the likelihood of success. Some of the obstacles loomed large just a few months before. There was tremendous risk, the partners felt, in waiting. On May 12 Goodlet advised Boschma that the Canadians were leaving.

The major conceptual issues had already been resolved with E&W. Negotiating the merger was simply a matter of formalizing what had been agreed on in the previous meetings. By late May the firms had an agreement in principle, which was presented to the partners of both firms. They approved it without a hitch. The firms spent June and July working out the details of compensation, governance, pensions, and leadership. On August 1, 1986—precisely on schedule—the merger was official.

The news broke on May 23. "Thorne Riddell, the Canadian affiliate of KMG Main Hurdman, the ninth biggest U.S. accounting firm, is defecting to join Cleveland-based Ernst & Whinney, according to sources close to both firms," reported the *Wall Street Journal*. While officials at neither firm would confirm the rumors, the Journal went on to say, "Meanwhile, reports are circulating among major accounting firms that KMG is again seeking a merger partner after its discussions with Peat, Marwick, Mitchell

& Co., the second biggest U.S. accounting firm, were aborted last September."[1]

As Palmer read the news in his Toronto office, he mused, *Isn't it ironic that we, by our actions, may have helped cause the very thing we wanted to happen—and we will be unable to benefit from it.*

Whether Palmer and the Thorne partners caused KMG to move more quickly back to the negotiating table with PMI is still conjectural. Informal merger discussions among the leaders (Horner, Butler, Brown, Havermann, Steenmeijer, and Boschma) were already well under way, and both sides were working vigorously to resolve any outstanding issues. But the Canadian situation did require the firms' leaders to go public with their partners sooner than they had planned, informing them that merger discussions were again under way.

---

1. Lee Berton, "Ernst & Whinney Said to Gain KMG Canadian Affiliate," *Wall Street Journal*, 23 May 1986, 27.

# Chapter Six

# Larry Horner and the Americans

As he looked around the room during the 1985 negotiations, Larry Horner realized that of the group, only he and a handful of others would remain in management roles beyond the next year. Most would be retired. Human nature being what it is, he thought, no one here is going to take a very long view of things. People generally avoid risk—and flexibility—in situations over which they will soon have little or no control.

Despite such reservations, Horner strongly supported the merger. The day before his election in October 1984 at the U.S. partners' meeting in Boca Raton, Fla., he pushed the PMI advisory committee very hard to pursue the KMG/PMI combination. It made sense to him from the beginning.

Soon after his election, he met with representatives of other Big Eight firms, including Arthur Young, Ernst & Whinney, and Arthur Andersen, to sound out possible interest in a merger. Those experiences, however tentative, convinced him that KMG was the best alternative, but he believed that he should at least test other options. In January 1985 he reported to the board of directors, "Other options would create serious problems that might weaken or destroy PMI, which we have worked very hard to develop and want to preserve. Even setting aside this matter, I don't believe AY or E&W will merge with us after the pressure of the DH&S and PW merger has been removed."

Horner went on to say he suspected that E&W and AY were considering a merger, but might have deferred action for the time being (the firms did merge in 1989). Horner viewed a merger with AA as a remote possibility at best. Other competitors had suggested PMI and AA should merge, observing wryly that these fierce competitors would destroy each other and open up the field.

Horner asked for and received authorization to pursue serious merger discussions with KMG. Strategically, it was a much better fit. A KMG/PMI merger would create a truly multinational organization with the largest national firms and possibilities for the best image, reputation, and clientele in the major countries in which they operated. These qualities, coupled with the firms' strong audit practices in several specialized industries—particularly finance and manufacturing—would create a powerful firm. In addition, PMI's strength in tax and consulting would expand KMG's capabilities in those practice areas. The firms' diverse client bases would also significantly expand referrals between countries. Horner strongly believed that this combination would yield much greater dividends than a similar merger between two Anglo-oriented firms. It had an added plus in that it was doubtful that any national regulatory body would object, because of the geographical diversity of the firms.

Because of his conviction that an international merger was essential for his firm to compete effectively in the global marketplace, and because of his leadership position in the international organization, Horner frequently shifted from U.S. to global issues as the merger negotiations took place. He delegated much of the responsibility for the U.S. combination to deputy chairman Robert Beecher, who in turn brought the U.S. firm's CFO and managing partner of its executive office, Harry Baird, into the loop. Horner and Beecher also enlisted Clifford Graese, retired vice chairman of audit, to help sort out the complex financial aspects of the transaction. Graese had headed the audit department of professional practice and was well known and respected throughout the firm and the profession for technical competence that bordered on wizardry as well as for his integrity. After a meeting in Harrare, Zimbabwe, Horner, on the flight home, laid out his thoughts to Graese.

The biggest problems in the United States were the vast differences in size and partner-to-staff ratios and the disparity in partners' incomes. Peat Marwick had U.S. revenues of slightly over $1 billion, 1,356 partners, and 10,356 professional staff—compared with Main Hurdman's $234 million in revenues, 529 partners, and 3,000 staff. Of most serious concern was the disparity in partner-to-staff ratios, the measure of a professional services firm's efficiency and profitability. KMG had 1 partner for every 5.7 staff members, while PMI's ratio was 1 to 7.9. Peat Marwick partners also earned almost double what their Main Hurdman counterparts earned.

Based on discussions with Main Hurdman during the first round, Horner figured the following conditions had to be met for the deal to work in the United States:

- All Main Hurdman partners would be admitted to the partnership and given a chance to prove themselves. Partner-to-staff ratios would be improved in the short term through an early retirement program. The leadership of the combined firm would then plan ways to make the ratios more compatible.

- Compensation would be equalized, for like functions,

over time. One way might be to allocate savings realized from the merger (such as elimination of duplicate costs) to the Main Hurdman partners.

- The firms would work together to retain senior nonpartner management and offer them opportunities to be admitted to the partnership.

- Main Hurdman partners would have some degree of economic protection in the event of termination.

- Offices would be reviewed on a case-by-case basis to determine which should absorb the other and who should manage the combined practice. Under special circumstances, in which leaders of the merged firm agreed, practices might be sold to their partners.

There would be problems internationally as well, the name among them. Horner and Hans Havermann had unsuccessfully attempted to strike a compromise on the name issue as the merger began to fall apart in 1985. They wouldn't let the name kill the deal again. KMG wanted its initials in the parent or international firm name; Peat Marwick KMG was acceptable, Horner thought. There would also be consolidation issues, such as combining offices, and PMI's Continental European Firm (CEF) would be most affected in a merger. No doubt the PMI firm would have to be merged into KMG's national firms, but the CEF's board of directors still supported the move, although with several reservations. Horner also believed that KMG was worried that the CEF would be given the authority to veto the merger.

KMG leaders were also seriously concerned about PMI's willingness and ability to merge in the United States and the United Kingdom. In a prophetic statement, Horner told his fellow directors, "From KMG's point of view, the two biggest problems appear to be in the United Kingdom and the United States. It is too early to say that these firms can be brought together, although it is very doubtful an overall merger can be consummated otherwise."

At KMG's 1985 annual meeting in early September in San Francisco, much of the discussion centered on the merger and the joint meeting of the firms scheduled to take place later that month in Amsterdam. PMI chairman Thomas L. Holton and incoming chairman James R. Brown went to San Francisco to discuss the major issues with KMG chairman Reinhard Goerdeler and executive partner Paul Boschma.

The situation in the United Kingdom—especially the partner-to-staff ratio—topped the list, Holton reported. KMG planned to go back to basics; the firm would trim the partner ranks in order to work out a full merger. Boschma reported that Bill Morrison, managing partner of KMG's U.K. firm (Thomson McLintock), promised not to accept a "no" answer without discussing it further with KMG's international office.

The name continued to be an issue. Peat Marwick KMG was acceptable for an international name, but not for local use. KMG preferred its initials before local country names, particularly in Holland and West Germany. Since most of the opposition seemed to come from KMG's Dutch firm, the group agreed it would be a good idea for Johan Steenmeijer, the KMG Dutch firm's senior partner, and Graham Corbett, who headed PMI's CEF, to discuss the matter prior to the joint steering committee meeting in Amsterdam.

Governance was a big question mark. The group talked about operating dual headquarters offices with one in Europe (probably Amsterdam) and one in the United States. The group eventually concluded that trying to run such a large organization with cochairmen would be difficult. The buck had to stop somewhere. There should be one head person and one head office. The issue was left open, however.

Professional standards were a delicate problem. Goerdeler was satisfied that the standards questions in France and Switzerland had been resolved. Holton didn't see it that way. He insisted on interpractice reviews before professional standards could be declared compatible between the firms.

KMG also wanted assurances from PMI's five largest firms and KMG's nine largest that they were not only committed to the concept of a merger, but would help solve problems that arose during the negotiating process. The national firms involved were (for PMI) the United Kingdom, continental Europe, Canada, the United States, and Australia; and (for KMG) West Germany, the Netherlands, France, the Nordic countries, Switzerland, the United Kingdom, the United States, Canada, and Australia. In the event of an impasse, both sides would agree in advance to accept some form of mediation.

It was a pretty long list of issues to be resolved in a short time, Horner thought. He was disappointed when the negotiations failed, but not surprised, given the situation. He was, however, determined to do all he could to get the discussions back on track. As the delegates left Amsterdam, he and Havermann both hoped they could revive discussions at the appropriate time. Both saw the wisdom of the combination and believed, in time, they could sell the idea to their firm.

A determined man who had risen from staff accountant in the Kansas City office to the top position in his firm, Horner was not accustomed to giving up simply because there were a few obstacles in his way. He had been to the mountain; he had seen the vision. And he was not going to give it up easily.

The vision belonged to Horner, perhaps more than to any of the others. It didn't come to him in a blinding flash in the middle of the night. It was, instead, a rather mundane and unsophisticated process, he thought. The world of the mid-1980s had changed, and he was responding to the changes. It was rapidly becoming essential for major accounting firms to have a strong international presence as their clients' operations spread around the globe.

Horner's view was more out of experience and intuition than a matter of long-term strategic planning. PMI had merged with various specialty firms over the years and begun new marketing initiatives to fuel internal growth. But a mega-merger was still a novelty. Horner had discussed the possibility with other firm leaders as he considered running for chairman in 1984, particularly after Price Waterhouse and Deloitte Haskins & Sells announced their intentions to merge.

KMG's European strength particularly appealed to Horner. Long before it became a popular topic in the U.S. business press, he believed the European Community's (EC) goal of free movement of capital, goods, services, and people between member countries by 1992 would have a major impact on worldwide business. The 1992 initiative would create a consumer market of some 325 million people that would fuel the growth of the already huge multinational companies located in EC countries. Accounting firms needed strength in Europe, and KMG would provide it. The KMG/PMI combination would be a balanced organization with a leading market position in most of the major countries in which it practiced. The merger fit the vision.

Such were Horner's thoughts as he left Amsterdam en route to Cannes for a CEF partners' meeting where he would no doubt be asked to explain recent events to a lot of angry CEF partners. Despite the difficulties the merger's architects had encountered, Horner was not discouraged. The merger still made sense. It fell apart because too many people with too many vested interests were involved. He was convinced that at some point he would be able to salvage the discussions.

The meeting met Horner's expectations. Discussions were heated at times, as partners demanded to know why they had not been informed earlier about merger negotiations, but Horner was a veteran when it came to tense situations. He dealt with the problems as they arose.

As things settled down at the meeting, Horner's thoughts

returned to getting the merger back on track. He wondered whether he should call Havermann to arrange a meeting to discuss their options. However, he knew he must be cautious. He could not put Havermann in a compromising situation with his partners. With the help of Dieter Lotz, senior partner of PMI's German firm, a phone call was arranged with Havermann. After exchanging pleasantries, the two got down to business, agreeing their firms would be foolish to lose this opportunity again. They agreed to meet in Paris on October 11 to discuss the alternatives. Horner returned to the States to go to Washington, D.C., to attend a small dinner party for a young, relatively unknown U.S. senator named Dan Quayle.

Havermann and Horner did meet in Paris, and with their wives they socialized and then talked business. Horner left Paris buoyed by the experience, convinced that by working with Havermann and a few others, the group could agree on the major points of the merger before anyone else got involved. By limiting the size of the group, they would minimize the problems that had plagued the earlier discussions. The two agreed they would meet again during the 1985 Christmas holidays when the Horners came to West Germany to visit Mrs. Horner's mother.

Horner and Havermann knew full well the problems to be solved if the merger was to be successful. The failed discussions had clearly revealed the differences that had divided the two firms. Name and governance issues could be negotiated. Partner-to-staff ratios, on the other hand, were a problem. The average among the Big Eight was around 8 to 1; if KMG was to merge with any of them, it would have to trim its partner ranks at least in the United States and the United Kingdom.

A little over a month after the talks broke down, KMG—in a shake-up of its U.S. operations—named James W. Hendrix, deputy director of operations in the Midwest, South, Southeast, and South Central United States, to head up the U.S. firm. Hendrix, who had a reputation as a mover, would relocate to New York to redirect the operational side of the business into more profitable consulting and tax work. John Thompson, who would continue as chairman and CEO, would then be free to focus on long-range planning. He told the *Wall Street Journal,* "Our goal is to boost consulting's share of total U.S. revenues to 15% from the current 10% and tax's portion to 30% from 25% over the next three years."[1]

The Journal went on to observe that Main Hurdman was "over-partnered" compared with the larger accounting firms. Hendrix responded that the firm traditionally had more partners per staff because, "We have less personnel in our offices than the Big 8. This could be a big plus for us as our business expands, but I do feel that partners can no longer expect to be good technicians. They've got to learn how to sell our vast array of services to clients, too."[2]

Thompson, who now heads his own interim executive placement firm in New York City, believed a KMG merger was inevitable; acceptable conditions would eventually be worked out. It might be PMI or another firm, but he believed KMG was destined for a merger. One of the founding principles had been strong national firms linked internationally, but at number nine in the United States, Main Hurdman was hardly dominant. Given the advantages the eight largest firms enjoyed in capitalization, training, marketing, recruiting, and virtually every other aspect of the profession, it would be impossible for his firm to overtake the others without a merger.

There was no magic about the Big Eight, he believed; they simply had the advantages that size brings. They were no different from the so-called Big Three automakers or Seven Sisters of the oil industry. Competing with them was like being in the NFL (America's National Football League). On any given day his team

---

1. Lee Berton, "KMG Main Hurdman Picks Hendrix for Post," *Wall Street Journal,* 25 October 1985, 20.
2. Ibid.

could beat any other given team. They had enjoyed some successes, such as winning the City of New York audit when Deloitte Haskins & Sells rotated out (the city is required to put its audit out for bid every four years), but they couldn't do it day in and day out. They simply didn't have the depth of resources.

Thompson knew KMG wanted better coverage in the United States, but he didn't get much in the way of specifics. Most of Main Hurdman's work came from KMG's large multinational European clients and the middle market clients it had acquired on its own. To grow large enough to compete with the Big Eight would require total reorientation of the firm and huge infusions of capital. The firm would have to invest in people and technology and resign from unprofitable accounts long before new clients in more profitable industry segments could be acquired. It would take time and commitment, both of which were expensive luxuries in a profession whose assets go down in the elevator every night.

One thing was plain, however. All indicators in the profession pointed to a major merger in the Big Eight. It was likely that others would follow. If they were to become a trend, Thompson intended to be on the front end of it, not left behind.

The next shoe dropped in late January 1986. It came in the form of a Main Hurdman announcement that it was reducing its New York executive staff by 10 percent, a move expected to save the firm between $2 million and $3 million a year. Hendrix was already making his mark. He told the *Wall Street Journal* the cuts would be achieved mostly through retirements, although some partners would leave for other reasons. According to the Journal, "KMG's moves [were] in line with cost-reduction efforts by other major accounting firms. Revenue growth has slowed as clients have pressed for lower auditing fees. 'Any accounting firm that can do the same job at a lesser fee is probably ahead of its competitors these days,' Mr. Hendrix said."[3]

---

3. Lee Berton, "KMG Reduces Executive Staff in New York 10%," *Wall Street Journal*, 30 January 1986, 23.

On the PMI front, Horner attempted to continue his international dialogue with Havermann after their Christmas meeting, being careful to maintain strictest confidence. At this early stage, he couldn't even advise his board of directors. As things became more promising and it appeared they might be able to resume discussions, Horner and Havermann widened the circle to include Brown, PMI chairman-elect, and Steenmeijer, senior partner of KMG's Dutch firm. Jim Butler, likely to become senior partner of PMI's U.K. firm, initially had to be excluded so as not to compromise him with his partners. Elections had not yet been held in the United Kingdom, and if Butler was elected as expected, he would not take office until July.

A merger strategy gradually began to evolve. The four major firms—in the United States, the United Kingdom, West Germany, and the Netherlands—would have to agree to merge. If they could agree, their unity would go a long way toward persuading the others to join them. The "big four" would provide attractive incentives, but would merge—pending the PMI council's approval—with or without the smaller firms.

The plan would be for KMG and PMI to work toward an international agreement, then work out the deals in their respective countries. But as a practical matter, international and domestic discussions would have to proceed concurrently. Horner advised his deputy chairman that he had resurrected the merger negotiations.

Things progressed relatively well into the spring of the following year. Horner, Beecher, and the U.S. team were cautiously optimistic. (KMG's negotiating team was headed up by Tom Leonard the first time and Phil McCormick the second time.) Then came the news from KMG that its Canadian affiliate was seriously thinking of defecting. Horner was at a General Electric shareholders' meeting in Kansas City on his way to a Stanford University Business School advisory committee meeting when Havermann called with the news.

A flurry of phone calls followed as schedules were hastily rearranged. Horner canceled his participation in the Stanford University meeting and returned to New York. He reached PMI's Brown, who interrupted a Florida vacation to attend the meeting. The KMG delegation stopped off in New York to personally deliver the bad news from Toronto to Horner and Brown and to ponder the future. The heretofore small, tightly knit group was about to expand. They would have to go public with their partners.

The next day, the group met at the Pierre Hotel to discuss their strategy. Despite the commitment both firms demonstrated, it had all been for nothing. The Canadians were simply too far down the road with Ernst & Whinney to change. The media reported the story on May 23 amid speculation that KMG was once again looking for a merger partner following the 1985 breakdown in discussions with PMI.

On May 12, the day before the urgent meeting with the international group, Horner had scheduled a lunch at the Links Club with Main Hurdman's Thompson and Hendrix to keep the U.S. discussions moving along. Main Hurdman was very receptive to a merger. Indeed, because of European pressure to expand coverage in the United States, some type of merger was almost a foregone conclusion, but Horner suspected that Thompson and Hendrix would not simply roll over and accept the first offer that came along.

His instincts were correct. KMG's U.S. firm had studied its options thoroughly. Most of Thompson's time for the past two or three years had been spent working on alternative strategies. He and his most senior partners had considered options ranging from redirecting their practice areas to "going it alone" in the United States. They ultimately concluded that a merger was their only real choice. But they would not give away the store. If they couldn't get a fair deal from Peat Marwick, they would go elsewhere. Thompson's take on Horner was that he would be tough, but fair.

On June 10 Hendrix asked Beecher to bring him up to date on the U.S. merger discussions. After looking over earlier discussion drafts, they reviewed the specifics in light of current discussions. They talked about a December 31, 1986, or January 1, 1987, date for the merger, although they agreed they probably wouldn't attempt to "move in together" until the end of the busy season.[4]

The nagging problems that had plagued the international discussions persisted with the U.S. talks. Some were financial; KMG's revenues in the United States were about 10 percent below budget, but Hendrix continued his "leaning and meaning" program. Unprofitable offices were closed, and partner-to-staff ratios were improving. Retiring partners were not replaced, and poor performers were leaving the firm. Beecher encouraged him to continue his cost-cutting programs.

As always, the name of the merged firm was a problem. Hendrix thought the name should be KMG Peat Marwick Main. Beecher responded that the idea had never been discussed by either firm's U.S. negotiating team, but that he would consult with Horner. Privately, Beecher thought having KMG in front and Main as a follower was a bit much. (Eventually, of course, the firms compromised and the merged firm was known as Peat Marwick Main & Co. in the United States. *Main* was dropped in 1989, and the name was officially changed to KPMG Peat Marwick to emphasize both international and national strength.)

The composition of the transition committee was an issue as well. Hendrix suggested that instead of three members from each firm as they had discussed previously, it might work better with three KMG and two PMI members. The two agreed they couldn't resolve everything at once and passed along the open issues to their respective chairmen.

Eventually the U.S. firms agreed that governance issues would

---

4. U.S. public companies are required to provide an annual report to shareholders shortly after year-end. Tax consultants' busy season continues until the April 15 federal income tax filing deadline.

be resolved by retaining Peat Marwick's basic format and structure. Positions would be added for Main Hurdman partners to
provide proportionate representation on the board of directors,
operating committee, strategic planning committee, and func-
tional and industry practice committees. With national and key
executive office positions, the Peat Marwick structure would
remain with positions created for key Main Hurdman executive
partners. Main Hurdman's regional partners would continue to
provide assistance on regional operating and personnel matters
during a one-year transition period. After a "reasonable" integration period, the organizational structure would be adjusted to an
optimum size with key positions going to those considered most
appropriate by the chairman and board of directors. The transition
period would also allow time for Peat Marwick and Main Hurdman partners to get to know each other and for Main Hurdman
partners to learn Peat Marwick policies and practices.

The merged firm's leaders would review the operating offices
on a case-by-case basis, considering economic, professional, and
client service issues, and select an ongoing management team for
each office. The new firm would attempt to obtain reasonable
representation from both predecessor firms. In locations where
only one firm had an office, the assumption was that it would
remain relatively intact.

A negotiating team would move the discussions forward to the
point of putting the merger to a vote of the general partnership.
After it was approved, the team would be responsible for resolving
any issues necessary to achieve actual integration of the firms. At
that time, a transition committee would come into being. Its
responsibility would be to address any problems brought to its
attention by the firm's board of directors or senior management
and to serve as a "protector" of partners in situations that
involved compensation, key administrative posts, transfers, client
reassignments, and poor performance. The committee would not

have final authority, but would have considerable influence and direct access to the chairman and board of directors.

Compensation would be adjusted over a period of four to five years through a complicated formula based on performance and profits. According to the memorandum of understanding, over a four- to five-year period all partners in the firm would receive comparable income levels for comparable contributions. The agreement also stated that the increase in compensation for Main Hurdman partners would focus on the compensation of Peat Marwick partners with similar responsibilities and performance.

In addition, Main Hurdman partners' jobs would be protected for three years except in those egregious situations that the transition committee felt would have called for termination in the Main Hurdman organization, even if the merger had not taken place. The deal also allowed for mutually agreeable early retirements or spin-offs of practice units.

Pension issues, always a touchy subject since most professional services firms fund pension liabilities out of current revenues, would be resolved by bringing Main Hurdman partners into the Peat Marwick plan effective on the date of the merger. Although no credit would be given under the plan for past service, years of service would be considered in determining vesting in the plan. The goal was to ensure that all partners were treated fairly and according to their contribution to the firm.

Horner, Beecher, and Graese blitzed the country. At regional meetings that included all U.S. partners, Horner laid out the international benefits while Beecher and Graese covered the Main Hurdman merger. The meetings, according to Beecher, were "enormously well received."

As the domestic discussions moved briskly along, the already delicate international negotiations were upset briefly on June 17, 1986, when a letter from Ernst & Whinney chairman Ray Groves landed on Boschma's desk at KMG headquarters in Amsterdam with copies to KMG central management committee members. The letter spelled out a detailed invitation for KMG to merge with E&W.

Groves recalled discussions about the profession with Goerdeler in 1984–1985, and they agreed on most issues. He noted that the merger of their respective Canadian firms (which was neither initiated nor participated in by either international organization) precipitated a discussion at E&W International about creating the first truly international accounting firm. Groves wrote, "I have been designated by our member firms to communicate to you and your partners E&W's very sincere interest in immediately meeting with KMG representatives to negotiate a worldwide merger of KMG and E&W, two strong international firms of equal and complementary strengths."

Groves attached a list of principles his firm would consider appropriate for a merger between their firms. These included such things as:

- "Balanced and broad" representation from both firms on an international management committee, with equal representation during a transitional period.

- Two international executive offices: one in Amsterdam and one in New York.

- Two cochairmen: one from each firm and, subsequently, each representing significant geographic areas of the world.

- A full-time executive partner in charge of each international office.

- Increasing responsibility for international direction and strategy on such matters as geographic coverage and research and development.

The name of the new firm would be KMG Ernst & Whinney and would offer advantages not present in mergers of other international firms. Besides, this was a deal that could be done quickly. Groves wrote, "Because of our knowledge of each other and the research and internal discussions that have taken place in arriving at these proposed principles, we believe that an international merger agreement could be negotiated in one month, and most national mergers within a few months thereafter."

KMG's central management committee discussed the E&W offer, but never seriously considered it. Bootleg copies of Groves' letter that found their way to PMI attested to KMG's commitment to the KMG/PMI merger. Besides, according to published reports, the PMI and E&W offers were two of five. Others were from Coopers & Lybrand, Deloitte Haskins & Sells, and Arthur Andersen.

Andersen was one of the earliest suitors. Soon after the discussions broke down in 1985, Duane Kullberg, Andersen's CEO, went to Amsterdam to meet Boschma and Steenmeijer. To avoid creating rumors and speculation, the three scheduled a luncheon in a small out-of-the-way restaurant on the outskirts of the city. Business was slow; there were only four other patrons in the restaurant. Before lunch was over, the trio knew they had been recognized, but they hardly expected the speed with which the news traveled. Back in New York, Horner had the news before dinnertime that Steenmeijer and Boschma had lunched with Kullberg.

Despite last-minute maneuvering by competitors, the merger moved along. PMI scheduled a special international council meeting for August 11 at New York's Carlyle Hotel to discuss particulars of both the domestic and international mergers. The committees and task forces had done their work. It was time to decide whether to proceed.

The PMI council overwhelmingly supported the combination and authorized the leadership to move forward. For Horner, the next seventeen days required nonstop meetings in London, Amsterdam, and New York as the final details were resolved. On August 28, the KMG/PMI joint steering committee met at the Carlyle Hotel, and at 3:00 p.m. in the East Versailles Room the delegates signed the international memorandum of understanding. That night, Horner invited the negotiating team to his home for a celebration dinner.

With the signing of the international memorandum of understanding, the national firms turned their attention to getting the merger together in their own countries. Horner and Beecher ironed out the remaining details of the U.S. merger with Thompson and Hendrix. When the moment came for Hendrix and Beecher to approve the U.S. memorandum of understanding before the final signing by the chairmen, Hendrix strode into Beecher's office, looked at the document, then said gruffly, "I suppose you want me to sign that paper just like it is." Beecher, well aware of his counterpart's unpredictable negotiating style, responded, "Well, yes, Jim. That would be nice."

"Then give me a pen and get out of my way," Hendrix barked.

On October 3, 1986, Horner and Thompson initialed the memorandum of understanding and forwarded it to their boards of directors for final approval. The U.S. directors approved the plan and set the merger date for January 1, 1987, with the physical combination of the firms to take place on April 1.

Reaction from the business community was immediate and positive. Horner's friends and business associates phoned and wrote to congratulate him on his achievement and to salute KPMG's expanded international capability. Over the next few months, Horner would log thousands of airline miles and reach many emotional highs and lows as he crisscrossed the globe selling the merger to the various national practices. But for now it was over. The vision was alive. There would be a merger.

# Chapter Seven

# Hans Havermann and the Germans

Few involved in the merger discussions appreciated its opportunities more than Hans Havermann. He himself had joined KMG's German firm, Deutsche Treuhand-Gesellschaft, through a merger and had risen to the position of CEO of West Germany's premier auditing and accounting firm. He knew firsthand the opportunities mergers presented to ambitious individuals, as well as the growth potential for two powerful partners.

Havermann knew many leaders of Big Eight firms well and had several friends at PMI. He had served on the International Accounting Standards Committee with Joe Cummings, PMI's international contact partner and deputy senior partner of the U.S. firm from 1972 until 1978. Havermann spent several weekends at Cummings' home in Connecticut, so it was natural that they would chat from time to time about the possibility of doing business together. Havermann also knew William Mecklenburg, PMI's Continental European Firm senior partner from 1972 until 1976, and had met Walter Hanson, PMI's highly respected U.S. firm senior partner for fourteen years before he retired in 1979. Havermann and Cummings had explored an affiliation between their firms, but were unable to work it out.

When the discussions with PMI rolled around in the mid-1980s, Havermann was in a better position to make things happen. He shared the view of most of the players (Larry Horner in particular) that the negotiating group that met in Paris in January 1985 was simply too large. Both firms considered themselves democratic organizations and wanted ample representation of their various constituencies. But eight people on either side—complicated by different languages—was an impossible situation.

More than anything else, Havermann thought the discussions had been premature. The senior leadership of both firms had been in place for a good number of years, and since several of the senior partners were near retirement, they were reluctant to commit their firms to something they wouldn't be around to complete. Havermann also felt that many of those involved simply didn't see the opportunities. Most accounting firms acquired smaller firms, merged with others, and worked out affiliate relationships regularly. It was the nature of the business when one had clients scattered around the globe. Often it made more sense to connect with an established firm staffed by resident nationals than to send expatriates from headquarters. Havermann felt that to many of the sixteen representatives in attendance at the Paris conference, it was just another merger discussion.

Havermann had trouble understanding all the quarreling about the name of the firm and its logotype. Participants had become so immersed in trivial details that they were willing to allow this marvelous opportunity to slip from their grasp. It was hard to imagine any client in any country really caring whether the firm was KMG Peat Marwick or Peat Marwick KMG or KPG or KPMG or ABC. Would the color of the logo help gain business?

Would clients stream through the door if its sign were KMG black and blue or reject the firm entirely if its colors were PMI burgundy and gray? Could clients care if the firm's colors were pink and violet so long as they got the highest-quality professional services available? Havermann found the whole business tiresome.

He was also concerned about the personality fit between members of the two organizations. It wasn't a matter of right or wrong, theirs or ours. Discussion leaders on both sides at times seemed to have difficulty relating to one another. Havermann thought it was just that some people like each other and can work together—they share a common view and understand each other—while others can't. It was a simple matter of chemistry, or lack of it, that caused the discussions to self-destruct.

One PMI representative seemed different to Havermann. Horner, chairman-elect of the U.S. firm, didn't need to be told what the Europeans were thinking; he instinctively understood. He appreciated the fact that PMI was an Anglo-American firm and KMG was European, with a different background, history, and philosophy. People could be different and still work well together. Horner was an American who—unlike most—could be a member of a club and not always have to dominate it. He was a man with whom Havermann could work. Havermann and Horner shared a view of a truly global organization, an international organization in which no single country or region dominated.

"Do you think PMI is a truly international firm?" Havermann asked Horner. "No," Horner replied. "It is an anglicized firm with worldwide operations, but it is by no means an international firm." "It's different with KMG," Havermann said. "We have been thinking internationally since our inception. We started with many independent international firms, and we were required to think and work globally from the very beginning."

Horner and Havermann each seemed realistic and practical to the other. They saw in this situation an advantage for both firms.

PMI had spent a lot of money trying to establish itself in continental Europe, but had never been accepted by the blue-chip companies; KMG, meanwhile, was very weak in America. Those two facts alone were enough to warrant a merger, but there were other advantages. Where neither was particularly dominant—South America, the Far East, the Middle East—they would be much stronger and more powerful together. But the real key, Havermann believed, was Europe. It wouldn't be the same strategic fit with any other Big Eight firm. There was only one dominant firm in Europe, and that was KMG.

As he conducted his personal postmortem on the failed discussions, Havermann concluded there was perhaps a faint shred of hope in this failure. Maybe people wouldn't realize what a great opportunity they had until it was gone. Under different circumstances the negotiators might concern themselves more with the opportunities than on gaining the advantage for themselves and their firms. You can take such an approach when it involves only your firm, he believed, but such an attitude will most certainly end in failure when other firms are involved. Havermann would allow a little time to elapse before broaching the subject with Horner. With their common views, perhaps the two could develop a more businesslike approach to a future merger.

Like many Germans, Havermann had learned to be flexible. As a consequence of the First and Second World Wars, fortunes abroad were lost, and runaway inflation at home rendered everything virtually worthless. Buildings and factories were razed, and the economy was in shambles. Everything had to be rebuilt.

The progress of KMG's German firm paralleled its country's history. Founded in 1890 by the giant Deutsche Bank as Deutsch-Amerikanische Treuhand-Gesellschaft, the firm's initial purpose was to look after its clients' investments in American railroads. (In 1893 the company's name was changed to its present name, Deutsche Treuhand-Gesellschaft [DTG].) Two years after it was founded, the firm withdrew from the United States and shifted its focus to audits of public companies, assistance with bankruptcy reorganizations, and trust work once the American railroads had been stabilized. Unlike accounting firms in many other countries, German auditing companies were initially organized as *Gesellschaft,* or corporations, with shareholders instead of partners as owners. The designation *partner* is an executive title. It is a tradition that continues today.

At the end of World War I, DTG followed its clients to Turkey and Russia. German companies built railroads, roads, and dams, and DTG began to expand internationally as clients began rebuilding their firms. The business of auditing got a boost in 1931 when emergency regulation established a statutory audit requirement for all public companies. Financial institutions, manufacturing companies, and retail stores all became potential DTG audit clients. Even small, privately held companies were potential tax clients. Business was good.

World War II changed all that. Entire cities were destroyed by Allied bombs, once again German companies lost their holdings abroad, and the economy was in ruins. Reinhard Goerdeler, a bright, young accountant who would one day head KMG, was in a Nazi prison camp. He was the son of Leipzig mayor Carl Goerdeler, a patriot who before the war repeatedly warned Western leaders about the Nazi menace and was a leader in the German Resistance. Reinhard Goerdeler, his mother, and the rest of the family were incarcerated as political prisoners following the elder Goerdeler's execution for his part in the plot to assassinate Adolf Hitler. The conspirators had organized a new government to replace the hated Nazis (upon Hitler's death) with Carl Goerdeler as chancellor. When a suitcase bomb failed to kill Hitler, Goerdeler fled to the countryside, assisted by the German Resistance. He was caught and hanged shortly before the war ended.

Young Goerdeler joined DTG in 1953, and the firm followed the German business migration, first to North and South America and eventually to the rest of the world. German companies, if left alone in foreign lands, would soon be acquired as clients by auditors in those countries. During the next two decades, DTG sent auditors to its client's locations, acquired a few local firms, and established representative arrangements with others.

By the 1960s Goerdeler was traveling throughout Europe, establishing small offices and forging alliances with other national firms that helped each other with international clients. DTG's relationship with Klynveld Kraayenhof & Co. (KKC) was the result of such an arrangement. The alliance was formed to look after Deutsche Grammophon, a record company formed through a joint venture of KKC client Philips and DTG client Siemens.

By the late 1970s Goerdeler saw that a more formal structure was needed, particularly in Europe, if the firms were to continue providing top-quality service to their international clients. On September 13, 1978, Goerdeler organized a meeting of the European representative firms at DTG offices in Frankfurt. Optimism ran high as the various leaders described their operations and talked about their clients: Shell, KLM, Philips, Carlsberg, Heineken, Pirelli, Crédit Suisse, Siemens, Daimler (Mercedes) Benz, and BMW were but a few of the European blue-chip companies on the client lists.

The meeting went extraordinarily well; by the time it was over, the firms had agreed to meet in Amsterdam on December 1 to sign a merger agreement. So certain were they that the deal would be consummated that the champagne was already chilled. But it didn't work. Too many people with too many different opinions and too many unresolved questions scuttled the meeting. "The second meeting was a disaster," Goerdeler recalled. "If you want to bring people together—for a large meeting, in particular—you must cover every detail. Everything must be arranged beforehand so that all you have to do is sit down and sign."

The signing was postponed until July 21, 1979, to allow sufficient time to work out the details. Despite last-minute activity in finalizing arrangements, the signing did occur. It was all done—except for a name. In an international partnership representing several languages and cultures, adopting a name acceptable to all was not an easy task.

Finally, the group settled on Logos—Greek for *word*. It seemed harmless enough; indeed, it had many positive connotations. Trouble was, it didn't work well around the world. In some languages *Logos* was used as a substitute in the Christian religion for the Bible, the Word of God. It was blasphemous.

Representatives from the still-unnamed organization met in September of the same year at a seaside resort in Holland. After much discussion, it was felt that the only workable solution was for the international organization to assume personal names. This was a problem for the Germans. DTG was a corporate name (roughly translates to German Trust Company). A Bavarian partner came up with the winning idea: "Let's use Dr. Goerdeler's name to represent the German firm," he suggested. "He is well known in the profession, he was the first president of the International Federation of Accountants, and he has friends around the world."

The name Klynveld would represent the Dutch contingent; Main would be used to show the American connection. Having selected the names that would be included, the group left it to the Dutch to decide in which order the names should appear. The Dutch experimented with the various arrangements, finally settling on KMG because it was the most euphonious. The firm became Klynveld Main Goerdeler.

Goerdeler and Havermann had been deeply involved in setting up KMG's international organization, and Goerdeler had served for several years as its chairman. These events affected KMG and the German firm. It was understood from the beginning of the exploratory merger talks that none of the stronger firms would leave the organization to merge separately. They would not abandon their weaker members; it was an all-or-nothing deal. The smaller firms might choose to go along, but they would not be forced.

This strong European organization attracted the attention of most of the Big Eight, many of which expressed an interest in working with KMG in some fashion. KMG leaders listened politely, but they really weren't too interested. Their very reason for being, after all, was to provide an independent, international accounting firm to serve clients based in Europe; it was an alternative to the Big Eight, not part of it.

Their resistance waned as demands for better coverage outside Europe increased. The U.S. problem was particularly troublesome. KMG needed a relationship with one of the large, prestigious American firms to crack the U.S. blue-chip market.

By 1984 Goerdeler and Havermann were listening carefully to senior Big Eight partners who came calling. The German firm was particularly attractive to potential merger partners because of its size, the dominant market position it enjoyed, and its outstanding client list. But DTG stuck to its KMG commitment; any merger would include the entire international firm.

Havermann was thinking about the international firm when Horner phoned from Cannes. Like Horner, he had planned to keep up the friendship and looked to the time when they could begin talking again about a merger. He planned to wait long enough for participants to reflect on what went wrong, but not so long that they would lose interest. Now, close on the heels of the breakdown in negotiations, Horner was calling. It was a good sign.

The first question on both their minds was the same. "Did we make a wise decision?" they asked each other. The answer on both sides was a resounding no. As they talked, they reviewed the problems that had seemed insurmountable just a few weeks before. They agreed that most of the points were trivial.

"To give up this opportunity because of such issues is stupid," Havermann said. "Is it absolutely important whether the firm is called KMG Peat Marwick or Peat Marwick KMG? Is this vital?" he asked. Horner chuckled. He agreed completely with Havermann's assessment. It was foolish for their firms to let a silly disagreement ruin a once-in-a-lifetime opportunity.

A merger made good business sense, the two agreed. To Havermann, it was simple. Although DTG was the largest accounting firm in West Germany, its clients operated all over the world. One Düsseldorf client operated in fifty countries. The client was headquartered in Havermann's backyard, and the firms had a good working relationship, but Havermann knew if he couldn't serve his client around the world, someone else would. DTG was committed to serving its international clients, but couldn't establish a worldwide firm on its own. There was simply not enough money and experienced people available to colonize the accounting world. Even KMG's alternative strategy of "going it alone" seemed unrealistic to Havermann. A merger with a Big Eight firm was the only reasonable answer.

Discussions continued on and off throughout the early part of 1986. Havermann had frequent conversations with Johan Steenmeijer, head of KMG's Dutch firm; Horner; and Jim Brown, PMI chairman. Things looked promising.

Springtime brought a problem with Canada. Havermann knew Thorne Riddell, the KMG Canadian firm, had received a good deal of pressure from clients to provide better coverage in the United States. And he knew its need was urgent; senior partner John Palmer had told him so when he visited Düsseldorf soon after discussions with PMI broke down. In fact, Palmer had been so insistent about resuming talks that Havermann considered Palmer squarely behind a KMG/PMI merger. Havermann saw no need even to discuss the resumption of talks with Palmer.

Havermann was shocked when he heard the Canadians were considering leaving KMG to join Ernst & Whinney. He had thought Palmer was one of the KMG/PMI merger's strongest supporters. And now, just two or three months before they could get a deal together, the Canadians were bolting. The immediate threat of losing clients had pushed them out the door. It fell to Havermann, in his position as a member of KMG's central management committee and senior partner of an outstanding national firm, to help keep the Canadian firm in the fold. Havermann joined the KMG delegation that made the pilgrimage to Toronto to try to dissuade Thorne Riddell.

The Canadian policy group members were polite as they listened to KMG's arguments, but Havermann felt they had already committed themselves. They may not have made a legal agreement, but mentally, the Canadians had already joined E&W. This was especially unfortunate, Havermann thought, because PMI's Canadian firm was totally prepared to merge. Because of its weaker position in that country, a merger with KMG would give it a significant boost.

Havermann also felt it was unfortunate because he knew Palmer strongly believed in the international firm PMI and KMG were attempting to create. It was a saddened Palmer who told Havermann, "My heart beats for KMG, but my brain tells me I must do something else."

There were some positives in all this, Havermann thought. The situation in Canada strengthened his determination to do all he could to persuade reluctant KMG national practices to "join the club." The apparent erosion in Canada coupled with some obvious trouble spots in other parts of the world could help convince KMG national practices that sticking together and merging as a group was the only viable alternative. They should stop worrying about becoming an American firm dominated by the large and powerful PMI. They should just design the merger arrangements so that KMG was assured equal influence.

Havermann was optimistic; there was a new breeze blowing through both organizations. Horner shared his views about the strategic sense of the merger, and Jim Butler would soon become senior partner of the U.K. firm. Horner spoke highly of Butler, who seemed receptive to new ideas, and Brown—the new chair-man of PMI's international organization—obviously favored the merger. On the KMG side, Steenmeijer had assumed the senior position in the Dutch firm. A small group of committed people might just get it done.

Shortly before Butler was to assume his post as senior partner of the U.K. firm, he hosted a dinner for Havermann, Horner, Paul Boschma, Brown, and Steenmeijer at an out-of-the-way restaurant along the Thames River, south of London. The group got on marvelously. It was apparent to all six that good things could come from this association.

After an exquisite dinner, Havermann summoned the waiter. "Would you bring me a cigar, please?" he asked. Ever the person-ification of British etiquette, the waiter responded expression-lessly, "Would you like to have your coffee outdoors?" He pointed to the announcement at the bottom of the menu that in tiny print whispered, "No smoking in the restaurant."

Havermann glanced at the window. It was raining. Seeing his disappointment, the waiter quickly advised him that there was a very nice covered pavilion—a boat house near the river's edge—where they could go to smoke and have coffee. "I have never been thrown out of a restaurant in such an elegant fashion in all my life," Havermann remarked. The others laughed. The camarade-rie that began at that dinner would grow and sustain them through the long and difficult months ahead.

KMG management committee members set out to explore all their options. They considered the "go-it-alone" strategy and examined all of the Big Eight to see which would be the best fit and offer the best deal. There was support for Arthur Andersen. Havermann had good friends in senior positions at AA, and the firm would have been an excellent partner. It was the largest firm in the United States and had a formidable consulting capability. In addition, AA was strong in many countries in which KMG was weak. The problem was that Andersen's "one firm worldwide" philosophy conflicted with KMG's decentralized, national approach.

Price Waterhouse was very much favored by the Dutch because of its long-standing working relationship on the Shell account. But PW had ruled out any discussions for a couple of years after its failed effort with Deloitte Haskins & Sells. Besides, the PW affiliation in West Germany with Treuarbeit, DTG's largest competitor, made PW totally unacceptable to Havermann. As it happened, Treuarbeit left the PW orbit soon after the KMG/PMI merger, but it was a very important issue at the time.

Ernst & Whinney was a possibility. It was not considered very strong on the Continent by the Europeans, but it was a major player in the United States. Chairman Ray Groves was likable and a mover. He made it known he was very interested in making a deal and would offer an attractive package.

Havermann felt a successful merger required the right combination of people, timing, environment, and circumstances. He never considered the failed negotiations more than a temporary glitch—a cooling-off period that gave everyone time to reevaluate their positions.

The failure had affected national practices on both sides of the proposed merger. Havermann found everyone much more reasonable in their expectations and more agreeable when it came to working out differences. By late August the firms had agreed on a memorandum of understanding outlining the terms and conditions that would govern the mergers of various national firms.

Havermann flew to New York to meet Horner, Butler, Brown, Steenmeijer, and KMG's executive partner, Boschma. At 3:00 p.m. on August 28, 1986, they sat at a table in the East Versailles Room of the Carlyle Hotel and signed the memorandum of understanding. That night they celebrated over dinner at Horner's apartment.

But the deal was far from done. The group had set a goal of January 1, 1987, for the individual firms to have worked out the details of the merger in their respective countries. Four months was not a long time to get 5,560 partners in 114 countries all headed in the same direction.

Havermann was asked to present the case to KMG partners at their annual conference in the fall of 1986 in Vienna. He reminded them that their primary goal in a merger was not size, but "first-class client service" around the world. The memorandum of understanding was "the result of strategic considerations by KMG." In a business that had only people—no machines or goods—it was far too important to make decisions based on anything else.

Havermann reminded the partners that KMG's goals in a merger were expanded geographic coverage; complementary strengths in services and industries served; an enhanced reputation in the financial markets; creation of a dynamic, innovative, growth-oriented organization that was willing to commit the resources necessary for sustained growth; and a truly multinational organization.

Havermann outlined the terms on which KMG was inflexible. First, KMG would negotiate as a whole firm, and each member firm would have the opportunity to participate. Second, the merged firm would not be dominated by any single group. It would be an organization of strong national firms bound by strong management. Finally, KMG would be recognized in the new organization's name. He dispelled fears that KMG would be taken over by quoting from PMI's international partnership agreement: "The purposes of the partnership are: to effect coordination among the firms without, however, becoming involved in their internal management of day-to-day operations . . . to promote the success and standing of each firm."

Havermann concluded with a personal note:

> I know a merger is always a difficult time. I was once the smaller partner in the merger with the much bigger DTG,

and therefore I understand very well the feelings of those involved. I also know that mergers entail not only professional and business problems, but also personal problems and feelings. I have come to compare a merger with a play. For a good play you need not only a good script, but also good actors. I had the advantage of coming into close personal contact, at a very early stage, with those acting on behalf of PMI. From this contact there soon developed a relationship of mutual trust.

I would like to assure you that from the beginning, I was very aware of the responsibility for us all. I would also like to tell you that, quite apart from all factual arguments, this relationship of trust is for me the decisive argument to recommend to you this merger with PMI.

At a very early stage we sat opposite each other not as negotiating parties but rather as partners who recognized the idea was right and who wanted to do everything to make this idea reality. We supported each other when one side or the other had to remove obstacles. I think you will discover this spirit of goodwill on every page of the memorandum of understanding. I am, therefore, entirely convinced that in PMI we have made the right choice.

Havermann's eloquent argument swayed many KMG partners. But he had problems back in West Germany that rhetoric could not solve. He had developed a cordial relationship with Dieter Lotz, the senior partner in PMI's German firm, during the course of the merger discussions. When it came to the merger agreement, however, they were very far apart.

It was apparent from the outset that without a merger in West Germany there would be no merger in Europe, and without a merger in Europe there would be no KMG/PMI merger. It was equally apparent that merging in West Germany would be difficult, regardless of how the senior partners felt. In addition to

PMI's Continental European Firm Versus KMG's national part-nerships, PMI's German firm was a general partnership that required a 100 percent positive vote before a merger could be undertaken. DTG, on the other hand, was a stock corporation. About half the stock was held by outside shareholders, yet a 75 percent majority vote would be required to approve a merger. The problem was eventually resolved by persuading outside sharehold-ers to convert their shares to nonvoting stock, a major accomplish-ment as far as Lotz and the PMI partners were concerned.

But there was still the question of money. Because of the way they were organized and compensated, PMI partners earned more than their DTG counterparts. It was a sticky wicket.

The firms explored several alternatives. The first was to trans-fer PMI's business to DTG in return for shares of stock. This wouldn't fly with DTG's clients. They estimated the merger would give PMI 30 percent of the voting shares, creating the potential for too much American influence.

The second option was to go with a competitor in West Ger-many. Several had come calling, and Arthur Andersen was espe-cially interested. AA saw a distinct opportunity in PMI and DTG's problem. If PMI's German firm could be lured away, it would strike a serious blow to KMG, PMI, and Havermann, one of the leaders of the worldwide merger. Success in West Germany could lead AA to other problem countries, such as France, and blow up the whole merger. It would be a public relations coup at the very least, one that could be trumpeted to the media and clients alike. Lotz believed AA would pay just about any price.

It was an emotional issue. Some partners felt they had made two bona fide attempts to merge with DTG and had been rebuffed; therefore, it was perfectly within their rights to go elsewhere. But when asked, "Are AA and the other interested firms the kind of people we really want to work with?" the answer was always no.

The third option was continuing to operate as separate entities, eventually combining the two. This would involve selling the PMI firm for cash and setting it up as a wholly owned subsidiary of DTG in West Germany; after five years, the two would merge fully.

The two firms finally realized they needed some objective advice. They engaged Roland Berger, a leading German consultant, to evaluate the potential merger and recommend a course of action. Berger's report provided independent verification that the strategy was sound, and Horner provided the persuasion. In a particularly tense meeting with Lotz , Havermann, and Horner in attendance, Horner told Lotz, "This is the best we can do for you, Dieter. We are going to go through with the merger. If you want to be part of it, you have to go along with this arrangement."

The deal called for PMI's German firm to be acquired as a separate DTG subsidiary in exchange for cash, which would allow the PMI partners to realize some personal financial benefit from their equity in the practice. The firm would operate independently as KPMG Peat Marwick Treuhand GmbH until 1992, at which time the former PMI firm would be fully absorbed into DTG. In the end, the PMI firm was still unable to get a 100 percent majority vote. Before the merger could be approved, the partners were required to buy out the single dissenter.

On September 30, 1987, Havermann and Lotz signed the papers formally chartering KPMG Peat Marwick Treuhand GmbH, a subsidiary of DTG. (Since 1987 DTG has gained several other subsidiaries, most notably West Germany's fifth largest CPA firm, Treuverkehr Aktiengesellschaft, which merged with DTG effective January 1, 1990.) "We must look ahead and understand the necessity and requirements of the future," Havermann said. "Whatever has happened is in the past. We can learn a great deal from history, but it does not mean this is the way to go in the future."

Back in New York, Horner moved West Germany into the "yes" column.

# Chapter Eight

# Jim Butler and the British

P. James Butler was in a difficult spot when negotiations began. As the likely successor to Sir John Grenside, the venerable senior partner of the U.K. firm (and chairman of PMI), Butler was invited to participate in the initial negotiations with KMG. But he was not yet senior partner; indeed, this appointment would not be made until several months after the first meeting in Paris in January 1985.

In addition, it was fairly widely believed in the U.K. firm that international affairs had dominated much of Grenside's time during his last years before retirement. Some of Butler's partners felt strongly that the senior partner should devote his time to problems in the United Kingdom, and Butler also saw the importance of getting out of London and spending time with his partners in the regions. Indeed, if there was one thing that could hinder his being elected senior partner, it was not being very well known outside London. Butler had spent his career in London and had for some time been active in the international affairs of his firm. But he hadn't spent much time in the provinces and was determined to do so.

Grenside sensed early on that Butler was skeptical about the merger. Butler foresaw a significant number of internal problems, and, given PMI's dominant position in the United Kingdom, there seemed little need to take on all the problems simply to increase the size of the firm. In addition, the British generally found the secrecy associated with a merger distasteful. They were a partnership with a long-standing tradition of openness and shared decisions. Because partners were always consulted on major decisions, it was difficult to know how far to go in discussions without consulting with and advising them. Grenside and Butler were also keenly aware of the problems Price Waterhouse and Deloitte Haskins & Sells had experienced. It was widely believed in England that one of the reasons for the difficulties was that the firms had kept the negotiations secret for so long it created a backlash. When the partners learned that their leaders had been considering such a major decision without their involvement, they rebelled and voted it down.

Grenside deplored doing anything behind the partners' backs, particularly the twenty-six members of the general partnership that served as the umbrella organization for the nine regional partnerships. Butler and Grenside did give the general partners a broad outline of what they were contemplating, but they were unable to provide much detail about the logistics and mechanics. Those would require considerable research before they could be presented in any sensible order. The idea of merging with KMG's U.K. affiliate, Thomson McLintock, received a mixed reception, even in the very early exploratory discussions with the general partners. Nevertheless, the group agreed it would be foolish not to explore the possibilities further.

Grenside had talked informally with Reinhard Goerdeler, chairman of KMG's German firm. Once when Goerdeler was in London with William Morrison, managing partner of KMG's

U.K. firm, to attend a Scottish CPA Society dinner, the two chairmen chatted informally about the possibility of combining their firms. Grenside recalled that much of the discussion centered on auditing standards.

By the time the two firms met in Paris, Grenside had warmed somewhat to the idea of a merger, but Butler was still skeptical. On the short trip from London to Paris, the two discussed the merger, and Grenside, for a fleeting moment, thought he and Butler were about to have their first and only strong disagreement over how to run the firm. "I hope this is not going to be an issue on which we are really going to fall out," Butler told him. Butler may have then been clearly opposed to the merger, but the Paris meeting changed his mind. He immediately saw the strategic sense of the combination, and he enthusiastically supported it.

When the talks fell apart in the fall of 1985, Butler turned his full attention to the United Kingdom. When the election for the position of senior partner was held, Butler received the overwhelming endorsement of his partners. He would take over as senior partner on July 1.

Through the spring of 1986, rumors floated through PMI's upper echelons that something was again afoot with KMG. Butler was in frequent contact with PMI's other firm leaders and occasionally heard information indicating that, at the very least, informal talks were under way to resurrect the merger discussions. Butler's friends were sensitive to his position; he was in favor of the merger and would soon assume the top post in his firm—but he was not yet in charge. Although both Larry Horner and Jim Brown suspected Butler knew exactly what was going on, they were careful not to tell him directly. If told, he would be faced with difficult questions about his responsibilities to Grenside, the international organization, and, most certainly, his U.K. partners. It is a peculiarity of the PMI culture (perhaps resulting from the tradition of discretion among accountants) that official notification almost never surprises anyone; it simply validates rumors. The grapevine transmits information with incredible speed and surprising accuracy.

When Horner phoned in late May to arrange a meeting, Butler had a pretty good idea what the meeting was about. The two had been friends for years; Butler invited Horner and his wife, Inge, to spend the weekend with him and his wife, Margaret, at their 500-acre working farm southwest of London. Unlike many Londoners who maintain large homes in the city and cottages in the country, the Butlers kept a flat in London and spent their weekends at their farm. It was a perfect out-of-the-way place for a confidential discussion.

Butler and Horner spoke at length Saturday evening. On Sunday morning, May 25, the two disappeared into Butler's study. Horner made it official, bringing Butler up to date on his discussions with KMG leaders.

One of the first points they considered was the likelihood of success if the negotiations were indeed revived. Both were new in their roles as senior partners of their national firms, and neither wanted to be associated with a massive failure during his first few months in office. "To fail once was terrible," Butler said. "To fail again would make us the laughingstock of our profession. There is no point in having even one meeting unless we truly believe that we can get to the end of the road." Horner agreed.

Butler felt Horner was sounding him out somewhat. He wanted to test his British friend's commitment to the merger and determine whether Butler could persuade his partners to vote for it. Was a merger the right answer? Were there other ways to achieve the firm's growth goals? They explored the alternatives.

Butler thought about his responsibilities to his partners. He had made it clear to them that if elected senior partner he would—because he, too, believed it was right—spend more time in the United Kingdom. He had already scheduled visits to the partnerships outside London and had promised to continue his rounds on a regular basis. His one goal as senior partner was to see more unity in the United Kingdom; he would look at the firm as a whole, not run the operation from London. Now, all the rules were about to change, and it would be extremely difficult—if not impossible—for him to live up to his commitments to his partners *and* help sell the merger around the world.

On Monday morning, Butler went into Grenside's office. "John, you're not going to believe this, but we're going to have another go at this merger," he said. "I don't bloody well believe it," Grenside replied.

Butler was almost instantly consumed by the demands of the merger. In his first year as senior partner he almost never visited the regional offices as he had planned, though there were discussions and progress reports. If not in London, he was traveling the world, meeting with PMI and KMG leaders. He became increasingly grateful for the unflagging support of his deputy, John Adcock.

Prior to being appointed to their firm's top leadership positions, Butler and Adcock had discussed extensively their approach to managing the firm; fortunately, they were in agreement on most major issues. The real test came with the merger with KMG. Because PMI's far-flung empire had begun in the United Kingdom, the British were especially sensitive to the organization's history and to what had become an extended worldwide family. It was an important part of the firm culture they didn't want to lose.

The U.K. partners were concerned about PMI's need to expand in Europe. They agreed the Big Eight's battles for dominance in the 1990s would be won or lost in Europe, and PMI was not strong enough to win. Despite a respectable client list, the firm was not gaining large European-based clients. To do so, the firm needed strong national firms, like those in KMG; however, the British partners were still reluctant to change. They knew the continental European partners' strengths and weaknesses and knew how to capitalize on their strengths. Plus, they sympathized with their

European brethren who were apprehensive about the massive changes the merger would require.

Butler knew Adcock's enthusiastic support would be a great help in selling the merger to the partners in the regions. Adcock started with the Firm's Birmingham office, and in his forty-six years with PMI has seen the office grow from one partner to forty-seven. He made partner in Birmingham and went on to become senior regional partner in the Midlands region, a position he still holds. He understood very well the role the regional structure played. In the United Kingdom, partners' incomes were directly tied to the results in their region—but problems involved more than that. The partners were proud of their respective regions and their freedom to make decisions and choose the best course of action. They wouldn't give up their regional autonomy easily. On the other hand, Thomson McLintock, KMG's U.K. firm, had only recently converted from a regional structure to a national partnership. It would be difficult to mesh the two firms.

The partner-to-staff ratio question had plagued the discussions from the beginning. In the United Kingdom, there was also an age differential; many Thomson McLintock partners were nearing retirement age. The failed negotiations helped with respect to the partner-to-staff ratios, which could have been a critical problem. The first round of discussions illuminated the differences between the two firms and allowed some time to rectify the problems.

Butler and Adcock realized they were very close philosophically. Both supported the merger. Butler would be required to travel extensively throughout the process, and Adcock would keep a steady hand at the helm of PMI's British empire.

Thomson McLintock had been blessed with inexperience when it came to mergers. A firm of Scottish origins, it had grown steadily without a merger until it was at one time the largest firm in Scotland and ranked fourth or fifth in the United Kingdom. Alan McLintock, grandson of the founder, served as chairman of the firm in addition to serving on the boards of several prestigious

U.K. banks and other organizations. The firm was proud of its traditions and independence. It neither needed, nor particularly wanted, a national merger in the United Kingdom. Like the other KMG firms, however, it was becoming more and more international in its work and was concerned about coverage in the United States. One of its largest clients, Grand Metropolitan, was acquiring companies in America and rapidly expanding there. Grand Met had indicated to Thomson McLintock that keeping its business would eventually depend on the firm's ability to provide consistently high-quality service around the world.

The United Kingdom was also beginning to see the effects of increased competition. Old-line companies that would not have considered changing auditors had become more receptive to proposals, and the British government concluded it was in its best interest to review the identity of the auditors of nationalized industries at least every five years. As a result, Thomson McLintock lost the audit of the National Coal Board, a client it had served since its inception in 1947. The National Enterprise Board, another audit client, had largely been disbanded by the mid-1980s. The situation was far from desperate, but it was changing. The firm's leadership knew it would probably have to do something within five years if it were to remain in the big leagues. When other KMG national practices began enthusiastically championing a merger, Thomson McLintock went along.

Alan McLintock had already decided that if a merger occurred, he would retire and pursue outside interests. He was within two or three years of retirement age anyway, and PMI's practice of restricting partners' service on corporate boards would have caused him to give up several directorships. Retirement from public practice was a bittersweet pill, however. Though sad that the firm that had so proudly borne his family's name for three generations was losing its independence, he was convinced it was the right thing for the firm to do.

McLintock was impressed with Butler. "He's a marvelous

leader," McLintock told his associates. "He's bent over backwards, really, to see the point of view of the smaller of the two firms—to get the whole thing through as a merger rather than a kind of swamping takeover. I give him the highest marks."

It wasn't enough, McLintock believed, for the international partnerships and the senior partners of the two national firms to simply agree this was the way to go. He shared Butler's belief that it was important for an overwhelming majority of the partners to support the merger and see the benefits of the combination.

"If we are going to put two groups of people together," McLintock said, "we have got to be particularly certain that the fundamental ground is going to be right. That, I believe, is the most important, single thing, and the most difficult part is establishing whether that is right or not. It's no good saying at the board or partnership level, 'We all get on like old buddies.' It's the people who are going to be running the show who count."

In retrospect, McLintock attributes much of the ease of the merger to Butler's having ensured that the much larger PMI firm was unselfish with its smaller partner. "For a merger like this to work," he said, "the bigger organization has to be generous, to a fault, with the smaller one. An extra seat on the board, for instance—even if it doesn't affect the overall balance of power—is important to the smaller firm. That kind of generosity makes an enormous difference."

The U.K. firms were combined smoothly because key decisions were made quickly. "We brought decisions on money and management to the center," according to Morrison, who served as McLintock's managing partner before becoming deputy senior partner in charge of the merged firm's operations in Scotland. "We communicated some of the key decisions about management very quickly. While this may not have been to everybody's liking—it couldn't possibly have been—it did clear the air."

U.K. leaders involved as many of the partners as possible in analyzing and combining the operations. The idea was to use as much brainpower as possible and to get the rank and file partners to "buy in" to the process. If they had a hand in shaping the new firm, they would be much more likely to support it. Working parties, or task forces, were assigned a host of responsibilities for combining the offices and functions—in short, the myriad details and activities that comprise two thriving, active businesses.

In Morrison's judgment, the task forces performed admirably. Self-interests were subjugated to the greater good of the firm; even those partners who thought they personally lost out on the deal felt the merger was the right thing to do. "I give them tremendous marks for what they did," he said later. "They did take a lot on faith and trust, so it became even more important for those of us at the top to make sure all commitments were honored."

Morrison and Butler understood and appreciated each other's problems. Both knew the other's job was no easier when it came to persuading partners that the merger would be good for both firms. Throughout the discussions they tried to balance their own concerns against the other's problems. They talked over difficult problems, thought them through, decided on a course of action, and stuck to it.

"People take their lead from the top," Morrison recalled, "and if the top men are fighting about who will do what and who should do this and that and the next thing, that attitude goes through the ranks, and everyone is scrapping. But if the top is a unified front and clearly in agreement—not under any kind of strain to be in agreement—it gives the proper signal to the rest of the firm. It means we are one, and nobody splits us on an issue. This is very important in negotiations of a merger of this size. If they can't split you, they'll try to work with the system, won't they?"

On September 3, 1986, PMI and KMG held a press conference in London. Butler told the assembled reporters that the firms "have agreed to a formal framework for negotiations intended to result in a full merger between the firms." He reported that since the talks broke down a year earlier, the senior partners of the firms had kept in touch and many of the difficulties that plagued the earlier discussions had been resolved. "Given the complementary nature of the two firms, it was perhaps inevitable that they would merge."

Butler outlined how the merger would proceed. "Because both firms have a democratic structure, many of the details of the proposed new organization have yet to be decided. They will be finalized through negotiations between individual firms in their respective countries, according to the agreed procedures of each practice. Following the negotiations, partners of each national firm will vote on the merger."

Joining Butler at the press conference were Brown, PMI chairman; Morrison, managing partner of KMG's Thomson McLintock; and Paul Boschma, KMG's executive partner.

Boschma, next on the agenda, pointed out that this merger "would create the largest accounting and consulting firm in the world by any measurement . . . a unique organization with unrivaled resources, expertise, and experience across an unprecedented range of territories and markets. For the first time, multinational clients will be able to call upon a single firm with authentic strength-in-depth in North America, the United Kingdom, and continental Europe and an extensive network of offices throughout the world." The new organization would have combined fee income of US$2.7 billion (£1.6 billion), operate in eighty-eight countries, and employ a staff of 60,000. The combined U.K. firm would boast revenues of £166.9 million (US$273.7 million), 428 partners, and 5,167 professional staff.

Brown stressed the importance of quality. "We would never compromise on the issue of quality," he said. "And with KMG, we know we will never have to. It, like us, is structured to provide clients with close personal contact at the partner level." He emphasized both firms' commitment to smaller, midsize, and privately owned businesses, as well as PMI's strength in insurance and finance and KMG's strong manufacturing and energy practices. Between them, the two firms counted among their clients ten of the top fifty companies listed on the stock exchange, including Grand Metropolitan, Imperial Chemical Industries (ICI), Boots Co., National Westminster Bank, and British Aerospace. The firms' senior partners expected the voting to be completed by January 1, 1987.

Voting on the merger was a complex issue. Because of the way the firms were organized and incorporated, approval would require a 75 percent favorable vote on the PMI side and an 80 percent yea vote on the Thomson McLintock side. To further complicate matters, each of the seven PMI partnerships was a separate legal entity, and each would be required to approve the merger separately; there would be no collective U.K. vote. The senior partner had to rely more on his powers of persuasion than his authority when dealing with a partnership. There was a protocol for approval of operating matters that didn't require a full vote of the partnership, but a merger of this size would require three quarters' approval. The merger was approved by over 99 percent of the partners of both firms.

Soon after the merger was ratified, the new firm got an unexpected opportunity to prove itself. It began with a telephone call to Alan McLintock in early November. The Thomson McLintock partner who handled the ICI audit was out of the office that afternoon, so it fell to the chairman to field a call from the treasurer of this major client.

Born in 1926 by the merger of four British companies that sought to create an organization capable of competing in world markets, ICI had, by the mid-1980s, grown to become the second-largest company in Great Britain, the seventeenth largest in Europe, and the forty-sixth largest in the world. Thomson McLintock, joint auditor in the United Kingdom with Price Waterhouse, conducted the majority of ICI's worldwide audit.

The news McLintock received was a shock. ICI decided the firm should be served by one auditor. The company would go out for proposals, and Thomson McLintock would be invited to participate. It was agreed that PMI and Thomson McLintock would submit a joint proposal.

It was an unparalleled opportunity for both. Without KMG, PMI would not have been invited to propose; and without PMI, KMG could not provide the kind of service ICI expected around the world. It was a unique and exciting opportunity to test the theory behind the merger. If the strategy was sound, this would give the firms the chance to prove it.

Unfortunately, the newly merged U.K. firm—known as Peat Marwick McLintock (*KPMG* was added later)—was in a weak position. The firm estimated it was doing only about a quarter of ICI's audit work, with the rest being performed by Price Waterhouse. PW clearly had the upper hand going into the proposal.

Alan McLintock asked Butler to nominate a senior partner to head the proposal process, and Butler turned to David Vaughan to serve as client service partner. Arthur Morison, the McLintock senior partner on the engagement, was due to retire at the end of March 1987, but, to ensure continuity, Morison would serve as a consultant to Vaughan for two years. When Butler asked him if he would take on the job, Vaughan retorted, "I'm not usually the type that enjoys championing lost causes." He surprised himself when he agreed to accept the challenge.

A senior partner in the U.K. firm, Vaughan had served a variety of multinational clients and was experienced in mergers and acquisitions, an area of interest to ICI. Vaughan, through what he labeled "a strange combination of good fortune and perhaps some small amount of skill," had never failed at a major proposal effort.

A 50-year-old veteran of the firm, Vaughan had been through many proposals and knew full well what he was getting into. When he evaluated the firm's chances in early December 1986, he stacked the odds against his firm by at least three or four to one.

Had he been an outsider, he would have figured the odds at about fifty to one.

A team headed by Vaughan and Morison was quickly assembled from the ranks of both firms. In the Americas, the team would be buttressed by northeast regional vice chairman Robert McGregor, a senior partner on the U.S. board of directors who had headed PMI's Latin American practice before assuming his current responsibilities. He would be the liaison with ICI's extensive operations in Wilmington, Del.

It was a strange situation. Although the firms, in December 1986, had agreed in principle to merge, it wouldn't be official until January 1, 1987, and the physical combination of the firms wouldn't take place until April 1. The ICI engagement team would pioneer the working relationship.

The proposal strategy was important. Vaughan believed it was critical to present to the selection committee the team that would actually do the work. Butler appeared in a leadership role to assure the client of its importance to the firm, but Vaughan and the engagement team made the pitch.

In the course of developing the proposal, the team had compressed the process of getting to know each other into less than a month. There simply wasn't time for the usual formalities. They had grown to trust and respect each other in short order. All of the team members pulled their weight throughout the process; the oral presentation would simply be a continuation of their outstanding team effort.

Despite the team's sterling performance, it was such an uphill battle that the most anyone expected was a commendable second place. A respectable finish would demonstrate to the combined U.K. firm and the rest of the KMG/PMI national practices that they could work together and that the merger made strategic sense.

With little to lose and a great deal to gain, Vaughan was convinced a little risk taking might shift the balance in his favor. He opened the team's oral presentation to the ICI selection committee by making the point that nobody on the KMG/PMI team was there by virtue of his seniority alone. "Everyone you see here will be actively involved in the audit," he told them, "and as far as I'm concerned, the affairs of ICI would be an absolute first charge on my time. You are seeing the people who are going to do the work, not some guys who will say an articulate three or four sentences and then disappear."

Vaughan tried to be provocative during the orals while following the strategy the team had adopted—emphasizing that KPMG was unique, not just another Big Eight firm. During the question-and-answer period following the presentation, the chairman of the ICI selection committee, Sir Alex Jarratt, an undisputed titan of British industry, addressed Vaughan: "One of the members of this panel," he said, "whom I will not name, has observed that you have brought to bear on the subject of materiality an attitude of mind that can only be described as brutal. How would you comment on that?"

Vaughan knew full well that this was a loaded question. It is the auditor's responsibility to determine whether an amount in question is material to the financial statements; it is often a point of discussion between the auditor and the client. Without hesitation, he responded, "Well, I would like to answer that question in two parts, if I may. First, let me say how much I admire the elegance of the language used by your unnamed colleague. Second, I have to say I deplore his judgment. And I deplore his judgment for the following reasons. . . ." The selection committee laughed at Vaughan's witticism; Vaughan then went on to address seriously the question of materiality. The team felt it had gained the advantage over the competition.

Indeed it had. Much to its delight, the team learned a few days later—on January 22, 1987—that Peat Marwick McLintock had won its first engagement as a combined firm. It would set a standard that would inspire and challenge other KPMG national practices. The merger strategy had been validated in the United Kingdom before the merger had even been consummated.

Butler and his British partners had come through with colors flying.

# Chapter Nine

# Johan Steenmeijer and the Dutch

**K**lynveld Kraayenhof & Co. (KKC), KMG's Dutch firm, was one of the earliest multinational accounting firms. Begun early in the twentieth century, it had developed an enviable client list that included KLM Royal Dutch Airlines and Philips, a Dutch manufacturer of electric appliances and electronic products. KLM grew into a major international carrier, and Philips grew into one of the world's largest corporations with operations that span the globe.

In many ways, KKC mirrored the companies it served. The Dutch heritage of world trade and expansion beyond Holland's small borders quickly led the expanding Dutch companies abroad. Philips, in particular, sought new markets in continental Europe, the United States, the United Kingdom, and virtually every other industrial nation. It expanded manufacturing operations into South America and other developing countries as well. KKC established offices to serve Philips and other multinational clients in the locations in which they operated. By the late seventies, KKC had established twenty-five offices outside the Netherlands.

In the early seventies, KKC merged with Frese Hogeweg, a Dutch firm with a comparable client base and common interests in Latin America. Several of KKC's clients had Latin American operations; the merger would allow KKC to share the costs of maintaining its offices in Buenos Aires, Rio de Janeiro, and other cities.

The Latin connection was one the Dutch firm had in common with the Germans. During the first half of the century, many Germans emigrated to South America; there are still many German-speaking communities in Brazil and Argentina. Their common interests there brought the Dutch and Germans together, and the South American connection became the foundation of their international networks.

The Philips audit was overseen by Jan Uiterlinden, a pleasant, outgoing Dutchman who had begun his professional career with Price Waterhouse. Fluent in English and a consummate client service professional, Uiterlinden was familiar with the audit approaches of both KKC and PW and knew the people, procedures, and personnel. He had been transferred from Amsterdam to Eindhoven, Philips' corporate headquarters, to work primarily on the Philips audit. Because of the Philips connection and his extensive experience in international relations (he served on a number of committees of the Netherlands Institute of Registered Accountants and became its president in 1976), Uiterlinden was one of the earliest advocates of a KKC international merger. With his major client regularly expanding internationally, he could readily see the need for a stronger presence in other countries, particularly the United States, where Philips had done business for years under the Norelco and Magnavox brand names.

The Dutch firm was particularly concerned about its position with Philips in the United States; Philips had, in the early 1970s, been audited by the relatively small firm of Smith & Harder. Uiterlinden and Dutch senior partner Geert Timmer had managed to merge the small firm into Hurdman and Cranstoun, which eventually merged with Main Lafrentz to form the U.S. firm Main Hurdman (then becoming part of KMG). Timmer and Uiterlinden did their utmost to keep the Big Eight out of Philips' U.S. operations; they were convinced that if one of the large firms got a foothold with their client, KKC's position in the Netherlands would be threatened.

Uiterlinden served in a variety of leadership positions in KKC, and he made his views known unequivocally. The firm needed a merger, he said, if it was to continue as a world-class firm capable of serving global companies like Philips. Uiterlinden was determined that one day his firm would be able to serve his client in every location without having to rely on Big Eight firms. He wanted KKC's international firm to conduct the complete audit. This determination eventually helped trigger the formation of KMG.

When Johan Steenmeijer rose to leadership, he shared Uiterlinden's interest in international expansion—but developed some reservations as the years went by. He was proud of the organization KMG had built in a short period of time under the leadership of Reinhard Goerdeler (chairman) and Uiterlinden (CEO), but he recognized that the firm was weak in some countries, particularly the United States. Although KMG's Main Hurdman was number nine in the States, there was a huge difference between number eight and number nine. Some of KMG's clients were refusing to use Main Hurdman, citing its relatively small size.

Steenmeijer knew that there had been some discussions about a KMG and Price Waterhouse combination. He believed KMG should consider a merger at some point, but for now it should build up its own national-practice network. National practices needed to have common policies and adhere to the same practices and policies if they wanted KMG to be viewed as a serious merger candidate. Otherwise, they would be perceived as a loose federation of independent firms.

The proposed merger between PW and Deloitte Haskins & Sells dominated much of the discussion at the 1984 KMG conference in Copenhagen. Steenmeijer agreed with the prevailing wisdom that if that merger went through, others were likely to follow. The partners agreed that the one thing they would like to avoid was being the last candidate involved in a merger. They should take a leadership role.

KMG then surveyed the Big Eight to determine which firms would best fit with each other and with KMG. They analyzed each firm's strengths and weaknesses in the countries in which they operated and speculated about possible scenarios. Just about any combination of Big Eight firms would work, but the best fit was always combining a Big Eight firm with KMG, primarily because of KMG's strong European presence.

The next step was deciding which of the Big Eight KMG should approach. Arthur Andersen was out, despite what Steenmeijer perceived as a keen interest in merging with or taking over KMG. It wouldn't work, however, because of AA's militaristic "one firm worldwide" concept. AA could take over local partnerships, but it was virtually impossible for the firm to have a merger of equals on a worldwide basis because of its commitment to its present operating philosophy.

Arthur Young would be difficult, especially in the Netherlands; a KMG/AY combination would mean merging the number one and number two firms in that country. The result would be more than 40 percent of the profession concentrated in one firm, auditing more than 80 percent of the listed companies. Clients and non-clients wouldn't stand for it.

PW wouldn't work in West Germany because of its affiliate relationship with Treuarbeit, a firm owned by various German governmental agencies. Even if it could merge with KMG's German firm, there was a size problem. As in the Netherlands, it would be a merger of the largest and second largest firms in that country.

Touche Ross and Deloitte Haskins & Sells were ruled out because of the KMG leadership's dislike of some of their policies or their image in some of the countries in which they competed. The firms were eliminated one by one, until only Ernst & Whinney, Coopers & Lybrand, and PMI remained. C&L was about as good a fit as Arthur Andersen, and E&W was an attractive option (Steenmeijer had the impression there was a general preference for E&W), but PMI would work if it could overcome its Anglo-American attitude and approach.

As the successor to Timmer (KKC's senior partner), Steenmeijer had long been involved in KMG management and had attended the 1985 Paris meeting with PMI. He was disturbed by his observations of the first negotiations. He strongly believed that most of the people there underestimated the problems and complexities involved in bringing the two firms together. He immediately saw the problems the two firms would have merging in Europe.

A conservative man who liked to think through problems in advance, Steenmeijer observed that the group considered the whole process too easy, an attitude that generated more problems. A superficial approach to problem solving only meant that problems would be that much more difficult when finally addressed in depth. He was aghast that some participants seemed to think all they had to do was strike a deal at a meeting and then go home and advise their partners. He preferred the KKC style of keeping the partners informed of all the firm's activities and involving them in all major decisions. He and his partners had already discussed at some length the desirability of a merger.

Steenmeijer was also troubled by KMG's willingness to accept the belief that the firm was in a weakened position because of Main Hurdman's problems in the United States. It went against his Dutch nature to accept the premise that the firm had to merge to survive. "We Dutchmen can be rather tough and stubborn now and then," he observed wryly, "but we believe strongly that we should never start merger discussions if we don't believe in ourselves. A merger based on weakness is not a good basis for the future."

Despite his reservations, Steenmeijer agreed to participate in the discussions. As the KMG national practices met and discussed the various aspects of a potential merger, it was obvious to him that there were too many people with too many views and too many different positions. Steenmeijer was also troubled by U.K. senior partner Sir John Grenside's ambivalence. Steenmeijer thought that while Grenside didn't say he was against the merger, it was apparent he wasn't at all happy about it. It would be difficult.

Steenmeijer was slightly encouraged by subsequent discussions with Graham Corbett, Dieter Lotz, and others about how to deal with the different structures of the firms in continental Europe, but he recognized that although the discussions were "on the record," they were just talks between a couple of people. They had not discussed the matter with the various national partnerships that would be affected. He had serious doubts that they would find the conditions acceptable. Nevertheless, Europe was crucial if the overall merger was to work.

As Steenmeijer evaluated the likelihood of the merger's working in other countries, he figured the United States was a given. Main Hurdman senior partner John Thompson believed that because of client losses and other problems, the best answer for his firm was to merge. "I think this is the best way for KMG, too," Thompson said, "and I think I can adequately deliver my partners, my people, and my organization to PMI."

The situation was similar in the United Kingdom. Thomson McLintock had an excellent reputation, but it was number ten in the country—and weakening a bit, Steenmeijer thought. No one doubted the quality of the firm, but profitability was not what it should be, and if the firm was to grow internationally, it needed to be larger. The toughest problem would be reducing the number of partners by 40 to 50 percent to get the ratios more compatible—a condition Thomson McLintock seemed willing to accept. Thomson McLintock leadership had resigned itself to the fact that massive changes would be required. At least that was the way it appeared to Steenmeijer.

The Dutch and German firms thought PMI's first-suggested conditions in the United Kingdom were unreasonable, and they didn't hesitate to say so. "Those terms are ridiculous," Steenmeijer said. "You should never accept them." Nevertheless, he recognized that drastic changes would have to be made if the merger was to work in the United Kingdom, and it must work there in order for the merger to work around the world.

By the time of the September 1985 KMG meeting in San Francisco, Steenmeijer had pretty well concluded that the firm was not yet ready to seriously negotiate with PMI. True, the firms had held several meetings and resolved several important issues, but the name question was still open, and the problems in continental Europe remained. He also disliked the conditions presented to Thomson McLintock in the United Kingdom. National practices had always supported each other, and he was not convinced that the British were getting a fair shake.

Despite Steenmeijer's lobbying to postpone negotiations, KMG went ahead with the next meeting in Amsterdam with PMI. Press attention was beginning to heat up as well, which intensified the pressure on all involved. It was difficult enough dealing with the sensitive issues, different cultures, and organizational structures in privacy and quiet. Reading articles in the newspapers and dealing with reporters' queries only complicated matters.

The major unresolved problem was Europe. PMI's Corbett believed that given enough time he could convince his partners that the merger was in their best interest, but it was a very sensitive issue. "Give me some time," he told Steenmeijer. "It's very difficult now." They agreed that if they began formal discussions in the various countries, they were likely to fail, and the merger would be lost. Then there was the U.K. question. There were simply too many obstacles to overcome. The timing was all wrong.

Steenmeijer was convinced that KMG was not yet ready for a merger. All the talk with PMI centered on KMG's internal weaknesses, he noted, which put his firm in a poor negotiating position. "We are considering this merger because of our own feelings of weakness," he told KMG leaders. "This is wrong. How can we work together in the future? If we continue this way, we will be taken over by the Americans. We are not ready to begin discussions in the national partnerships. The Dutch firm is not prepared to join in any further discussions." This time he prevailed. The discussions were dropped, and the participants went home.

After negotiations broke down, Steenmeijer turned his attention to the McKinsey report and the "go-it-alone" strategy. He was particularly interested in McKinsey's observation that

> There is a risk that some partners in certain member firms may feel skeptical as to the value of an assessment of the steps needed for KMG to pursue independent development—because they may be convinced that the best option is to merge with a Big 8 firm. Such partners may be even less enthusiastic about the thought of converting this preliminary assessment into a detailed business plan. However, we urge that KMG continue this process for two reasons:
>
> • Having a picture of a feasible alternative—independent development—will measurably strengthen KMG's confidence and hence its psychological bargaining position in any merger discussions and negotiations.
>
> • Given the partnership makeup of a likely merger partner and qualified majorities needed—on a country-by-

country basis—KMG should be conservative in assessing the likelihood of any specific merger to be actually consummated. It is imperative, therefore, that KMG have a contingency plan ready in case merger negotiations would not be successfully concluded.

McKinsey was right on the mark with those observations, Steenmeijer believed. The strategies should be aimed at "going it alone," but with the real intent of strengthening the entire organization. Its goal should be to get back to believing in the future.

Steenmeijer talked over his beliefs with Hans Havermann, CEO of KMG's German firm. The two agreed that discussions should be resumed shortly, possibly with PMI and perhaps with other Big Eight firms. They decided that whatever course KMG chose, the two of them would have major roles. They arranged a meeting of a few key people from the Dutch and German firms to discuss some of the terms and conditions they would insist on in future negotiations. Gradually the group developed a "hypothetical letter of intent" that contained the conditions they would find acceptable. The document, which addressed such issues as the name of the organization, how the group felt the executive committee should be formed, and the location of the merged firm's world headquarters, would provide a basis for discussion in future merger talks. The small group agreed they were ready for a new round of discussions.

Havermann didn't tell Steenmeijer about Larry Horner's phone call attempting to resuscitate the discussions with PMI, an act Steenmeijer later characterized as "very careful." The timing still wasn't right as far as KMG was concerned. Right or wrong, KMG leaders believed that the U.K. senior partner, Grenside, opposed the merger—or if he didn't actively oppose it, he at least wasn't in favor of it. They preferred to wait until he retired to resume discussions, believing they would have a better chance of working out problems in the United Kingdom with Grenside's successor,

Jim Butler.

Steenmeijer liked Jim Brown, incoming chairman of PMI. Brown was more diplomatic than Tom Holton, his predecessor, Steenmeijer thought, and had the added advantage of being Canadian. His involvement might mitigate some of the fears the European firms had about an American takeover. Besides, Brown seemed to have a better feel for European issues than some of the PMI people with whom they had dealt in the past.

Then, of course, there was Horner. Steenmeijer liked the fact that Horner had lived in Europe and married a European. He seemed to have the right attitude and experience, and he certainly had the ability to get things done. His experience as a managing partner, regional vice chairman, and senior partner of PMI's German firm had given him a rare perspective—and a sense of urgency. He was a man accustomed to setting goals and achieving them.

On the KMG side, some of the players had changed as well. Goerdeler and Paul Boschma had been heavily involved in the first discussions. This time around Havermann and Steenmeijer would run things. They would be tougher and better prepared. By the spring of 1986, when Horner again called Havermann, Steenmeijer and the others were more receptive. They had completed their draft letter of intent, and they were ready to talk.

From Steenmeijer's point of view, his first meeting with Horner, Brown, and Havermann went very well. Members of the group liked each other, and the chemistry was good. They decided that the best way to approach a merger was for them to agree, then invite the others to join in. They would make it easy for the other countries, and they would allow plenty of time to get it done.

They were in no hurry to resume formal talks; in fact, the reverse was true. They needed to delay for a few days to allow Butler to assume the top spot in the U.K. firm. Elections had been held, but Butler would not take office until July 1. If they began negotiations now, it would be impossible for Butler to participate.

The four didn't talk to anyone. Steenmeijer and Havermann didn't even inform KMG chairman Boschma that they might resume discussions with PMI at some point in the future. They continued to build the KMG organization and kept the merger discussion group small so as not to compromise anyone. Only a handful of people from the two firms knew what was going on.

They would have kept their activities quiet longer had it not been for the Canadian defection. When John Palmer, senior partner of KMG Thorne Riddell, notified Boschma that his firm was seriously considering joining Ernst & Whinney, Steenmeijer and Havermann had to let their partners know that they had been in informal talks with PMI leaders.

Steenmeijer and the others made the trek to Toronto to inform the Thorne Riddell policy group that the firm had another option. Instead of merging with E&W, the Canadians could join in the discussions with PMI to help put together a deal. The Canadians opted out. They had already determined that E&W was their best option.

Despite the acceleration in merger activity following the Canadian defection, Steenmeijer was unwilling to compromise on certain points. One was the possibility of a takeover by the Americans. "Some Americans are just too American," he said. "And we don't want to be taken over by them. We want to build a truly international firm. Some Americans are simply incapable of understanding what an international firm is; they think it is one in which everything is done the American way. How do you explain this to them?"

Horner was different. Even if he didn't fully understand, Steenmeijer thought, he tries to understand, and he accepts it even if he doesn't believe it. And Brown was a great help to the Dutch cause. He did his utmost to remain an independent discussion leader, and he delved into complex problems and tried to understand thoroughly what was going on in the minds of the Dutch participants. He seemed able to grasp the real issues and explain them to others in terms the Dutch could accept.

Because the leaders of the second round of discussions were more flexible, and because the conditions for the merger were more favorable, the talks went better all around the world. The problems in the United Kingdom were worked out over the course of the summer of 1987, and gradually Steenmeijer began to believe a merger could be successful. He did not doubt, however, that KMG could "go it alone" if its leaders chose to do so. There would be problems, to be sure, but they could survive at least a few more years without a merger. That was important to Steenmeijer; it gave him the assurance he needed to negotiate from a position of strength.

On the PMI side, Harald Kessler, the newly elected senior partner of the Continental European Firm, studied Steenmeijer and analyzed his motives. It seemed to him that Steenmeijer was the quintessential Dutchman. He fully understood the implications of living in a small country that had prospered by expanding well beyond its own borders, but he also saw his country's limitations. Companies huge by Dutch standards would be considered small or midsize on an international scale. Banks, insurance companies, and manufacturing firms alike fell into this category.

The way Kessler read it, Steenmeijer was a strategic thinker looking to the future. Unless KKC became part of a large international organization, his firm's position would be eroded. In 1992, when borders would be erased and competition in Europe intensified, Dutch companies would be bagged, rather than be on the firing line.

Horner's motives were different, Kessler surmised. If one believed the cynics, Horner was a driven leader who no longer wanted to be number two. He wanted to be number one in the United States; failing that, he wanted to be number one in the world. Whatever the cynics believed, Kessler thought the strategic objectives made sense; the questions revolved around assessing whose interests needed to be protected, and at what price.

Nevertheless, it seemed to Kessler that Horner and Steenmeijer shared common interests, whatever their true motives may have been. It was definitely to both their advantages to merge. Horner and the U.S. firm would get the size and strength they wanted in Europe, and Steenmeijer would be able to tell his clients that he had excellent coverage in the United States. Kessler didn't know if PMI was Steenmeijer's first choice in the Big Eight, but Steenmeijer seemed to think PMI was a good, professional firm in whose people he had trust and confidence.

Kessler's mission was to convince PMI's CEF partners that Steenmeijer and Horner's interests could parallel their own. His firm was small in comparison to KMG, but it was very profitable and had achieved some notable successes in recent years. Nevertheless, in Europe PMI was basically a foreign firm. It was stronger in some countries than in others, but it would take years to achieve the critical mass and momentum that could be gained instantly with a merger.

What other PMI leaders thought about the merger wasn't enough for Kessler; he was a man who made his own decisions. He would not ask his partners to support something in which he did not believe. Kessler later reflected:

*We could make a quantum leap by merging, but what we would effectively be saying is that what was there was not good enough. We will be admitting that we cannot achieve what we want through our own organization.*

*Who will be the winners and who will be the losers in a merger? I have always said, when confronted with such questions, that life is all about change, and being successful in business is all about change. It means adapting to change*

*and environments that change. It involves changing atti-
tudes. A merger crystallizes the element of change. It accel-
erates it, makes it more brutal in a way, because it condenses
it in time. No doubt people will be affected in dramatic ways,
and there will be those who can adapt faster and those who
will adapt less well.*

Kessler would support the merger, and he would try to get his
partners to support it. Many would be asked to change their views.
He would approach this leadership challenge the same way he had
approached others. He would try to get people to identify with his
objectives. Only when people reach for the same objectives can a
leader generate the energy necessary to take people beyond what
they thought was possible. It would be the greatest challenge of
his career.

In Steenmeijer's view, many of the problems on the Continent
stemmed from the naive belief of many PMI partners that international growth would come easily. It had been true for PMI in
Europe initially because 70 percent of the CEF's work was
referred by the United States, the United Kingdom, and Japan.
Future growth would not be so easy. Kessler understood that, but
many did not. They would have to be educated.

Compared with the mergers in other countries, the Dutch
merger proceeded extremely smoothly. The partners had been
informed about the merger as events happened and had been
involved in the planning. When it was put to a vote of the partnership, it was passed by an overwhelming majority.

Steenmeijer then turned his attention to problems in other countries. There was no satisfaction in the knowledge that he had been
correct in his assessment of the January 1985 meeting—that the
merger was going to be far more difficult than some had assumed.
KKC had merged in the Netherlands, and Steenmeijer supported
the merger worldwide. He wanted to help bring the firms
together.

He and Brown went to Singapore, Hong Kong, and Australia attempting to help the local partners resolve their differences. Because they held senior positions in their respective firms and would be in leadership positions in the merged firm, the duo could address problems from a variety of perspectives, and each could reassure his partners of the honorable intentions of the other side.

Steenmeijer got a huge dose of culture clash in Australia. After he and Brown met with the partners from their respective sides, both sides got together to discuss the problems that had caused the first discussions to fall apart and to see if they could start again. "Let's put the issues on the table," Steenmeijer said, "and, hopefully, we will be more successful than the last time."

Before this meeting, Steenmeijer had not met George Bennett, the senior partner of PMI's Australian firm. After everyone was seated at the conference table, Bennett opened the meeting. After a few pleasant introductory remarks, he talked for a quarter of an hour, regaling them with what Steenmeijer perceived to be the reasons he opposed the merger. Steenmeijer was stunned.

*Okay, I can go back to the Netherlands now,* Steenmeijer thought, *and Jim can go back to Canada. This man doesn't like the merger at all. His remarks are very hostile. I would never talk to someone that way during a first meeting. We need to meet some more and get to know each other better before we begin that kind of talk.*

Steenmeijer looked around the room. The others were smiling and nodding, obviously pleased with what Bennett was saying. It was just the Australians' way of talking to each other. Nobody was angry, nobody was hostile, and apparently nobody opposed the merger. It was Bennett's blunt Aussie way of speaking that gave Steenmeijer a totally wrong impression.

There would be other misunderstandings over the course of the next few months on both sides, but the strategic sense of the merger would withstand the most intense scrutiny. It was the one element that KMG and PMI leaders alike could point to as the underlying reason for merging.

As he reflected on the merger's success, Steenmeijer thought the accomplishment of a merger with all its complexities in the 114 countries in which the firms operated was nothing short of amazing. He later reflected:

> *It is very difficult to bring together such diverse cultures in so many firms. When you consider the number of partners, the number of offices, and the different languages involved, it seems like an impossible task. I doubt that another set of similar circumstances will ever occur. As I look back, I think we had the opportunity, the chance to do the right thing at the very right moment. It was an opportunity that probably none of us will have ever again.*
>
> *But we did it.*

The name of the firm continued to be an issue up to and including the signing of the international memorandum of understanding. The KMG partners preferred Klynveld Peat Goerdeler; eventually the firms compromised on Klynveld Peat Marwick Goerdeler for the international firm. The Klynveld partners commissioned special commemorative plates from a client in Holland. Pictured above are: 1 — Larry Horner, U.S.; 2 — Hans Havermann, Germany; 3 — Paul Boschma, Netherlands; 4 — Jim Brown, Canada; 5 — Johan Steenmeijer, Netherlands; 6 — Jim Butler, U.K.; 7 — Guy Smith, South Africa; 8 — Harald Kessler, Netherlands; 9 — John Gath, Denmark; 10 — Randy Noonan, U.S.; 11 — Robert Piard, France; 12 — David Gairns, Hong Kong; 13 — Bill Morrison, U.K.; 14 — John Callaghan, Ireland; 15 — Peter Valentine, PMI Secretariat; 16 — Geoff Kelleher, Australia; 17 — Ross Walker, Canada; 18 — Graham Corbett, France; 19 — Victor Earle III, PMI general counsel; 20 — Athol Mann, PMI Secretariat; 21 — Michael Speer, KMG International Office; 22 — John Thompson, U.S.

**Larry Horner**

**Jim Brown**

**Jim Butler**

Harry Wilks

Horner and Merlin Dewing (vice chairman, audit) at PepsiCo headquarters.

W. Frankehaiser

Hans Havermann

Johan Steenmeijer

Steve Harlan (vice chairman, international), Horner, Dane Brooksher (vice chairman, Midwest region), and Bob Galvin (KPMG client and chairman, Motorola, Inc. Motorola was the inaugural winner of the Malcolm Baldrige National Quality Award).

Steenmeijer, Butler, Brown, Paul Boschma, Havermann, and Horner.

Henry Kissinger (KPMG client and former U.S. secretary of state), Horner, Lord Cockfield (KPMG adviser; considered architect of EC 1992), and Caspar Broeksma (KPMG international executive).

# Chapter Ten

# Problems in France

$\mathbf{F}$rance almost always reserves for itself a special place in history; this history is no exception. The merger there was extremely difficult. The two firms had very different practices, and the KMG firm dwarfed PMI in France. It would be a takeover of dimensions that the PMI partners were unwilling to accept. Their principal fear—one that they shared with other Continental European Firm partners—was that they would be swallowed by the much larger KMG firm. This scenario was repeated around the world on both sides of the merger. The partners and employees of the smaller firms feared domination by the larger one and worried that they would have limited influence and few career options with the merged firm.

Robert Piard, who headed up the KMG firm in France, saw the size difference as an advantage. "Is there any point in merging similar and balanced parties?" he asked. "If there is no strategic advantage, if the strengths of one organization do not complement the strengths of its merger partner, the only reason to merge is to create a larger organization. Just being bigger doesn't necessarily benefit the clients."

In the end, persuasion and some strong guarantees (job security, career development, practice support, quality of work, audit standards, and compensation) solved the problem, but not before most of the accounting world knew about the difficulties in France. Competitors seized every opportunity to discredit both the PMI practice and Fiduciaire de France, the KMG firm. A KMG/PMI combination there, as in most other parts of the world, would create a fearsome competitor.

French history is riddled with great events precipitated by people quarreling among themselves. The French have a well-earned reputation for tenacious opinion. They are a proud, independent people in a society where individual thought is cherished and encouraged. Inevitably, there are differences of opinion. Charles de Gaulle used the variety of cheeses produced by his country as an illustration of the impossibility of trying to get his people to behave as one: *"Que voulez vous, cher ami, on ne peut pas rassembler a froid un pays qui compte 265 specialites de fromage?"* ("My dear friend, how can you make a country that has 265 varieties of cheeses behave, in normal times, as one?")[1]

In France, as in many other countries, the accounting profession tends to divide itself into two segments: those that provide accounting services (usually for small to midsize companies) and those that conduct audits. All limited liability companies (corporations), except for certain very small businesses, are required by law to have an audit. Although accounting services providers and auditors are overseen by different professional bodies, as a practical matter most professionals are members of both groups and commonly provide accounting advisory and auditing services, although never to the same client.

In the mid-1960s the French statutory auditing requirements were expanded to bring them more into line with generally accepted auditing standards followed in other countries. The

---

1. Luigi Barzini, *The Europeans* (New York: Simon and Schuster, 1983), 137–138.

immediate effect was that auditing fees would have to be increased considerably to allow for the increased time and testing procedures necessary to meet the new standard. Client managements, who would have to foot the bill, balked at paying the huge fee increases.

The pragmatists in the French government and in the profession quickly realized that it would be impossible for all companies to meet the standard overnight. Instead they agreed on a series of changes that would allow the requirements to be implemented over time.

In the years that followed, the KMG organization in France grew into the country's largest provider of accounting, tax, and audit services. KMG representation in France consisted of three firms:

- Fiduciaire de France, the largest accounting and auditing firm in the country, had 3,800 people, including 400 partners, and blanketed the country with its 150 offices. At the time, its revenues were Fr1.035 billion (approximately US$180 million). The firm's lines of business included review and examinations of middle market companies, accounting and management consulting services, and the preparation of financial statements. The firm had an audit department in the greater Paris area of approximately 130 people and several specialized teams in the provinces that worked on statutory audits. Fiduciaire de France had a list of distinguished clients in the banking, agribusiness, merchandising, construction, public works, and high technology industries. Sixty of its client companies were listed on French stock exchanges.

- Fiduciaire de France also owned the majority of the shares of Frinault Fiduciaire, which it acquired in 1978. Frinault's primary purpose was to conduct statutory audits, usually of listed French companies. This subsidiary, which operated only in Paris, posted revenues of about Fr70 million (US$11.5 million) and had a staff of about 150 people.

- A legally separate company with its own organization and staff, Fidal was a law and tax firm composed primarily of experts in business law. The firm had many clients in common with Fiduciaire de France. Fidal had approximately 1,600 people, including 400 partners, and revenues of Fr450 million (US$76 million).

PMI France was part of the Continental European Firm (CEF) and included three legal entities, one for each of the typical PMI audit, tax, and management consulting disciplines. Its client list consisted mostly of subsidiaries of companies the firm served in other countries, although the practice had made progress in penetrating the French market.

Despite the differences in services offered and the clientele they served, KMG's Piard believed a merger could work in France. A thirty-four-year veteran with the firm, Piard had worked his way up through the ranks, becoming regional director in 1958, vice chairman in 1973, and deputy chairman in 1976. Chairman since 1986, he knew his firm and its potential. In addition to his responsibilities with the French firm, Piard was also a member of KMG's central management committee and had been involved in the international merger deliberations. A delegate at the ceremony in New York when the international memorandum of understanding was signed, he returned to Paris buoyed by the experience and ready to work on a deal.

He talked the situation over with the operating committee (directoire) of Fidal and the chairman of Frinault Fiduciaire. They agreed that the merger should be fairly simple in the tax and consulting areas. PMI's tax practice would fit nicely within Fidal, and KMG did not have a similar management consulting practice. Accounting and auditing, however, were a different story. Fiduciaire de France leaders believed that synergies with Frinault had not been realized, and they saw in the merger an opportunity to consolidate Frinault's statutory audit operations into the mainstream firm. Accounting services and audits of small to midsize firms would be provided by one department—Fiduciaire de France's international audit department, Frinault—and the PMI practices (each of which were approximately the same size) would be combined into a single department that would conduct statutory audits, including those for listed clients and large multinational companies. It would be a formidable combination, the largest firm in France by any measure.

Thus, PMI's French firm negotiated with KMG as three separate entities. As expected, there was little difficulty in working out a merger with the consultants. PMI consulting senior partner Jean-Claude Cohadon and Jean-Claude Petit, who succeeded him as senior partner, negotiated an agreement that would allow the consulting practice to join KPMG as an independent unit. It continues as such today.

PMI's senior tax partner Loïc Steunou and his fellow tax partners negotiated with Claude Colin, deputy chairman of Fidal at the time. They, too, had comparatively little difficulty in coming to terms. They reached an agreement in principle in October 1987 with an effective merger date of January 1988.

The real difficulty was on the audit side. PMI's French auditors believed, as did many Continental partners, that the CEF was making significant progress and that the French firm was making a substantial contribution to PMI's growth. It had made inroads into some of the larger French businesses, and the partners believed that given enough time, the firm could help build itself into a European power. In a merger with KMG, they believed, they would be bargaining uphill.

PMI leaders, on the other hand, saw limited growth

opportunities—particularly in Europe—if the CEF continued alone on its present course. It could take decades for PMI's firm to reach the size of the merged firm, if indeed it ever could. The situation was exacerbated by the competition that existed between PMI and all the French national firms.

There were misunderstandings on both sides of the merger around the world, but nowhere were they more pronounced than in France. The PMI and KMG firms were more than competitive. Their wariness of each other was rooted in the deep divisions perceived between the French firms and the international firms with offices there. Fiduciaire de France, dominant in the marketplace and a leader in the profession, saw PMI as little more than an expatriate representative firm. PMI partners, on the other hand, because of their professional confidence (some said arrogance), appeared to be condescending toward the French firms. They were satisfied with what they described as their "high profile, value-added services" compared to their perception of Fiduciaire de France as a storefront provider of accounting and tax services. Now they were going to be merged (or submerged, they believed) into one of those firms, and they didn't like it very much.

In fact—as is often the case with such closely held misperceptions—both were wrong about the other. The truth was likely somewhere in the middle. PMI was making progress in its efforts to recruit more French professionals and increase its market penetration, and Fiduciaire de France had far more statutory audit clients (more, in fact, than the PMI firm) in France than the PMI partners first believed. It was an ominous beginning.

The PMI audit partners made their feelings known early on. "Right or wrong," they told PMI leaders, "there is no way we ever want to get into bed with Fiduciaire de France." Discounting Fiduciaire de France's accounting practice, the PMI partners focused on the differences they saw in the audit practices. "A merger with Fiduciaire de France would create a major image problem for us," they said. "They have very little proper audit practice, and the French market knows it. Their business, offices (PMI had 3, Fiduciaire de France had 150), and clientele are totally different from ours." By the end of September 1986, just a month after the signing of the international agreement, the merger seemed hopelessly stalled.

PMI audit partners, convinced that they could never live with the deal Piard proposed, met with Larry Horner and Jim Butler to seek "an undertaking that they would never be asked to negotiate with Fiduciaire de France; they would negotiate only with its subsidiary, Frinault." They intimated that unless they got such assurances, the entire CEF would vote against the merger. After much debate and discussion, the PMI partners felt that they had the assurances they needed and that they could go forward with the merger discussions.

It was the first of many misunderstandings that would plague the discussions. Given the number of people, partnerships, and special interests, it was virtually impossible to determine precisely what was said in every discussion, meeting, phone call, and conversation. Selective recall was the order of the day, as people interpreted the events in light of their own preferences and experiences. It may be that, as one wag observed, "There are no truths; there are only perceptions of truths."

Armed with the belief that they had an agreement with the PMI firm leaders, French senior partner James Shaw and the PMI audit partners set out to strike a deal directly with Frinault Fiduciaire. Since Frinault had been founded as an audit firm, the PMI partners believed their cultures were more compatible.

It should not have come as a surprise to anyone that this did not sit well with Fiduciaire de France, which—despite its majority ownership of Frinault—was not invited to participate in the discussions. Piard was advised that Frinault was in preliminary discussions with PMI as well as with Arthur Andersen and Coopers & Lybrand, although it was never made quite clear who would pay Fiduciaire de France for the shares it held in Frinault if

Frinault went with AA or C&L. It was common knowledge on both sides that AA was Frinault's preference. The good relations between the two firms had been developed during the course of several engagements in which they served as joint auditors. (In France joint audits are required in certain situations, for example, with financial institutions.)

The PMI partners sensed the strained relationship between Frinault and Fiduciaire de France, but attributed it to Frinault's resistance to Fiduciaire's attempts to more fully integrate the auditing firm into its operations. The PMI audit partners' strategy was to work out a deal with Frinault, then try to establish their firm as a separate unit of KPMG. They would be the statutory audit firm, and Fiduciaire de France would be the accounting services firm.

It didn't work. In April 1987 Frinault announced that it had struck a deal with AA. This created a complex problem since it wasn't clear to anyone whether Frinault's actions were legal. Technically, Frinault was owned by Fiduciaire de France. Nevertheless, the last thing anyone wanted was a protracted dispute. Later, after much discussion and even after the Fiduciaire de France and PMI merger had been completed, a deal was eventually struck, and Frinault departed from the Fiduciaire de France organization.

The move left a great deal of confusion and uncertainty in its wake. With Frinault gone, Fiduciaire de France intimated that it was time to begin serious negotiations with PMI. The audit partners resisted, convinced that they had a firm understanding with PMI international leaders that they would never be asked to negotiate with Fiduciaire de France. With Frinault's departure, they also recognized that they were clearly in a much stronger bargaining position.

Horner, Butler, Jim Brown, and other PMI leaders were trying to hold the merger together at all costs; France was simply too important to the international network. The new situation required a change in tactics. PMI leaders met with the French audit partners to clarify their understanding and to strongly encourage them to seriously negotiate with Fiduciaire de France.

The PMI audit partners were incensed. At a raucous CEF meeting in Frankfurt, the partners insisted that their feelings be documented in the meeting's minutes. They wanted it known that they did not trust the word of senior PMI partners. "Two key guys gave us this undertaking," the French partners said. "We had a specific meeting with them, and they said that under no circumstances would we be asked to negotiate with Fiduciaire de France. Now, six weeks later, they come to a partners' meeting here and tell us that if we want to be part of the merger, Fiduciaire de France is our only remaining option!"

Dissension was rampant at PMI. Audit partners openly discussed leaving the firm and taking their clients with them. "We've been screwed by Peat Marwick," they said, "so screw them! Let's go with Coopers & Lybrand or Ernst & Whinney."

Despite the PMI audit partners' initial resistance, in May 1987 a meeting was arranged to begin exploratory talks with the KMG firm. KMG would be represented by Fiduciaire de France chairman *(president du directoire)* Piard and deputy chairman *(directeur general)* Arnaud Bertrand. On the PMI side it would be audit senior partner Claude Briolay and audit partner Dickin Drew.

A structure was proposed and discussed by both sides. The PMI practice would be part of a KPMG audit department that would have its own identity within Fiduciaire de France. A working group composed of representatives from both firms would be assigned to study the problems of merging. It would address such questions as how the department would be organized and managed, the kind of clients it would serve, who would be audit partners, responsibilities of partners and various levels of staff and management, compensation issues, which clients would be audit clients and which would be served by the accounting services department, and how audits would be signed.

As the controversy swirled about him, Drew saw an opportunity in the midst of the disorder and disarray. British by birth, he had begun his career in London and knew the PMI leaders well. A partner in the CEF since 1971, Drew had been based in Paris for more than two decades. He met his American wife in Paris and planned to stay there.

Drew took it upon himself to draft a paper outlining the options. Addressing it to all the remaining audit partners—including those who were contemplating leaving—he began by pointing out that they now owned the audit practice and that "whilst we might not like the thought of negotiating with Fiduciaire de France, there might be an option that would be acceptable to us. If we could negotiate with specific objectives in mind, and specific requirements for staying, we might be able to strike a reasonable bargain."

Image was a concern. The departures of PMI people and rumors that more were on their way out had so seriously damaged the firm's public image that Drew believed the entire French audit practice was at risk. "If we could get sufficient, well-negotiated assurances with regard to image, quality control, training, management of the audit practice, and proper professional standards, we can save the firm," Drew told his partners.

Reaction to Drew's paper was mixed. Some questioned its logic, some favored its approach, and some opposed the idea, thinking it would never work. "You're wasting your time, Dickin," the dissenters told him. "You will never achieve your financial objectives or the professional, quality control, and image goals. You just don't understand the realities of life. You were brought up with PMI, and you've been with them too long. You're no longer objective."

"My first reaction," Drew recalled, was to say, 'Fine, off you go.' " But it wasn't that simple. First those partners who seriously wanted to leave had to be bought out. They had to either be compensated for their interest in the firm or be allowed to take their clients with them. After a good deal of wrangling, a deal was finally struck where partners who wished to leave could do so, but they could take only domestic clients with them. They could not pursue clients referred through the international network.

Eventually, seven audit partners did leave the firm, further charging the already tense atmosphere. Charges and counter-charges flew amid rumors that at least one or two of the partners had secretly signed agreements to join competitors before they told their PMI partners. The remaining partners heard stories about how the partners in question had misrepresented their intentions, participating in merger discussions after they had already made the deal to leave and recruited twenty-five staff members to go with them. The rumors gained credibility with each departure; in the end, about twenty staff members left the firm.

The exodus of clients was less extensive, despite persistent rumors that some of the firm's largest clients were receiving phone calls from former PMI partners encouraging them to change firms. Reportedly, they were being told that PMI had broken up in France, and that regardless of how they felt about PMI, there would soon be no PMI representation in France.

Few actually left. PMI estimated that of a Fr95.6 million (US$16.0 million) practice, the seven partners who finally left took about Fr7.2 million (US$1.2 million) worth of business with them. For the most part, clients stayed with PMI.

Audit senior partner Briolay, Drew, and the remaining audit partners set out to negotiate with PMI and Fiduciaire de France. They knew that even though the French firm would be responsible for working out its own merger in that country, the international organizations could help. They told Horner and Butler, "We will undertake to negotiate with Fiduciaire de France in good faith—provided we have your assurance that you will help us meet our professional and financial objectives. We don't think these are unreasonable requests, but we believe we have been screwed once, and we want to make damn sure that we aren't going to get dumped on again."

In truth, they were not overly concerned that they would be cut out. France was simply too important to the international firm, particularly in view of the increased merger and acquisition activity as French companies began expansion plans in anticipation of the "borderless Europe" by the end of 1992. Business was good, and no one would walk away from such a substantial practice. Besides, given the uncertainties so far, it was logical to assume that PMI had some sort of contingency plan.

It was a shaky beginning, but a step in the right direction. Both sides were cautious, taking time to get better acquainted before tackling the problems and misunderstandings that faced them. Neither side wanted a replay of the events of recent months. The negotiating teams understood very well the importance of eliminating ambiguities that could create problems later on. They knew that things said and actions taken during the negotiations would live long in memory. As he looked back on the tumultuous events in France, Piard reflected:

> If I were advising someone else about such a merger, I would tell them to consider carefully the interests of the people involved and do everything possible to retain the right people. Throughout the process, maintain a positive attitude, and don't be discouraged by the merger events. Find ways to motivate people during the process, but try to move the discussions along in a spirit of continuity and good harmony. That will be very important later when you find yourselves together in the same firm. You must remember through all the difficult times and discussions that these are the people you will be working with in the future.

As the negotiations continued, PMI partners made the rounds, visiting clients to squelch rumors about lost clients and staff members leaving the firms in droves. They assured the clients that they would continue to receive quality service from the senior partners who were committed to keeping the practice viable. In addition, there were experienced senior managers who would be made partners in a year or two and very capable young managers who were on the job every day managing the engagements. Plus, the partners assured clients, "We have the open-ended support of the worldwide organization." It wasn't business as usual quite yet, but things were beginning to stabilize.

By the time the dust had settled, PMI's French firm had lost close to 40 percent of its staff. Those who went told stories of chaos at PMI; competitors used the information to try to lure away clients. The stories worked their way through banks, stock exchanges, and other financial institutions, raising questions about the ability of the two firms to ever get together.

In the cold light of logic, however, it was clear that both firms needed the merger, but for different reasons. Fiduciaire de France had not changed throughout the turmoil at PMI, but it needed to reinforce its audit practice. There was plenty of statutory audit business if the firm had qualified people; PMI could provide some of those people as well as its internationally known auditing techniques. In France, as in much of Europe, PMI wanted to change its Anglo-Saxon image and create a strong national practice; KMG was strong nationally and on the Continent, but needed to expand its audit capabilities internationally. A merger could work to the advantage of both.

PMI leaders Horner, Butler, and the newly elected CEF senior partner Harald Kessler made numerous trips to France to show support and help solve the problems there. KMG's Piard was unyielding in his determination to persuade PMI partners that Fiduciaire de France was a quality firm. He was convinced that their combined resources together with Fiduciaire de France's penetration of the French market could create an invincible firm, more powerful than seemed possible at the time.

Butler, who in the division of responsibilities among PMI leaders was given responsibility for France, credits Piard with much of the eventual success there. He said, "The situation in France was one of the most difficult problems I have faced in my professional career. Despite the efforts of many people to strike some sort of reasonable compromise, there were times I doubted it would be possible to reconcile the interests of everyone involved. Robert Piard was enormously helpful in eventually resolving the issues. Without his cooperation, it would have been impossible to conclude the merger in France."

Butler, Piard, Bertrand, Briolay, and others toasted the merger when an agreement in principle was reached in October 1987, but there were no champagne corks popped when the deal was finalized in December of that year after many tiring negotiating sessions and late-night international phone calls hammering out the details. Mostly, the key players felt a sense of relief that this phase was ending and apprehension about the long, hard road ahead. The public image needed a great deal of work, there were offices to be combined, the common audit manual had to be introduced, and the auditors needed to be trained in the new KPMG audit approach.

Although the auditors didn't physically combine their offices until October 1988, they began working together on January 1, 1988, the effective date of the merger. Initially, a great deal of time and money was spent teaching staff members the KPMG international audit procedures and familiarizing them with KPMG's automated approach to the audit. One of the conditions of the merger that the PMI partners had negotiated was the purchase and installation of Apple Macintosh computers for the auditors. The "Mac" had become an integral part of the KPMG auditor's toolkit; with the proprietary software that the firm had developed since introducing the Mac, staff accountants could perform in minutes calculations that formerly required hours with a calculator. KPMG is so committed to the microcomputer that it now boasts one for every three employees—around the world.

Despite the difficulties in putting the pieces of the merger together, the French firm prospered. The audit practices, now combined as KPMG Audit, department of Fiduciaire de France, had been about the same size when they merged. By 1990 the firm had added 9 partners and 150 staff members. Revenues for the fiscal year ended September 30, 1989, the first full year together, showed a 20 percent increase. The momentum continued into 1990 with revenues that year increasing 30 percent over the previous year.

The record growth was fueled by the impetus of the 1992 movement, the development of international business, and the acquisition of new audit clients such as Auchan, a longtime client of Fiduciaire de France and a major French department store chain. Auchan, prior to the merger, had rejected the idea of one firm providing audit services around the world, preferring instead to deal with the firm it believed to be the best in each country in which it operated. With the new KPMG firm, Auchan management was convinced that the company would receive consistent, high-quality service around the world.

KPMG Audit stretched to meet the demands of new work created by clients' inbound and outbound investments, as well as cross-border investments in Europe. French companies went on a shopping spree, buying companies in the United States, in the United Kingdom, and on the Continent.

With the increase in business, recruiting became increasingly important. As the audit department grew from 250 to 400 people in just two years, it needed a regular supply of university graduates. The growth of KPMG Audit helped to dispel earlier campus rumors about problems during the early tumultuous days of the merger talks.

One notable success came when KPMG was selected as the statutory auditor of Caisse Nationale de Prevoyance (CNP), France's largest life insurance company. Another resulted from the key role the French firm played in regaining Motorola as a client in Europe. French partner Jean-Luc Decornoy led the proposal team that regained the audit from Arthur Andersen in France; Motorola had defected to the competitor when it became disenchanted with PMI in Europe prior to the merger.

The firm further expanded its strength in France with the acquisitions in 1989 and 1990 of two smaller audit firms. The first, a firm based primarily in Paris, expanded KPMG's high technology capability in Paris and the surrounding area. The second acquisition added another dozen quoted companies to the client roster and gave the KPMG firm a strong foothold in the Rhone Alp region, a rapidly developing industrial area of France.

These successes prompted Piard to muse, "I wonder what might have been accomplished in France if the communication had been better and the misunderstandings avoided from the outset?" One thing was clear as the firm moved into the 1990s: KPMG in France had made the long, hard climb to the next pinnacle.

# Chapter Eleven

# A Confusing Situation

In many countries, the KMG/PMI merger accelerated changes already being driven by social, economic, and competitive conditions. Once people accepted change as inevitable, they explored every option. Joining forces became the order of the day, and a spate of mergers swept the accounting profession.

Contrary to many firms on the Continent, Italy was a model of cooperation. PMI senior partner Giuseppe Angiolini and his KMG counterpart, Henry Glogg, enthusiastically endorsed the merger and quickly struck a deal. They hoped that their early and lasting commitment would shine as a beacon of success to other countries that were having difficulty hammering out a deal.

They quickly resolved the issues dealing with a complex ownership structure in which KMG's Swiss firm owned part of its Italian firm. Discussions were wrapped up by the end of December 1986, and on March 20, 1987, Italy became the first firm in continental Europe to finally sign the agreement.

In Sweden the merger was a nonevent. Fourth-largest Reveko, the KMG affiliate, swallowed the tiny PMI firm without a hiccup.

Indigestion came from the events that followed.

At the time of the merger, Sweden was enjoying a tremendous amount of success. The economy was booming, and accounting firms struggled to keep up. Because of its small size and geographic location, Sweden had long ago developed an international outlook. In preparation for 1992, Swedish companies streamlined and reorganized their operations. As they bought and were acquired by foreign companies, they needed merger and acquisition advisory services, acquisition audits, valuations, and other consulting services. Their activities fueled growth among accounting firms that reached rates of 20 percent and beyond.

The leading firms competed vigorously for the best new accounting graduates, driving up salaries by percentages that equaled or exceeded the firms' growth rates. There simply were not enough good people to meet the burgeoning demand for accounting and consulting services.

The leading accounting firm in Sweden was Bohlins, the Deloitte Haskins & Sells affiliate. It led its nearest competitor by a scant Skr35 million (about US$5.7 million), but boasted more than 30 percent of the quoted companies (those listed on the stock exchange) in that country. Prior to its DH&S affiliation, Bohlins was for thirty years a PMI firm. Larry Horner had known senior partner Caj Nackstad's father when the elder Nackstad headed Bohlins while Horner held the top post in West Germany. In the early 1980s Bohlins leadership became increasingly concerned about the Anglo-American domination of the firm. Nackstad didn't like the Continental European Firm (CEF) being built into an empire that was being run out of Paris "by a bunch of British expatriates."

All of the Big Eight suffered under Anglo-Saxon domination, Nackstad thought, but he believed he could cut a better deal than he had with PMI. When he eventually took his firm to DH&S, he left the PMI office with about twenty-five people.

By the time of the KMG/PMI merger, Bohlins was a third

larger than fourth-place Reveko, the KMG firm. Bohlins posted fee income in 1988 (the first full year after the KMG/PMI merger) of Skr460 million (US$74.8 million), compared with Reveko's Skr314 million (US$51.1).

The event that set in motion a reshuffling that would continue for months as accounting firms jockeyed for position was the news in December 1988 that Hagström & Sillén (the Arthur Young affiliate) was merging with Bertil Olssons (the Ernst & Whinney affiliate). Shortly before the international firms AY and E&W announced their intention to combine, their Swedish firms independently decided to merge and join the AY network.

Reveko, part of the KMG family since 1980, had been in continuous operation since the turn of the century. It had grown through a series of mergers with local firms as well as sustained internal growth. But being in fourth place didn't fit well with KPMG's strategy of being number one or two in its major markets.

Over the years Reveko had received polite inquiries from Öhrlings—the Coopers & Lybrand firm—largely, Reveko audit partner Katja Elväng suspected, because of the Philips audit. For some fifty years, Öhrlings had audited the Swedish subsidiaries of Philips, one of its oldest and most prestigious clients. When KMG was formed in 1979, Öhrlings feared that because of Netherlands-based Philips' strong ties to Klynveld Kraayenhof & Co., KMG (and later KPMG) would persuade Philips to move its audit in Sweden to Reveko. They eventually did in 1988.

Elväng would run into the Öhrlings chairman in connection with their joint audit of a Swedish quoted company, AGA AB. (In Sweden, quoted companies are often audited by two firms.) Now and again the subject of a merger between their firms came up, but Elväng deflected the inquiries, saying, "It's not the right time yet. We're not prepared. We only joined KMG in 1980. Give us time to mature."

Following the KMG/PMI merger, KPMG's goal of market

dominance made Reveko more receptive to Öhrlings overtures. When Öhrlings inquired again after the combination of AY and E&W, Elväng, who served on KPMG's CEF board and other international committees, responded, "Maybe this is the time. Why don't you call our chairman? But remember, there are two very important things. First is our relationship with KPMG. We want to preserve that. Second, we want equal ownership."

"No problem," came the answer. "Let's negotiate."

The Reveko firm was a young partnership and very democratic in its approach. As was the usual procedure, a three-partner team was set up to negotiate with Öhrlings. This cumbersome arrangement required the negotiating committee to report back to the partnership and ensure support for any deal it might strike.

During the last week of 1988, Elväng went skiing in Switzerland. Her vacation was interrupted by a disturbing telephone call. Instead of bringing Öhrlings into the KPMG family, her partners were seriously considering merging Reveko into the Coopers & Lybrand network.

Elväng considered her options. Öhrlings was a good firm, and its leaders had promised a fair deal regarding ownership and compensation. The two firms were about the same size, but Öhrlings had a few more blue-chip clients than Reveko. On the other hand, Öhrlings had been experiencing some personnel problems. Because of its heavy client load, overworked managers were leaving for other opportunities. Reveko was a little more flexible, more tolerant, and, Elväng thought, a more pleasant place to work.

As Reveko partners vacillated, Elväng phoned Hans Havermann in Düsseldorf who in turn advised Horner. They arranged a meeting in New York to map out a strategy. Soon afterward they met in Sweden with the leaders of both KPMG and C&L in a futile attempt to either bring the C&L firm into the KPMG family or at least retain Reveko. The Swedish firms insisted on strict confidentiality. Havermann and Horner were not to tell anyone of their discussions.

Over the next few weeks, the Reveko partners debated. Finally, on the weekend of February 24–25, 1989, they put it to a vote, and the partners voted their pocketbooks. They agreed that, effective September 1, Reveko would merge with Öhrlings and join the C&L network in a deal that would offer the partners a level of financial independence they had not yet achieved with KPMG. For the average line partner it made little difference whether the firm was affiliated with KPMG or C&L. International strength was an abstract idea that did not affect their daily lives—or their pocketbooks.

The following Monday, Horner reported Reveko's defection and took his lumps for keeping the confidences entrusted to him. In a memo to the board of directors, he wrote in part:

> [The Swedish firm's] interest in the merger was solely based on its desire to create a firm with a greater market presence in Sweden. Both firms readily acknowledge KPMG's worldwide position is superior. We had hoped that our partners would convince the Coopers partners to switch from the Coopers International firm to KPMG. They say they are still considering this alternative but I am doubtful that KPMG will be successful.
>
> A further complication is the fact that Hans and I kept the matter confidential as requested. A week ago the possible merger leaked to the Swedish press, and several partners who were not aware of the situation became very upset. [We] are working to get the relationships back on track.
>
> Currently it appears that Katja and perhaps one or two other partners will not be part of the merger and will remain with KPMG. She will probably take staff from Reveko and be able to serve our clients. There are other possibilities for a major firm to join KPMG. All of these options are being pursued at this time.

Horner placed a call to Nackstad. They exchanged pleasantries and reminisced briefly about their former affiliation. Encouraged by his warm reception, Horner asked Nackstad if he would be interested in talking about an affiliation with KPMG. He would. Horner phoned Jim Butler in London and hastily arranged a stopover in Stockholm on his way to a meeting in Japan.

The timing was fortuitous. Nackstad was already worried about Deloitte Haskins & Sells' disinterest in dealing with competitive pressures brought on by the KPMG merger. Most of the firms expected the merger to fall apart because of culture clashes. Early difficulties in France gave the other Big Eight firms hope that it was going to be virtually impossible to get KMG and PMI to work together in a meaningful way. Such hopes were dashed with KPMG's success in the United Kingdom with ICI. When they examined the situation more closely, competitors saw something disconcerting. Against all odds, the merger seemed to be working.

Nackstad had become increasingly concerned. A second-generation senior partner at Bohlins, he had made his way to the top by consistently outperforming his peers. He was determined to dispel any suspicions that he was getting preferential treatment because of his father's influence. Plus, he had seen the Big Eight from both sides of the Atlantic, having served two years in San Francisco.

"We need another merger in our own international organization," he told DH&S leaders, "to make sure we can compete with KPMG on an equal basis."

The defection of Reveko from the KPMG ranks left KPMG without representation in Sweden, and Nackstad was making little progress with DH&S. "Perhaps we should team up with a firm that already has its act together," Nackstad told his partners. "KPMG has achieved what we want—a presence as strong internationally as it is in Sweden."

The meeting with Horner and Butler went well. It wasn't diffi-cult to renew old PMI relationships in the new KPMG. Though he wasn't surprised when Horner phoned, he was nevertheless cau-tious. He did not want a repeat of 1981, when the CEF chafed under Anglo-Saxon domination. As he examined the merged firm and talked with Horner and Butler, Nackstad liked what he saw. The merger had changed the culture. American and British firms shared leadership roles with strong European firms. It was an organization with which he could work. Nackstad later reflected:

*It's ironic that we left PMI in 1981 because of its weakness in continental Europe. Now we're coming back because of its strength here—a critical asset with the approach of 1992. We can't yet imagine the total effect 1992 will have on our clients. Sweden will see immediate effects because of its international trade. We are more eager to tear down the boundaries between countries than are some of the EC mem-ber countries.*

*The leading companies in Sweden—Volvo, Electrolux, and others—are trendsetters for the whole economy. They are very internationally minded and set the example for others. Their internationally oriented managers establish the culture for others around them. Our own strategy is to stand out from the other firms—to be the most international of all the accounting firms. If we can establish that perception here, we will be the international accounting firm of the future. That's the vision we have to articulate to our people and our clients.*

Over the course of the next few months, Nackstad and Butler sketched out a deal that would include Elväng and a handful of former Reveko people joining Bohlins. Nackstad first attempted to negotiate a joint arrangement that would allow Bohlins to work with both DH&S and KPMG in a representative capacity. It was not to be. With the Touche Ross/DH&S merger, Bohlins would be required to merge with the TR firm, TRG Revision, Sweden's sixth-largest firm—something Bohlins was unwilling to do.

On January 1, 1990, Bohlins became a full-fledged member of KPMG.

For many of the smaller countries, the KPMG merger was like the post–World War II Yalta conference. The "big four"—the United States, United Kingdom, West Germany, and the Netherlands—had met and divided up the world. The smaller countries could either go along with what had been decided or deal with the consequences of not cooperating. They had few options.

Nowhere was the influence of the "big four" felt more keenly than in Latin America. In the PMI organizational structure, the Latin American firm was controlled by the U.S. firm. When it was time to merge, there was no discussion, no dissension, and no voting. Word came down from on high that the firms were to merge, and that was it. Senior partner Randy Noonan tried to save something of the old organizational structure (which was similar in design to the CEF), but it was not to be. The merger would become a merger of national practices in Latin America as it had around the world.

"The impression we had was that it was a done deal between the 'big four,'" said G. M. "Rae" Scanlan, who now heads up KPMG's Latin American technical support group. "They hoped everybody else would merge, but in the final analysis it wouldn't matter if the smaller firms didn't go along. The 'big four' were going to merge anyway."

PMI's Latin American firm had to be dissolved since it was, after all, a legal entity. As a practical matter, however, since the Latin American firm was a creation of the U.S. firm, dissolution was little more than a formality.

National mergers weren't even necessary in several countries. In Guatemala, Honduras, El Salvador, the Dominican Republic, and Haiti, there was no KMG firm. In Costa Rica, Panama, and Colombia, the PMI firm was dominant by far; KMG had only very small representative firms. Only in Mexico, Venezuela, Ecuador, Chile, Argentina, and Brazil did the size of the KMG and PMI firms approximate each other.

Things progressed smoothly in most countries. Mexico was an exception. In the end, the KMG firm opted out of the merger and the PMI firm became the KPMG member. And in Chile, the firms merged because considerable international pressure was exerted on them to do so. Even though the combined firm had only six partners, it had pronounced differences, and within a year two of the three KMG partners had left the firm.

KMG's firms in Latin America in many ways reflected the culture and business of the European clients they audited. Both the Dutch and German firms had representatives in Brazil and Argentina as they followed leading Dutch and German international firms to those countries.

PMI for many years had a joint venture with Price Waterhouse in South America in the countries south of the equator. Before the days of regular air travel, the distances were simply too great to travel frequently, so firms that competed vigorously in other countries solved time and distance problems by working together in South America. PMI and PW were joined by a predecessor firm of Touche Ross when the partnership was formed in 1915. The name was changed to Price Waterhouse Peat & Co. in 1930 and operated under that name until 1977, when PMI decided to establish independent firms in Brazil, Argentina, Chile, and Peru.

At the time of separation, Price Waterhouse Peat had thirty-nine partners in Brazil. Thirty-six stayed with PW; three came with PMI. One of them, Dickran Derian, built the PMI firm into an organization with offices in São Paulo and Rio de Janeiro. Derian later became senior partner of KPMG's Brazilian firm.

Before the merger, the KMG firm in Brazil was headed by

Roberto Dreyfus, who had built his firm from a one-man operation into a national firm. The firm did a good deal of KMG referral work, particularly for German and Dutch clients, in addition to serving local clients. In his late sixties at the time of the merger, Dreyfus had been "in the process of retiring" for several years. Although the merger gave him the opportunity to do so, he continued to serve as chairman of the KPMG Brazilian firm's advisory committee.

The two firms were so compatible that after the failed negotiations in late 1985, they considered an independent merger in Brazil. Eventually they were dissuaded by assurances that the international firms would return to the negotiating table when the timing was appropriate.

When talks did resume, the issues that had to be resolved in Latin America centered on fees and technical support. The KMG firm would in some cases be required to double and triple fees to be consistent with PMI practices. This, of course, would take time to accomplish. In addition, the PMI firm had long enjoyed the technical support provided by Latin American Headquarters in Montvale, N.J., and wished to continue to do so.

At a PMI Latin American partners' meeting in Panama in October 1986, the issue came to a head. One by one the managing partners asked, "What will happen to the technical support? The merger is fine, but we need the technical support to ensure continued high-quality service and to be competitive."

The fact that each one repeated the same basic message served to illustrate the depth of their concern about this issue. Horner, eager to contain costs and continue building a base of strong national firms, tried to deflect the questions. He quipped, "We can always give you the phone number for the U.S. firm's department of professional practice."

It didn't fly. After the meeting Harry Baird, the U.S. firm's chief financial officer and managing partner of the executive office, and Walter O'Connor, international vice chairman, met with Horner. They believed technical support would be critical to the success of the merger in Latin America and told Horner, "Larry, the number of DPP is not the answer these partners are looking for. They want much more. What they are interested in is the same kind of support they have now. They understand there will be no management or financial support and no profit sharing, but they insist on maintaining the technical support."

Horner agreed. They discussed the pros and cons and how long support should continue. Eventually they decided that three years would be about right. It was in keeping with compromises made in other situations around the world. The three-year "license" ended June 30, 1990, and was promptly renewed.

As the Latin American firms considered the structure of the new organization, they planned to build on the best of both predecessor firms. KMG was strong nationally, and PMI had a more centralized international structure. They would take advantage of the strengths of each by building a regional organization governed by representatives of the strong national firms. The regional board would be responsible for providing general direction to practices in the region without getting involved in daily operations, it would promote the success and standing of practices within the region, and it would facilitate and maintain high, uniform standards of performance in all practice areas. The regional board would report to KPMG's international office.

The plan was adopted on schedule when the firms formally merged on July 1, 1987.

When the final chapter is written about the history of Homo sapiens on this planet, Australia will no doubt go down as one of its most interesting experiments. In a scant 200 years, the descendants of British penal colonists have grown to a position of world leadership while preserving the cultural heritage of the aborigines, one of the world's oldest peoples. Australians are a tough, independent, and proud people given to a decisiveness and directness that sometimes unnerves the uninitiated.

At the KMG/PMI conference in Paris in January 1985, the Australians were among the most optimistic supporters of the merger. Anthony Kewin, KMG's chairman of the regional board for East Asia and Australasia and international partner for the Australian firm, and Geoff Kelleher, chairman of PMI's Australian firm, hit it off immediately. Each recognized the strategic sense of the merger, and each believed his partners would agree. Their optimism and confidence increased as they discussed the key points of a merger during their twenty-six-hour flight home. They concluded that the combination offered great opportunities.

The KMG/PMI merger would allow the new firm to vault over number-one Coopers & Lybrand and number-two Price Waterhouse into first place in the country with $A160 million (US$120 million) and 240 partners. The expanded coverage would be a decided competitive advantage both in Australia and around the world.

The issues that eventually divided the firms were similar to those in other countries. There was a question of size; PMI was almost twice as large as Hungerfords, as the KMG firm was known. PMI leaders saw it as their right to be the dominant partner; KMG didn't want to be taken over and insisted on "reasonable" (more than proportionate) representation on the board of directors and other governing committees. There were also questions about the direction the new firm should take and substantial differences in the firms' pension plans. Eventually they reached an impasse.

Having tried to merge once and failed, KMG's Australian partners decided to explore other options. They had already accepted the idea of a merger and the opportunities it presented. If they couldn't work out a deal with PMI, they would try elsewhere. The most promising candidates were Coopers & Lybrand, Arthur Andersen, and Deloitte Haskins & Sells. Informal talks were held and possibilities explored, but the two never really got into serious negotiations.

Around October 1986, PMI's Kelleher was admitted to the hospital with cancer. The ensuing series of tests confirmed that he was seriously ill. He quickly relinquished his management responsibilities to devote the time required for treatment of the disease. (He died three years later, in August 1989.)

Fifty-six-year-old George Bennett, who had been with the firm thirty-six years and was a member of the executive committee, was appointed chairman. Bennett joined the firm at age nineteen and, except for a one-year stint at IBM in 1955, had spent his entire career at PMI. A modest, plainspoken man, Bennett said, "I became chairman by default. If Geoff had not become ill, I never would have become chairman, because I would have never stood for election against him. I was happy being a managing partner, and becoming chairman wasn't an ambition of mine."

By the time the January 1987 deadline for the international merger had passed, KMG's Australian firm was receiving increasing pressure from its international organization to take action. By that time, KMG Hungerfords had been approached by every Big Eight firm in Australia. The partners said to Bennett, "We must have a good international connection. Our clients are telling us so. Why aren't we talking to PMI? That's the easiest connection. The partners who have done our international work wouldn't have to change. If we can't get a merger together, KPMG is going to choose the larger of the two firms here, and we will be left out in the cold. PMI is a damn good firm. Let's talk to them."

When Bennett received the inquiry, he quickly advised Jim Brown, Horner, and Butler of the new developments in Australia. Their response was urgent, unanimous, and pointed: "For God's sake, if you are going to negotiate a deal with them, please go get them. The fact that they have come back to you indicates that they are willing to give some ground at least on positions where they were intransigent before."

With Horner and Butler occupied in Europe, Brown and Johan Steenmeijer quickly concluded that a trip to Australia might be worthwhile. When they arrived, Brown went directly into a meeting with PMI partners; Steenmeijer did likewise with the KMG contingent. The two groups had a joint meeting that afternoon.

Brown, like Steenmeijer, was taken aback by the Australian style of negotiating, which he later described as "extraordinarily forthright. At times it seemed to me that it passed from forthright to downright abrasive. George really lit into them. He hit them right between the eyes. He told them that 'this time we will discuss things in our sequence, and these are our conditions. We would love to go into negotiations, but let's not have any illusions about how easy it is going to be.' As I watched Johan slide down in his chair, I doubted that we would ever get to a point where we would be able to negotiate."

Both Brown and Steenmeijer were astounded at the benign response of the KMG representatives; they didn't seem at all offended by Bennett's remarks. Much later Brown learned that Bennett and Kewin had known each other for years and that Bennett had sponsored his KMG counterpart for membership in their city club. It was a long-standing relationship that could stand considerable frankness. They understood each other quite well. Only the foreigners were nonplussed.

The spirited discussion continued through dinner, interrupted only briefly when Cliff Graese, the U.S. vice chairman of auditing and the man responsible for working out many of the details of the U.S. merger, wandered into the restaurant. Graese and his wife were on vacation in Sydney and had come to try this out-of-the-way restaurant with a reputation for excellent food and service. Neither Brown nor Graese had any inkling that the other would be there.

By the time dessert was served the Australians had concluded that they should begin serious negotiations.

The next morning, at Bennett's request, Brown paid a courtesy call on Evan Cameron, chairman of the KMG firm, and Kewin. Brown told him he believed their firms could work a deal, and

PMI was more than willing. PMI had great respect for the KMG firm and its people.

Both sides gave a bit, and over the course of the next few months the remaining details were thrashed out. KPMG Peat Marwick Hungerfords was signed into being on October 19, 1987. It was not, however, without its casualties. The western region of the KMG firm, which operated out of its Perth office, opted out of the merger, choosing instead to join Arthur Andersen.

Most of the issues that might have created problems were resolved in the frank discussions that preceded the merger. No rival political camps sprung up to impede the transition, and the commitment of both firms to share in the governance assured fair and equitable representation by partners of both predecessor firms.

As 1989 neared its end, KPMG's strategy of building leading national firms bound by a strong international organization yielded yet another dividend. Touche Ross partners in Australia, irked that their U.S.-dominated firm was attempting to force a merger with Deloitte Haskins & Sells, responded favorably to KPMG overtures when they concluded that discussions with DH&S would be unfruitful. DH&S began talks with Coopers & Lybrand.

By December 1989 KPMG and TR had a deal. TR's Australian firm would be merged into KPMG by July 1, 1990, following approval by the boards of directors of both firms. It was a move that would give the firm a dominant market position in most specialized industry categories, including banking and finance, food and agribusiness, manufacturing, energy, merchandising, transportation, and construction. TR's $A87 million (US$65 million) contribution to revenues would push KPMG to the top spot in the country with $A283 (US$213 million) in revenues and 329 partners, well ahead of second-place Ernst & Young ($A203 million and 234 partners) and third-place Coopers & Lybrand ($A194 million and 221 partners).

The January 1990 issue of *International Accounting Bulletin* reported that "The combination of Touche Ross and Peat Marwick Hungerfords came as a surprise to many accounting professionals, as PMH had only recently completed the combination of Peat Marwick and Hungerfords. But PMH saw that the timing was right, as talks between Deloitte and TR, initiated by the announcement of the Deloitte Ross Tohmatsu (DRT) international merger, had stalled with neither side convinced of the benefits of a merger."

# Chapter Twelve

# Consolidation

What was supposed to be a tale of wedded bliss was more like a shotgun wedding, according to *International Management* magazine. KMG and PMI's brilliant strategy almost produced a disaster, the author opined, because of the firms' organization as separate partnerships that had to individually approve the merger. The article stated, "Accusations of betrayal, bruising squabbles over precedence, and many defections were the result. In a number of countries, no merger occurred because either the KMG or the Peat Marwick office refused to join the combined mammoth. In the United States, the KMG subsidiary has lost a quarter of its partners, including chairman John Thompson, because they decided they wouldn't fit within the bigger organization." [1]

In the end, the firms estimated that less than $50 million in volume out of $2.5 billion in revenues was lost at the time of the merger, and KPMG retained the strongest firm in each principal country. But journalists could always find a disgruntled person or two willing to speak on the record. It was good fodder for stories.

1. Jane Sasseen, "Shotgun Wedding," *International Management*, September 1988, 27.

Although the international memorandum of understanding was signed in August 1986 to become effective January 1, 1987, reports of problems began to surface soon after the beginning of the new year. A *Wall Street Journal* article published January 6 reported that "the projected merger between [PMI and KMG was] beginning to show major strains," listing Australia, New Zealand, West Germany, France, Switzerland, and Spain as problem countries. Speaking for PMI, Continental European Firm (CEF) senior partner P. Graham Corbett attributed most of the problems to differences in compensation and organization, while KMG executive partner Paul Boschma cited cultural differences as the principal roadblock.[2]

It was one of the great ironies of the merger that two people who had key roles in Europe had both held the same position and left the firm before it began to reap the harvest from the seeds they helped to sow. Corbett, who was instrumental in getting the discussions under way in 1985, left KPMG after serving twelve years as senior partner of the CEF over what he called "sharp differences of opinion over how the merger was being put together." He recalled:

> I don't think I had a decent night's sleep for a period of fifteen months or more. And normally, I'm someone who can cope with crises and sleep well. But crises that are as personal to the people for whom you feel responsible . . . God, that's difficult.
>
> It just never let up. The personal antagonisms and tensions are not something I would ever, ever wish to go through again. I see these other international firms putting together their mergers—and knowing what they are going to have to do in continental Europe, I ask myself, "How will they survive it?" I hope they find it easier than we did.

---

2. Lee Berton, "Peat-KMG Merger Proposal Strained As Units in Some Countries Drop Out," *Wall Street Journal*, 6 January 1987, 7.

Corbett left the firm in July to accept a position as financial adviser to Eurotunnel, the British and French venture to construct a £7.5 billion (US$12.3 billion) tunnel under the English Channel between Dover and Calais. He is a KPMG client.

Harald Kessler, whom Larry Horner once described as "a super professional and a wonderful guy," was elected to succeed Corbett. He assumed responsibility for the CEF when negotiations were in trouble in several countries. Horner recalled later, "I have a good deal of admiration for Harald. He was tremendously helpful. I'm not sure we would have gotten there without him."

Despite Horner's accolades, Kessler left the firm in 1989. When he concluded that he would not attain the position of chairman of KPMG–Europe—as had been the plan—he resigned. Looking back, he philosophized about the merger:

> A merger is a revolution in business. It's that simple. It may have the effect of crystallizing something that might have happened anyway, but you didn't know it was going to happen. In the course of a revolution things change. Positions are consolidated or eliminated altogether, and people's lives are affected. That's just the way things are. I was disappointed in the outcome of some of the actions that were taken, but through it all, I supported the merger. I still do.

By February 1987 problems were beginning to surface in the United States. The news broke early that month that KMG Main Hurdman had been dragged into the so-called Wedtech scandal in which a South Bronx (New York) minority-owned defense contractor was charged with paying bribes to officials in exchange for favorable treatment on military contracts. Main Hurdman had reported on the financial statements for the years 1981 through 1984, and, in the process, its opinions had appeared in connection with $175 million of public offerings.

Manhattan district attorney Robert Morgenthau said that his

office was investigating the relationship between Wedtech and Richard Bluestine, a Main Hurdman partner who left the firm to join Wedtech.

Charges and countercharges flew. Various investigations were conducted. Civil suits and criminal charges were filed. The cases have dragged on for years. During this time, Wedtech would be declared bankrupt, and the scandal would result in jail terms for two Democratic Congressmen, Reps. Mario Biaggi and Robert Garcia, and tarnish the image of U.S. Attorney General Edwin Meese. No criminal charges have been filed against Bluestine.

Litigation continued into 1990, but at this writing, there have been no settlements or judgments in the civil cases.

The next one-two punch came less than two months later. On March 25 the Securities and Exchange Commission censured Main Hurdman for what it called "improper professional conduct" in connection with two audits in the state of Texas. The firm's partners settled with the SEC without admitting or denying guilt in an attempt to put the matter behind them prior to the merger.[3]

As the April 1 merger deadline approached, the California State Board of Accountancy charged that Main Hurdman's 1985 audit of Technical Equities Corporation violated professional standards. A San Francisco-based firm, Technical Equities specialized in financial management and packaging tax shelters. It generated a great deal of publicity because of the wealthy show-business personalities and professional sports figures among its clientele. The scandal first made news when it became public that Technical Equities head Harry Stern had defrauded his clients of millions and, in the process, deceived his auditors. By 1990 Main Hurdman had settled several suits; others remained unresolved. The state board's accusation was tried before an administrative law judge who found in favor of the Main Hurdman professionals and

---

3. Cynthia S. Grisdela and Lee Berton, "KMG Main Hurdman Censured by SEC for 'Improper' Conduct in Two Audits," *Wall Street Journal* , 26 March 1987.

recommended dismissal of the state board's accusation. The state board, however, refused to follow the finding of the administrative law judge, and the individuals involved—faced with additional and costly litigation—decided to accept minor disciplinary action and settle the matter with the state board.

In America's litigious society, however, lawsuits are filed against virtually any and every individual and organization with money. Plaintiffs' lawyers file amid much hoopla knowing accountants' ethical standards preclude their commenting about client matters. The lawsuits are often dismissed or quietly settled later. PMI professionals, only too familiar with the routine, discounted the negative press coverage.

In an upbeat message to employees on April 1, Horner told KPMG people that the PMI/KMG merger would be discussed for many years. He cited experts in the industry who hailed the merger as a "combination of opportunity," pointing out that PMI's strong U.S. and U.K. business in tandem with KMG's formidable European presence made good sense for both firms and for the new firm's clients.

In the United Kingdom, the firm engaged Aspen Television to produce a video to tell the staff about the merger. It was an independent look at the PMI and KMG firms that examined the merger's impact on the staff and explained the new firm's structure and philosophy. Andrew Harvey of BBC Television News narrated the report. The firm borrowed the nearby Unilever theater and for days screened the video continually for clients, friends of the firm, and employees.

There was some frivolity despite the solemnity of the occasion. The irreverent *London Daily News* noted, "When it begins operations on April 1, the giant merged accountancy practice of Peat Marwick McLintock will become the second largest recruiter of university graduates in the U.K. Only the civil service will take more. The only hope of salvation for our keenest minds lies in suggestions circulating at yesterday's launch press conference.

Namely, that senior partner Jim Butler will stand up on the appointed day and shout: 'April fools.' "[4]

Would-be comedians on the other side of the Atlantic had their say, too. One story making the rounds in the United States was that the April 1 date was appropriately selected to commemorate the new firm's initials—KPMG—which stood for "Kiss Peat Marwick Good-bye."

Mostly, however, it was serious business as the new firm began working through its lengthy "to do" list. The audit department introduced an audit transition manual aimed at standardizing approaches without any disruption to clients. The manual included notes on the audit process, microcomputer considerations, accounting and review services, prospective reporting, and independence. The idea was to provide a general framework that auditors could follow while moving toward a complete transition.

The final product, the *KPMG International Audit Manual,* was four months in the making. An audit process task force composed of representatives from the Dutch, German, U.K., and U.S. firms released a draft for review by the national firms in early September. The final version was distributed at the first international partners' conference in October in Amsterdam.

The consolidation was a test case for the accounting profession. It was the first time a merger had taken place on such a grand scale. Previous combinations with Big Eight firms usually involved the acquisition of a much smaller firm, and it was clear who was driving and what the rules of the road were. It came as a surprise to no one that by late April, the consolidation was beginning to show some cracks. KMG affiliates in Ireland, Mexico, Spain, and Colombia opted out, as did a PMI office in Norway. Problems continued in Australia, Belgium, Switzerland, and France.

In the United States, despite the fact that over 100 partners had retired from Main Hurdman before the merger, an exodus began

---

4. "Where Angels Fear to Tread," *London Daily News,* 2 April 1987.

soon after that and continued for months. Some took advantage of an enhanced early retirement plan or a special compensation package offered after the merger. Some just didn't like the huge new firm and quit.

At the end of December 1988, Charles Johnson, chairman of the transition committee, sent a memo to former Main Hurdman partners reminding them that they had one year remaining on the three-year security period provided for in the merger agreement. The guidelines, designed to ensure fair treatment of all partners, basically provided for up to one year's severance depending on when they elected to leave. Departing partners would be entitled to compensation until March 31, 1990; those who left on March 31, 1989, would get a full year's severance. The amount would decline with each month that elapsed until September 30; those who left after that date would receive six months' severance.

Partners who elected to retire early as part of the deal would be allowed to "purchase" years of service or age in order to enhance their retirement benefits. Retiring partners would also be eligible for medical, dental, and life insurance benefits. Johnson suggested to the partners that they evaluate their long-term career goals, talk to their managing partners, and consider their options carefully. Partners selecting either severance or early retirement had until June 30, 1989, to make up their minds.

Although the tone of the memo was measured, and Johnson encouraged the former Main Hurdman partners to talk over their situations with the firm's management as well as the transition committee (which had unimpeded access to the board of directors), there was a fair amount of grumbling in the ranks. Some partners viewed the program as a thinly veiled attempt to get them out of the firm, but most partners on both sides of the issue seemed to think the arrangement was fair. More than 100 former Main Hurdman partners left under the provisions of the departure arrangement.

KMG's Boschma found himself in a difficult spot at times.

Senior partners unhappy with the way the consolidation was going turned to their former executive chairman for help—but to no avail. "We can always support you in spirit," Boschma told them, "but unless there is some injustice done—something contrary to the memorandum of understanding—that is all we can do. Your own ideas are your best protection. It is your obligation to work it out."

It pained him to turn them away. An empathetic man who as a sixteen-year-old during the German occupation of Holland during World War II lived a couple of days with his brother underneath the floor of their home to avoid capture and deportation to a Nazi work camp, Boschma liked helping people. He became a teacher to help others, and he entered the accounting profession with similar motives. He joined a small firm in Amsterdam whose primary business was helping Jewish clients who survived the Holocaust to start business again after the war. His management style was similar to his teaching style. He got close to people and tried to help them. He said:

> I made a lot of friends at KMG—I still have them—and I believe this was because I always tried to get people close to my heart. I was sincerely interested in their special concerns, and if I could help them find a solution, I would.
>
> After the merger, I had some pretty dramatic experiences, particularly with some of the Main Hurdman partners. No one is to be blamed—the decisions were made by both PMI and KMG—but America is so different from the rest of the world. I wouldn't say that the American way of doing business is wrong. It's just different from what we grew up with in Europe. Here, we are not so bottom-line-oriented.

There were a few smaller KMG offices in the United States that did opt out. St. Louis and Buffalo—and later Topeka, Duluth, and

El Paso—went quietly; Waco went with the merger, but was later sold to the local partners at their request. Wichita raised a ruckus. Managing partner Paul Allen told the *Wall Street Journal,* "My five partners and I felt we just couldn't mesh with the local Peat office. All six of us are native Kansans. We all started at the bottom here. The Peat partners were mostly from out of state. They had come into town with fancy salaries and big jobs."[5]

On April 1, instead of moving in with PMI, Allen and his partners started their own firm and filed suit in a Kansas court to stop the merger. KMG responded with an allegation that Allen's new firm owed its former firm $3 million in lost client revenues. Allen denied it. Eventually, the two reached agreement.

In Europe, of course, it was the other way around. Frank Dolan, a former PMI Paris partner, told the *Wall Street Journal,* "We were the Lilliputians and KMG was Gulliver." Said the Journal:

> Some Peat partners threatened to break up the firm's European operation. Top American and British Peat officials went to bat for them and convinced KMG that the entire merger might fall apart if Peat's European partners weren't protected.
>
> P. James Butler, the head of Peat's United Kingdom practice, spent hundreds of hours with KMG people trying to bring the two sides together. Mr. Butler says the negotiations were "the toughest period of my working life. I often had to fly [throughout] Europe. I hardly saw my wife." Even at his farm, he couldn't get away from the pressure. "My wife often had to drive out to the fields to bring me to the phone," he says.[6]

Horner also spent considerable time in Europe. He and Butler

---

5. Lee Berton, "Mixed Marriage: Accountants' Merger Tests Idea of Meshing Partners World-Wide," *Wall Street Journal,* 22 April 1987, 1.

6. Berton, "Mixed Marriage," 1.

divided up the countries in an attempt to maximize the coverage and minimize the difficulty, but it stretched them both to their limits to fulfill their management responsibilities while simultaneously stitching together the largest merger ever in a professional services firm.

Even as things began to settle down and the national practices started coming together, there were predictable stresses and strains as sometimes bitter competitors moved into the same offices. Firms that once said, "Peat Marwick? Never!" found themselves partners, said KMG's Boschma. "It was good that those words were sugarcoated," one wag observed later. "It made them easier to eat."

In Holland KMG's Kees J.I.M. van Tilburg found himself in a particularly interesting situation. After the merger had been approved, he, as head of KMG's marketing efforts, was designated to coordinate publicity in the Netherlands and with his colleagues in other countries. Right away, he phoned PMI's Martin Lewis and introduced himself as the KMG partner who had just a year ago taken away one of his largest clients, TNT Ipec.

As it happened, TNT was an Australian transport company audited by KMG; Ipec was a PMI European client. When TNT acquired Ipec, management wanted the new subsidiary to be audited by the same firm as the parent company. PMI, which had a long-standing client relationship with Ipec and several alumni employed there, balked. Rumors reached Van Tilburg that PMI partners were attempting to discourage the change, saying KMG was an old-fashioned firm with a bunch of old partners. The KMG Australian senior partner told the new client, "Well, maybe they aren't all old. I know a young one. Go to Amsterdam and contact Van Tilburg." Van Tilburg recalled later:

> So they came, these three people from the eastern part of the Netherlands, believing that ours was a boring, old-fashioned firm. So it took quite some effort to convince

these people that we had young partners, people who could speak English. It was quite easy for PMI to create an unfavorable image about our firm with the client. We were, more or less, a bit of an arrogant organization—not so much anymore—but at the time we were called the "Price Water-house of the Netherlands." We were very different from PMI, which had a very aggressive image in the Netherlands.

Lewis and Van Tilburg joked briefly about how interesting it would be to tell the client they were now part of the same family, after which they set a meeting to discuss publicizing the merger. For Van Tilburg, it was the first time he had seen—up close—the difference between the perception and the reality of their two firms. He was surprised to learn that the firm he had always thought was very keen on publicity and marketing hadn't given it much thought. PMI was surprised in reverse. Here was a partner from what they perceived to be a stodgy firm talking to them about how to generate the most publicity for the merger. It was incongruous.

As they talked further about joint marketing efforts, Van Til-burg asked to see a copy of PMI's client list. He looked over the list and handed it back to Lewis. "This is your target list," he said. "I want your *client* list."

Lewis responded, "That's it." It turned out that they shared several clients, and each had many of the other's clients on its target list.

In one of the happier stories in the consolidation, Lewis now serves on the KPMG Netherlands' marketing committee that Van Tilburg chairs and sits in for him when Van Tilburg is unable to make a meeting. The key to a successful merger, Van Tilburg says, is to be understanding and learn from each other. "Each firm has positive characteristics, and the art is to combine the good points of both, especially in those cases—as it was here—

where one firm is several times larger than the other. We have acquired several of those positive PMI characteristics, such as its aggressiveness and exceptional planning ability. That's why it is important to be kind even during the toughest negotiations. It makes it much easier to work together later."

On June 30, 1987, the book was closed on KMG and PMI, as the Peat Marwick International Secretariat's office in New York closed its doors. The office was headed by executive vice chairman Athol Mann and partners Richard Worrall and Peter Valentine. Their staff had been responsible for international practice development, worldwide standards, personnel development, international communications and visual identity, funding of PMI projects, and overall international guidance.

Many of the secretariat's activities were assumed by KPMG's first international executive, H. Caspar Broeksma; director of administration Michael Speer; and their staff at the new international headquarters in Amsterdam's World Trade Center. In the first-ever international move for a PMI communications professional, the U.S. firm's director of media relations, Pamela Middleton, transferred to Amsterdam to help with the formidable task of organizing the new international firm's marketing communications department.

Mann, who became one of the first casualties of the merger when his job was eliminated soon after he began it, returned to New Zealand to become dean of the faculty of commerce and business administration at Victoria University of Wellington. Worrall served three years as management consulting international coordinating partner before moving up to become partner in charge of information technology consulting. Valentine returned to the Netherlands as a line partner in KPMG's Dutch firm.

In December KPMG–Switzerland proved it had gotten its act together when a team headed by Hugh Matthews was appointed auditor of Asea Brown Boveri (ABB), the firm that resulted from the worldwide merger of Asea of Sweden and BBC Brown Boveri of Switzerland. The Zurich-based holding company would be one of the largest electrotechnical companies in the world, with annual revenues of Sfr24 billion (US$17 billion) and operations in 90 countries. Representatives from KPMG firms in Switzerland, Sweden, West Germany, the United States, and International Office in Amsterdam assisted with the proposal effort.

In a grand understatement, Matthews said at the time, "Winning this engagement is a great boost to KPMG in Switzerland and internationally. Our ability to demonstrate that KPMG could commit resources to meet that challenge was critical to our success."

Industry observers later credited KPMG's success with ABB as being partly responsible for setting off the accounting profession's great feeding frenzy, which began as other accounting firms eyed KPMG's new international prowess. Competition was already beginning to heat up in Europe. Price Waterhouse announced it was talking with Dijker & Doornbos (the Dutch affiliate of the U.S. firm Seidman & Seidman), and Ernst & Whinney merged with Dechesne Group (the former Dutch affiliate of another U.S. accounting firm). Industry observer Arthur Bowman of *Bowman's Accounting Report* speculated that the moves were in response to the KPMG merger.[7]

As the year of consolidation ended, Thompson elected to retire as executive vice chairman of KPMG's U.S. firm, saying:

> I've had a very rewarding career experience, and I've done everything that can be done within public accounting. I think this is the time of my life, from a point of view of both age and opportunity, to use the skills I have acquired to go into something that is very intriguing.
>
> I have had a lot of personally rewarding experiences. There were the professional challenges of building a strong operation in New York, developing a team of strong part-

---

7. Lee Berton, "Major Accounting Firms Seek to Expand by Lining Up Mergers with Dutch Firms," *Wall Street Journal*, 1 October 1987, 12.

ners, running a multinational firm, working with clients like Union Carbide during the Bhopal crisis. We were breaking new ground, facing new issues that created a feeling of being on the leading edge.

But I would say that overall the most satisfying thing was to be part of an organization that was moving ahead . . . being associated with a group of partners who were willing to work hard to achieve our goals . . . and to have their recognition and the privilege of leading them.

Thompson, who now heads his own firm, which provides interim management to businesses and not-for-profit organizations, questions some of the actions taken during the consolidation. "I think it could have been handled better," he said.

"We are still in the process of capitalizing on the strategies that we created," Horner said. Looking back on the consolidation, he recalled, "I anticipated that it would evolve more quickly than it did, and there were some costs that I considered out of line—but they were related to the time involved. But even though the merger cost more and took longer than we thought it would, the basis for success has been built. I think time will show how successful we were in what we created."

The *Big Eight Review* (now *Emerson's Professional Services Review*) was more effusive. Said publisher James Emerson:

Peat Marwick has never been a firm to follow the crowd. They have a history of charting new ground and that philosophy continues today. The firm has also attracted critics and that also will likely continue. Based on our analysis, however, it should be said that Peat Marwick has invested heavily to be a leader in information technology, it has invested heavily to deliver industry specialized services, it provides a very personal level of service to all sized clients, it has unparalleled international reach and scope, it is bold, it is aggressive, it has tremendous business savvy, and is the first firm ever to exceed the $3 billion threshold in world-wide fees.

The question was whether the recent decisions made by Peat Marwick represented reactions to the present or a vision for the future. Based on our analysis KPMG Peat Marwick is a firm which is leading today and extremely well-positioned for tomorrow.

*Congratulations on a great first year of worldwide combination.*[8]

---

8. James C. Emerson, "KPMG Peat Marwick—Leading Today, Positioned for Tomorrow," *Big Eight Review,* March 1988, 1.

# Chapter Thirteen

# The Feeding Frenzy

The year 1989 may well be remembered in the accounting profession as the year of the feeding frenzy. Big Eight accounting firms merged or considered merging so often that one newspaper columnist speculated the mania would continue until the Big Eight became the Big One.[1]

One of the peculiarities of accounting firm partnerships that complicates mergers exponentially is that seldom is just one merger involved. The firms are often separate partnerships in the regions and countries in which they operate, and they may have smaller partnerships within those partnerships. In addition, a merger of two offices in the same city will involve meshing the audit, tax, and consulting practices at the local level. A deal can't be struck by the chairmen of the firms, then forced on the partnerships. The result appears to the uninitiated as an incredibly unwieldy organization that is often disrupted by renegades unwilling to go along with management's wishes.

---

1. Louis Trager, "Money Talks: Thought, Talk, and Speculation," *San Francisco Examiner,* 27 August 1989, D1.

Price Waterhouse and Deloitte Haskins & Sells learned this fact the hard way when they tried to get together in the early 1980s. PMI and KMG's experience was little better the first time the firms attempted a merger in 1985, and even with the benefit of experience, they had trouble in some countries. Accounting firm partners are accustomed to giving advice, not taking it. They are an independent lot who keep their own counsel.

Nevertheless, the KPMG experience had proved it could work. Said Lee Berton, the *Wall Street Journal* reporter who covers the accounting profession:

> Prior to the KPMG merger, there was a great deal of skepticism in the profession that any Big Eight firm could pull off a merger with KMG. A lot of the people I interviewed at the time were also skeptical because of the difficulty in merging a partnership as opposed to an industrial corporation.
>
> When the report first surfaced, I felt it would be a very difficult thing to do, and I wasn't surprised the idea didn't work the first time. The Price Waterhouse and Deloitte Haskins & Sells merger didn't work because of their British partners, so I thought it could be a problem for PMI and KMG in other countries. Even if a merger agreement could be worked out, it would be an immense undertaking with a huge number of problems.
>
> As the story progressed, KPMG officials increasingly gained confidence in their ability to overcome the problems. They felt that merging a strong American firm with a strong European firm was a solid strategy—and, in this case, a particularly good fit. Some of the partners I talked to thought it was a farsighted effort, especially with the unification of Europe coming up in 1992. They thought the prospect of EC 1992 would spur some to action, making it easier to get various firms to agree to the merger.

The competitive firms, according to a *Wall Street Journal* report, saw only KPMG's successes in acquiring international clients and felt compelled to merge to expand their own international capabilities. Close on the heels of the merger, KPMG's British firm acquired the giant Imperial Chemical Industries (ICI), an engagement neither PMI nor KMG could have gotten without the other. Donald Hindson, ICI's controller, told Berton, "It's a great advantage to have an auditor with such a global presence."

Juergen Kraemer, president of Bertlesmann Inc., the U.S. subsidiary of Bertlesmann AG which bought the Bantam and Doubleday publishing operations in the United States, was even more complimentary. Explaining why the firm switched its audit business from Arthur Andersen to KPMG Peat Marwick, Kraemer told the Journal, "There are enormous advantages since the merger of Peat and KMG to having Peat do our U.S. audit.

"We feel that its merger with KMG was a major reason for our decision to hire Peat. In fact, a recent merger of Peat in Germany with Treuverkehr, a major German accounting firm, will give Peat our West German audit business too, meaning that Peat will be auditing 70% of our worldwide net sales. We couldn't be more delighted."[2]

Other successes followed: KPMG was chosen over Arthur Young to audit Asea Brown Boveri, the company formed through the combination of the Swiss company Brown Boveri (KPMG's client) and Swedish company Asea (AY's client). Georgia Bonded Fibers, a Newark, N.J., company, changed from Ernst & Whinney to KPMG.

Accountancy income showed dramatic increases as well. For the year ended September 30, 1988, KPMG posted revenues of $3.9 billion, a 20 percent increase over 1987 figures.

Such lessons were not lost on the other large firms. In a confi-

---

2. Lee Berton, "Bottom Line: Peat Experience Shows Why Accountants Are Rushing to Merge," *Wall Street Journal*, 17 July 1989, A1.

dential document distributed to its partners, AY, the sixth largest accounting firm, and E&W, the third largest, said:

> Companies throughout the world face significant challenges in responding to the opportunities presented by the dynamic business environment. Globalization of both production and marketing is causing many companies to establish a presence in key markets worldwide, either through direct ownership or strategic alliances. Capital markets are also global, allowing instantaneous movement of multiple currencies and the proliferation of new products. The opportunities available are greater than ever before, but so are the challenges. As companies seek assistance, opportunities are expanding rapidly for professional services firms. And those firms able to respond effectively will develop reputations resulting in significant advantages in the future.
>
> Both Arthur Young and Ernst & Whinney are following clearly stated strategies and achieving success. However, the rapidly increasing service opportunities—particularly in the fastest growing markets in the U.S., Europe, and the Pacific Rim—and increasing competitive challenges have led both firms to consider ways to accelerate the pace of progress on their respective strategies.
>
> The current position and direction of three of our competitors present the most significant challenges. Arthur Andersen and KPMG are by far the largest Big Eight firms, and while pursuing markedly different strategies, they are currently positioned to respond to the increasing service opportunities. Arthur Andersen has a significant worldwide consulting presence, especially in information systems. In key markets—most notably the United States, the United Kingdom, and Continental Europe—it has established the

leading information systems practices. As a result of its merger, KPMG currently has the greatest number of personnel on a worldwide basis. It is able to offer a broad network of professionals to deliver the traditional Big Eight scope of service in virtually all key markets in the world. And Coopers & Lybrand recently has had several large mergers in Europe.

The merger of Arthur Young and Ernst & Whinney recognizes that a combined worldwide practice would accelerate a response to the opportunities presented in the market.

On May 19, 1989, the two firms announced they had reached an agreement in principle to merge, subject to approval by a two-thirds majority of each of the firms. The combination of the two would make Ernst & Young the largest accounting firm in the world, with 1988 revenues of $4.3 billion compared with KPMG's $3.9 billion. The merged firm would be jointly run by E&W CEO Ray Groves and AY CEO William Gladstone. (KPMG later overtook E&Y in late fiscal 1989, when KPMG consummated mergers in West Germany, Sweden, and Canada.)

On May 23, KPMG chairman Larry Horner issued a statement to the financial press:

> When Peat Marwick International and KMG announced plans to merge in 1986, our competitors said they would take a wait-and-see approach to determine how well our combination worked before undertaking one of their own.
>
> The announcement by Ernst & Whinney and Arthur Young of their intention to combine underscores the strategy we took approximately three years ago. It is indicative of the need for accounting and consulting firms to achieve broader global coverage and the economies of scale that this coverage provides.

We regard both firms as able competitors, possessing their own unique strengths and corporate cultures; we will watch with interest to see how well those cultures blend.

If the merger does take place, it will mean the creation of a very large organization and heightened global competition among accounting and consulting firms. We feel quite comfortable in this competitive environment; one of the major strengths of KPMG is our geographic reach and balance, which provides a clear point of differentiation, as do our leadership in market specialization and our commitment to technology.

The pattern E&W and AY followed was essentially the same one KMG and PMI had successfully followed. Rather than requiring a successful vote in a number of countries identified in advance, the firms said in effect, "We're going to try to merge internationally. We will first ask the major countries to see if they can make a deal, and once we get the critical mass of countries necessary to make it work, we will declare it a deal internationally."

E&W's and AY's U.S. firms held discussions in the spring and concluded relatively quickly that they could make a deal. They already had a relationship dating back to the 1984 Price Waterhouse and Deloitte Haskins & Sells merger attempt. According to industry sources, they had concluded then that if PW and DH&S got together, they would attempt a merger.

By the time the U.K. and U.S. firms concluded that they could make a deal, it was evident to most of their national firms that the two would indeed make an international deal. If the two largest national firms could make it work, they were close to having the critical mass they needed to merge internationally.

In Canada, problems were beginning to emerge between Thorne Ernst & Whinney and Clarkson Gordon, the AY firm. There were large cultural differences between the two, and they were bitter competitors. They had fought for the top spot in their country for years. Clarkson had dominated the Canadian market until 1986, when Thorne overtook it, a fact Clarkson resented.

By the end of June, it was apparent that the combination of these two competitors would be more negative than positive in Canada. The principal sticking point seemed to be that the Thorne firm under John Palmer's leadership tried to operate in the true spirit of a partnership. Partners were involved in task forces and committees, and they voted on all major issues. On the other hand, the AY firm, Palmer believed, was run by nine people who had immense power and authority.

"The nine guys allocate all the income. They have all the dealings with the partners," Palmer said. "The electoral process is really what the Clarkson partners describe as a 'Russian election.' There are no alternative candidates, nor is there any capacity for there to be an alternative candidate. The partners simply ratify the selection the committee makes from its own membership. And these nine guys are not about to give up the power that they have. Nevertheless, it's a system that works for them. I can't be critical of it in their context. It works well, and they are a good firm. But it's a very foreign system to us."

Structure and governance also seemed to be problems. Clarkson was centralized with a great deal of authority in Toronto; Thorne's power and authority resided in the regions and the operating offices.

Things were also beginning to heat up in West Germany. In what some industry observers called a move to secure its number-one position, KPMG's German firm, Deutsche Treuhand-Gesellschaft, merged with the Touche Ross firm, Treuverkehr, Germany's fifth largest.

In a June 23 announcement, the firms said they were merging to combine their expertise and experience in order to meet the needs of international clients and the challenges of the single European market in 1992. DTG chairman Hans Havermann chose not to elaborate on the combination, prompting an "industry source" to speculate that the initiative came from Treuverkehr. Said the *International Accounting Bulletin,* "This raises the question of whether Treuverkehr's move gave the impetus to the proposed Deloitte Ross Tohmatsu merger or whether it is the first casualty of that merger."

The Bulletin quoted Touche Ross' Richard Murray as denying that either was the case. His opinion was that KPMG wanted to regain its top spot, which it lost when two other large German firms—number-two Treuarbeit and number-four Treuhand-Vereinigung—were merged into Coopers & Lybrand earlier in 1989. According to the Bulletin, "Murray characterized Germany as 'a country where power and size have a great significance in the marketplace.' He continued, 'The acquisition of Treuverkehr by DTG was a national response within the German profession by which DTG, the previous long-time number one, was able to reestablish its size.'"[3]

The terms of the deal allowed Treuverkehr's shareholders (professional accountants in the firm) to purchase 25 percent of DTG's stock and merge the boards of directors of the firms. The combined firm would have a total staff of 3,300 with fee income of DM530 million (US$265 million). The merger would become effective January 1, 1990; the firm's name would continue as KPMG Deutsche Treuhand-Gesellschaft.

In early July the profession got two more jolts in rapid succession. Shortly before noon on July 6, Arthur Andersen and Price Waterhouse released an announcement that they were in merger talks. Reuters, the Associated Press, United Press International, Dow Jones, and PR Newswire carried the story.

The combination of those two firms would have put them at the top of the heap with $4.9 billion in worldwide revenues. Ernst & Young would be a close second at $4.27 billion, and KPMG

---

3. Kathleen Barrington and Tom LaFreniere, "Touche Ross Loses Treuverkehr to KPMG in Germany," *International Accounting Bulletin,* August 1989, 1, 6.

would be third with $3.9 billion. Once again the accounting world was topsy-turvy.

AA and PW, taking a cue from the mergers that had gone before, planned to keep a lid on news about their discussions. They signed confidentiality agreements and said in a statement, "There will be no public comment during the 60-day period of discussion."

In a later story, UPI reported the firms' reasons for the merger: "Arthur Andersen and Price Waterhouse said their talks were initiated to analyze possible business benefits from the globalization of world economies, the pace of technological advances, and a need for new financial services."[4]

Shortly before 5:00 p.m. the same day, Dow Jones broke the story that Deloitte Haskins & Sells had announced plans to merge with Touche Ross. The story, quickly picked up by the other wire services, was that these two firms had also reached an agreement in principle to combine. The new firm, to be known as Deloitte & Touche in the United States and Deloitte Ross Tohmatsu internationally, would replace KPMG in the number-three spot with revenues of $4.0 billion.

It appeared that the Big Eight, as it had been known for decades, had in the space of a couple of months been collapsed into the Big Five. By all public indicators KPMG in the same short time span had slid from the number-one spot internationally to fourth place.

"The Big Eight is gone," said Arthur Bowman, editor of the Atlanta-based industry newsletter *Bowman's Accounting Report.* "I'm already calling it the Giant Five."[5]

The craziness increased. It occurred to someone that no one had heard from Coopers & Lybrand lately. The media rounded up the usual suspects, and more rumors bubbled to the surface.

---

4. United Press International, "Arthur Andersen and Price Waterhouse in Merger Talks," July 6, 1989, 2:30 p.m. EDT.
5. "Big 8 Now 6 After Deloitte, Touche Ross Merger," *Denver Post,* 15 August 1989, 2D.

Bowman was quoted as saying that he wouldn't be surprised if C&L were on the prowl, since it otherwise risked being the smallest of the Big Eight. Industry seers speculated that C&L, not wishing to be left behind, had abandoned its attempts to merge with the number-thirteen firm Spicer and Oppenheim (about $400 million in revenues) and was instead "stalking a possible merger with the much larger KPMG Peat Marwick."[6]

Both firms' marketing and public relations people denied the reports, but Steven Oppenheim, the chief executive partner of Spicer & Oppenheim, was a little more forthcoming. "Frankly, any firm that is not reviewing its strategic plan or position at this time is almost an ostrich," he told the *New York Times*. Nonetheless, he admitted there were no serious talks going on.

KPMG's Horner and Butler, in meetings with their managing partners to report on the state of the firm, as well as to discuss marketing opportunities created by the confusion in the profession, stated emphatically, "We are not in talks with Coopers & Lybrand. We still have plenty of work to do to consolidate our own merger and take advantage of the opportunities we have now. We don't need another mega-merger at this time. Our strategy is to 'cherry pick' the partners, practices, and national firms that fit into our plans."

C&L began to position itself as an island of stability in a sea of turmoil. In a letter to a U.S. client, a C&L partner identified the reasons for the mega-mergers among the Big Eight as "better service to global clients, technology, capital, and economies." He went on to explain that C&L had a thirty-year history of providing "in-depth, multidisciplined expertise needed to serve multinational clients. . . . New multinational clients like Avon, Cadbury Schweppes, Kraft, Sanyo, and Unilever know we understand the global issues they face—and can deliver the range of services they need to succeed," he wrote.

---

6. Alison Leigh Cowan, "Coopers & Lybrand Is Said to Seek a Bigger Merger," *New York Times*, 21 July 1989, D10.

His firm was a technological leader in the profession, and he and his partners had always been able to generate plenty of capital and didn't need a large merger to provide efficient service. He concluded with an observation by one of his U.K. partners "who likened mega-mergers to the World War I Battle of the Somme when he said, 'What has now happened is like the Somme in 1916: Everybody is locked in, and nobody is ahead of anyone else. The difference is, they are all in the mud, and we are not.'"

Meanwhile, back in Canada, the Arthur Young and Ernst & Whinney merger was in trouble. Thorne Ernst & Whinney had for some time been exploring other options. As CEO John Palmer and his partners had done when they decided to go with E&W rather than wait to see if KMG and PMI would indeed merge, they looked at the pluses and minuses. They considered having discussions with firms other than AY, but decided that their already-low chances of success with AY would be entirely destroyed if they were having parallel talks with others.

When they finally concluded that a deal with Clarkson was impossible, they began ranking the other firms. Once again, for the same reasons it had in 1985, KPMG rose to the top of the list. The only thing that had changed over the years was that KPMG had gotten stronger in the Canadian marketplace. When Thorne compared its competitive successes with major proposals against other firms in Canada, Thorne always came out ahead— except when going against KPMG. Thorne's record against Clarkson was three to one in favor of Thorne; with KPMG, it was a fifty-fifty split. KPMG had become a major force in Canada and Thorne's toughest competitor.

Thorne respected KPMG not only because it was an able competitor, but also because it was a very professional firm with a reputation throughout the country as a firm that maintained the highest ethical standards. It had all the characteristics Thorne partners liked in an accounting firm.

Despite the tough competition, the personal relationship

between Palmer and KPMG's Canadian senior partner, Ross Walker, had continued to be strong. They saw each other fairly often, and Palmer had watched Walker grow from a relatively new senior partner in late 1984 to a confident leader. Walker had developed a stature in the Canadian marketplace and in the profession. In addition, he had been elected president of the Ontario Institute of Chartered Accountants. In Palmer's view, Walker had become a decisive, objective, respected leader in his firm and the profession. Palmer and his partners liked Walker's style.

Walker and KPMG chairman Horner, in the meantime, were in relatively serious discussions with the AY firm as well. Clarkson had also recognized it would be very difficult to merge with Thorne and had been contacted by Walker to express an interest in opening talks with KPMG. Walker was receptive. As the talks progressed, it became increasingly apparent that while either firm could probably come to terms with KPMG, they would have a tough time with each other.

Walker described it as having KPMG in the center and Thorne and Clarkson on either side. "In a very simplistic sort of way, you've got Clarkson here and Thorne there, and KPMG somewhere in between with respect to governance, style, and the attitude toward disclosure to partners. We could move a little either way and find common ground, but between Clarkson and Thorne was a huge gap. That gap didn't exist with us because we are more centrally managed than Thorne, but not as centrally managed as Clarkson. In addition, our culture was closer to either of them than their cultures were to each other."

Walker recognized that the discussions Clarkson had initiated with KPMG resulted largely from the partners' desire to keep their options open. Their first choice would have been to merge with Thorne, as their international firm had done. Nevertheless, Walker did come very close to a deal with Clarkson. It began to fall apart when the new Ernst & Young sweetened the pot in an attempt to keep Clarkson in its family. Walker, sensing a shift in attitudes, wanted assurances from Clarkson that they could make a deal; Clarkson was unwilling to give them. They determined that, perhaps, the best option was to part as friends.

As the talks began to founder, Walker received discreet inquiries from other Canadian firms that were also exploring their options in light of the new developments in their country. He preferred the opportunity presented by a merger with Thorne Ernst & Whinney. He liked and respected both Palmer and his firm.

The discussions were a breeze. The 1985–1986 experience with Thorne and the discussions with Clarkson in 1989 had given KPMG's Canadian firm a definite advantage. Most of the problems had been identified and several alternative solutions developed. The major players already knew and trusted each other. It was simply a matter of choosing the best option under the circumstances. Issues of governance, compensation, pension plans, and professional practices that could have been serious points of discussion were quickly resolved and agreed upon.

In other parts of the world, Ernst & Young continued its steady pursuit of growth, driven largely by its desire to be part of the leadership of the industry, according to James Emerson, publisher of *Emerson's Professional Services Review* (formerly the *Big Eight Review*).

> It would clearly be a stretch for any other firm to be in KPMG's league. They have to have a new strategy. They have to do something other than just sit there. Doing nothing is tantamount to a slow disbanding.
>
> And they're a very competitive group, I think, particularly the Ernst & Whinney element. You don't find someone from Cleveland who isn't going to scrape and scratch. These people are tough competitors. They just could not see themselves in what might have become known as the second tier of the firms.

So we said, in predicting something that might happen, that Ernst & Whinney was very likely to respond to the success of the KPMG merger. And I think that's exactly what happened. In fact, since they haven't refuted that comment, I assume they agree.

The other thing that I really believe—it wasn't so much of a factor when the KPMG merger came together—is that technology is increasingly driving American business. Technology is driving what is happening for clients, and consequently it has to drive what's happening at the accounting firms. I think the perception from the clients' point of view is that "I need my key business advisers to be on the leading edge of technology." The practical aspect of the demands for new technology is that firms need substantial amounts of capital to maintain a leadership position because of the rapid pace at which technological developments are occurring. By mid-1989, several firms could not sustain that position. KPMG changed the marketplace because it now had the resources to deliver what clients wanted in the technology area, and the competitors had to respond.

By late August there were rumors of trouble in paradise. The business press reported that the Ernst & Young merger was having problems in Canada and Japan. Industry sources were quoted as speculating that Clarkson Gordon would most likely merge with KPMG, while Thorne Ernst & Whinney would stay with E&Y. Not likely, the firms said. "Mort Meyerson, a spokesman for Ernst & Young, denied that the firm was having any trouble enlisting support in either Japan or Canada. 'These are just rumors,' he said."[7]

The next day, KPMG issued a press release datelined Toronto, August 24, 1989:

---

7. "Ernst & Young Merger Hits Snags," *Cleveland Plain Dealer,* 23 August 1989, 2F.

> Thorne Ernst & Whinney and Peat Marwick today announced that they have signed a Memorandum of Understanding proposing the merger of their practices into a new firm, Peat Marwick Thorne.
>
> At the same time, Peat Marwick Consulting Group and Stevenson Kellogg Ernst & Whinney announced their intention to merge their consulting practices to form Peat Marwick Stevenson & Kellogg.
>
> Partners of the firms will be asked to approve the merger within the next two weeks. . . . "The merger will create Canada's largest professional services organization, with a network of offices in 61 cities across the country, over 800 partners, and 5,600 staff. Combined annual fees are expected to exceed $450 million," said Larry D. Horner, Chairman of KPMG, the international accounting and consulting firm of which the two firms will be members.

The vote of the partners was one of the most enthusiastic of all the mergers. An overwhelming 90 + percent of the partners voted in favor of it. Only a handful of partners from both firms voted against the combination.

Thorne Ernst & Whinney, which as Thorne Riddell had served as a catalyst for getting KMG and PMI together, had now played the role of spoiler in the Ernst & Young merger. Its move was a harbinger in the profession.

Ten days before KPMG and Thorne announced their intentions, the Deloitte Haskins & Sells and Touche Ross partners approved their own merger. Cable News Network anchor Bill Hartley reported on the Business News broadcast: "Another accounting giant was born over the weekend. Deloitte Haskins & Sells and Touche Ross are one, that merger approved by the U.S. partners of both firms yesterday. Together they employ 65,000 people. They have revenues topping $4 billion. Even so, Deloitte & Touche, as it is now going to be called, falls short of its even more giant rivals. The new Ernst & Young tops the list of accounting firms.

Then comes Arthur Andersen and KPMG Peat Marwick. And the new Deloitte & Touche ranking is just ahead of Coopers & Lybrand."[8]

On September 5, the day before Arthur Andersen and Price Waterhouse's self-imposed news blackout expired, the news media speculated that things weren't going quite so smoothly and the firms might need additional time to work things out. "Sixty days was quite ambitious," Stewart Kohn, an Andersen alumnus who quit to start his own consulting firm, told the *New York Times*. "They're not necessarily ready to agree, nor are they necessarily ready to call the party off yet."

The story went on to describe some of the difficulties facing the two firms. "In a small, but perhaps telling, example of the larger issues that still divide them, the two sides do not even agree on when the self-imposed deadline officially expired."[9]

Industry watchers attributed the problems to differences in philosophy and finances. *Bowman's Accounting Report* explained the two major issues:

- "Philosophy—AA operates as one firm worldwide and PW has 26 different partnerships, each run differently. PW began moving toward a one-firm concept a few years ago; it has further to go than AA anticipated.

- "Finances—AA partners have individual retirement funds and get only about $30,000 from the firm, which is accrued. PW pays partner retirement, about three times AA's, from current earnings. PW's liability, which may equal equity, scared AA."[10]

---

8. Bill Hartley, "Business Morning," Cable News Network, August 14, 1989, 6:30–7:00 a.m. EDT.

9. Alison Leigh Cowan, "Slow Talks by Anderson, Waterhouse," *New York Times*, 5 September 1989, D1.

10. "Philosophies, Financial Issues Kill Andersen–Waterhouse Talks," *Bowman's Accounting Report*, October 1989, 3.

There was also at least one big client problem. Andersen Consulting had enjoyed a long-standing relationship with International Business Machines (IBM) in its information technology practice. Price Waterhouse had been IBM's auditor for years at a fee reputed to be in the neighborhood of $24 million annually. One of the relationships would have to be given up unless the firms could persuade the Securities and Exchange Commission to change its independence requirements. They couldn't.

In late September, Arthur Andersen CEO Lawrence Weinbach sent a memo to all personnel, with a copy of a press release to be distributed on September 26, advising them that the discussions with Price Waterhouse were over.

> After a lengthy discussion process, we have determined that a number of central issues could not be resolved within a realistic time frame. Accordingly, we have decided that client, personnel, and Firm interests will best be served if we do not combine the practices.
>
> Given recent events in our profession, we would have been remiss not to investigate the feasibility of the combination. Even though these discussions have not resulted in a merger agreement, they have been worthwhile. . . . However, our analysis concluded that the detriments outweighed those benefits. These discussions have reaffirmed the soundness of our integrated global structure, our organization, and our commitment to auditing, tax, and consulting services.

The firms took issue with the published explanations for the breakup. In response to an October 9 *BusinessWeek* article entitled "Why Andersen Dumped Price," Shaun F. O'Malley, chairman and senior partner of Price Waterhouse, wrote, "No one was dumped. . . . Business relationships that Andersen Consulting has with several of our audit clients would have impaired our independence of those clients and restricted our future markets for audit and tax-consulting services." Citing a recent action by Securities and Exchange Commission chairman David Ruder deferring consideration of a petition to permit some of the relationships, O'Malley said, "We believed that to consider merging in this uncertain regulatory environment would have violated our historic commitment to all of our clients."[11]

Over the course of the next few months, some of the national firms would defect, rejecting their own international organizations in favor of joining competitive firms. The DH&S firms in the United Kingdom and the Netherlands joined Coopers & Lybrand, and the Touche Ross Australian firm struck a deal with KPMG.

As the firms moved into the 1990s, the confusion that followed the feeding frenzy of 1989 began to abate, and the accounting profession once again brought order to chaos.

KPMG remained at the top.

---

11. Shaun F. O'Malley, "Why Did Price Waterhouse and Arthur Andersen Break Up?" *BusinessWeek*, 30 October 1989, 7–8.

## The Great Feeding Frenzy of 1989

| | |
|---|---|
| January | KPMG reports that its expected merger with the Japanese Century Audit Corporation (under negotiation for several months) has been delayed by at least two years. (The merger was completed in July 1990.) |
| | Arthur Young's Swedish firm, Hagström and Sillén, merges with Ernst & Whinney correspondent Bertil Olssons. |
| February | Arthur Andersen's managing tax partner says in a published interview that his firm is "open to mergers." |
| March | Ernst & Whinney announces plans for several mergers in Latin America. |
| | KPMG's Swedish firm, Reveko, leaves to merge with Coopers & Lybrand affiliate Öhrlings. |
| April | The German firm Treuarbeit leaves Price Waterhouse and joins Coopers & Lybrand's Treuhand-Vereinigung. |
| May | Ernst & Whinney and Arthur Young announce that they have reached an agreement in principle to merge.. |
| | Deloitte Haskins & Sells affiliate Bohlins Revisionsbyra joins KPMG. |
| | Rumors begin circulating that the AY/E&W merger in Canada is in trouble. |

| | |
|---|---|
| June | Price Waterhouse acquires a French firm that was formerly associated with the smaller firm of BDO. |
| July | Deloitte Haskins & Sells and Touche Ross announce plans to merge. |

TR's German firm, Treuverkehr, defects to join KPMG's Deutsche Treuhand-Gesellschaft.

Arthur Andersen and Price Waterhouse report that their firms are in merger discussions.

Japanese Ministry of Finance quashes Arthur Young/Ernst & Whinney merger but approves the TR/DH&S combination.

PW forms a joint venture with West Germany's third largest bank, Commerzbank, to provide consulting services in that country.

Rumors circulate that Coopers & Lybrand is seeking a merger with KPMG.

August      Ernst & Whinney's Canadian firm defects to join KPMG.

Deloitte Haskins & Sells and Touche Ross partners approve the combination of their firms.

Arthur Young and E&W national practices in Belgium announce plans to merge.

September      Price Waterhouse and Arthur Andersen call off merger discussions.

October      Deloitte Haskins & Sells' U.K. firm refuses to merge with Touche Ross and instead joins Coopers & Lybrand.

DH&S's Dutch firm announces that it, too, will join C&L.

Rumors circulate that other DH&S firms may bolt, including the Australian firm and some others in Europe.

November     Deloitte Haskins & Sells firms in Belgium and Austria join Coopers & Lybrand.

The Canadian partners of Deloitte/Samson and Touche Ross agree to merge.

DH&S's national practice in Luxembourg joins KPMG.

December     The Touche Ross firm in Australia announces plans to merge with KPMG.

Arthur Young's Irish tax staff defects to join KPMG.

AY's national practice in Denmark joins KPMG.

*International Accounting Bulletin* reports that Ernst & Young is temporarily the world's largest accounting firm. E&Y will be passed by KPMG when the full annual effects of the acquisitions in Canada, West Germany, Sweden, and Australia are reported in KPMG financials.

# Chapter Fourteen

# Moving Forward

**S**omeone once described it as being similar to turning an aircraft carrier around in the Chicago River. It can be done, but it is a long and tedious process and some of the superstructure may be re-arranged before the carrier is headed in the right direction. As the events following the merger unfolded, some observers wondered if the people who built the machine could drive it. The characteristics necessary to get the deal done might not be the same ones needed to make it work after the firms were combined. The drivers of the merger had to be almost dictatorial at times in order to move things along, while the leaders of the merged firm had to be able to inspire and motivate followers.

There are three phases to a merger, says Harald Kessler, PMI's last Continental European Firm senior partner:

> Phase one is when you get together a small group with a commonality of interest. They are convinced that the merger will ultimately add value, and they push for it. Through it all, it is essential for them to recognize that no

matter how hard they have to push to get the deal done, they will need others to make it work.

Phase two is molding and building commitment. Because of their conviction, those behind the merger move it forward, but they know they need the commitment of others. The key is to bring others into the process—to expand the size of the group that shares the commonality of interest. In phase two the cultures of the merged firms are shaped into a new culture. Otherwise, what is the point of merging?

Phase three is integrating the business aspects of the firm. It is realizing the potential inherent in the merger. It is referring business between the national practices, expanding market penetration, adding new clients to the list, and selling value-added services to existing clients. That is the real test of the success of a merger.

Few would argue that achieving such noble goals in today's business environment is difficult. Changes in the world occur with such frequency and speed that even the most informed leaders are hard-pressed to keep up with them. Traditional organizational structures are crumbling. Hierarchical, pyramidal organizations are giving way to small work groups linked—like atoms—with workers revolving around a nuclear manager and moving from atom to atom as skills are needed. Managers become teachers and coaches who empower their workers and trust them to make the right decisions.

It is a management style with which accounting firms are comfortable. For decades, client service teams have been headed by a partner with the requisite technical expertise and staffed with managers, supervisors, and staff members who complete one engagement and move on to the next. Partners and managers may have several engagements staffed by different professionals; management remains constant to ensure continuity of client service.

The direction of an accounting firm is driven by the chairman who, with the board of directors and other oversight committees, is both steward of the partners' assets and their leader. He sets the tone, style, goals, and pace. He also, together with the board and other senior committee members, heavily influences partners' incomes. In addition, he attempts to solicit feedback from the partners about major issues that affect the firm and to involve the partners in the management of their business.

Larry Horner never doubted before, during, or after the merger that he was doing the right thing for the firm and its clients, partners, and employees. But the pressure was incredible at times. Most of his 1986 Christmas holiday was spent on the phone with Jim Butler and others wrestling with problems in France. His lowest point was the difficulty in getting the PMI and KMG firms to merge in West Germany. Horner had invested a lot of himself— he still had ties to Germany from his days as managing partner as well as a friendship with Hans Havermann—and Germany was strategically important to the international merger.

It was tough, too, to deal with the criticism from the U.S. partners. The idea was fully developed, and it would work; yet there were the Monday-morning quarterbacks who second-guessed decisions based on their view of a small piece of the puzzle. Those with very little experience working in a foreign environment or trying to negotiate many different deals in many different parts of the world couldn't fathom the complexity and difficulty. Horner understood their feelings, but sometimes the questioning and criticism got to him. At times he thought it would be easier just to forget the whole thing and walk away—to go back to the beginning and leave PMI the way it was.

But like others who make their way to the top, Horner is a man who, having committed to something, will not rest until it is done. He despises giving up or not accomplishing something in which he believes. To reach such goals, he says:

> One needs a lot of persistence, patience, and an almost fanatical belief in the vision. It takes a tremendous commitment and willingness to devote a great deal of time and effort. One needs the flexibility to roll with the punches, and if everything doesn't work exactly as hoped, to take another shot at it. It's necessary to accept others and appreciate the differences in cultures, backgrounds, and personalities. One has to believe that through diversity—and adversity—one grows strong.

No one can say for sure how such attributes are developed, but they seem an innate part of successful leaders. Another part of the equation may be the simple unwillingness to accept defeat. For the major players in this merger, to have tried and failed twice would have been unacceptable. It would have been extremely expensive and would have resulted in a competitive disadvantage that Horner personally would not allow. He was convinced KMG would merge—with either PMI or a competitor.

What kept Horner going was the vision he shared with the others. They had within their grasp the opportunity to create a unique organization. Psychologically, or egotistically, the merger's architects liked the idea of being number one around the world; but as a practical matter, as long as the firm had a critical mass of people, financial resources, and adequate geographic coverage, being the largest was unnecessary. The vision was the international strength and market position of the global firm they saw at the end of the process. It was their light at the end of the tunnel.

There were high points in the process to be sure. The first was when Havermann, Horner, Johan Steenmeijer, Butler, and Jim Brown realized they had the structure of a deal each could live with. The next major milestone was the approval by KMG's and PMI's international organizations for the national firms to initiate formal negotiations. The first international conference of the merged firms in 1987 in Amsterdam was an uplifting experience for Horner. When then-KPMG chairman Brown introduced him, Horner looked over the podium at the hundreds of partners assembled there, and he felt great relief that they had come so far but was gripped by the realization that this was more of a beginning than an end. The challenges they had overcome would pale in comparison to those that lay ahead.

New "people networks" had to be established, new standards manuals developed, and new marketing literature published. Those wounded in the merger and the ensuing consolidation had to be healed, and those who lost the faith along the way had to be restored. More than anything else, former competitors had to learn to trust each other and work together.

While the executive committee members had established a good working relationship and quickly established the overall direction of the firm, the spirit of cooperation and harmony that its members enjoyed had not yet begun to move through the rest of the organization. A good deal of the responsibility for improving relationships and capitalizing on the opportunities the merger presented rested with the newly formed international marketing committee.

The committee was chaired by Colin Sharman, who headed up marketing in the United Kingdom. The original committee consisted of Sharman, Ronald Ashworth from the United States, Kees van Tilburg from the Netherlands, and James Johnson from international office. Johnson resigned a few months after the merger, and the committee was expanded to include Dieter Lotz from West Germany and Anthony Kewin from Australia. Clarence Schmitz transferred from the United States to Amsterdam to head the international marketing effort.

All had been line partners before moving into management positions. They brought a variety of perspectives and a wide range of experiences to the task at hand. Sharman had lived and worked in several countries in Europe, reporting to Horner when both were based in West Germany and competing with KMG in the Netherlands. Schmitz was head of the Cleveland office's mergers and acquisitions practice, Kewin was international contact partner for KMG's Australian firm, Lotz (who had also reported to Horner in Germany) was senior partner of PMI's German firm, Van Tilburg enjoyed such marketing success in the Netherlands that he was placed in charge of the effort in that country, and Ashworth had garnered a national reputation for his success with the health care practice and was appointed vice chairman of marketing and specialized industries in the United States.

One of the first problems the group grappled with was the identification of the new firm. One of the conditions of the merger insisted on by KMG was that the merged firm would adopt its logo—with a slight modification. The three blue boxes that served as a backdrop for the firm's initials would be expanded to four for the new abbreviation, KPMG. The style and color would remain the same. Peat Marwick's stylized *P,* as well as its burgundy and gray, would be jettisoned.

Most of the new marketing committee members found out about the logo agreement at the first meeting. But even with a logo, there was still no stationery, business cards, office signs, or instructions. Identity standards had to be developed immediately in order for the firms to begin printing stationery, business forms, and marketing materials. Signs had to be designed, and a visual identity manual had to be distributed to guide national practices in their often-substantial publishing endeavors. Hundreds of details needed attention before the new firm could get in business. Then it could begin paying attention to the business opportunities the merger afforded.

After the initial flurry of activity required to handle such tasks, the committee turned its attention to more important matters. One of its first and most important jobs, Sharman thought, was getting the new firm to look ahead. He recalled:

One of the great things about a merger is that it changes the game rules for all time. All of the things that had been difficult, for historical reasons, in either firm went away. We were in a new game with a new team. Ron Ashworth and I have known each other a long time, and in Kees van Tilburg we found an unusual Dutchman—a very marketing-oriented person. The group's affinity—established right away—was quite astonishing.

We all saw the opportunity right away. We had a fresh team. Kees had been involved in KMG's marketing efforts, but Ron and I had not been involved in PMI's international marketing endeavors. We never really had a marketing committee in PMI; I think KMG did, but it was mostly concerned with referrals. We had to create a new entity with a new image, and referrals are only part of that. We needed to put marketing, in all its forms, very firmly on the international agenda.

The group had an unusual opportunity. In addition to having a new team, it had virtually an open playing field. To a large extent, it could determine the marketing strategy and tactics needed to execute the new firm's plans and help it realize the merger's inherent potential. With the exception of Kewin, the committee also had the advantage of not having been deeply involved in the merger itself. Being new on the scene gave the committee members the distinct advantage of not having strained any relationships along the way. Schmitz, whose M&A experience gave him a unique perspective, explained it this way:

In mergers in general, founding fathers sometimes become hamstrung after the deal is done and have difficulty moving things forward. They are perceived as having a vested interest because it is their legacy. After the deal is done, they may be reluctant to push too hard or do anything that might exacerbate the situation. If you look at mergers generally, those that fail are those that get stalled after the merger and don't move ahead to fully integrate the companies. Most mergers and acquisitions fail to meet original expectations. Problems are swept aside during the euphoria of the merger to be dealt with later, after the deal is done. Those things have to be dealt with during the integration phase.

As the group began analyzing the competitive position of the new firm, they realized effectively communicating the advantages to clients, potential clients, and the world at large would mean quantifying those advantages. It wasn't enough to say, "We're the biggest." Selling is usually low-key because accounting firms take very seriously their professional commitment not to make any marketing claims that cannot be substantiated. Professional societies in some countries (and some states in the United States) even go so far as to forbid the use of such words as *expert, specialist*, or any derivative of either when describing professional capabilities. KPMG's description of the attributes that differentiate it from the competition must be easily recognizable, and it must be true.

Ashworth took on the task of identifying and quantifying KPMG's unique attributes. He called on Scott Showalter, a partner from Norfolk, Va., on rotational assignment to the U.S. executive office, and John Higgins, the U.S. senior director of firmwide communications, for assistance. In an afternoon brainstorming session, four themes began to emerge: KPMG was obviously the strongest firm internationally. The merger had given it unparalleled strength, particularly in Europe. Industry specialization was another unique characteristic. Other firms touted specialized industry practices, but it was a matter of record that PMI had pioneered the field. Another novel attribute was the firm's approach to technology. It was the first to automate the audit by providing portable computers to staff members. Calculations that formerly required hours with a calculator could be performed in a few minutes with the firm's microcomputers and proprietary software. KPMG also offered an unusual brand of strategic information technology consulting through its Nolan Norton subsidiary. The final differentiating characteristic was a little more difficult to quantify, but it was well established as the top priority of the firm: superior-quality client service. Higgins drafted a white paper outlining the four differentiating characteristics.

The U.K. firm had recently launched a quality measurement program that was receiving rave reviews from clients in that country. Under the chairmanship of Stephen Harlan, the U.S. firm's strategic planning committee had developed a definition of quality service: meeting or exceeding the client's expectations every time. The U.S. committee, after painful introspection, had also developed a formal program of measuring and monitoring client satisfaction. KPMG was the first in the profession to distribute questionnaires to its clients asking them to evaluate the quality of the service the firm provided. It was a competitive advantage that the firm extolled in advertising, publicity, and speeches.

"Global reach and coverage" was the descriptive message developed to describe the firm's international strength. By the time the consolidation phase was complete, the firm had the dominant market share in fourteen of twenty-two critical markets and had 5,050 partners and 63,700 staff in 650 cities and 120 countries around the world. KPMG's client list numbered 180,000 and represented virtually every facet of the world economy—commercial, financial, educational, governmental, and service industries.

The firm's leadership in market specialization grew out of its early dominance in the financial services industry, a position it still enjoys. In the United States, for example, KPMG Peat Marwick audits 25 percent of *Fortune*'s top 100 banks and 42 percent of *Fortune*'s top 50 thrifts. Other specialized industry practices emerged over the years; KPMG went on to become a leader in insurance, real estate, merchandising, health care, high technology, merchandising, manufacturing, state and local government, and higher education.

KPMG could also point with justifiable pride to a number of firsts in information technology. It was the first to use microcomputers on-site to conduct audits (it now has more than 15,000 microcomputers in use); integrate microcomputers and mainframes into audit test procedures; develop proprietary audit software; and automate the audit process.

In addition, the firm was a leader in the development of artificial intelligence for use as an audit tool, and its Nolan Norton subsidiary was a pioneer in helping businesses transform themselves into twenty-first century organizations through the strategic use of technology. Gradually the four messages worked their way through the firm until they became part of the culture.

By the fall of 1989, when the firm held its international partners' conference at New York's Waldorf Astoria Hotel, KPMG had made substantial progress in reshaping itself and was poised to create and take advantage of new opportunities. The mood of the meeting was decidedly sunny despite a rainstorm that hung over the city for the duration of the conference. At the opening ceremony, Horner welcomed West Germany's Treuverkehr, Sweden's Bohlins, and Canada's Peat Marwick Thorne to the KPMG family, along with new clients Credit Suisse First Boston, Hitachi Data Systems, Bertelsmann, Inc., U.S.A., Klockner, Asea Brown Boveri Group, Landis & Gyr, and Dentsu.

Horner used the occasion to share some personal thoughts with the assembled partners:

> The KPMG merger gave PMI the opportunity to make a quantum leap toward achieving the goal of moving beyond its Anglo-Saxon network of offices to become a balanced firm with strong national practices managed and staffed by resident nationals. The balance we have achieved has given us a definite advantage over our competitors, which say they

are merging for the same reasons we did. It is impossible for them to achieve that kind of balance because the firms that are merging have a great deal more redundancy, not only in the United States, but also in Europe and around the world. And where there is no redundancy, there is a void.

While being the world's largest has a nice ring to it, it doesn't describe what we are all about. What's important to our clients is that we have a critical mass of people, technology, and experience to deliver superior-quality client service. We need to continue to target and win top multinational clients. We should be able to expand our portfolio of clients that are among the world's top multinationals. We need to maximize international referrals.

We need to emphasize industry and service specialization throughout KPMG. When our clients engage us, they should know they are getting the very best business advice possible. We help them by developing realistic competitive strategies, improving quality, incorporating advanced technology, and putting the power of our people to its fullest and most productive use.

It is one thing, Horner and the marketers thought, to persuade yourselves and your partners that you have a pretty good thing going, but it is quite another to sell it to a skeptical marketplace that is already inundated with far more marketing messages than it wants.

The ultimate test of the merger's validity came with the March winds of 1990. When Arthur Young, PepsiCo's previous auditor, merged with Ernst & Whinney (which audited archrival Coca-Cola), Coke reportedly told the new Ernst & Young that it must choose between its two clients. In February E&Y, in an unprecedented move in the profession, decided not to renew its audit relationship with PepsiCo. Based on speculation that this might happen, Ashworth and the marketing department had already distilled mountains of information about the company, and Horner had already begun assembling an engagement team.

When the invitation to propose came from PepsiCo headquarters in Purchase, N.Y., work began in earnest. Based on previous conversations, Horner thought D. Wayne Calloway, chairman of PepsiCo, would like the style of the U.S. vice chairman of audit, Merlin Dewing, and would appreciate his experience and stature in the organization. But first, Dewing had to get past the selection committee, most of whom Horner did not know. Nevertheless, he figured that Calloway's key people were similar in approach and style to the chairman. If Dewing could fit with Calloway, he could fit with the committee. Dewing would resign from his vice chairman's position to take on the new challenge of heading up the worldwide PepsiCo engagement team. He would be assisted by New York office tax partner in charge Robert Decelles, who would serve as tax engagement partner. Dozens of people around the firm assisted with the massive task of organizing and writing the firm's plans for serving a company with revenues of $13 billion and 235,000 employees in the soft drink, snack food, and fast food industries.

The scope of PepsiCo's operations was staggering. Major products and trade names included Pepsi, Diet Pepsi, Mountain Dew, 7Up, Slice, Frito-Lay (Doritos, Ruffles, Lay's, Fritos), Kentucky Fried Chicken, Pizza Hut, and Taco Bell. Its international operations included soft drink sales in 150 countries and territories, 700 bottling plants outside the United States, 2,862 Kentucky Fried Chicken Restaurants in 58 countries, and 1,005 Pizza Hut and Taco Bell restaurants in 50 countries. Dewing was given complete authority to make all decisions relating to the PepsiCo engagement. He could deal with professional staff résumés and transfers and talk to people at all levels in the firm. He described it as being "lean and mean and free from bureaucracy."

All the major accounting firms except Ernst & Young had been invited to propose, and the whole accounting world knew it. It would be a major coup for the firm that won the engagement. From the beginning, it was apparent KPMG had several advantages. KPMG was the largest accounting firm in thirteen of twenty key PepsiCo markets outside the United States. And of five key U.S. markets, KPMG was the largest in four and had the largest audit practice in the fifth.

KPMG's strategy paid off. In announcing KPMG's appointment to the firm's partners and employees, Horner said, "Winning PepsiCo in head-to-head competition with Arthur Andersen and Price Waterhouse validates the strategies we have been pursuing to differentiate our firm. These include taking full advantage of our balanced global delivery network and our steadfast commitment to superior-quality client service."

Echoed industry observer James Emerson, "Certainly there were many key factors which led to the KPMG selection, including the Dewing commitment; however, you must speculate that the KPMG global organization was also crucial. In terms of strength in the major worldwide markets, Peat Marwick was a clear leader over Arthur Andersen and Price Waterhouse. This success would seem to be a significant confirmation of the vision Larry D. Horner and his partners pioneered."[1]

While the PepsiCo proposal was under way, northeast regional vice chairman Robert McGregor was going up against Deloitte Ross Tohmatsu, Ernst & Young, and Price Waterhouse for the audit of Varity Corporation. Headquartered in Toronto, Varity was relocating its headquarters to Buffalo, N.Y. It was another opportunity resulting from the firm's expanded international reach.

The $3.4 billion Varity Corporation is composed of three business groups: Massey-Ferguson, a U.K.-based manufacturer of tractors; Perkins, a British manufacturer of diesel engines; and Kelsey-Hayes, a Detroit automotive and hydraulic component

---

1. James C. Emerson, "PepsiCo Selects KPMG Peat Marwick," *Emerson's Professional Services Review,* April 1990, News and Views.

manufacturer. When Varity acquired Kelsey-Hayes in November 1989, Varity already had two accounting firms, and Kelsey-Hayes had a third. The company decided it was time to work with a single firm. It invited its three current auditors to propose, and because Massey-Ferguson and Perkins had worked with the U.K. firm in the past, KPMG was invited to the party.

Horner, McGregor, and Butler mapped out a strategy. Paul Gordon, a Short Hills, N.J., partner with extensive multinational experience and strong working relationships with several U.K. partners, was tapped to serve as engagement partner. He would be assisted by several senior people in the Buffalo, Detroit, London, and Cambridge offices.

Gordon and his team jumped aboard airplanes and in six weeks visited thirty Varity locations around the world, assembling information for seven proposal documents that focused on the company's specific needs and how KPMG would meet them.

Word that Varity had chosen KPMG arrived the same week PepsiCo announced its decision. It was another major victory.

Meanwhile, in Tampa, Fla., managing partner Hilliard Eure III was pursuing his own commitment to quality client service with St. Petersburg–based Florida Progress Corporation, a $2.129 billion holding company with interests in electric power and fuels, insurance, financial services, and real estate. Although Florida Progress had been an Arthur Andersen client for forty-nine years, KPMG Peat Marwick convinced the company that the firm's dedication to client service extended beyond the pretty words in its brochures. Dennis Bongers moved the national public utilities practice he headed to Florida and promised to transfer any other experienced public utilities professionals necessary to staff the engagement. Eure would serve as client relations partner for the company.

Back in New York, Herbert Morse (vice chairman of the New York region and managing partner of the New York office), Frederick Turk (national director of the education and other institutions practice), and Herbert Folpe, audit partner, were battling the rest of the Big Six for the audit of the March of Dimes Birth Defects Foundation. The engagement team used the firm's proprietary ratio analysis technique to compare the organization's finances with competitive health and welfare organizations, and the proposal included a resource audit, a unique KPMG strategic planning approach not-for-profit organizations use to acquire and manage resources.

Although the research took place at the height of the busy season, KPMG professionals from twenty offices visited local March of Dimes chapters to help with the winning proposal effort. It was teamwork at its finest.

The next week, the firm scored its fifth major success with the acquisition of Beckman Instruments Inc., a Fortune 500 company that manufactures, sells, and services laboratory instruments and consumable products for life sciences and clinical diagnostic labs. Beckman had been a client of the Orange County (California) office before its parent company, SmithKline Beckman Corp., changed auditors in 1987. Orange County managing partner Ronald Merriman and several of his partners kept in touch with Beckman officials after the formal relationship ended and in 1988 assisted Beckman management through its initial public offering during its spin-off from SmithKline.

In the fall of 1989, Beckman went out for proposals. A round of qualifications statements and oral presentations narrowed the field to incumbent Coopers & Lybrand and KPMG. The proposal effort involved more than thirty people in the Orange County office and KPMG professionals around the world, including U.S. and European high technology directors Tom Moser and Rodney Dowler. Horner went to California to stay in contact with audit committee members he knew and to visit Beckman during the proposal process and participate in the final presentation.

On March 29, Beckman chief financial officer George Kilmain announced that KPMG had been selected. He said, "[We were] impressed that Peat Marwick did not take for granted its excellent relationship and proven record of quality service to Beckman. Instead, the team demonstrated a strong commitment to an even higher level of service with its strengthened global capabilities."

In the United Kingdom, another client service drama was beginning to unfold. The story began decades earlier when partner David Vaughan (the partner who successfully led KPMG's first international proposal effort with ICI) was a senior manager in London. One of his clients, John Thompson Ltd., a Midlands boilermaker, had by 1970 gotten itself badly overextended through a series of "disastrous acquisitions." As a result, the firm was acquired by an aggressive northeast England engineering group, Clarke-Chapman Ltd., whose auditor was Deloitte Haskins & Sells. Clarke-Chapman's reputation for swiftly removing the professional advisers of firms it acquired was well known. After lengthy representations, however, Peat Marwick McLintock was retained as joint auditors of the merged group on a trial basis. A sterling engagement team was assigned, and in short order, the firm had effectively replaced DH&S as Clarke-Chapman's accountants in all its acquisitions.

In 1977, to maintain its strong Northeast engineering base, Clarke-Chapman merged with Reyrolle Parsons, a firm that in the accounting profession was widely regarded as the jewel of Price Waterhouse's Northeast practice. This time there was little debate; over the protests of both PW and DH&S, Peat Marwick McLintock was appointed sole auditor of the merged firm, which was renamed Northern Engineering Industries (NEI). It was, said Vaughan in an uncharacteristic immodest moment, "a triumph of sheer professionalism, commitment, and hard work; it was also a triumph for success decisively devised and decisively implemented."

The world changed again in 1989 when NEI was acquired by Rolls-Royce plc—a company whose very name symbolizes quality—as part of of its plan to diversify into power generation.

Coopers & Lybrand was Rolls-Royce's auditor, and once again KPMG found itself in a competitive situation.

It was an enormous opportunity. Although the automobile business that helped make the company's name a household word was sold several years ago, Rolls-Royce continues to be a leading manufacturer of aircraft engines. It produces power plants for the Boeing 747, 757, and 767 aircraft; the Airbus A320; and McDonnell Douglas MD90. The Rolls-Royce Olympus engines power the Concorde. Its largest engine, the Trent, will power the Boeing 767X, the Airbus A330, the MD11, and advanced derivatives of the Boeing 747. Its smaller engines power the Gulfstream, Fokker 100, and B.Ae 111. Rolls-Royce added yet another in a long list of achievements when a Qantas-operated Boeing 747-400 powered by Rolls-Royce engines gained the world-long-distance record for commercial aircraft by flying nonstop the 11,000 miles between London and Sydney in twenty hours and nine minutes.

The company is also a leading producer of military aircraft engines. The Tornado, Harrier, Harrier V/STOL, Jaguar, Hawk, and AMX attack aircraft sport Rolls-Royce power plants, as do Trident nuclear submaries and many naval vessels.

The company would be an exceedingly important client. Its 1989 results, adjusted to include seven and one-half months of NEI revenues, reported sales of £2.962 billion (US$4.864 billion) with pretax profits of £233 million (US$383 million). Rolls-Royce operations would provide important business to KPMG offices in the United Kingdom in the London, Midlands, Northeast, Northwest, and Scottish regions. Internationally, service would be needed in Australasia, Brazil, Canada, South Africa, and the United States.

Despite strong competition from C&L, KPMG had a good hand. Rolls-Royce's board of directors was chaired by Lord Tombs of Brailes and included Sir Philip Shelbourne, who had been instrumental in securing the joint appointment with Clarke-Chapman; Harold Mourgue, chairman of the audit committee of

Turner and Newall; and Terry Harrison, chairman of NEI. The board formerly had been chaired by Sir Arnold Hall, who had been a supporter during the ICI proposal.

Vaughan and U.K. senior partner Jim Butler fielded an impressive team. Vaughan described the engagement team selection process: "Clearly, my number one had to be Michael Steen, whose performance on Turner and Newall had brought him to the highest regard by both Lord Tombs and Harold Mourgue. It had to include Philip Hardaker, whose reputation within NEI was of the highest order. It required the unparalleled tax input of Robert Berg. And, in my view, to tackle the immense complexities of the aeroengine business we needed the technical excellence, incisiveness, and commitment of Ted Awty."

On March 15, 1990, Lord Tombs notified Vaughan that KPMG had won the audit. In a statement prepared for KPMG publications, Vaughan said, "The selection is a particular distinction to KPMG. Rolls-Royce and its chairman, Lord Tombs of Brailes, are renowned for a commitment to a policy of technical excellence and the highest quality standards throughout the group's operations."

It was a major coup. In just two weeks in March 1990, KPMG added six major clients to its roster.

Several other victories followed in rapid succession. In early June, KPMG was selected over incumbent Arthur Andersen as the auditor and tax adviser for the European operations of Motorola, Inc., number forty-eight on the Fortune 500 list and a $10 billion worldwide manufacturer of advanced communications and semiconductor products.

KPMG had lost the European work to AA in 1986, and several leading U.S. partners, including Midwest region vice chairman and Motorola client relations partner K. Dane Brooksher, were determined to get it back. Moser, national director of the high technology practice and Motorola client service partner; Gerald Finnell, Chicago audit partner; and Eugene Midlock, Chicago tax partner—along with Taipei partner John Sim, who was the Motorola service coordinator for Asia—all came onto the scene and demonstrated their commitment to providing the best possible service to the company.

When the merger was completed in 1987, KPMG established European audit and tax teams for Motorola with the objective of rebuilding relationships and instilling confidence in the firm's expanded capabilities in Europe. On May 3, 1990, KPMG and AA presented their qualifications to Motorola Europe at a meeting in Geneva. Brooksher, Moser, Finnell, Midlock, and fifteen KPMG European partners—including Jim Kerevan of the Reading, U.K., office, who would fill the role of services coordinator for the twelve KPMG European offices that would serve Motorola—participated in the presentation. Despite the fact that Motorola had already informed KPMG that a change would be very unlikely, the company was impressed with KPMG's new worldwide strength, the benefits of a single worldwide audit and tax firm, and the firm's commitment to quality. And a month before, KPMG–France had already won the audit and tax work there in competition with AA.

Three weeks after the presentation, word came from Motorola that KPMG had been selected.

Meanwhile, U.S. international vice chairman Harlan was inching toward the successful conclusion of the firm's expansion plans in Asia. Harlan had become a regular fixture on the New York to Tokyo route as he worked to culminate the merger with Japan's Century Audit Corporation and attempted to accelerate the negotiations to strengthen KPMG's presence in key Japanese markets.

In May 1990, the firm signed a merger agreement that went into effect in July of the same year. To be known internationally as KPMG Peat Marwick, the firm would continue to practice domestically as Century Audit Corporation. The merged firm has eleven offices and a staff of 966, with 760 in audit and accounting, 176 in tax, and 30 in management consulting. Its client list of some 1,100 includes such Japanese notables as All Nippon Airways, Dai-Ichi Kangyo Bank, Dentsu, Hitachi, Matsushita, Nippon Credit Bank, Taisho Marine and Fire Insurance, and Tokyu Group.

It was an important achievement for Horner and Harlan and a significant step in the firm's Japan strategy.

On June 13, KPMG, which established its first office in China in 1983, issued an announcement that it had signed an agreement with the Chinese Institute of Certified Public Accountants to establish before the 1990 year-end the first joint accounting firm ever sanctioned by the government of the People's Republic of China. The new arrangement was designed as a test for the Chinese institute. If it works (and Horner says KPMG is committed to its success), the institute will enter into similar arrangements with other firms. The firm will be known as Hua Wei in China and KPMG Peat Marwick China elsewhere.

The accounting firm was created to provide audit services to both local companies and Sino-foreign joint ventures. Until the firm was established, all companies—including joint ventures with foreign partners in the People's Republic—were required to be audited by Chinese firms. Chinese authorities would not accept audit reports signed by foreign-based firms, and such firms could not charge their fees to the joint venture. Foreign partners paid foreign audit fees independently.

The agreement was signed at a solemn ceremony in Beijing on June 5, 1990, by Horner and Yang Jiwan, president of the Chinese institute. Observing the signing ceremonies were China's Minister of Finance, Wang Bing Qian; Harlan; KPMG Hong Kong senior partner David Gairns; and KPMG Peat Marwick China partners Aloysius Tse and Walter Kwauk.

As he reflected on the first six months of 1990, Horner could hardly conceal his delight. The firm was beginning to capitalize on the opportunities inherent in the merger. It had been a long, uphill struggle, but it was worth it.

The vision was alive and well.

# Epilogue

It was Shakespeare in *The Tempest,* another politically charged drama, who observed, "What's past is prologue," and noted that "what to come is in our discharge." What a dynamic future awaits us. We awake in a new world every day. At no time in history have so many momentous events occurred in such a short period of time.

We have seen the USSR and Eastern Europe lift the iron curtain to allow the rest of the world to peer inside, and they have asked for help in reforming their stagnant economies. Nationalism is crumbling in the face of the relentless advance of a global economy.

It is not yet easy to do business in these countries, despite legislation passed in 1989 in several of them that allows foreign investment and provides for repatriation of foreign currency and profits. The word *profit* doesn't exist in Hungarian, for example. When a New Jersey company negotiated a joint venture in Budapest, it solved the problem by writing "profit" in German.[1] Capitalism is still a very mysterious and theoretical concept in most Communist countries.

Communications technology has opened broad new vistas and

---

1. Julia C. Martinez (The Associated Press), "A New Land of Opportunity Loaded with Risk," *The Record* (N.J.), 18 Feb. 1990, B1.

inspired ordinary citizens to rise up against oppressive regimes. People are not content to stand in breadlines after they've seen the opulence of "Dallas" on satellite television, and it's far more difficult to manage events when news floats uninhibited through the sky and through telephone lines to fax machines.

The effect on business is that conditions change so rapidly the question "What next?" has been replaced by "How fast?" Increasingly sophisticated products work their way through the world's markets in equally shorter life cycles, and ever-fickle capital moves electronically with lightening speed between companies, industries, and countries.

No one yet knows for sure what the likely effect of a single European market in 1992 will be on the world's economy, and much of the public interest quickly shifted to a unified Germany when the Berlin Wall crumbled. Nevertheless, the march to 1992 continues, driven by economic necessity. Most informed observers believe that EC member countries will adopt most of the proposals by the December 31, 1992, deadline. Says KPMG international executive H. Caspar Broeksma:

> Whatever happens in 1992, it is likely that Europe—that little old lady—is a little more awake and has economic strength that will be much more visible. And the competition with the Japanese and the other countries will be much stronger. We've been through a stage of euphoria that was moderated by the recent events in Europe, but things would have probably slowed anyway of their own accord.
>
> It's difficult to fight bureaucracy with bureaucracy. When you compare the simplicity and length of the Ten Commandments or the American Constitution to a very specific Brussels directive, you begin to get the idea. One EC directive regarding fishing—who may fish for what kind of fish on what days using which nets on a small fringe of the western part of the nation—is 1,045 pages long!

For such reasons, I am pessimistic about the political aspects of getting Europe together; but most of 1992 is business driven, so I am optimistic about that. It is silly that a truck from New York can drive to Los Angeles in seventy-two hours while a truck from Amsterdam to Copenhagen (which is about half the distance) takes twice or three times as long because one has to go through the formalities at the German and Danish borders. Those kinds of problems must be resolved if Europe is going to compete effectively on a global basis.

Europe does not have a monopoly on change. Booming Asian economies fueled industrial growth and brought increased wealth and savings and burgeoning equity markets followed by expansion into other countries. Japan's cross-border mergers and acquisitions are showing phenomenal growth, up 55 percent in 1989 over the prior year.

Despite their impressive growth, however, the Asian countries have begun to feel the pressure of the competition. Products once "Made in Japan" moved to Taiwan or Korea, which experienced the same pattern. As their economies grew and modernized, manufacturers moved to emerging countries in search of cheaper labor. Taiwanese and Korean manufacturers set up shop in Thailand, which may in a few years occupy the same position Korea or Taiwan does today, as the rapid industrialization of Asia forces nations to look at Indo-Chinese countries that are just beginning to build industrial economies.

Globalization has wrought massive change in Australia and New Zealand as well. As little as ten years ago, their undercapitalized and protected economies depended mostly on the United Kingdom and the United States for survival. Today, despite volatile currencies, high interest rates, nervous stock markets, and fluctuating economies, Australia and New Zealand attract a good deal of foreign investment. The bargain-basement prices brought on by the October 1987 stock market crash forced some companies into hurried divestitures.

Nevertheless, Australian companies were active participants in the "great American buy-up" in which foreign investors spent $A72 billion (US$54 billion) on more than 700 purchases of U.S. businesses. The Australians forked over some $A10 billion in the buying spree, trailing only the United Kingdom, Japan, and Canada.[2]

For its part, the United States began to think more about its own participation in an emerging North American trading bloc as the world shrinks and American industry continues the transformation to a service-based economy. Large, mature companies have been forced to reach further out internationally to sustain growth, and even small and midsize companies are drawn into the maelstrom as business becomes more competitive and more global. Worldwide competition is forcing all companies to become more productive and efficient. It is a global world not only for corporate giants, but also for emerging companies and the middle market.[3]

As clients move into new markets, so will accountants. However far-flung the empire, history has repeatedly demonstrated that multinational companies expect their accountants to be able to audit even the most remote operations, know the local tax laws and their effect on home-country headquarters, and provide consultants who can assist with the thorny problems of doing business in unfamiliar territory. But expansion alone doesn't create the need for accounting services. Change does. Whether it is new tax legislation, a change in accounting procedures, or a major investment, when money changes hands, accountants are involved.

Despite the rush to globalism, fundamental change in the accounting world occurs slowly and after much debate, and the

---

2. "The Number of Cross-Border Deals Comes Down While Their Value Goes Up," *Deal Watch,* December 1989, 1.

3. John A. Higgins, "The Globalization of Professional Services Firms," a KPMG perspective on consolidation among public accounting firms, speech presented October 23, 1989.

practice of accounting may vary from country to country. Practices differ not only in language and technical interpretation, but in culture, approach, and attitude toward investment and taxation. National standards are sometimes as different as the nations in which they are set.

Reasons vary, but most differences can be traced to historical precedent. By and large, accounting standards evolved out of legal systems established centuries ago. In the English-speaking countries, standards are generally based on common law, fairness, and precedent, while on the Continent, the standards are often a subset of the law as determined by the Napoleonic Code and the Commission of European Communities.[4]

Some of the greatest contrasts in accounting standards revolve around what the Germans call their national pastime—avoiding taxes. It's common practice in several European countries, for example, to set up hidden reserves to cover contingent liabilities. Such reserves, considered sound business practice, help to smooth out earnings during tough times. In the United States, the same practice isn't allowed by generally accepted accounting principles.

How goodwill is handled in business combinations is another major difference. Defined as the "excess of the fair value of the consideration paid over the fair value of the acquired company's identified net assets," goodwill is what makes a business worth more than the stuff it owns. In the United States, Canada, and Japan, goodwill is capitalized as an asset and amortized against future income. Canada and the United States allow an amortization period of forty years while Japan allows five. West Germany and the United Kingdom give companies a choice between capitalizing and amortizing goodwill and writing it off against shareholders' equity. International accounting standards allow either method with no minimum or maximum period specified if the

---

4. Chris Nobes, "Why Accounting Differs Internationally," *International Accounting Bulletin,* April 1986, 2.

company elects to capitalize and amortize. The net effect is that an identical transaction, purchase, and business would be reflected very differently in the financial statements, depending on the country in which the transaction occurred.[5]

Will we ever see uniform international accounting standards? "Probably not in my lifetime," says U.K. senior partner Jim Butler. He adds:

> We should see such standards in our lifetimes, but I am not at all sure we will. Except at a very low level, we haven't even got EC accounting standards. And when they start, they will start from a very low base and work up. It's very sad, I believe, that the United States and the United Kingdom haven't been able to amalgamate accounting standards. Had that been possible, it would have been a very good base for the rest of the world.
>
> In accounting for goodwill, for example, it's nonsense having companies traded on the New York and London stock exchanges and actually having to report different profits for them. There are other minor differences in standards, but goodwill is a major difference. It would be logical to have the same standard, it would be right, and it would be sensible, but it is going to take some time to achieve.

Echoes KPMG chairman Larry Horner, "If I had to guess, I would estimate that it will be twenty years before the standards are consistent. The only thing that might accelerate the process would be pressure from the world's stock exchanges to adhere to a specific set of standards and accounting principles. Otherwise, it will be very difficult to overcome the national parochialism that exists today."

Closely linked to the differences in accounting standards is the

---

5. Leonard P. Novello, "Steps Towards Creating an International Language," *New York Law Journal*, August 31, 1989.

difficulty of moving information across national borders. According to Teddy L. Coe, chairman of the accounting department at the University of North Texas's College of Business Administration, questions surrounding the movement of information have profound implications for the accounting profession of the future:

> Integrating economies, developing international accounting standards, and educating accounting graduates are all related to a better and more complete understanding of how our economies and societies use information, gather it, process it, and then act on it.
>
> Restrictive national laws and international treaties greatly limit the type of information that can be exchanged electronically. These restrictions affect the way business is done and are in reality a form of export control. Transnational data flow restrictions will have an important impact on the future of the accounting profession.

Technology will influence our lives in ways we can't even imagine today, John Sculley, chairman and CEO of Apple Computer, Inc., is fond of saying. He compares the evolution of computer technology to that of the automobile. In the early days, drivers had to have a pretty thorough understanding of their cars because they often did the repair work themselves. The infrastructure was poor or nonexistent, roads were bad, technology was experimental, and the cars often broke down. Now one doesn't think about pistons, valves, and spark plugs; one just gets into the automobile, turns the key, and goes. The same is true for the personal computer. When the technology becomes so transparent that we no longer have to think about how to use it, we will be just beginning to tap its potential.

James Emerson, editor and publisher of *Emerson's Professional Services Review,* puts it this way:

Technology is increasingly driving business, and it has to drive accounting firms. Clients expect their business advisers to be on the leading edge of technology. It's expensive, but it's not really an option. What are firms that are having trouble sustaining such capital investment going to tell their clients? "I'm an audit firm but maybe Peat Marwick or Andersen Consulting can help you on the technology." That isn't a very viable strategy.

By 1989 everyone realized that fact, and it was a key factor in the accounting firm mergers. I think it impacted Ernst & Whinney and Arthur Young—and definitely Touche Ross and Deloitte Haskins & Sells. Now, Price Waterhouse is saying that one of its strategic imperatives is information technology. The firm may be dropping something else to focus its money there. It doesn't have any choice.

James Corboy, chief financial officer of Dresser Industries (a multibillion dollar supplier of energy-related products and services for oil, gas, chemical, and mining concerns), also sees technology as an essential competitive tool.

You have got to use technology; you cannot survive in the new customer environment using the old system. Clients who are feeling cost pressures themselves are not going to pay the same fees for an audit as they have in the past. You have to become more productive if you are going to retain the ability to live a long time.

You still have to produce the same end product, but you are going to have to sign the audit certificate for less revenue in the future. Accounting firms are not alone in this regard. You are right in there with the rest of us. We've got to reduce the cost of producing automobiles and machinery while in competition with others who are doing it more efficiently. For those of us who have been through it, who have experienced those kinds of pressures, we have to say, "Welcome to the club."

Such intense competition takes its toll on people. Accounting profession leaders and observers agree that the human resources part of the equation will become increasingly important. The pressures to do more with less, to become more productive, have the effect of discouraging entry into the profession. The best and brightest will have other options available to them; they may choose other professions that allow more income with less effort.

Recruiting good people is essential, particularly to Anglo-oriented firms that require regular infusions of new university graduates to replace those who do not make it to the partnership or at various stages of their career decide that a public accounting career isn't for them. Because most large firms have highly regarded training programs and offer an opportunity to get a wide range of experience in a variety of industries, many accounting graduates enter public accounting with an exit plan already in mind. They plan to get some training and experience, then move on to a career in industry.

North American firms are finding that they have to compete hard for the smaller number of accounting graduates. According to the *International Accounting Bulletin,* many of the best graduates are choosing careers in investment banking and marketing over accounting.[6] The American Institute of Certified Public Accountants has found that the number of accounting graduates has dropped from a high of 57,000 in 1984 to 52,500 in 1989.

It is a problem in other parts of the world as well. German firm chairman Hans Havermann points to the opportunities that have been opened up by East Germany's move toward unification with the West.

---

6. Bob Lavine and Gundi Jeffrey, "North American Firms Fight for Quality Graduates," *International Accounting Bulletin,* February 1989, 14.

In a country of sixteen million people, there is practically no accounting profession, and not a single tax adviser. They have only six hundred lawyers. At present, there is a dramatic shortage of qualified professionals in several fields.

I would hire three hundred to five hundred people right now if I could find them. We have to open three to five offices in East Germany, and we don't know where we will get the people. We don't have them in our firm now, and in the short run there aren't enough trained people available in East Germany. We have to recruit them and train them, but this will take time.

In Scotland—the cradle of the profession—where it took fifty years for the independent Scots accountants to merge various societies into one institute, Ian Percy, president of that body, led his colleagues in a move to broaden educational requirements for accountants. He says, "An accountant should be a man of business, educated to think. At present there is a danger that he may become an auditor, simply applying as rulebook. In Scotland we want an accountant to be able to think before they learn standards. The standards are there only to give him guidance. For that reason, I think that it may be useful for accountants to learn non-accounting subjects in their first year of study, like language or philosophy."[7]

Percy would no doubt find a kindred spirit in Professor Joseph Gibson at the University of Virginia's McIntire School of Commerce, who asks, "Is it possible that the entry-level person in accounting should be recruited at the level of a paraprofessional, with a truly liberal arts background and a minimum of technical training? Is it not time that accounting establish itself as a true profession?" He opines:

---

7. Pratap Chatterjee, "Stirring the Pot in Scotland," *International Accounting Bulletin*, February 1990, 15.

We must face the fact that in the present political climate, there is no practical solution to the social advancement policy of elementary and secondary education. The high school graduate will continue to be poorly prepared. The colleges and universities will have to continue to remedy these failings. But businesspeople, especially professional accountants, must not only be able to think, to understand technical jargon but to communicate effectively with the uninitiated.

Increasingly, the accountant must be better prepared! The professional accountant must know, understand, and appreciate the culture of the United States and that of other countries. He or she should be able to read, write, and, hopefully, converse in at least one foreign language.

It would be convenient if the problems of accounting education were simply those of the schools and the larger firms. Together, I think we could solve most of them. However, to my mind, it is a very serious disservice the profession is foisting on the public—that is, clothing a student with a minimal educational background and extremely modest practical experience to hold himself or herself out as a professional, a certified public accountant. I shudder to think of the quality of service offered by these persons as they sally forth particularly as sole practitioners or as partners with others of their ilk.

Johan Steenmeijer, senior partner of KPMG's Dutch firm, says quality is the single highest priority in the profession. Without quality service, accounting firms will not survive. It is not simply a matter of differentiating one firm from its competition. "We are a little earlier in our approach than the other firms," he says, "but the others—the Price Waterhouses and Coopers & Lybrands of the world—will follow."

Quality service transcends language and culture, Steenmeijer believes; clients in every country like to be a part of the process of evaluating the service that is provided to them. The commitment to quality must permeate the staff functions as well, Steenmeijer says, from the senior partner to the telephonist—every employee of the firm.

It can be a double-edged sword, however, says Australian senior partner George Bennett. Clients expect quality, they hear the buzzwords, they have quality circles themselves, and they expect quality from the firms that serve them.

> Any reasonably intelligent person can work out what he or she needs to do to give that service. Service, in a very large sense, is in the eyes of the beholder—it is meeting or exceeding your client's expectations. Over here if you don't do that you are at a disadvantage. It is terribly important—almost like motherhood. The firms that provided the best service are the ones that have the clients now.
>
> It is a trend that is very worthwhile for everyone. It is the bottom line. Quality reduces the waste of resources because things are done right the first time. It is more efficient and therefore a better utilization of resources.

Quality service is likely to be on the minds of the profession's leaders for a long time to come. As the firms expand in size and geographic reach, quality must be institutionalized in order to ensure delivery of consistently high quality service to clients around the world. Says Horner, "We need to burn quality into our minds, our everyday habits, and our thought processes, until it becomes second nature. Then it becomes real, it becomes a part of our culture. We need to develop more quantifiable methodologies for measuring the impact of quality, and we need to better reward those who provide quality service and penalize those who don't."

As the accounting profession looks to the twenty-first century, what's to come may indeed, as Shakespeare said, be "in our discharge." Says KPMG's first chairman, James Brown, "We proved it could be done, and our success sparked other mergers. We showed them it could be done and how to do it, but the KPMG merger is substantially different from the others. Strategically, our firm is in a much better position because of the expanded global coverage. There were many strategic reasons for an Arthur Andersen/Price Waterhouse merger—for example, better consulting capability and a very distinguished client list—but it still wouldn't have offered the worldwide balance KPMG has.

At this writing, it seems very unlikely that another merger of the type reported here will occur in the foreseeable future. The day of the dramatic mega-merger is over, says Germany's Hans Havermann:

> Of course, one cannot be totally sure, but I can't see the Big Six becoming the Big Three or Four. The authorities everywhere, particularly monopoly commissions, have become nervous about what's going on in the profession. It has become very public as a consequence of the mega-mergers, and several commissions—including the European Commission in Brussels—are investigating the field.
>
> More important, I think, is that clients would become more and more critical. In Germany, when we established KPMG, they told us, "This is exactly what we want you to do. It's a great thing—congratulations." When we had one or two more mergers in Germany, we still had our clients' support, but if we were to continue to—from their point of view—eliminate our competition through merger, we would face a great deal of criticism from both our clients and the monopoly commissions.
>
> My personal feeling is that the time of the mega-mergers is over.

Debate and discussion continue. As American folk hero, baseball great, and master of the malapropism Yogi Berra is said to have observed, "Predicting anything is difficult, especially when it involves the future." There is no doubt that the future of KPMG will be shaped by many people, some of whom have yet to emerge on the national and international scene. KPMG's Brown is retired, and the other four architects of the merger—Steenmeijer, Butler, Havermann, and Horner—would under ordinary circumstances retire within the next three to four years.

As Horner looked back over his achievements, he considered his future. His six-year term as chairman would end in October; the partners would elect a new chairman on October 4, 1990, at their annual meeting in Orlando, Fla. At fifty-six, Horner would be eligible to serve an additional three-year term before reaching the firm's mandatory retirement age.

Speculation swirled throughout the firm, but the conventional wisdom was that the popular chairman could have the three-year term if he wanted it. Horner considered his alternatives, and at a special U.S. board meeting held August 7 and 8, he notified the directors that he would step aside and would not seek reelection. He told the board, "The firm needs a chairman who can serve a full six-year term to implement its strategies."

He also advised the KPMG executive committee that he would not seek reelection as chairman of KPMG when his term expired December 31, 1990. The executive committee tapped Butler to succeed Horner as chairman and chose Steenmeijer to fill the new post of chief executive and deputy chairman. Two of the founders would continue to lead the international firm into the 1990s.

The August 9 edition of the *New York Times* carried the story about Horner and paid tribute to his achievements:

> For Mr. Horner, the decision caps a brief, but accomplished, tenure in which his firm more than any other

American accounting firm has positioned itself for the increasing globalization of business. His biggest accomplishment was widely viewed as the merger he led in 1987 between his old firm, Peat Marwick, and KMG Main Hurdman, which had extensive European operations. That huge combination created a wave of copycat mergers, and also helped KPMG Peat Marwick attract several important multinational audit clients, including PepsiCo in the United States and Rolls-Royce in Britain.

Horner said he had contemplated his decision for some time and that he wanted to make way for a successor who would have a longer period "to address and burn in some of the solutions" to problems like maintaining a partnership structure as the firm grows in size.[8]

A spirited campaign followed in the United States, in which partners interested in the top leadership positions described their visions for the firm. During a whirlwind, eighteen-city tour, straw polls of more than 1,000 partners showed two clear favorites: Jon C. Madonna, 47, managing partner of the San Francisco office, and James G. Brocksmith, Jr., 49, managing partner of the Chicago office.

Before the board of directors met to choose one of the two as its candidate, Brocksmith and Madonna got together. In view of the strong support for both, they reasoned, they would be a formidable team. On September 7, 1990, the board enthusiastically endorsed the combination and presented the slate of Madonna as chairman and Brocksmith as deputy chairman to the partners. At the meeting in Orlando, the partners united behind the team and swept them into office with a clear mandate. The new leadership team would implement the firm's mission by differentiating it

---

8. Alison Leigh Cowan, "Chairman of KPMG Peat Marwick Is Giving Up His Post," *New York Times*, 9 August 1990, B3.

through quality, industry specialization, technology, and its international presence; and manage the business for profitable growth. "Our overriding goal," they told the partners, "is to be the best and most profitable accounting and consulting firm in the world."

Whatever the future holds, one thing is certain. The accounting profession seems to be predestined to fulfill the ancient Chinese curse:

*May you live in interesting times.*

# Index